PSYCHOTHERAPY FOR THE WHOLE FAMILY

Case Histories, Techniques, and Concepts of Family Therapy of Schizophrenia in the Home and Clinic

PSYCHOTHERAPY FOR THE WHOLE FAMILY

ALFRED S. FRIEDMAN
IVAN BOSZORMENYI-NAGY
JEROME E. JUNGREIS
GERALDINE LINCOLN
HOWARD E. MITCHELL
JOHN C. SONNE
ROSS V. SPECK
GEORGE SPIVACK

SPRINGER PUBLISHING COMPANY, INC., NEW YORK

The authors

ALFRED S. FRIEDMAN, PH.D.

Program Director "Family Treatment of Schizophrenia in the Home" project; Director of Research, Philadelphia Psychiatric Center.

IVAN BOSZORMENYI-NAGY, M.D.

Family Therapist, Philadelphia Psychiatric Center; Director of Family Therapy Project, Eastern Pennsylvania Psychiatric Institute, Philadelphia; Associate Professor of Psychiatry, Jefferson Medical College, Philadelphia.

JEROME E. JUNGREIS, A.C.S.W.

Family Therapist, Philadelphia Psychiatric Center; Chief, Psychiatric Social Service, Philadelphia General Hospital; Instructor, University of Pennsylvania School of Medicine, Department of Psychiatry.

GERALDINE LINCOLN, M.ED.

Family Therapist, Philadelphia Psychiatric Center; Family Therapist, Eastern Pennsylvania Psychiatric Institute.

HOWARD E. MITCHELL, PH.D.

Senior Research Psychologist, "Family Treatment of Schizophrenia in the Home" project; Director, Human Resources Program, University of Pennsylvania; Assistant Professor, Family Study in Psychiatry, University of Pennsylvania.

JOHN C. SONNE, M.D.

Family Therapist, Philadelphia Psychiatric Center; Associate in Psychiatry, School of Medicine, University of Pennsylvania; Staff Member, Institute of the Pennsylvania Hospital, Philadelphia.

ROSS V. SPECK, M.D.

Family Therapist, Philadelphia Psychiatric Center; Clinical Associate Professor, Department of Psychiatry, Hahnemann Medical College; Consultant in Family Therapy, Eastern Pennsylvania Psychiatric Institute, Philadelphia.

GEORGE SPIVACK, PH.D.

Family Therapist, Philadelphia Psychiatric Center; Director of Psychological Research, Devereaux Schools, Devon, Pennsylvania.

Preface

The family, as Weston LaBarre* points out, is the source
of all human institutions; improvement of family life will
help individual human beings achieve the measure of
humanity set for them biologically and socially. Today,
the family as an institution appears to be torn apart, and
may even be in the early stages of dying, exposed as it is
to the dehumanizing aspects of our culture. Jules
Henry** has colorfully highlighted the "ramifying ma-
lignant consequences" of some of our cultural traits:
"Such prevalent American personality characteristics as
shallowness of involvement, vagueness, the tendency to
sacrifice tenderness to strength and to read life off in
terms of a dominance-submission struggle, and a tendency to defend one's self by criticizing and humiliating
others, may combine in a husband and wife in a lethal
form to produce a dreadful, unplanned and unintended
but nevertheless pathogenic entanglement of parents and
children that has the quality of destiny and tragedy."

This book is the outcome of work done in the belief that human society
has the potential for progress and growth, and that family life can become
more satisfactory. We are only beginning to appreciate the importance of
the family dynamics and structure, and of the totality of the family
environment for the development of each of its young members. A long-
standing cultural taboo against close clinical examination of a whole
family and of the intimate aspects of family life is now being superseded
by scientific and clinical study and treatment of the family. Our efforts,
at Philadelphia Psychiatric Center, are part of the development of this
new era.

Dr. Howard E. Mitchell, as the research consultant for this project,
first conceived the idea and plan for this book. He planned the procedures
for the evaluation of the families and of the results of the treatment. He
coordinated and edited the initial draft of the manuscript. He would have
continued to fulfill this central role if not for a change in his professional
responsibilities at that particular time.

Now in the Summer of 1965, we have finished the rewriting and
editing of this book. Most of the family case histories and chapters had
been written one or two years earlier; there followed a process of re-
composing according to our latest experience, and a period of integration,

* See Reference 66 for La Barre, W.
** See Reference 50 for Henry, J.

vi

of joint discussions, commitments and decisions. To achieve a fusion of the democratic process with the creative effort is notoriously difficult and time consuming. It is with much satisfaction, therefore, and also with some relief that the eight of us, having each one started with his independent ideas, attitudes and feelings, have worked out a joint statement of our experience and our thinking.

This is not a collection of papers loosely drawn together by an editor from contributions by persons who have worked separately in related areas of a field of interest. We have each been shaped by each other and by a mutual experience. The book represents a part of each of us, and a part of our joint psyche and our mass ego. We have grown and changed in the process. But the individual did not become wholly submerged in the group. Differences in opinion, emphasis, expressive style and therapeutic method will be found from case history to case history, and from chapter to chapter. The topics of the book were not assigned, but were chosen by each project team member on the basis of his interest and the contribution he felt he could make. As it turned out, the particular professional background of the team member, whether medicine, psychology or social work, was not a factor in the selection of topics.

Our therapeutic approach to the family and our theoretical conception are not the only possible ones; rather, to us they make the most sense in light of our current knowledge. Since detailed case histories of family treatment, such as those presented here, have not been available in the literature, we hope that they will convey the process and the problems of treating disturbed families more vividly and more concretely to those in the family treatment field.

While the family treatment we describe was conducted mostly in the homes of the families, many of the techniques and principles demonstrated are applicable, or adaptable, to the conducting of family treatment in other settings, such as clinic, hospital, social agency and private office. We believe that what we have reported here will stimulate the thinking and the criticism of members of the various academic and professional disciplines concerned with the family.

July 1965   The Authors
Philadelphia Psychiatric Center

Acknowledgements

We are indebted and grateful to many persons for their help in the development of this book. First of all, we are indebted to the troubled families who shared this new experience with us, who risked revealing themselves to our inquiring minds, and who granted us permission, while protecting their anonymity, to publish their stories for the benefit of others.

Mrs. Gertrude Cohen, the assistant administrator of the project, was truly the indispensible person in this endeavor. She was a unifying, organizing and supporting influence. She was both expediter and friend to the family treatment staff. She gave valuable counsel, assistance and devotion beyond what can be repaid to the planning, integrating and editing of this book.

Mrs. Nadine Mitchell helped to get the book started by compiling a file of appropriate references and reprints, and continued her help through editorial work.

Mrs. Tybie Levit made a valuable contribution in her efficient and accurate transcription and compilation of the manuscript and its revisions.

To Silvan Tomkins, our research colleague, who participated in the germination of the ideas for this project, we are indebted for sharing with us his creative insights into human nature, and for his personal warmth and encouragement.

We wish to express our gratitude to the National Institute of Mental Health (Grant #MH-00154) for affording us the opportunity to do this work. Not only financial support, but wise consultation and guidance in planning the project were provided by three officers of NIMH: Mrs. Ruth Knee, Chief, Clinical Facilities Section; Dr. Harry McNeill, Regional Director; and Dr. Harold Hildreth, Chief Psychologist, Community Services Branch.

To the following persons on the staff of the Philadelphia Psychiatric Center, we are grateful for their cooperation and their interest in the project: Dr. Philip Mechanick, Medical Director; Zvee Einbinder, Executive Vice-President; Ina D. Saft, Administrator; Dr. Robert Nathan, Clinical Director; Dr. Louis Alikakos, Director, Out-Patient Services; Robert Fishman and Edward Fish, Directors, Social Service.

We extend thanks to the following journals for permission to reprint parts of the indicated materials

Family Process: Sonne, Speck, Jungreis; "The Absent-Member Maneuver as a Resistance in Family Therapy of Schizophrenia"—Vol. I, No. 1, March 1962.

Family Process: Sonne and Lincoln; "Heterosexual Co-Therapy Team Experiences During Family Therapy"— (In Press)

The International Journal Of Social Psychiatry: Friedman, A.S., "The 'Well' Sibling in the 'Sick' Family: A Contradiction"—Special Edition No. 2, August 1964.

Contents

Therapeutic Techniques

IV

Issues, Problems, and Concepts in Family Treatment

V

The Emerging Picture

VI

Introduction and overview

Howard E. Mitchell and Alfred S. Friedman

In the summer of 1958 Alfred Friedman invited Silvan Tomkins and Howard Mitchell to Philadelphia Psychiatric Center, as research consultants to discuss the development of a research program at that institution.

For several months this threesome met weekly in delightfully argumentative bull sesssions and the initial outlines of the demonstration project, entitled "Family Treatment of Schizophrenia in the Home," began to evolve. The final phases of these discussions were then drawn together by Friedman, and submitted to the National Institute of Mental Health under the Public Health Service Act which provides for the financing of new approaches to the problems of mental illness. The project proposal, submitted by Alfred Friedman as program director, was approved under grant number OM-154 in November 1958, and we were on our way to what has proved a great adventure. The original aim of the project was to demonstrate that it is possible to treat the schizophrenic patient by a method of group psychotherapy of the whole family in the home, and to evaluate the effectiveness and the unique values of this method. Simultaneously, we were intrigued with this new opportunity to gain deeper understanding of man in terms of his most fundamental relationships, those of the family, and to gain additional conceptual clarity regarding the problem of schizophrenia.

In this book we seek to evaluate our experience, and to add to our understanding of family functioning. In so doing, we have also taken the opportunity to adapt and test several test instruments used in studying family and personality dynamics. As the reader will see, the techniques used had to be designed and applied in accordance with the complexity of the situation; in other words, techniques were selected which could be administered to the entire family whose ages and abilities are variable.

The family is conceived of as the unit of treatment, and the therapy of the schizophrenic member thus becomes an integral part of the total family treatment. By focusing upon the family as the unit of illness, we hoped to demonstrate not only improvement in the health of the family member primarily ascribed the sick role, the schizophrenic, but to make a contribution toward the improved mental health of the other family members through their active engagement in the treatment process.

There is ample clinical evidence demonstrating that the therapeutic progress made by the patient in the hospital is often lost on his return to the same family environment.

At the time we began our experiment in 1958, evidence was also being reported to support the view that schizophrenia in an individual is indicative of probable pathology in the social organization and dynamics of the family. The defects in the primary patient's way of perceiving, communicating, and relating are derived from characteristics of the family's social system through identification, modeling, learning, and other socialization processes.

A theoretical framework that justifies viewing the family as the unit of treatment has been gradually developing in sociology, social psychiatry, and social psychology. The family as a social system has global and institutional characteristics beyond the simple summation of the individual personality of its members. The life of each family has its own history, its own character, its own climate, its own style, and its own social structure. Each family member's role and his own self-concept are significantly influenced by the expectations of the family. Crucial to understanding the dynamics of the family is an appreciation of its reciprocal role interactions and the extent to which they become fixed. Of particular interest also is the character of the reciprocal role relationship that exists between the member ascribed the sick role (the schizophrenic) and the key or dominant family member.

We began with the conviction that the psychosis of one family member may well be thought of as a crisis affecting the entire family group. The illness may result in the withdrawal of the whole family from its usual activities and social contacts. The family often cannot tolerate the social stigma related to the mental illness of one of its members. Of greatest importance is the effect of the acute stress experienced in the intra-family environment. It forces a restructuring of each member's perception of his intra-familial role and of the shared perception by the entire family of its status and role in the community. In order to assist the family to overcome the crisis and proceed toward a more effective functioning level, it is necessary first to study the particular family's organizational pattern and to capitalize on its inherent strength. Observation of the family in the natural habitat of the home, rather than in the outpatient clinic, gives a more comprehensive and accurate behavioral picture of the family's characteristics and organization; it may also provide a short-cut to understanding the patient and his illness. It gives immediate tangible meaning to the primary patient's behavior and symptoms, and enables the therapeutic team to differentiate more quickly and accurately between what is reality and what is distortion in the patient's thinking than they can by interviewing him in the clinic or hospital. In the observation of the family interacting together in a therapeutic milieu over a period of time, new insights into the intimate relationships of human beings are developed.

There is a possible advantage in maintaining the responsibility for the patient and his illness within the family—no matter how "sick" one may judge the family unit to be. Thus, in theory, the family is not permitted to deny or exorcise the "sick" or "bad" part of itself by sending the patient to the hospital. It is very tempting for the family to push the major responsibility for their problem onto the therapist and then to suffer guilt for this action.

We intend in this volume to demonstrate—via a series of case histories—specifically the following:

1. The effectiveness of the family therapy method in modifying the psychotic illness of the schizophrenic member and improving his social adjustment.

2. That it is possible to conduct the treatment of the schizophrenic patient in the family milieu in the home as an integral part of the group treatment of the family.

3. That this method of treatment can achieve a more effective family group functioning and a more satisfactory family life by which family members other than the primary patient benefit.

The reasons given for treatment of the family as a whole, rather than the individual with behavior problems or symptoms, are: a) individual therapy has often failed with a particular type of case or problem and it is argued that the family environment may be preventing change and should be treated; b) when a patient relapses after return to the family from the hospital, the relapse may be considered the result of the pathogenic family environment; c) when a patient improves, other family members have often been observed to develop increased stress or symptoms. This apparent "transfer of illness" raises the question of the therapist's responsibility to the other family members. It may be that the appearance of symptomatic behavior in an individual member is necessary for the continued functioning of a particular pathological family system. A change in the "problem" member's behavior, therefore, is only likely to occur if there is some intervention and change in the family system. The cause of the behavior problem or illness is no longer seen as the "fault" of the child or patient, or the mother's "bad influence" or the father's "inadequacy" or "lack of role responsibility"; the current point of view is that the whole family system is disordered or pathological, and that the whole system must be influenced to change if any of the elements are to change.

The family interaction as it occurs in the home or clinic setting is the strategic point for intervention against the emotional and social forces which determine maladjustment and mental illness. We have come to realize that the traditional child-guidance clinic procedures approached the problem from the wrong end. The family was treated as an extension of the child, rather than the child being treated as an extension of the family. The whole burden of the treatment and the responsibility for change had been placed on the child. By bringing the symptom-free family members into family treatment, we are beginning to involve the people who, while they are themselves an integral part of a problem, succeed in bringing others into treatment and never seek it for themselves. We know now that the child that came to the clinic, or was brought to the attention of the public authorities was often a family representative, and that the message, conscious or unconscious, was that the family was seriously maladjusted or sick and needed help. We consider the family, instead of a noxious agent from which the individual must free himself, as a unit needing help and as containing the potential for possible change which can be capitalized upon.

This book, therefore, is concerned with mental illness in the context of family living. We seek to understand how the social environment of the family can play a part in the maldevelopment of personality. For reasons made clear in Chapter 1, we have tried to develop a frame of reference in both intrapersonal and interpersonal terms. Particular attention has been paid to the literature and experience of others who have attempted to understand the relationship of family dynamics to mental illness. It has not been our intent to review comprehensively *all* the literature in this general area; the work of Bell and Vogel[13] has done this adequately. Our review is rather limited to those reports which have aided us in developing a conceptual model of family functioning that is meaningfully related to the goals of our therapeutic efforts.

The central body of data in this book consists of the histories of several of the families which are presented in some detail in Section II. The method of exposition used is the case method. Our attempts at theory-building arise out of and will be supported by specific detailed observations of these families. In our approach to these families we are concerned with their whole situation. By this we mean what Homans[52] would call both the external and internal relations of the family system. It is our belief that if one wants to develop a theory of family behavior as related to family therapy that shows how elements of the intrafamilial environment are related to the therapeutic approach, then the material collected must be connected to the broad outlines of some reference system. As Homans points out—if you are going to show connections, there must be connections.

We shall examine, therefore, the histories of four families in family therapy. Each study will be a description of a particular family and deal with one or more distinctive features, as well as with common elements in the experience with all families.

Moreover, we intend this book to be more than a report of family treatment of schizophrenia in the home. Our additional objective is to report the experience of our interdisciplinary team who met and pooled their knowledge and professional skills, in attacking an old problem (schizophrenia), in a unique manner (therapy of the family unit), in foreign territory (the home). This experience was informative and challenging, exciting and frustrating, anxiety-producing and ego-building. One of the most exciting aspects of this experience for the team members was the realization that they might contribute a little toward bridging the gap between clinical psychiatry and the social sciences. In the weekly team meetings we often argued vehemently from opposite sides of intrapersonal psychodynamic frames of reference. The complex issues became clearer although not necessarily resolved in these discussions. What was more important is that we realized more fully the complexity of the questions raised and the paucity of neat, simple answers from any theoretical frame of reference.

It is our hope that the reader will be challenged as we have been. We hope he will be stimulated to join our quest for answers that may help us understand man's relationship to man in the intense personal atmosphere of family relationships. Our fundamental goal in this search is to learn more about how families function. Much will be said about both the techniques of treatment and the evaluation of family pathology. We believe that techniques can be derived from theoretically based experience by an inductive process; we also believe that a reverse process can occur in which the empirical results of techniques, applied experimentally, lead to the formulation of hypotheses and to theory-building. We shall, however, proceed according to the former sequence, identifying the concepts we had at the beginning, describing how they developed as we went along, and reporting our methods of studying and evaluating the families treated. At a later point emerging treatment concepts are dealt with, propaedeutic to the development of new hypotheses regarding family dysfunction and psychopathology.

I

THE BEGINNING

The search for a conceptual model

Howard E. Mitchell

Howard E. Mitchell

Chapter

1

One particular evening early in our experience the project team assembled to review and discuss the current treatment of one of the families. The immediate focus of discussion concerned the therapeutic handling of a family in which one key member, the father, had manifested his resistance to family therapy by his physical absence from the two previous sessions. Opinion was divided both between the family co-therapists, and among the project team members, as to whether the family should continue with therapy or wait until the absent member returned. Subsequent discussions centered on the goals of family psychotherapy in the home and on how the father's resistance related to these goals. As later experience demonstrated, these discussions of therapeutic technique and goals eventually led to consideration of even more basic issues. Of paramount importance, for instance, was the concept each project team had of the family as a sociological and psychological unit. Questions frequently raised were: what constitutes a well functioning family, what constitutes a poorly functioning family, and in what ways are family units that have a schizophrenic member unique from other inadequate families?

In these debates, opinions and speculations flowed freely. In our collective ignorance little was withheld, and our notes and transcriptions of these sessions are evidence of a hodge-podge of anecdotal material and theoretic speculation. The latter represented the variety of professional orientations and training of the interdisciplinary project team.

After a number of such meetings and discussions, the team recognized and began to make explicit the need to develop some concepts of family functionings as related to the disorganized family units being treated and studied in the home setting. It was agreed that more therapeutic headway could probably be made if a frame of reference was developed which combined sociological and psychological considerations. Such a frame of reference also was needed in order to register and chart more systematically our experience and insights.

Accepting the fact that the team needed to develop a rough conceptual model of the family along the lines of what Bell and Vogel[13] have termed a structural-functional analysis of the family, a beginning was made. There was general agreement that the family, despite its structural properties, be viewed as a gestalt of personalities interacting in a small social system. Moreover, viewed as a small social system, the family may vary in the extent to which it is in articulation with external social systems. The fact that each family may develop a style or value orientation that transcends generations was also recognized and needed to be accounted for in our conceptualizations.

Naegele[85] raises that issue in a larger context, criticizing the mainstream of family research. "At the present time," he writes, "family research seems on the whole to have made little consistent use of the leads of kinship analysis and to have by-passed a cumulative effort at spelling out the empirical details of the social structure of various types of American families. As it is, we hear much about the family as a 'unity of interacting personalities,' about processes of accommodation or conflict, or about the kinds of "valuation that marital partners place upon one another; yet we hear little of the intervening details, which in their fullness, would give us a sense of how indeed a family as an ongoing concern functions, and how the emergent demands of its social structure are met, how the social structure of a family is related meaningfully or functionally to the rest of the social system, and how any family of orientation dissolves into successive families of procreation" Bell.[13] In reference to the progressive dissolution of the family of orientation into successive families of procreation, we would like to attach importance to the fact that values are unconsciously transferred from generation to generation in some family strains.

Moreover, the staff felt that a conception broad enough to allow full communication of our experience should account for the inroads of the therapeutic team into the family system and provide a basis for explaining changes brought about by such intervention. For example, in our initial contacts with these families in their home, the therapeutic teams were impressed how some families sought to absorb them immediately into their internal network of sentiments, affects and communications. The teams would return from family treatment session and report how they were really "let inside" the family, "felt a part of it," and had experienced the ebb and flow of its emotional currents. In fact, Spivack deals specifically with this aspect of the co-therapists' experience in Chapter 13, where he discusses the demands of family therapy upon the therapists.

But there were also instances where these same teams remained on the periphery of family units, with key members or the family as a unit attempting to keep them at a safe emotional distance. Often this was done by trying to change the therapy into a social situation, by having refreshments ready to serve when the team arrived, or by talking about superficial issues. Perhaps the greatest need for an emerging conceptional model was due to our awareness of the complexity of the personal and social phenomena with which we were dealing. In developing a model, we sought to avoid the experience of others who have viewed interlinking personal and interpersonal factors solely in personal terms.

Maas[75] effectively points out how investigators, ten to fifteen years ago, had to struggle to deal with the social and interpersonal factors that are important in the etiology and maintenance of schizophrenics without a conceptual model. In an evaluation of Tietze's "Study of Mothers of Schizophrenic Patients,"[109] he writes, "One sees Tietze struggling with an awareness of social and interpersonal factors in schizophrenia which she is apparently unable to study because she cannot conceptualize them." He goes on to say that although Tietze refers to particular relationships and family constellations, she is obliged to present her findings in terms of individual psychodiagnostic patterns.

In a theoretical paper Floyd Allport[6] draws attention to another aspect of the same issue as being still prevalent in the everyday parlance of social scientists. He feels that there is "something unfortunate" in the practice of employing psychological (that is, individually oriented) concepts as personifications applying to groups. If, for example, it is said that a group "convenes," "thinks," "feels," "decides," "achieves solidarity," "becomes organized," "legislates" or "adjourns," either the expression is a tautology, a borrowing for a group of a term that has meaning only at the level of the individual organism, or else it refers to some kind of "concerted doing" performed by an alleged agent for which we can find no unique referent. An individual can be said to "think" or "feel"; but to say that a group does these things has no ascertainable meaning beyond saying that so many individuals do them.

With these reasons in mind more attention was given in our project team discussions toward developing the broad outlines of a conceptual model. This model would serve not only as a base from which we would be able to sharpen our therapeutic procedures, but would be necessary in order for us to appreciate more systematically the many layers and levels of phenomena with which we were working. The latter process was empirical and because of the many clinical and administrative problems that arose in the conduct of the program to which priority had to be given, the development of the model could be pursued only at intermittent intervals. Nevertheless, it was pursued, and the issue of delineating a common frame of reference remained a major preoccupation throughout our experience. Moreover, by developing a rough initial conceptual model we sought to avoid the somewhat strong but timely criticism made by Rosenthal[95] in his review of two books of clinical papers on the treatment of schizophrenia. He remarked that in reading the papers he had the feeling that artists were at work: "It is as though one had asked a group of distinguished painters or sculptors to represent their perceptions of a common entity—in this case, schizophrenia—and each has done so in his own unique way. . . ." This resulted, however, in a low level of substantive communication among the therapists, and Rosenthal sums up his critique of these "reference-less" artistic productions by concluding that, "One must therefore raise the question whether reliance on clinical impressions re-formulated in metapsychological, literary, mythological, and sometimes metaphysical language can hope to advance prospects in these matters any further. This is not to deny the contribution and potential value of clinical observations made during psychotherapy, but to indicate that the models and concepts with which these observations are based, must eventually be integrated into the basic sciences rather than in the literary and philosophical arts." Browning[28] has stated similarly that stumbling blocks in delinquency analysis would be substantially resolved by attention to systematic and definitive qualitative and descriptive analysis. The lesson gleaned from Rosenthal's statement was that our conceptual model certainly needed to be developed from a broader base than our therapeutic efforts constituted.

The parameters of this frame of reference began to take form as we examined the literature of clinical psychiatry, the social sciences, and mental illness. It became apparent that there was general agreement on conceptual viewpoints of some issues, for example, that the family be conceptualized as a dynamic social system—although one investigator may give more emphasis to some properties of the system than to others. Furthermore, if we are to understand adaptive and maladaptive behavior of family members, we will have to arrive at some integrative concepts which tie together the dynamics of the individual with interpersonal phenomena operating within the familial environment, as well as with the structural properties of the family system.

Some investigators have devoted their energies to developing elaborate classificatory systems of family diagnosis. A major contributor in this respect has been Nathan Ackerman.[3] The principal service of these family diagnostic schemes has been to draw attention to the wide variety of personal and interpersonal factors involved. Titchener and his associates[110] have gone one step further and have begun to test the adequacy of their classificatory system via the collection of empirical data as they investigate the complex relationship of family life to adolescent personality development.

There is a growing amount of research concerning the breakdown in the relationships and dynamics between the mental patient and his family. Representative of more meaningful studies in this direction have been the theoretical propositions of Robert S. Albert,[4] and some of the notions expressed by Freeman and Simmons,[37] at the Community Health Project at the Harvard School of Public Health.

Finally, important contributions are being made by a number of the early pioneers in family therapy with the schizophrenic, who have developed specific theories which, if they do not explain the etiology of schizophrenia in the family, at least account for its maintenance. This work may be classified with those studies that seek to show the significance of family environment in the etiology of schizophrenia, studies that comprise a large part of the current psychological theory concerning schizophrenia. Here we refer to the Palo Alto group's[9] concept of the "double-bind" and "family homeostasis," Lyman Wynne's[117] theory of "pseudo-mutuality," the concept of "marital schism and skew" developed by Lidz and his associates,[71] and Murray Bowen's[19] point of view that the schizophrenic psychosis of the patient is a symptom manifestation of an active process that involves the entire family ("undifferentiated family ego-mass"). Therefore, the family unit is regarded as a single organism and the patient is seen as the part of the family organism through which the overt symptoms of psychosis are expressed. Bowen's concept is extremely important as regards the manner in which the family of the schizophrenic is approached and treated. It will become clear to the reader that initially the co-therapists had varying degrees of confliction as to whether "the whole family was sick" or mainly the family member diagnosed as schizophrenic. As Bowen did in his report of his first four years of research, we too moved more toward viewing schizophrenia from a family rather than an individual orientation. And in so doing we agree with Bowen that "the schizophrenia did not change; the only change was in the eyes that saw it. In a sense the family concept provides another position from which to view one of man's oldest dilemmas."

The presentation of a beginning working model will help the reader to understand the origin of our ideas and the scope and limits of our conceptualizations as we approached these disturbed families in their homes. We will subsequently discuss our initial frame of reference, our method, some family histories, objective evaluative data as well as clinical and theoretical concepts, and finally the emerging conceptual model.

A Beginning Model

George Homans[52] quotes Elton Mayo, a pioneer in the field of industrial psychology and sociology, as saying "It is better to have a complex body of fact and a simple theory—a working hypothesis—than a simple body of fact and a complex theory." This was the position in which we found ourselves at the beginning of the project. We were faced with an amazing, somewhat confusing array of human phenomena possessing fragmented concepts, none of which was broad enough to encompass the problem. The team brought to the project a wide variety of clinical experience gained in individual and group psychotherapy, marital counseling, and in working with psychotic as well as neurotic populations. Moreover, the work of the early family therapists cited above was beginning to be published, and thus expanded the body of fact available to us. From this emerged a working conceptual model, which essentially served as a baseline for therapeutic operation as well as systematic observation. The working model viewed the nuclear family as a social system embedded in a larger social system. The family social system has important structural characteristics among which are subsystems comprising groups of family members in dyads and triads. The mother-father-child subsystem makes up a crucial triangular system which we viewed as the fundamental determinant of personality. Other dyadic and triadic relationships may impinge upon and modify this basic triangular relationship.

The family social system is viewed as a dynamic social organism which, like the human organism, is never in a static condition. Its components are in a continual state of reciprocal transactions. The term "transactions" as used here is distinguished from the term "interactions" and follows the definition offered by Kluckhohn and Spiegel:[61] a complex network of processes which determines behavior rather than an individual personality or even a group. These transactions are conceptualized at two levels: the covert level which deals with the family's imaginary fantasies and infantile matters, and the overt, immediately observable level which reflects itself in verbal and non-verbal communication patterns of a current situation. Moreover, the gestalt-like quality of these transactions may be described along a continuum of equilibrium-disequilibrium.

Equilibrium is used here synonymously with family stability, which, according to Zelditch[120] and his cultural anthropological studies is in part dependent upon differentiation and adjustment to present and future roles in the family environment. According to Zelditch, "If the nuclear family constitutes a social system over time, it will differentiate roles such that instrumental leadership and expressive leadership of the system are discriminated. . . . If the nuclear family consists of a defined 'normal' complement of the male adult, female adult and their immediate children, the male adult will play the role of the instrumental leader and the female adult will play the role of the expressive leader."

Family instability and disequilibrium is often the result of lack of clarity of perception and allocation of instrumental and expressive leadership to the husband-father, wife-mother and siblings by family members. This disequilibrium particularly manifests itself when rules are altered or changed by forces internal or external to the familial environment.

The family system also has its external and internal boundaries. Through its external boundaries, family members, individually or collectively, articulate with other reference systems in the larger social system of which the family is a part. These articulations are largely made through the operation of kinship systems and the family's pursuit of work, recreation, and religious experience. The therapeutic team's entrance into the home represents a somewhat unique intervention of the family social system from the outside. The manner in which a family mobilizes to cope with this special type of intervention is of considerable interest and may in some way be predictive of the success of the therapeutic efforts since fundamental changes in the family's behavior will depend upon the extent to which the therapists are able to get beyond the family's external boundaries into its inner network of sentiments, feelings and fantasies. The principal therapeutic goal is then to move the family as a unit toward a fuller and more meaningful participation in the larger society. The latter will depend upon changing the character of shared psychopathology in the family. A principal feature of the above is the "scapegoating" of the primary patient into the sick role by all family members so that they might carry out a marginal adjustment. In other words, a degree of adaptation is achieved, both internal and external to the family system, as a result of the mutual perception of the sick member.

At the same time we accomplish our larger goal of evaluating family pathology and potential for healthy adjustment. The family viewed in this way is a dynamic organism and is evaluated in terms of its ability to change and make accommodations and adjustments to its internal and external pressures. This ability enables the family as a unit, or sub-unit, to move toward fuller and more meaningful participation in the larger society.

It will be noted that in our beginning working model we did not conceptualize about specific theories with which to tie together the intrapersonal and interpersonal, nor did we suggest the agent or the intervening variables to account for the etiology or maintenance of schizophrenia in the family setting. The family case histories will hopefully guide the reader toward more definitive statements in this direction than we were prepared to make when we started our adventure.

The family and schizophrenia

Alfred S. Friedman

Chapter

2

There are many divergent and conflicting reports in the clinical and research literature regarding the attributes of parents of schizophrenics, their child-rearing practices and their relationships with their schizophrenic offspring. Some of these studies report statistically significant differences between these parents and parents of normal control or non-schizophrenic subjects; and other studies are unable to replicate these differences. The results are thus equivocal regarding the effects of parental personalities on the development of schizophrenia. (A part of this confusion, incidentally, might be clarified by careful studies using adequate samples which separate the parents of female schizophrenics from the parents of male schizophrenics.) Some of the attributes which have been reported, but not cross-validated, for mothers of schizophrenics are: overtly and covertly rejecting, dominating, hostile, overpossessive, overcontrolling, overprotective, cold, unyielding, rigid, ignoring, impervious, anxious, helpless, irrational, and distrustful. Some of the attributes which have been reported, but not cross-validated, for fathers of schizophrenics are: weak, dependent, passive, withdrawn, indifferent, ineffectual, remote, cool and tyrannical.

It may be that in attempting to discriminate schizophrenic families from non-schizophrenic families, we shall find no one consistent personality profile for each type of mother and father. It also may be that other factors are more discriminating than the specific parental personality characteristics, such as the degree of personality disturbance, the maladjustment or distortion in the individual parents, the faulty milieu of the family, the distorted structure of the parents' marital relationship, certain global characteristics of a pathological family system, etc.

No single factor, such as a faulty mother-infant relationship, seems likely to cause schizophrenia by itself but rather it seems to be the structure, milieu and interaction of the family that are detrimental to the ego development, the personality and the social adjustment of the children raised in them. Lidz et al[71] reported that they found the parents were often struggling with incestuous and homosexual tendencies within themselves: "The parents are unable to form a coalition as members of the parental generation, to maintain their appropriate sex-linked roles, or to transmit instrumentally valid ways of thinking, feeling, and communicating suited to the society into which the child must emerge." They described the parental marriages in these families as being either "schismatic," with associated mutual distrust and derogation and the parents' hostilities dividing the family into opposing factions, or "skewed," in that one spouse goes along with the aberrant ways and child-rearing practices of the more disturbed partner; the parental alliance is thus based on these distorting pathological defenses. The overt parental alliance succeeds in masking the underlying disagreement and conflict to achieve what Wynne has called "pseudo-mutuality." In either pattern, an "emotional divorce" exists and there is a lack of a basic, warm, affectionate and sexually satisfactory relationship. A review of this matter by our therapeutic team over the six-year period of working together led to the consensus that in most cases the pathological dyadic relationships between the grandmothers and grandfathers in both of the parents' families of origin, and in the current parental marriage relationship, are all in conflict with each other.

We also have seen families where the parents maintain an apparently exclusive complementary relationship with each other; they parentify each other and anxiously protect each other in a narcissistic pact against a hostile world. They are unable to admit their child into this world, and emotionally isolate the child. Some schizophrenic families shift back and forth from one type of dyadic alignment to the other, and correspondingly from "schism" to "skew" in the parental relationship.

The efforts at resolution of parental conflict point in one of two directions. The conflict may remain largely between the parents with comparatively little involvement of the children, or it may transmit itself primarily to one of the children, leaving the other children less involved, and leaving relatively few problems between the parents. In either case there is an inability to establish a stable, mutually gratifying triadic relationship, or to develop an adequate family image. Regardless of which phase the parental relationship may be in, the common underlying attitude, and the common family sense accords no existence to the real self, the real feelings and impulses, of the scapegoated child. This child is not allowed to project any of its "bad" self onto the parents. Rather the parents need to project their "bad" introjects, derived originally from their own parents, onto their child.

The relative distribution of power between the parents has an effect on the behavior of a child, quite independent of the absolute level of authority exercised by the parents collectively. Thus, if we were to test Lidz's observation that both "schism and skew" characterize the marital relationships of the parents of schizophrenics, we might expect to obtain a bimodal distribution of scores on a measure of degree of marital conflict and disagreement. In the "skew" condition the avoidance of relationship by one partner from the other, which is maladjustive, nevertheless results in a very low conflict score.

Schizophrenia appears to arise from an intense pathologic family relationship, rather than from neglect or the absence of a relationship. Often—especially in the tightest family systems, those with an only child —all the significant emotional exchanges are contained within the closed, complete social system of the family, and there is little meaningful contact with the outside world. Some of the characteristics which have been variously attributed to schizophrenic families, in addition to genetic factors, are: 1) excessively closed family systems, in which the schizophrenic symptomatology serves a homeostatic function within the rigid family structure; "pseudo-mutuality," and isolation of the family affectively from the rest of the community, 2) shared family myths or delusions, 3) paralogic modes of thinking in all family members, 4) lack of individuation and self-identity of members from the family "ego-mass," 5) intense pathological symbiotic attachments of child to parent and of parent to grandparent. There is also some suggestive evidence that schizophrenia is a process that may require three or more generations to develop. Family therapy has uncovered in some families specific delusional or highly unrealistic, fixed attitudes or myths which originated at least two generations ago, and which have been transmitted unchanged through the parent to the current young schizophrenic patient.

Bowen[19] has described the symbiotic pairing as a "being for each other," usually most intense between the mother and the designated patient, and emotionally excluding the other parent and the siblings. There is a long-standing conflict or alienation between the two parents, and the child has been misused by them, either in the role of an essential communication link, or to fill the emotional void in their relationship, or as a narcissistic extension of one of the parents—"to be for the other." One of the children born into this climate of parental emotional divorce is selected for this special role, for reasons which are not yet too clear, but which may have something to do with the sex of the child and the stressful situation in the parental marriage at that time. This child becomes engaged in a prolonged and consuming symbiotic relationship with the more aggressive, demanding and needy parent. The overprotective and rejective "mothering one" seems to be allowed by the weaker spouse to mould and coerce the child in a way that grants almost total control. The symbiosis appears to be the only workable solution for the child in this situation. The child gets trapped into this relationship, but also accepts it in order to insure a less anxious and more predictable mother.

A major life theme of the schizophrenic child is his unsuccessful effort to liberate himself from the pull of the symbiotic attachment to the mother, and to overcome his fears of differentiating, growing up and separating. He has to deal first with his mother's efforts to hold him, and his own urge to stay with her; then, when he gets partially free, he faces outside social relationships without a self of his own.

Bowen has also described these children as functioning as extensions of the "undifferentiated family ego-mass." They might separate themselves from the family and function as dependent attachments to others. They do not "grow away" from the family ego-mass. Instead, after reaching physical maturation, they may "tear" themselves away, maintaining a kind of pseudo-separateness by means of angry rebellion or distant, indifferent positiveness. They may function adequately in school or work, but when they marry they immediately find themselves "fused" in a new undifferentiated family ego-mass with its characteristic overdependence, overdistance and emotional turmoil.

Despite the allure of the dependency gratification of symbiosis, home and parents, the parents' fears of being overwhelmed and of the primitive uncontrolled destructive and cannibalistic impulses within the family, including their own, sometimes lead the schizophrenic child to regress into psychosis or unusual behavior as a way of signaling for outside help. He offers himself in the sacrificial role and denies that he wants change, since he greatly fears the final rejection by, and separation from, his parents. He has little confidence that outside therapeutic forces are powerful enough to change the forces that are driving his parents and are maintaining the family system.

Scheflen and Birdwhistell have recently, in a personal communication, used the colorful analogy of "a tar-baby, Siamese-twin" to describe the symbiotic relationship between the mother and schizophrenic child, referring to the lack of ego-differentiation between the two, and to the manner in which each member of this dyad engages in isolating the other from a meaningful emotional relationship with a third party. We ourselves, through our observations in family treatment, have conceptualized the schizophrenic family as composed of multiple psychopathological dyadic alliances. We shall describe the interpersonal relationships in these families as typically split and compartmentalized—characterized by stereotyped, static and symbiotic dyads—rather than integrated into flexible triadic or four-person maturational functioning units.

Bowen[19] also reported that he has found it virtually impossible for parents of a schizophrenic child to work therapeutically on their own marital relationship problem, without having the child-patient physically present in the therapy. The parents and the child present themselves to the therapist as a pseudo-triad which appears healthy on the surface. While the parents genuinely believe that their main interest is to help their child, they actually find it necessary to make a project out of the child's illness, and to work on that project as a flight from the anxiety inherent in their own marriage relationship. We ourselves have encountered similar difficulties in our work with the parents in such families, but we have sometimes succeeded in helping these parents to give up their view of the child as something to project their problems on, and to face some of their personal anxieties which blocked improvement of their marriage relationship.

The family organization of the schizophrenic has been characterized by us and others as rigidly stable; excessively impervious to the external environment; controlling and distorting the interaction of family members with the outer environment; distorting the usual, culturally defined role expectancies within the family while maintaining superficial conformity to external standards; suffering from overcontrol, suppression of affect, massive denial and shallowness of affect inappropriate to the situation; from vagueness, blurring and fragmentation in the family communication; and as an organization where the members often do not hear each other or reach each other. Seen in the context of family treatment, some of the most incomprehensible and bizarre thoughts and behavior of schizophrenic patients may begin to make sense.

Methods and plan of treatment

Alfred S. Friedman and Howard E. Mitchell

Chapter
3

In spite of enthusiastic attempts in recent years no generally effective and definitive therapeutic approach for schizophrenia has been developed. The project on which our experience is based, was planned as one of many efforts currently being made to acquire new knowledge and find new approaches to this major mental health problem. As we stated in the "Introduction," our thinking about the actual treatment plan to be followed was based upon the concept of the family as the primary unit of mental illness. Our approach, therefore, was to treat the schizophrenic and his family as a unit via a group therapeutic technique in the home setting.

Work Setting

The Hospital of the Philadelphia Psychiatric Center is a 144-bed, non-sectarian, non-profit community institution, dedicated to the short-term treatment of the mentally ill. Half of the beds are set aside for ward, part-pay and free patients. Approximately 1400 patients are admitted to the hospital annually, approximately one-fourth of whom are young schizophrenic patients. In addition to the hospital, there is a large adult out-patient clinic and a modern child care facility. The Philadelphia Psychiatric Center is a member of the Health and Welfare Council of Philadelphia and is affiliated with the Federation of Jewish Agencies of Philadelphia and with the United Fund. The Wurzel Institute for Research and Training which is attached to the hospital, supplied a modern comfortable setting for our project. There were several large offices to accommodate families in treatment and a room, equipped with a one-way screen and sound and tape recording facilities, for staff observation and analysis of family treatment sessions.

Referral and Selection of Families

The plan *per se* was to accept referrals of families who have produced a young schizophrenic member in his teens or early twenties, and evaluate them for treatment. One requirement was that the presenting patient was unmarried and living with the parents. Generally speaking, we accepted cases only where the family was intact and living together; where both parents were available and agreed, together with the siblings of the patient, to participate in the treatment. Occasionally, we made an exception of an older married sibling who lived in another city, or of a sibling who was away at college. If these were not too far distant we made an effort to get them into the treatment unit, and succeeded in doing this in several cases. No cases were ruled out on the basis of sex, race, religion or socio-economic status. A broad range of social economic status, roughly representative of the distribution in the greater Philadelphia community, accordingly characterized the group of families with which we worked. We had no very wealthy families who would be rated as Class I on Hollingshead-Redlich's SES Scale, but we did have several professional families, who would qualify as either Class I or Class II on that scale. Our sample also contained a fairly broad representation of the national, sub-cultural, religious and racial groups of the total community, except for the fact that about one-third of all our families were Jewish and lower middle class, which is of course a greater incidence of this type of family than occurs in the general population.

The fees charged to the families for the treatment ranged from nothing to twenty-five dollars per session. We generally tried to set a fee which would represent a meaningful amount of money to the family, but would not cause them great difficulty or sacrifice. Rather than letting the fee become a focus of resistance at the outset of therapy, we set it at a nominal amount and raised the question of increasing it at a later stage, when the family was ready to deal on a more realistic basis. We never turned away a family because they could not pay a fee.

Following the evaluation and review by the project personnel, family treatment in the home would be offered to the family. If the parents accepted the offer, work was begun even if the young schizophrenic patient refused. It is interesting to note here that in all such instances the patient eventually entered actively into the treatment process. In general, families evaluated accepted this new treatment arrangement when it was offered to them. In some cases, the parents began to maneuver to avoid the family treatment after one or several sessions, and to get the patient into individual treatment, especially when they saw that the problems in their marriage would be exposed and that they would have to undergo psychotherapy for themselves. Most typically the mother would telephone to say that the family treatment could not proceed because of her husband's lack of interest, or some external reason, rather than admit and discuss her own personal anxieties and resistances.

The majority of the families were referred by the Out-Patient Service of the project's host hospital, or by the Psychiatric Reception and Evaluation Center of the Commonwealth of Pennsylvania, in Philadelphia.

Some cases were on waiting lists of public mental hospitals in the area, and family treatment was offered in lieu of the hospitalization of the adolescent schizophrenic member. Later on, as the project became known in the community, families were referred by other clinics, social agencies, and psychiatrists in private practice. These referrals were frequently made at the point when the diagnosed schizophrenic patient was hospitalized or re-hospitalized, or when hospitalization was recommended. We accepted cases regardless of whether the patient had had a previous psychotic break or not, or whether he had been hospitalized prior to the current schizophrenic illness. In a number of the cases in which family treatment was initiated, the young schizophrenic member had withdrawn and isolated himself from the community by having refused to go to school, to work, or to an out-patient psychiatric service for long periods of time. In these cases treatment in the home was the only treatment possible, other than hospitalizing the patient by force which the parents had not and would not accept.

We did not accept cases where a parent rather than a child was in an active psychotic phase at the time of referral, nor did we accept cases where a parent in addition to a child was in an active psychotic phase. And yet, in spite of this restriction, we had a number of cases where we had to deal with the psychotic conditions of parents as well as children.

The diagnosis of schizophrenia was established by the referral source and confirmed independently at Philadelphia Psychiatric Center, in accordance with the regular American Psychiatric Association diagnostic criteria, by a qualified psychiatrist who was not a member of the family treatment staff. This psychiatrist interviewed the patient in the clinic, completed the Multidimensional Rating Scale for Psychiatric Patients (Lorr and Jenkins), at the time of interviewing the patient, and established the diagnosis. These ratings, obtained before and after treatment, constitute one of the measures of the patient's condition and serve as an evaluation of the effects of the treatment. The MSRPP is composed of items which are behaviorally based, quantitatively defined, homogeneous, and mutually exclusive. It yields a total "morbidity" or psychopathology score, as well as syndromes (factors) and type-profiles of psychopathology. In two cases where the patient refused to come to the clinic, the independent psychiatrist went to the home for testing, as did the psychologist who administered the psychodiagnostic test battery.

Psychological Testing

A psychological test battery consisting of the Wechsler Adult Intelligence Scale, Rorschach, Thematic Apperception Test, and Draw-A-Person Test was administered separately to each family member. This provided us with some leads regarding the distortions of the perception of each family member, his defense mechanisms, his assets for therapy, and his adaptive functioning. These leads add to the therapists' understanding of the psychodynamic implications of the family's interaction, especially during the early sessions. In the projective test protocols of the parents we usually found evidence of psychopathology which cued us to the specific ways in which the parents had contributed to the development of schizophrenia in their offspring. Some siblings who superficially appeared quite intact in their behavior, often revealed surprising distortions and disturbances in their projective responses.

The Multiple-Impact Method

We employed the Multiple-Impact method of family evaluation in addition to the more traditional evaluative methods referred to above, and in addition to the evaluation of the family in their home setting. This method was developed at the Galveston project of the University of Texas Medical Branch of Psychiatry,[76] whose members have found it effective in uncovering the dynamics of the family in cases of juvenile delinquency and behavior disorder, and in accelerating the family's involvement in therapy. We have found it to be equally effective and powerful with our families of schizophrenic adolescents. After individual family members, in separate interviews, express different opinions regarding the family problems, they are encouraged to talk through and reconcile their differing versions in paired and total family interviews. The irrational projections of the one member onto the other are thus frequently exposed and dissolved. This method furthermore tends to quickly unsettle joint family resistances, and to remove the façade which the family usually presents to outsiders. As a rule, four members of our professional staff spend four consecutive hours with the family in a sequence of individual, pairing, and overlapping interviews, and an intervening conference by the treatment team to plan strategy; a joint family-team session finally reviews the findings and discusses a plan of treatment.

Definition and Boundaries of the Family Treatment Unit

Since the term "family treatment" has been used to connote a variety of therapy arrangements, we wish to define our use of the term here as a procedure in which the same therapist or the same therapy team works with all members of the family treatment unit at the same time; neither the designated patient, nor the problem child, nor any other family member is seen in any concurrent or separate individual therapy sessions, except for some very special or unusual reason. The terms "conjoint family treatment," "family group treatment," and "family unit treatment," have also been used to designate this approach, and to distinguish it from "family oriented," collaborative forms of treatment in which individual family members are seen separately by the same or different therapists. The family treatment unit is defined as including members of the nuclear family, as well as significant relatives or non-relatives who share the living experience, or who exert an important influence on the total family system even when living elsewhere.

Some families had living grandparents who were important members of the nuclear family unit, and on whom the parents were still fixated—whether they lived under the same roof or not. Several of our mothers called their mothers on the telephone every day; they were still very dependent on them and could not act contrary to their opinions. Sometimes it was necessary to include such grandparents in the family treatment sessions.

We also included in the family treatment unit, as a standard practice, the married children of the nuclear family. Less regularly we included the spouse of the married child, and only, when this appeared indicated. (The mother in the nuclear family may be in a close dyadic alliance with her married daughter, and be in daily contact with her, creating a separate mother-daughter involvement that has a splitting effect on the total family relationship. Unless this is brought into the treatment and explored it may serve to maintain the emotional divorce between the parents or have other pathological effects.)

For special therapeutic purposes the family treatment unit was occasionally broadened to include a key relative or close friend who did not live under the same roof, or some peripheral person of influence such as the family physician or the attorney. In general, we tried to maintain a flexible and exploratory approach. In several cases we included the fiance of the patient during a phase of the family treatment. For example, in one family (see Chapter 5), the twenty-four-year-old schizophrenic boy was about to marry a girl who had recently had a child out of wedlock by another man. Everyone agreed that this particular marriage was ill advised, including the treatment team, the parents, and the boy's rabbi who was his adviser. The young man was in no condition to assume the responsibilities of marriage and it was difficult to see how the marriage could succeed. Nevertheless, he insisted that he was going to proceed with the wedding as scheduled. Three weeks before the wedding date, the treatment team decided to bring the intended bride into the family therapy sessions so that she could see for herself what was going on between the patient and his family. As anticipated by the team, both she and the patient decided after two such sessions to cancel the wedding. In one of these sessions the boy's rabbi was also included, since the boy at the time was in a fanatically orthodox religious phase and believed that it was his religious duty to take a wife.

In another family we might have achieved additional results if a key uncle had been involved in the family therapy—the mother's eldest brother, a widower, who lived with the family. He was a businessman and by far the most successful, respected, and influential member of the household. If we were working with that family today we would probably take a more definite stand in including him in the therapy unit than we did originally. However, more will be said about the emergence and understanding of such clinical issues later on.

FAMILY TREATMENT PLAN

Schedule of Therapy

The family therapy sessions are one and one-half hours in duration and are scheduled regularly once a week. Special additional arrangements may be made as required to control acute behavior of the patient, or to guide the family in handling an acute problem. Treatment sessions are usually started in the home, unless the designated patient is already hospitalized. If after home treatment starts, the family feels unable to tolerate or control the patient's behavior, even when supported to do so, the patient may be admitted to the hospital for a short period of time. Family therapy sessions are continued in the hospital during this period to maintain the integrated family orientation to solving the problem. The patient is returned to the home and to family therapy in the home as soon as possible.

Organization of Co-Therapy Teams

The project treatment staff is composed of eight members, including four psychiatrists, two psychiatric social workers, and two clinical psychologists. A therapy team assigned to a family may be composed of any two members of this staff of eight family therapists: a different pairing may be decided on for each new family in the project, depending primarily on the availability of therapist time, and the type of family or problem in which a particular therapist has an interest and is most successful. At the first treatment evaluation session the family-problem concept and the family-treatment concept are discussed; the composition of the treatment unit is determined and a schedule of sessions is set up. The initial evaluation session is sometimes attended by more than two therapists. Subsequently, two therapists who have chosen to work together or in whom the family has evoked more response and interest than in the others, are assigned to work with the family. We prefer heterosexual therapy teams whenever possible, as this provides a more natural identification model for the family. However, sex difference in the team is not required to obtain transference reactions from the family, (*see* Chapter 14). Teams composed of two male therapists have successfully worked together, but we have not as yet tried to team two female therapists. Eventually each staff member will have had an opportunity to work with several different partners, an arrangement that will broaden his therapeutic experience and technical armamentarium.

The therapy of each family is reviewed in weekly conferences of the entire project staff. The thinking of each team member is stimulated by the exchanges of therapeutic problems and strategies with the other teams, as well as in consideration of theoretical issues. The co-therapists share in the problems and decisions and learn from each other about the many things that happen simultaneously in a session. They confer with each other at the end of each session, reviewing it and planning future strategy. We consider our clinical observations and formulations of a family system to be more reliable when they are the result of the thinking of two skilled clinicians, rather than one, that have checked each other on their impressions of and reactions to the family.

While it is possible to conduct family therapy with one therapist, our project team members usually prefer to work with a partner rather than going it alone when coping with a very disturbed family. The presence of another therapist helps to check and counterbalance all the countertransference phenomena which can be intense in family treatment be they negative, positive or ambivalent. A team is less likely to be "swallowed up" by a pathological family system than is a single therapist. Using a therapy team seems to give us a lever to loosen up the tight formation of pathological dyads in the schizophrenic family; family members can be shown how to enter into a healthy triadic relationship by relating positively and simultaneously to the two therapists.

To the extent that the co-therapists become a harmoniously working team, they serve as a positive identification model for the family. They plan some sessions in advance, and may decide that it is advantageous for one of them to take the lead in handling a certain family problem; for example, one of the co-therapists may be more likely to get a positive response from a particular mother who is resisting change. They are secure enough in their working relationship in the presence of the family even to present different views on a specific problem, and the family becomes aware of the respect with which each therapist considers the other's views. One therapist can support the other by talking to him in a calm way when there is intense family anxiety. This exercises a strong control over the family system and permits effective therapeutic interaction. Among the many other ways in which the therapists can complement one another is for one to play the reassuring role of the calm observer and evaluator, while the other stimulates affective interaction. Both work toward a balance of their authority and support each other's position with the family when indicated. The family tends to select one of the therapists as the leader of the therapeutic enterprise and it is up to the co-therapists to realize that this may be a neurotic need or a maneuver, and not necessarily to go along with it. A major requirement for team work is the ability to trust the co-therapist, to be able to depend on him for cooperation, and to respect him as a person and a therapist.

Therapeutic Method

Regarding the question of a therapeutic "method," approach or technique, we make no attempt to adopt a uniform method or technique of treatment to be applied to all families and adhered to by all therapy teams. We have therefore no special brand or label with which to identify our particular therapeutic approach. Haley[47] has referred to our approach to family treatment as "The Brotherly Love School." We do not completely disavow the "brotherly love" aspect of our approach, even if it is not in the height of psychiatric fashion. We certainly do become very actively and empathically involved with the families and their problems.

We start from a minimum baseline of an ego-supportive approach and an orienting of the family toward working as a family in the solution of family problems. But the methods used in the treatment are varied and flexible, and range widely on the activity-passivity continuum of therapist role. The therapists' activities include, among others: neutral observing, reflecting, interpreting, confronting, active empathic participation, functioning as a communication and problem-solving expert, and providing direct authoritative leadership. We may also engage at times in the uncovering of intrapsychic conflicts, unconscious material, family myths and fantasies, primarily by means of free association and dreams. Many examples of the foregoing are provided in the subsequent detailed case histories. The therapist, for example, may temporarily adopt the role of the authoritative superego figure, and lecture to the family about their uncontrolled aggressive acting-out or sexual behavior, in an effort to neutralize the excess of tension and aggression and to bring order out of chaos. In non-verbal families we may facilitate expressive and interpersonal skills. In lower socio-economic and culturally-deprived families we give attention to real life environmental problems, task assignments, job counseling, development of motivational incentives and rewards, and many other aspects.

We have sometimes found the purely neutral understanding of the observer's role to be insufficient to control a disturbed or acting-out family, or to overcome very rigid family resistance and denial. During the course of our experience with these rigidly pathological families we have moved toward the employment of more active techniques. We do not believe, however, that our therapeutic techniques have usually been as actively intervening and authoritative as those described by Ackerman, or as controlling as those described by Haley and Jackson. We permit or stimulate, as required, considerable free interaction among family members, and do not keep the attention of the family focused on ourselves.

In our orientation toward positive family goals, we engage in such techniques as: making group goals explicit; effecting compromise and integration; improving communications; helping members to express feelings and to listen and hear; correcting distortions; acting as a communication bridge; reflecting feelings of the family members toward each other; focusing attention on non-verbal reactions; providing feedback and mirroring; verbalizing for the group; and providing information.

Finally, the therapist makes constructive use of his own personality, his feelings and his creativity. To the chaotic destructive family he presents himself as a definite integrated personality and a factor to be reckoned with; to the stereotyped, repressed or "dead" family he presents the vibrant, involved, challenging and exploring aspects of his personality.

The above-mentioned techniques are by no means the only ones that are used in our family treatment; additional methods and treatment procedures are discussed in Section IV.

EVALUATIVE TECHNIQUES

Rationale and Scope

The main purpose of the project was to demonstrate how effectively the schizophrenic and his family could be treated as a unit in the home. The objective measurement of the effectiveness of the demonstration is based upon the nature and degree of change of psychopathology of the individual family members and the restoration of the family as a unit to a more effective functioning level. For both the individual family members and the family as a unit a rationale was developed consistent with our conceptual model, and our treatment plan, and with practical considerations of the administration of the evaluative techniques. The treatment situation, for example, demanded that the evaluative techniques given to all family members be simple and direct both in language and manner of presentation.

The rationale developed to understand the effectiveness of the demonstration for individual family members as well as for the family as a unit drew considerably upon the thinking of Koos.[63] He reasoned that the severe mental illness of the primary patient creates a crisis situation for the family as a unit. The degree and speed with which the family unit recovers from such crisis depends upon the pre-crisis level of internal and external functioning. Therefore, effectiveness for both the individual and the family unit, is defined relative to baseline measures of the patient, his family and their articulations to the community. For the schizophrenic this means that we are interested in the degree to which there is a reduction of symptoms, an alteration of distorted perceptions and disorganized behavior, and an increase in positive object relationships.

The areas of quantitative data obtained from the family members can be divided into four categories as follows: 1) psychodynamics of individual family members; 2) internal family interactions and transactions; 3) family interactions with community; 4) sociological and biographical facts about family and home environment.

To appraise the psychodynamics of each family member, its personality structure and assets for psychotherapy we utilized the Wechsler-Bellevue Adult Scale Form, the Thematic Apperception Test, the Draw-A-Person Test, the Rorschach Technique, and Lorr's MSRPP, as already indicated. The data pertaining to areas 2 and 3 above were mainly obtained from two types of family evaluative techniques, which were administered to all family members as an adjunct to the therapeutic process. The first type consisted of two instruments derived largely from a schedule developed at the Marriage Council of Philadelphia.[84] The second type consisted of a Family Participation Index and a Family Disagreement Scale.

Family Participation Index

This index lists a large variety of activities; family members are asked to indicate whether they participate in them singly, with other family members, with relatives or friends, or not at all. The 20 types of activities included in the Family Participation Index to which the respondent indicates the extent of his engagement are as follows: 1) motion pictures; 2) dances; 3) competitive sports; 4) spectator sports; 5) outdoor activities; 6) social gatherings with friends; 7) reading; 8) artistic and creative; 9) political-civic; 10) hobbies; 11) membership in clubs and organizations; 12) business or professional activities; 13) meals; 14) talking together; 15) religious activity; 16) snacks; 17) household maintenance and repair; 18) listening to radio or watching TV; 19) gardening; 20) family-circle meetings and parties. (See Appendix.)

Responses were obtained in the initial phase of the family treatment and at subsequent follow-up points. This enabled us to observe the degree to which family members consciously perceive change in their activities and the activities of other family members. Moreover the data is suggestive of the relative integration or isolation of the family as a unit, or of its individual members, into or from the community. The data will show rather strikingly the degree to which the parents in particular see themselves as isolated from participation with anyone except their immediate family.

Family Disagreement Scale

The second area of inquiry is the amount of family conflict, the intensity of specific conflict areas and the discrepancy in reports of family conflict areas by individual family members. Previous research (Gianopulos and Mitchell,[43] Mitchell et al.[82]) has demonstrated that the 22 areas of marital disagreement may be empirically classified into the following four categories: 1) domestic-economic; 2) socio-biographical; 3) personal; 4) parental-social relationships. (*See* Appendix.)

It was originally reasoned that an effective demonstration of the therapeutic method of the project would result in a reduction in the amount of conflict, a decrease in intensity of specific areas of conflict, and in greater agreement among family members as to the amount of their disagreement. This hypothesis naively was based upon experience with neurotic families and did not take into account the massive conscious denial of conflict by members of very disturbed families.

At the level of the family members' interpersonal perceptions of themselves and other family members we obtained a series of perceptual pictures via an administration of the Interpersonal Check List (ICL) developed by Leary and his associates.[68] Later we asked a number of the families also to give their perceptions of the co-therapists on the ICL. These percepts have been scored and plotted on the two major axes of the Leary sytem: dominance-submission and love-hate. In Chapter 8 we present our analysis of this perceptional data. One of the hypotheses tested was that the achievement in therapy of better self-understanding and communication among family members should result in a reduction in the discrepancies between self-image of a family member and the modal picture of the family member held by all the other family members.

II

THE EXPERIENCE WITH THE FAMILIES

The Island family

The early phase
Jerome E. Jungreis

The late phase
Ross V. Speck

**Chapter
4**

We all meet at some time or other in our lives a family that seems much like any other family, except that one member is mentally ill. The Island family was much like that. It seemed that all was well and could again be well, but for the blundering happenstance of nature that blindly struck their daughter with a critical illness. To their neighbors, and initially to us, the Island family seemed mature and poised, both as individuals and as a family. Their well-being seemed evident by their stated interests and relationships with the community and with us, by their concern with each other, and in particular, their concern and interest in their sick daughter Cass and in her treatment. They seemed eager to undergo treatment and have their daughter do likewise. The parents presented their marriage as a very happy one, and wanted their children to grow up, get married, and be as happy as they were.

However, as we became enmeshed in their lives, it became increasingly clear that what appeared to be strengths were actually weaknesses. Their stated family closeness and good marriage turned out to be physical closeness, but with an underlying emotional divorce. Their collective image of themselves as an outgoing family was a denial of their basic isolation as a family. They had almost no visitors, no friends, and minimal contact with relatives. Their wish to see their children mature concealed deep ties that bound the children to the home. We eventually learned that part of the bind to the home was a not-so-latent intense incest problem.

In contrast to their apparent willingness to cooperate in therapy, to do *anything*, all family members had a tenacious need to maintain sameness and to thwart even the mildest suggestion of change. Their concern for Cass therefore represented a need to be in control, because as soon as she moved toward health, they became anxious and even physically sick. We became impressed with the evidence that Cass's illness was not just a vagary of fate, but that the Island family generated forces that tended to cause Cass to become schizophrenic and, more clearly, to keep her that way.

This, then, is the case history of the Islands, whom we have known for three and a half years in family therapy. We are going to report about this family chronologically, the way we gathered the information, so that the reader can share with us what we experienced and learned in family therapy with a clinically identified schizophrenic child. Almost all of the therapy was conducted in the home in accordance with the project plan. In the case of the Island family, it could not have been conducted elsewhere. The therapy team consisted of a male psychiatric social worker (Therapist A) and a male psychiatrist (Therapist B).

Before seeing the family, we knew relatively little beside the patient's diagnosis and medical history. The family consisted of four people: a fifty-year-old father; a forty-eight-year-old mother; the schizophrenic patient, Cass, age twenty-four; and her nineteen-year-old brother, Harvey. This was a middle-class Jewish family, living in a nice residential neighborhood of private homes. Mr. Island was an executive in a small real estate office in a nearby city; his wife was the homemaker, their son Harvey was going to college, and Cass had secluded herself in the home for about six years prior to the onset of treatment. She had no social contacts outside the home during this period. She had been hospitalized for two weeks in a private psychiatric hospital two years earlier, with little improvement. During the phone conversation with Mrs. Island to set up the first appointment, she informed us that she doubted that Cass would be present at the sessions.

Initial Impressions

In the first session with the family, every member was present except the sick daughter. We can still recall the father as a strikingly handsome man, the image of a successful corporation executive, with the manners of a proper Bostonian. He gave the impression of being a reasonable, flexible person who would do *anything* to help his daughter. The mother was a rather plain-looking woman, neatly dressed, with a nice figure, who also was well-spoken, rather bright, and knew how to act the hostess. Harvey was a young man of about medium build, dressed without any distinctive style; he wore glasses, and generally spoke in a very low voice, at times almost inaudibly. He had a marked tendency to deal with all manner of things in a detached intellectual way.

We sat in the living room, grouped in a circle. Harvey sat apart in a corner, but he listened and participated. The interview started with general conversation about Cass and how hard they were trying to help her. They also expressed bewilderment as to why Cass was the way she was. They indicated they had tried everything. The mother mentioned that she had sought help at a number of agencies and other community resources, but they had always disappointed her. She could not remember where she had been and why she was unable to use these services. She almost gloatingly told us how right she was that her daughter would remain in her room and would not come downstairs to the living room or speak to us. After a while Therapist B went up to talk to Cass for some time. She spoke to him from behind the locked bathroom door. His attempts to get her to talk to him were almost futile. She felt that she was hopeless and that any kind of therapy was valueless. During the time Therapist B was trying to talk to Cass, the other members of the family moved in close to Therapist A. They were then able to talk about their ideas concerning Cass. They claimed that the shabbiness of their previous living quarters was the reason Cass had been unable to entertain friends. They spoke about the great financial risk they had undertaken in buying this house in a new neighborhood. They had thought the move would do the trick in getting Cass out of the home and helping her acquire some friends. Her sickness restricted them quite a bit. Actually, as their conversation developed, it appeared that Cass's illness had hardly changed their life pattern of isolation. We both wondered about the father, for as well-spoken as he appeared to be, with the manner of a senior executive in a very large firm who had long since "arrived," he did not seem nearly as financially successful as his demeanor would indicate. Indirectly both parents raised the question of the therapy upsetting and exciting their daughter. It seemed terribly important that no one upset her. At this time too, while Therapist B was upstairs, Harvey really opened up on his parents, accusing them of living a cloistered life with no outside interests. He also said that his mother had an inferiority complex and was extremely "nervous." His remarks seemed to slide off the parents' backs, and they would reply to him gently. He did not sustain this attack but would get his point across angrily and then withdraw somewhat until another point arose to excite him.

On the return of Therapist B, the discussion focused on what could be done for Cass, and revealed the fact that she had refused individual therapy. There was also great hesitancy about hospitalizing her again, even though the family recognized that her previous hospitalization had done her some good while she was in the hospital. They said that if Cass didn't want to be hospitalized, that was that. They indicated an interest in using themselves therapeutically as possible participants in the family therapy group. When we pointed out the possible changes that would occur within the family, upsetting their equilibrium, they denied that this would discourage them. They saw our offer to help as being better than nothing, and insisted that they wanted to do "anything" that would help. We felt that they weren't really listening to us as we spoke about changes that would take place in the entire family.

In discussing their daughter further, we became aware of the degree of their denial of the seriousness of her illness. Her attitudes and behavior were seen as normal and understandable. They tended to minimize gross symptoms. For instance, the family could appreciate Cass's feeling that people might think there was something physically wrong with her, even though they couldn't point to anything specific that was physically wrong. The father insisted that she was only in a "rut," that once she stepped out of the house for the first time, she would be fine. Harvey was the one who was most convinced that his sister was not ill. He seemed angry when the therapist suggested that she was. Cass seemed to be the dominating force in the home because of her problems, and in indirect ways the family gave the impression that the entire home revolved around her. Our initial interview ended without our having seen Cass.

In the following session, we elicited more detailed information on the family's isolation and also discussed with the family the importance of having Cass join the therapy. Mrs. Island told us that she herself was not a very sociable person, had no friends, didn't want any, and had been this way for many years. Her husband refused to accept this concept of herself. He insisted that she was an *extremely* sociable person, that she could easily have a host of friends any time she wanted. At this point, Harvey angrily joined in to state that the entire family was highly neurotic and his sister crazy. When Mr. Island challenged Harvey to explain himself, Harvey reeled off a number of symptoms he had noted in his father: fear of dentists and of riding in a car or boat, friendlessness, and many other disturbances. The father blandly denied that these fears existed and joked about Harvey's summation in a belittling way. The mother remained aloof from the father-son dialogue. Mr. Island was skillful in handling Harvey, so that the angry tirade petered out into a desultory discussion.

In the first two sessions we had discussed with the family Cass's failure to come down. At the third session we finally suggested that the entire family go up together with us to see Cass, wherever she might be. This upset the mother and in her rather flat, bland manner she suggested that we might hospitalize her daughter. She then suggested that if she left the house and went away somewhere, somehow, for some length of time, her daughter might be forced to get better. She also expressed fear that if we coerced Cass in any way, the whole home would be upset. The therapy team did insist, however, that we all go up and at least try to talk to Cass. The mother said that she would not go up but would wait for us. As the two therapists got up and started to walk toward the stairs with the father following, the mother quickly ran on ahead and while seemingly wanting to lead the procession, actually blocked us and started to push us back. After a few moments of this, we all went up. Cass was locked in the bathroom and did not speak to anyone. When we came down, the mother expressed strong, sympathetic feelings about how Cass was reacting; the empathy was almost extreme, as though she were pleading her daughter's case in her absence, as though she were the daughter. Later in the same session, one of the therapists again went upstairs alone to talk to Cass. This time she talked. She seemed extremely angry toward her family and said she did not want to come down because if she went on talking, the entire family would see the extent of her fury and this would be very upsetting to them. She suggested that she was staying upstairs to protect the family, and intimated that it was best that she be ill to prevent anyone else's getting sick. When the therapist came downstairs, the mother was crying.

When we came in for the fourth session, Mr. Island announced that he had taken the lock off the bathroom door, so that Cass could not lock herself in during the session. (Twenty-five sessions later we learned that it was actually Harvey who had insisted that the lock must come off, and in fact had taken it off himself.) After the father's announcement, the family started to discuss Cass's domination of the household. We could hear her behind the wall, on the stairs leading to the second floor. In the midst of the complaints about her, she suddenly popped in.

Most striking to the therapists were her extreme obesity (she looked considerably younger than twenty-four, closer to seventeen), her thick eyeglasses, and her disheveled appearance. Her pajama-like clothing appeared to have been slept in and worn for several days. Her hair, a pretty golden-brown, was unkempt. She came in without greeting, sat down, and talked as though she had been a regular member of the family meetings. In a very tense, vibrating way, yet in a low and controlled voice, she said that it was clear from what she had overheard that we didn't understand her or appreciate her condition. Her feelings of inferiority, for example, were too deeply ingrained. We could not understand how utterly impossible it would be for her to change. She was physically different from other women, marred in some indefinable way. All this was said coherently. She seemed well oriented and in contact. After telling us about herself, she turned on her parents and attacked them for misrepresenting her and the family situation. Again, there were no loud voices or strident tones. Cass talked in that low, tense voice while the rest of the family talked in a measured conversational way. She insisted that it was not her fault that the family did not socialize; in fact, she had frequently urged the family to bring people in and try to live as normal a social life as they possible could, and not let her illness hinder them. She said her parents would not even try, and then they claimed it was because of her that they could not socialize. We pointed out to Cass that her parents had told us that she always said she wanted people in the home, but that after they came, she would have a tantrum. She denied that and went on to launch an attack on her father because of his overprotectiveness. She angrily asserted that he had never let her live a life like other girls her age. She recalled that there had been times before she got sick when she had had some girl frinds and had gone out with them in the evening. Her father insisted on accompanying her, even on bus rides where she would feel ridiculous because he would be the only parent present, sitting beside her. The father flushed, tried to keep calm, and admitted that it might be true that he had been overprotective in the past, but he wanted to talk about the future. At this point the mother intervened, stating that she didn't think it was right to blame the father, for actually, long before the father had started protecting Cass, she had been the dominant person and had contributed to her daughter's illness. She seemed almost eager to acknowledge her direct intervention and involvement in Cass's pathology. We sensed that what she was saying, perhaps, was that she was the most important person in Cass's life, and not her husband. We were impressed also with her sense of detachment as she spoke about being responsible for Cass's illness. There was no real feeling of pain, anxiety, or guilt. She went on to say that she had been extremely upset during her earlier married years, describing herself as being schizoid in many ways, suspicious of neighbors, staying at home at all times, wanting Cass to be around her in the house. She would not permit Cass, even as a little child, to go out and play with other children. She admitted some of her rationalizations were not really valid.

We attempted to draw her out further by asking her about her feelings and attitudes prior to her marriage, but she became evasive. She said that early in her marriage they had not been well off financially; she was always very upset and the entire family was unhappy. Mr. Island would work long and hard hours; he was discouraged and discontented, and when he finally did get home from work, everyone felt it. The family mood was one of unease and depression. Mr. Island denied that he was ever pessimistic and said that his "profession" was a great one. He enjoyed every moment of it and in fact, would recommend it to Harvey or any eager youngster. Cass responded by mentioning that she had seen a psychiatrist several times during the previous year, but had stopped because the expense had been too much for the family. At this point the conversation gradually flagged.

Emergence of Family Patterns

During the fifth session Cass came in late. The family had changed the seating arrangements somewhat, with both parents sitting in individual chairs and the father's chair next to Cass. Whereas before Mrs. Island had sat at one end of the couch, and Cass at the other end, near the stairs, tonight's seating arrangement placed Cass by herself on the couch. Both parents could look directly at her and facilitate the non-verbal communications that were obviously there but so hard for an outsider to pick up.

Several themes seemed to accentuate and delineate the problem areas. The father started by saying that he hoped Cass would want to be helped and would show some initiative. The therapists strongly indicated that the family was expecting a great deal from a very sick person, and suggested that they, rather than Cass, should show initiative. The father seemed deaf to this and appealed to Cass to encourage him. The therapists repeatedly pointed out to Mr. Island, whenever he indicated that Cass had to seize the initiative, that he was asking her to be the strong one. Cass mentioned that shortly after her parents' marriage, her father had supposedly had some kind of "nervous breakdown." Her mother immediately defended the father, saying that he was under a strain but was able to function, which was more than Cass had been able to do. This theme of the mother's intervening and protecting her husband, and his doing the same for her, was one which persisted for quite a while in the family therapy. We repeated our recommendation about the family's need to show some initiative toward increased socialization. Later on Harvey attacked his father's passivity, claiming that his father's role in the family was that of a passive negativist who could do nothing constructive, and giving numerous examples of his father's refusal to seize the initiative on any problem. There was something provocative and enormously frustrating in his denial in the face of overwhelming evidence. It was interesting that no one in the family substantiated Harvey. While not disputing the facts, Mrs. Island defended her husband and tried to change the subject. When any specific incident or family issue was mentioned where Mr. Island could have used some initiative, he would say that he worked very hard in his office, was very tired when he got home, had special problems, or had been under a strain. All these themes continued for some time; obvious again was the family's feeling of hopelessness, their passivity, and their need to maintain static roles.

Other themes that appeared in these early sessions were the family's forgetfulness and Mrs. Island's suspiciousness of the therapists. The memory loss was particularly true of the parents, who seemed to have forgotten many significant things both in the family history and current family events. This was in sharp contrast to Cass's extremely fine memory for incidents affecting her. She questioned, for instance, the family's necessity to live in a shabby apartment immediately following the war, where they had continued to live until they had bought their present home. The father's reaction was that the rental situation was tight right after the war. Cass reminded him that this was no explanation as to why they had remained there for ten years. The father, in particular, disagreed with Cass about other incidents in the family history, such as the length of her illness, whether she ever was really normal or not, and how many friends she actually had before she became overtly ill. Both parents seemed to think that her pre-morbid state had been characterized by her normality, by having lots of friends in the house and, in general, leading a satisfying existence. Even though Cass provocatively challenged the parents on this, there wasn't much give and take. Talk lagged. The two therapists tried to highlight the contrast in the memory of these events, and pointed out that the parents didn't seem willing to take up the challenge or to substantiate their own point of view. In fact, the session tapered off to general apathy on the part of the parents, leading to a family mood of drowsiness. The therapists, after much exertion at stimulating family interaction, also became tired and apathetic. Near the very end of the session, the mother challenged the father because he had recently told someone at his office that Cass was mentally ill. Although this person had responded sympathetically, the mother had been extremely angry. She suddenly became aware that there was hostility in her tone and stopped, but denied that she had any angry feelings. When we asked a direct question to further clarify this incident, Mrs. Island wanted to know why we were asking, what we had in mind, what purpose the question would serve, and how it was going to help. Harvey backed her up, while her eyes looked a little frantic.

During the next few sessions, we were again struck by the family's ingenuous art of not remembering and their need to make any stressful activity as meaningless as possible. We found out indirectly that Cass had made a number of suicidal threats and dramatic superficial attempts both before and even *during* the time of our earlier visits. We learned about it at this time because Mrs. Island mentioned that Cass had asked her for an overdose of sleeping pills so that she could kill herself. Only as we probed further, did we find out that she had slashed her ankles with a razor blade, but mostly skin-deep. When we asked why we hadn't heard about it sooner, we were told, in an offhand way, that they had simply forgotten.

In one session, shortly after the family had filled out some forms we had given them, we noted that all had mentioned only one family area of disagreement—the father's cigar smoking. He supposedly had a heart condition, which had never been verified, and was not to smoke. When we pointed out that we had observed numerous differences such as between Harvey and his father about the father's negativism, and between Cass and the father about his overprotectiveness toward her, the father spoke for the family who agreed that there were some mild differences of opinion, but not "disagreements."

In these ways too, they were telling us that we were outsiders who couldn't understand, and only wanted to stir up trouble. Sometimes when we came in, we discovered changes in the seating arrangements, designed to keep both therapists off in one corner. Occasionally we would ignore these arrangements and seek chairs in the family circle. Although Cass started to come regularly to the sessions we noted two things: 1) she would come late and her mother would have a faint smile of satisfaction which said "I told you so;" all would wait for *us* to handle the lateness; 2) Harvey started to miss sessions. When we persisted in wanting to know about these absences, indicating that it was significant, it came out that he wished to avoid challenging his father. He, as well as his mother and Cass, thought that if they openly discussed their angry feelings toward the father, he would "go to pieces." Mr. Island tossed this off laughingly. In the main, however, they all wanted to talk about Cass, not about themselves. When Cass did speak, the content was very restricted. There was almost no fantasy material—only her hopelessness and a fear of leaving the home.

Some Family History

From about the 12th interview on we started to get more historical material. It should be remembered that this was not revealed as an orderly sequence of events, but seemed to pop out here and there over the next forty to fifty sessions. Mr. Island's parents were separated when he was about fourteen years of age, and he had to go to work. His father was supposed to have had a number of extramarital affairs; his own sympathies were with his mother whom he saw as a martyr. We later learned from a relative attending one of the sessions that Mr. Island's mother had also been promiscuous. He spoke about his sister who, when she was fourteen, had gone "bad" and because of her sexual promiscuity had ended up in a state hospital where she still was. During the separation of his parents, Mr. Island lived, for unexplained reasons, with strangers. He had thought then that after he married, he would devote his life to keeping his own family together. He was determined not to permit his children any sexual experience. One of the therapists pointed out quite directly how this was related to his feelings about Cass. His initial reaction to this was to say that we must be thinking about the future rather than the past; but as we continued to press this point in session after session, he started to deal with it somewhat more directly. We also learned that he had been hypertensive for many years.

We learned too that Mrs. Island had been seriously depressed for many years. Since the age of twelve she had felt that people were saying horrible things about her and excluding her, but she denied having any specific idea of what they might be saying about her. She thought that her older sister had started the rumors. Another fact that emerged was that she had a spastic colon. Although she knew what particular foods would cause her to have diarrhea, she would frequently eat these foods. We learned too that Harvey at the age of seventeen, out of sheer recklessness, had smashed up two cars in a brief period of time. He had been unable to keep friends. Only after the family had moved to the present house and he had started to go to college, had he formed some friendships. We noticed an emerging dyad of Harvey and Cass against the father—they would exchange smiles over the father's stuffiness.

In session 14 we got our first dream material. It came out spontaneously near the end of the session, apparently unrelated to any immediately preceding discussion. The mother and father mentioned that Cass had had many nightmares in the past, although none recently. Cass couldn't remember the content of any of them, but Harvey reminded her that she used to have dreams in which she felt that an elephant was running after her. He then recalled his embarrassment concerning several of his own dreams, in which he would find himself walking the streets without his shoes on.

In session 15 Harvey announced he was going to have a weekend guest. The mother's initial reaction was to try and make Cass as comfortable as possible upstairs; she thought of bringing the television set into Cass's room and making other arrangements so that Cass would not have to come downstairs and meet this friend. It was clear that Mrs. Island was not making any effort to help Cass to socialize. She challenged us as to how she was going to explain Cass's mental illness to this friend and to others, explaining that this would hurt Cass in the long run. Cass said she didn't believe that her mother really cared about her, preoccupied as she was with her own problems. The parents tried to handle this by increasing their efforts to make Cass feel guilty. They said they couldn't take a vacation because of Cass; Cass challenged them this time, saying that she would go to a state hospital so that they could take their vacation. Harvey was seeking a summer job, but admitted that he was procrastinating and wasn't looking very hard. No one in the family seemed bothered by this. Then Harvey started to talk about his shyness, denying that it was on an emotional basis, and admitted that he never had any friends until he was about sixteen years of age. Typically, the father denied this and said that Harvey had always had many friends; he couldn't understand why Harvey talked this way.

As further family history emerged, increasing attention was paid to some of the mother's paranoid ideas. She had an older sister, Bertha, and two brothers, one older and one younger than she. The older brother had always been the family "black sheep," never having married and never having established anything for himself. The youngest brother was the most successful member of her family financially, and Mrs. Island's father had lavished most of his attention and money on him. He was now fifty years old and unmarried, and the family saw him as a "man about town." The main theme in the mother's discussion of her family was a conspiracy between her sister and father against her. She was convinced that her sister had told their father that the Islands were well off and needed no financial help, but that she, Bertha, did. After the Islands moved to their present house, Mr. Island asked his father-in-law to live with them and help with some of the expenses. Here too, according to Mrs. Island, Bertha conspired, and succeeded in stopping this plan. When we asked for more details about Bertha and herself, Mrs. Island became anxious and said people might think she was crazy for talking this way. She attempted to block further discussion by daring us to challenge her ideas, implying that if we did, we would be joining the ranks of Bertha's supporters. Cass was very provocative towards us at this time, and was supportive of her mother. Both mother and daughter were convinced that their current neighbors, whom they scarcely knew, were talking about Cass. They did not appreciate our remarking that such talk was natural and not necessarily malicious, especially since they knew Cass lived at home, but had never seen her.

Mr. Island's pervasive concern with Cass's virginity continued to creep in. During one session Harvey recalled an incident, substantiated by Cass, of a family outing at the movies when Cass was still a child, and the father insisted that the women sit between Harvey and himself. Cass said, "Father, you have always been frightened that someone would take sexual advantage of me." The rest of the family agreed with her, and the father finally reluctantly admitted it, but would not pursue it further. Mother suddenly announced that she had a headache and sent Harvey out for some aspirins.

Another interesting situation, typical of the family's attempts to deal with the world outside the home, came up somewhat later. Father's vacation time was approaching, and his sister had invited the family to join her at a nearby resort. In the discussion Cass stated that she wouldn't mind if her parents went, but that she would like to be hospitalized forever; she denied that she wanted to prevent the family from going. The parents started to elaborate on all the necessary plans and details, making the small preparations sound like moving to a distant country. The simple project of traveling an hour and a half and staying for a few days finally seemed insuperable and overwhelming; it was talked to death, and nothing came of it.

As a result of our attempt to see what effect increased frequency of therapy would have on a family, we recommended therapy twice a week and continued this for over a year. We had telephoned the family before the 22nd session to inform them of our decision to meet twice a week. When we arrived, Cass was not present—she had slashed her ankle rather superficially with a razor. The therapy team insisted that the family take responsibility for keeping razor blades away from Cass. The father really seemed most angry about it, showed genuine emotion, and was supported in this. However, instead of reacting to this support in a postive way, he started backtracking with various rationalizations, claiming he didn't understand the situation too well. In strong contrast to the vigorous, angry reaction and discomfort of the father, Mrs. Island discussed the incident in a flat, detached way. Harvey thought it was a deliberate act on Cass's part to provoke the family. It was impossible to generate a fruitful family discussion on this topic. Harvey then stayed away from the next four sessions.

As we pushed for more and more family socializations outside of the home, we started to get a picture of the mother constantly complaining about being sickly and tired, giving fatigue as the reason for her inability to get out and meet people. We questioned her because there seemed to be nothing physically wrong with her. She complained of pains in her side when she lifted things, and blamed the fact that she tired easily because of a standard gynecological operation four years before. As the sessions continued, we pointed out more and more directly that the entire family was sick. As we asked each one individually about his own reaction to this statement, the mother replied that she was extremely uncomfortable talking about herself, and that it was much easier to focus on Cass. Having said this, she was then able to say that she actually thought, and still thinks, that people were already talking about her when she was about twelve years old. The father stated that he didn't discover his wife's paranoid preoccupation until about ten years ago. The mother then laughed and said she had told him nothing about this before their marriage. Although Mr. Island remained superficially relaxed and pleasant during the session, we did sense his increasing, although unverbalized, resentment towards his wife. He related his resentment in some way to the onset of Cass's symptomatology as well as to the fact that, since that time, Mrs. Island never again accompanied him to any of his rare business or social functions.

Cass then related that she had dropped out of school at the age of sixteen because of some kind of "nervous breakdown." She fantasied that people thought she was pregnant. Actually she was failing in her grades and thought it best to leave school. Her parents initially thought she should be forced to attend, but her mother finally agreed that she couldn't really force Cass to do anything at all. As a result, Cass never went back to school. The family never thought of this experience as an emotional illness. Additional items of the chronological history of Cass's illness then appeared, with Cass doing most of the talking and the parents filling in here and there. It was clear that the father had forgotten a number of significant occurrences.

Cass Tries

At the age of seven, Cass had the measles; upon returning to school she complained of visual difficulty, even though she wore glasses. The nurse at school suggested that Cass go to a sight-saving class. The family accepted the nurse's recommendation without checking any further or seeking the opinion of an eye specialist, and never consulted the doctor who had originally prescribed the glasses for Cass. Cass remained in the special sight-saving class until her first year of junior high school. At the age of ten, she noticed that she could not sit through a class without difficulty; she would often have to get up and pace back and forth. The mother had taken Cass to a doctor because she was overweight and apparently was "growing too fast." The doctor had given Cass some hormone injections which the mother said were related in some way to Cass's nervousness. At any rate, Cass was unable to complete the school year. She remained at home in close contact with the mother, and both of them stayed home all the time until the end of that academic year. The following fall Cass returned to school. It is interesting to note that the father had no recollection of this episode, partially because of his usual blocking of painful events, and partially because he was traveling quite a bit during that time and was not very much involved with the family.

This then led into a discussion of the father's own fears, with Cass pointing out his fear of open spaces. While the father insisted that this was a physiological reaction, he did not seek treatment. As the discussion increasingly focused on the father's fears, both Cass and Harvey indicated that it was very difficult to reach their father because he saw everything through rose-colored glasses. Although he tended to minimize problems, he finally did admit that he was having some difficulties in his office. Specifically, three men had been fired because of embezzlement and had started to impugn his reputation as well as that of his company. He was obviously upset but denied concern. He saw himself as a strong person in the office, though actually he was very indecisive. When he spoke about his employers, we got the distinct impression that he saw the company executives as really great, almost world-renowned figures and elder statesmen. He spoke of them with a good deal of awe. As we tried to pinpoint some of the details, it seemed that only in the past three or four years had he been making an adequate salary, and that for the previous twenty-one years his income had been mediocre. We pointed out that throughout all these years his work had taken him on the road most of the time, and had left him exhausted, with little time to spend on family activities when he got home; it hadn't provided a decent income until recently. All our efforts were in vain—he still maintained that his life at work was at all times a wonderful experience.

The next six sessions were rather hectic ones. Cass started again to look disheveled and to seem disorganized. She slashed her ankles several times during these weeks. The family's way of handling her agitation was to plead with her to give them some encouragement. At one point Mr. Island, provoked by Cass's cutting herself, retorted, "I'll slash the dog if you continue to slash yourself." Cass merely answered that she didn't believe him. People suspected she was mentally ill, she said, and were constantly watching her to see if she would do something crazy. The family agreed with her. Futhermore, everyone admitted that to get close to people meant to get hurt in some way. In this discussion, it was also revealed that Mrs. Island was making some attempts at socialization, but that it was her husband who was hindering her at this point. Typically, he denied this, and said that he was a sociable person who loved to be around people. His wife then backed down, saying that perhaps it was her fault, and that she really was the one who didn't want to socialize. She was rather withdrawn during these sessions; Cass was tense but seemed more relaxed by the end of each session.

In session 33 Cass pleaded with her family, particularly her mother, to get her some suitable clothing since she had nothing to wear. We pointed out that it had been at least six or seven weeks since we had talked about clothes for Cass and the mother had promised to get her some stylish and well-fitting things. The father made a somewhat sharp comment about his wife's failure to buy Cass any dresses; the mother smiled and said, "Well, I guess I'm a witch." During the next session Cass spoke further about herself, voicing her feeling that she was ugly and stupid, and had always done poorly in school. She had dropped out of a secretarial course after two weeks. She told how she had once wanted plastic surgery on her nose, and how the family had refused it. Cass related her feeling about being repulsed and unwanted to experiences many years ago when she and the family had lived elsewhere. On Sunday mornings, for instance, her father would take Harvey fishing. Cass and her mother would plead with the father to take Cass along but he insisted he could not do this. The mother did not persist because she always thought that taking care of two children on a morning's outing would perhaps be too much for the father. We pointed out that each member of the family had the fantasy that every other member was extremely fragile, that if any tension were provoked or one person tried to deal with another person directly, that person would crack up. This was similar to Cass's feeling, early in the therapy, that if she started talking and acting more normal, someone else in the family would go crazy. Cass remembered that in the fishing incident, her father had once said to her quite directly, "When I look at you it makes me sick." The father vehemently denied this but Harvey wondered how he could be so sure he never said this, when he seemed to be so forgetful and vague about other things. As we tried to push this discussion further, with Harvey actually trying to deal more directly with his father, Mr. Island finally said that the reason he hadn't taken Cass was that it was muddy in some places along the shore where they fished, and he didn't think it was fitting for a girl to be in these kinds of places. At this point, with Harvey directly disputing the father, the mother announced that she had stomach pains and was not well.

Beginning with the 35th session Harvey could come only one of the two nights we were with the family because he had obtained a part-time job. Simultaneously, Cass started to dress more neatly and to seem more spontaneous, less angry. As Mr. Island's own role became increasingly clear, the therapy team was able to point out to Cass that he was actually giving her two messages, both mutually contradictory. On one hand he tells her that the world is a wonderful place where business and work is fascinating and that he loves people; on the other hand, what she sees is her father coming home from work every night, exhausted, talking only about the problems he is having at the office and his worries, and never going out or having friends.

Session 37 marked the first time that Cass actually wore a dress that fitted her and was becoming, though it proved to be a dress purchased several years before. Shortly after she joined the group, she said she didn't feel that her mother wanted her to improve. Her mother's reaction was that she'd heard these accusations many times. Cass then observed that her mother became less depressed as she (Cass) became more ill. Father commented in a somewhat incredulous voice that it was fantastic for Cass to think that her mother or father really wanted her sick. Cass's response was, "You heard me." Father lapsed into a stunned silence and did not participate in the rest of the session. Therapist B quite directly pointed out that judging from the family's delay in getting Cass some attractive clothes and their lack of offering Cass encouragement in small practical ways, there certainly seemed to be substance in Cass's statement. The mother was even more disturbed by Cass's saying that if she got better, the first thing she would do would be to move out of the house. Cass added that she thought her mother wouldn't want her in the house if she were well.

In the following several sessions Cass again wore the same unfashionable but becoming dress. During this time too, the mother's involvement with Harvey came out more patently. He had not appeared in several sessions, and the therapists questioned the family at length about this and more forcefully than before. It was clear that the family was discussing the sessions with Harvey and was listening to his opinions on family matters of importance, while telling the therapy team that his presence could not be important. It was also clear that the mother had deliberately encouraged Harvey not to be present. At the same time we noted that Cass was improving, that she seemed well ahead of her parents in therapy, dressed much more appropriately, and was losing weight. One of the mother's reasons for not wanting Harvey to be present came out that night. The day before Harvey had invited a girl friend to have dinner with the family. Cass helped with the preparations. Shortly before the meal Harvey said that he and his friend were going to take a brief walk. While they were out, the mother insisted that she, father and Cass start to eat. When Harvey and his friend returned, they ate alone; Cass was not able to socialize with them but rather acted as a waitress. Thus Harvey's position as a possible pipeline to the outside world was again being minimized. Cass did receive much encouragement from the therapy team, and for the first time seemed pleased rather than angry about it.

For the 41st session Cass appeared well-dressed and for the first time had used lipstick; she had had a big weekend socially, although her father had made some attempt to sabotage it. However, toward the end of that session and during the following session, the father was finally able to talk about his inability to really enjoy a vacation. He admitted to feelings of loneliness; he had gone shopping one vacation day and found he had no one to visit and no one to talk to. He spoke with considerable affect about this. One therapist suggested that perhaps one of the reasons Mr. Island was so busy and exhausted was that it kept him from thinking about his loneliness and his social isolation. The therapy team encouraged him to relax a little, take off more time and leave work a little earlier on certain days. As we discussed some of the details of the father's job, we learned that he chose to be the last one to leave the office because he had to check everything before leaving. He was unable to delegate responsibility and kept himself unnecessarily immersed in the trivia of office routines. This was connected in the following session to his needs at home to check closely on everything, his general fearfulness, and his compulsiveness. Although Cass continued to show improvement over the next several interviews, she still talked about being totally discouraged. She occasionally mentioned suicide. Harvey seemed to be having more difficulty studying, and blamed the family because they stayed up late to watch television. His mother was supportive of his rationalization. With Cass looking better and socializing somewhat more, Mrs. Island complained to the therapy team that Cass was getting sicker; she also speculated about hospitalization.

In the 50th session we learned that Cass had had another exciting weekend, going places and accomplishing many things. Near the end of the session the mother said that perhaps it would be best if Cass went to a state hospital. She said this because of some trivial incident that had occurred earlier in the day. At this session we also asked the family to come to the hospital for psychological testing. The reaction was interesting: Cass and her mother wondered whose I.Q. would prove to be higher.

In the following session Therapist A launched into an exhortation, pointing out that the family had been talking for a long time about the need to socialize but nothing had been done. Mrs. Island's reaction was that Therapist A was right; the family did have a tendency to talk and to procrastinate. Harvey became angry for a moment but couldn't speak about it directly. Later on both therapists attempted to be supportive by recognizing that socializing was difficult for the family, while at the same time encouraging them to talk about their inability to establish friendships. During the course of the ensuing discussion we learned that Mrs. Island was very uneasy with all the women she had met or expected to meet, feeling that she would be drab, have nothing to say, and be uninteresting. This was what Cass frequently said about herself. We were surprised to learn also that Harvey seemed to identify with the father in discouraging visitors to the home by stating—as his father had done—that he disliked certain people who dropped in, and that others bored and irritated him.

In the next session the mother mentioned that she had suffered from severe headaches all week and that Cass had regressed. This came on top of Cass's getting a letter from her uncle's girl friend, who was approximately Cass's age, announcing that she was coming to town for her vacation and would like to visit Cass. The mother tried to discourage this visit, stating that Cass might embarrass the girl by refusing to appear downstairs. During the same session we learned that Mrs. Island's father was seriously ill in the hospital. She had visited him but was very much in conflict about these visits because of meeting her hated sister Bertha, who also went to see him. Her only way of handling her discomfort was to stay away from Bertha and try not to think about her. As the mother discussed her sister, it became clear that this sister was all the things the mother felt she was not. Bertha apparently was vivacious, interesting, competitive and aggressive, had lots of friends, belonged to many organizations, and was very popular. In the following session Cass mentioned that she had written a courteous letter to her uncle's girl friend saying she could not spend any time with her.

Emerging Therapeutic Techniques

From about the 40th session on, some techniques that had been attempted earlier but somewhat sporadically became more crystallized and sustained. We pushed for the parents to act as a married couple and to have a life of their own, independent of the children. We offered to help them with their difficulties in executing this program. Each family member was encouraged to express his thoughts and feelings. We attempted to explore some of the relationships in the family: the symbiotic mother-daughter tie and the latent incest between Cass and her father. Cass was encouraged to act in a more normal way, to dress appropriately, to keep normal waking and sleeping patterns, and to try to meet people who came into the home. Therapist B adopted for his specific role that of a mother figure for Cass. He spent much time discussing women's clothes, styles, how women sat, flirted, aroused interest in themselves. To assist in this, Therapist B confronted the parents with their attempts to undermine his role. Harvey was encouraged to invite his friends into the home.

In session 57 Harvey announced that he was planning to have a party in the home. He was very enthusiastic about it, and Cass offered all kinds of help. Typically, the mother was against it, raising various objections. The father was rather passive, but both therapists strongly supported Harvey, challenging his mother at several points. The party was held and proved successful. Cass was able to socialize somewhat and assisted considerably with the preparations.

In the next session we continued with some topics that had been discussed earlier, particularly the mother's wearing the same black dress, while Cass now wore more attractive clothes and changed them more often. At that time we noted that, simultaneously, Mrs. Island was gaining weight and Cass losing. The mother denied this, and she and Cass argued; the father sat back, seeming to enjoy himself. The therapy team added that it was interesting to observe that the mother first started to feel better when Cass started to get sick. The mother vehemently denied this, despite the fact that her denial directly contradicted earlier statements by her and other family members. We tried to get the family to pick up these disagreements. Although the mother and father never seemed to be directly contradicting each other, the discord was apparent. We wondered aloud also if Cass was too afraid of her mother's hostility to directly disagree with her and defend her own point of view. Cass said she didn't know, and then added she didn't understand why her mother should be tired all the time since she, Cass, did most of the household chores.

In the following session we discussed, in a very general way, the results of the psychological tests at the hospital. The family knew we would be doing this; when we arrived Cass complained of stomach trouble, and her mother complained of a headache. They *all* spoke with extreme anxiety about the tests, yet *all* denied any feelings of anxiety. We present here some excerpts from the report of the testing psychologist:

Mr. Island: "There were a number of suggestions from the psychological material that thought processes are autistic to the point of borderline psychosis."

Mrs. Island: "The subject appears to be a self-doubting, unrealistic, schizoid individual whose object relationships are fragile and conflictual."

Harvey: "There were several striking pathological responses on the Rorschach which reveal underlying autistic perception, dissociation and fluidity of thinking."

In session 60 Cass observed that the father would sometimes be very playful with her, chasing her around the house. We sensed, as she talked, an underlying sexual excitement; however, neither Cass nor the family could discuss this further. At the same session Harvey announced his plans to leave home, set up his own establishment with a friend, and buy a car. There was considerable feeling expressed about his leaving. Only after a good deal of discussion did it come out that Harvey planned to do this after two more years of college, followed by two years of military service. However, the father was extremely hurt, and asked Harvey if he was unhappy with his family. Harvey said that it wasn't so much that as his need to fulfill himself. The father's reaction was that Harvey was really saying that he wanted to live away from home because he wanted to have a gay time, including sexual experiences.

In the next session the mother again urged Harvey to leave the session, suggesting that he had to study for tests. At another point she said that Cass had regressed and went on to note that Cass's increased activities and social participations were "small things." This time the father mildly challenged his wife and said that Cass had made remarkable progress. Looking at her mother, Cass said that she would like to go back to the hospital, that she felt hopeless. The mother then stated that she was extremely frightened of Cass when she got angry. Cass said she didn't believe it. The mother felt that Cass could lose control of herself, smash furniture, possibly kill her. She also wondered whether Cass would harm her during the night when she was sleeping, although nothing of this sort had even remotely occurred. The father then suggested in a playfully sexual way that if Cass got angry, he would hold her. Cass laughed and said she knew what would happen—the two of them would end up in a struggle that was part wrestling, part chasing, part teasing. In the next session both Cass and her father seemed to be avoiding each other. The father then took the offensive saying that he couldn't understand why Cass should be annoyed at him because he loved her and wanted the best for her. The mother wondered if Cass was ever going to get better. She thought Cass was too dependent upon her and it might be best if she and Cass were somehow separated. Attempts to get at the mother's and father's fantasies were not very fruitful. Cass again complained about not having nice clothes. This time the father defended his wife, saying she was doing all she could to get Cass an attractive wardrobe.

In the next few sessions we concentrated on trying to understand Mrs. Island, offering support and letting her know that we were as interested in her as in Cass. With this, she was finally able to say that were we to start probing her interpretations of important events in her life, her assumptions about other people, her certainty that others had been talking against her, it might reveal that her life had been a horrible waste. This she could not face and did not want to . It would be too painful.

Concomitantly, Mrs. Island became more direct in discouraging Harvey from coming to the sessions, although she did make some mild efforts to get Harvey involved in the treatment. Cass complained that although she was feeling better and wanted to continue her improvement, her mother seemed to be more and more discouraging. At the same time, the therapy team noted that when Mrs. Island made some efforts to get out of the home with Cass, Cass herself canceled these excursions. Thus, it was clear that both mother and daughter tended to project some of their own difficulties onto the other, but structured the events in such a way as to make it appear that although each was trying, she was being held back by the other. Nonetheless, the urge to improve seemed stronger in Cass than in her mother.

In session 68 only Cass and her mother were present, since Harvey was sick and Mr. Island had explained the previous week that he would be attending a business affair. The mother mentioned that several days before she had called up the Philadelphia Psychiatric Hospital to arrange for a bed for Cass. She projected all of this arrangement on to Cass, saying that this was something Cass had wanted. Cass was not admitted because neither of the therapists agreed that Cass needed hospitalization. When Harvey did appear at the following session, he started to talk about a problem he was having, almost as though he were offering the therapy team a gift. The father immediately tried to suggest that Harvey really had no problem and that Harvey's reactions were fairly normal. However, this dialogue did lead into a discussion of dreams Cass had had a few nights ago. Harvey actually spoke about the fact that he daydreamed too much, but his father disagreed. Only after a long discussion, in which the therapy team pointed out Mr. Island's own obsessive ruminations, did we explore Cass's dream. In one of the long dream's sequences, Cass finds herself at home, close to the kitchen. The kitchen is a complete mess, and the entire family is in the living room. She runs into the kitchen to straighten out the mess. This ends the first sequence. In the second one, she is approached by Albert Einstein who appears to resemble her maternal grandfather. He says he has a problem for her which she can easily solve. The problem is to divide eight by either one, three, four, five, or six and get as an answer a five-pointed star. He said it would be easy for her to find out which of the numbers would have to be divided into eight in order to get the five-pointed star. In the dream Cass feels stumped, ridiculous and incompetent. Albert Einstein sadly tells her that the answer is one. In recounting this dream, she spoke in an almost inaudible voice and was not very productive in elaborating on fantasies about the dream. It was interesting that Harvey also spoke in an extremely low voice, and both therapists had difficulty hearing Cass and Harvey. Other members of the family, however, had no difficulty whatsoever. It almost seemed then that even in the context of conversation, the family could exclude outsiders.

In session 70 the father for the first time sat on the couch and said that in this position he could see more of what was going on between Cass and her mother in terms of non-verbal communication. When pressed for further explanation he could not elaborate. Cass then said she had something she wanted to discuss but was afraid to talk about. The mother's attitude was to support her not talking about anything that would upset her. Finally Cass said that in her attempts to reduce, she had regurgitated her food on a number of occasions. She denied that she had any thoughts, feelings or fantasies about this. There was a brief pause, and suddenly Therapist B asked Cass about masturbation. There was a hush in the family for a few moments, and then the father said this was something the family had never discussed. Mrs. Island seemed very tense and anxious. Cass denied that she had ever thought about or engaged in any masturbatory activity. When this was questioned by the therapists, Cass tried to turn it into a verbal duel but Therapist A, who had last questioned her, immediately disengaged himself from the discussion. At this point Therapist B pointed out that the therapy team had been coming to this family for over a year now, and most of the family still did not want to get involved in painful or anxiety-producing discussions. Mrs. Island agreed, but no one wanted to pursue the topic.

In session 72 the father was talking about Harvey's wanting a car and his denial that he was concerned about riding in Harvey's car. Cass started to ruminate about being in a car with Harvey and remarked that she would not be anxious, but then went on to talk about her own body image. She said that when she was about ten she was much larger than the other children in her class and more physically developed; she had started to menstruate before the age of ten. Moreover, she had always thought that there was something physically grotesque about her and that people made comments about her body when she passed them on the street. Even before the age of ten, she had the feeling that she looked much older, almost like an old lady, and many times when she was with her mother she imagined that people thought she was the mother and her mother the daughter. The discussion seemed to encourage the others to talk more about themselves in the next session. Harvey joined the family and started to talk about himself again. He said that he had a sense of failure about himself. The family, particularly the father, seemed very surprised. Mother said she knew what Harvey meant since he had been talking to her about himself. He said he had always been a rather solitary fellow, particularly in elementary school and high school, but in college he had managed to make some friends. His sense of failure, he thought, came from his inability to organize himself properly. He then showed us a picture he had painted which he said he intended to give to a friend as a gift; he wondered if it were appropriate. The colors in the painting were characteristic of those seen in the works of Gauguin, the subject and background being reminiscent of the South Sea Islands. The painting revealed a nude girl against a bright green background consisting partly of a kind of forest. The girl was rather muscular and almost masculine in her physique, although her breasts were prominent; Therapist B seemed to think that she was pregnant. The most remarkable aspect of the picture was the girl's face. Her eyes were extremely intense, almost psychotic-looking; her teeth were so obtrusive that they appeared to have a life of their own. Father remarked that it seemed more like a mask than a face. Mother thought it would make a good gift because it was a striking picture and would be a conversation piece. She then went on to talk about her own sense of failure. For the past several years, particularly in the past year, she had the feeling that there was no point in living; that she was "dead" inside; that whatever experience in life she had longed for, she had already had. She thought that her only purpose now was to offer help in some way. The family was taken aback by this, but no one was actually extremely surprised. Father verbalized some anxiety but didn't really show it. Therapist B pointed out that actually the family had known about the mother's depression for quite a while and that it seemed to coincide with the onset of therapy. Mother then said she thought she wasn't doing Cass any good and that Cass would be much better off without her. She quoted a psychiatrist with whom the parents had consulted a number of years ago, who had said that Cass would get better when the mother died. She thought that Harvey was the only person who really needed her, and she felt instinctively that Cass was a stronger person than Harvey. Therapist B then pointed out that he thought the mother had made a significant contribution by opening up various areas of discussion and revealing ways in which the family could help each other. We were struck by the fact that the mother should make this statement at a time when Cass had lost a considerable amount of weight, was now really good-looking, was dressed neatly, and was much more presentable generally. It seemed as if she were saying that perhaps she had to die so that Cass might be born and also, that she could no longer compete with Cass for her husband but could hold on to Harvey. This was a reversal of the usual situation in which Cass said that her life was empty and she could see no purpose for living, in a sense asking her mother and father, particularly her father, for reassurance.

In the following session we learned that right after our previous session the mother had had a severe attack of colitis.

Over the next several sessions more historical material was revealed, with further implications of the Oedipal struggle typical in this family. Initially, Mrs. Island spoke about her unhappiness when she first married; she and her husband had had to live with her parents. She was aware of the fact that her husband never even knew she was so unhappy, that he was not very sensitive to her needs. It was in this session too, with Harvey's support, that she was able to admit that she had been angry with her husband for many years, but had come to terms with him in the last few years because she understood him better. As it developed, what she meant by this was that she was able to manipulate her husband in such a way that things would remain on a more even keel for her. She did not mean that she was able to talk to him and share her thoughts and feelings with him. Mr. Island was not particularly responsive to this. The therapy team gave Harvey much credit for initiating that night's discussion and following it up with questions.

In the next session the mother looked much more cheerful. There were some Oedipal interpretations made in this session. Mention was made, for instance, of the fact that Cass seemed to be getting more and more attractive. Certainly, this was a difficult situation for the father, although he denied it. Harvey then pointed out that his father seemed to show affection only toward Cass, that he put his arms around her, teased her, and ran after her in the house. The father said that this was true but indicated that he still had great affection for his wife, and went on to say that this was actually an affectionate family. Harvey said it was essentially a cold family and described himself as a rather cold person. He regretted this but thought it was his fate to be cold.

In the following session there was further discussion of the mother's neglect of herself and of her not dressing properly. Her only response was that she would never embarass her husband if people came to visit; that she would certainly be dressed neatly and attractively for visitors. Therapist A suggested that she was more concerned with impressing other people than with trying to be attractive, pleasing, interesting, and sexy for her husband. She admitted this but said that as she got older she was less and less concerned with interesting her husband. Cass then said the better she seemed to get, the worse her mother became, as though her mother was going in the direction she once went. Mother denied there was any correlation between Cass's condition and her own. At this point, Harvey came home from his job; having overheard the last part of the conversation, he undid what had been discussed by stating that his mother could be attractive any time she wanted to. The therapy team suggested that possibly the father might prefer to escort Cass to his business social functions rather than his wife. The mother hotly denied this, although actually she hadn't accompanied him to any function in the past ten years.

In the next session, Mr. Island said there was a business affair coming up and he was sure his wife would come with him. When the therapy team wondered why he was so sure in view of the past experiences, he seemed unable to respond, except to say that he was sure she would go. He also denied increased interest in Cass, now that she was actually quite attractive, took care of the home, did some of the shopping and assumed much more the wife's role. We noted that Cass always commented on how unattractive she looked so that her father would tell her how pretty she was. Therapist B suggested that little children have these kinds of thoughts about parents of the opposite sex, and that perhaps even the father himself, when he touched his daughter or thought about her, had some vague warm, close feeling about her. Mr. Island seemed shocked but his wife did not. The father refused to discuss this matter further.

The next session was an extremely dramatic one. Harvey was present throughout the entire session. It started off with Therapist A wondering whether the family had any additional thoughts about Cass's fantasy that if she got better her mother would get sick. At this point Cass denied that she had said this. She did notice and comment upon the fact that her mother seemed to be better dressed this evening and was slightly more cheerful. The mother then told how Cass had been extremely upset the previous evening, saying that she wanted to go to the hospital. As the mother started to talk further about what had happened, the father said that he would have to be excluded from this evening's discussion, even though he would be physically present. He was feeling very tired and had pressure in his chest, and indicated vaguely that he might have some heart trouble. When the therapist showed interest in his physical condition and talked about a possible examination, he refused to consider it, insisting that he would stay in the session but would not participate. The mother then said that the previous evening Cass had been quite demanding of her, and she didn't know what to do. She said that this frequently happened and she often just took the dog and ran out of the house. Cass denied that she was as upsetting and angry as her mother described it. The therapist wondered why Cass was nagging so constantly and why the mother couldn't take some effective steps to stop it. The mother said she could not; that Cass chased her all over the house, demanding answers about things that she simply couldn't answer. She was terribly afraid that Cass was going to smash things up and possibly even try to kill her. Cass said that she did sometime have uncontrollable impulses and was afraid that she might act them out. We felt that she seemed to be saying that if she stayed sick and immobilized she could not murder her mother, or, that the mere process of getting well would make her mother so sick as to cause her death. This seemed to be the therapeutic plateau. As she got better she became more frightened and fearful of her own impulses, of her mother's getting sicker, and of her increased attractiveness to her father. She then demanded to be hospitalized, or the mother demanded that her daughter be hospitalized. As the sessions developed further, there was considerable talk about strong feelings of hostility and murderous impulses. No one seemed extremely surprised when the mother spoke about this. Harvey seemed the most comfortable in this discussion about control of feelings and said that he was rather free about smacking Cass and calling her names, knowing that he would not lose control over himself. The same evening that Cass—according to her mother—had gotten very angry, the mother could not sleep the entire night. She denied that she was worried about Cass and what she might do to her. Particularly worthy of note is the fact that the father detached himself from this session, pleading physical disability, and Harvey showed increased activity by participating more and more.

In the following session the family refused to discuss previous topics, and went off on various tangents. However, mother did say she felt Cass was bigger and stronger than she was, although it was obvious that she appeared to be physically capable of handling Cass.

In the next few sessions Harvey and Cass continued to attack their father for his massive denials of family realities and his acting out his neurotic needs at the expense of the family. Their mother remained silent. They complained that their father had interfered with their activities by his need to control. Both mentioned that he always knocked on the door when they were in the bathroom, wanting to know what they were doing. He was puzzled when, after numerous exhortations from them to stop his bathroom hounding, they had refused to speak to him. Cass made note of her father's particular attention to her when she bathed, often knocking on the door six or more times. He also embarrassed her when they went to a restaurant, because he sat across from her, grinning at her, wriggling his nose, smiling at her, and acting quite seductive. She said it was just like the way he acted at home when he tickled her and chased her around the house. Father shrugged and said that none of this meant anything. Harvey supported Cass during much of this, repeatedly pointing out that father merely wants to have the family present in the home but has no further interest in them. Cass said she would take it one step further—she would say father wants all in the living room where he could watch them but doesn't really want to have much to do with them otherwise.

This topic of father's controlling and checking up on everyone, constantly asking questions without really wanting to know the answer, and never telling much of his own thoughts and feelings, was a theme that persisted throughout most of the therapy and one that Harvey and Cass would mention repeatedly. Both women also complained that the men in the family didn't want them to act as women; they gave several examples, one of them an instance when they had invited a nearby couple in for dinner and both men acted annoyed.

In the following session the father started to talk about himself, about some of his business concerns and his feelings about his future. He felt he was getting older and life was slipping by him, that he had missed out on some good times. The mother then attacked the father, stating that he always tried to make an overly good impression on people: they had once taken a cab for just a few blocks and he had extravagantly overtipped the driver. When Mr. Island reacted with mild annoyance at this, his wife immediately retracted and made several statements supportive of her husband.

In session 92 it was revealed that Cass had called up Therapist B and insisted she be hospitalized. She said she was taking a cab right down to the hospital as soon as she hung up. Therapist B was very forceful in telling her that he would not recommend hospitalization and there would be no bed available. He suggested that perhaps the sexual discussions in the past sessions had distressed her. She denied this. We also discovered at this session that an elderly male neighbor had frequently been coming to the home, bringing Cass flowers. The entire family denied that this meant anything and then went on to express some annoyance at the therapy team for the sexual discussions. The father said that we had our minds in the sewer, and categorically denied that he had any sexual thoughts or feelings about Cass. Cass then suggested that her father talk about his feelings to the therapists individually rather than in front of the family. Therapist B pointed out that the father was a very denying person about his own feelings and probably wouldn't talk about them in individual therapy either. The team then went on to point out that every member of the family, including Harvey, seemed to have some sexual problem. Whenever he was asked about his relationship with girls and what his dating pattern had been, Harvey became extremely reticent, and did not attend the next few sessions. We also suggested to the father that his rigidity made it difficult for other members of the family to talk more freely about sex. Between this session and the next, the mother called up Therapist B and told him that Cass was extremely upset and was again demanding to be hospitalized. Following this, Cass got on the phone and said she was going to commit suicide right then and there if she were not hospitalized. Therapist B again was not intimidated and said we would talk about it in the next session. Following this rebuff, the mother called up a general practitioner who came to the home and prescribed some tranquilizers for Cass.

In the next session, when Cass did not come down for a while, Therapist B suggested that he go upstairs and talk to her. Everyone in the family thought it was a good idea but when he headed for the stairs, the mother again fluttered on ahead of him and blocked the therapist. When Therapist B finally did get upstairs and spoke to Cass for a moment or two, she came right down. She said she felt people would never like her, she had nothing to offer, and therefore wanted either an overdose of sleeping pills or to be put in a state hospital. It was also interesting to note that once, in a previous session when Cass had again been doggedly nagging her mother and speaking about her helplessness, her mother had turned on her and told her in a very forceful way that she was not going to take this from her any more. Cass then had left and had not bothered her anymore.

In session 97 it was announced that Harvey had gotten a regular job and was satisfied. The family had all gone to a resort for the weekend and Cass had actually put on a bathing suit, had gone on the beach and had swam a little. When they got home, Cass was rather upset; while her father was out taking the dog for a walk, she started to have a temper tantrum, ran upstairs and tried to smash things in the bathroom. Harvey ran after her and prevented her from hurting herself or from smashing things. When the father returned, he was very angry at Harvey, stating that he had the impression that Harvey was losing control of himself.

In the following session the mother was able to express fairly directly some angry feelings toward her younger brother and her husband. She said that her brother wanted the Island family to help pay for the medical expenses of their father, but she felt very angry because her father had given her brother almost all of his money. She felt therefore that her husband ought to tell her brother that he should assume most of the responsibility for the care of his father. Mrs. Island complained that her husband wouldn't do this because he preferred to put up a big front and impress people. Typically, the father denied this. The therapists pointed out he had done the same thing with the family, denying any anxiety on the subject of learning to drive a car, denying fear of water, of having his teeth pulled, etc. We pointed out too how the mother reinforced the father's pathology by defending him most of the time, not letting him really talk about himself or allowing the therapy team to help him understand himself. We pointed out that his constant denials set the tone for the whole family, and made it difficult for anyone to talk about himself or get involved in therapy.

In the following few sessions Cass did not come down until Harvey brought her. The father's reaction was that this resulted from a sexual discussion which was very upsetting to Cass. He denied that the sexual discussion had any effect on him. The mother started to talk more freely about her own family background, stating that her parents had never been able to protect her from her younger brother or older sister. She described how they had manipulated the parents, particularly how her older sister Bertha had deceived her father. The fact that her mother had never bothered to protect her, annoyed her, but she did not feel that her mother was against her. It seemed clear that Mrs. Island was reproducing her own mother's patterns. She also stated that she wished Cass would get better and out of the home so that she could completely regress into what she would like to be, namely a recluse, lying around the house most of the day. She seemed to be saying that Cass's pathology forced her to act in a somewhat more "normal" manner; that if Cass were to get better she would gratefully sink into complete regression.

Before the next session the mother's younger brother, Mort, came to visit with his mistress. This was the brother who had demanded that the family help pay the expenses for his sick father. The mother now told him for the first time in her life exactly how she felt about their sister Bertha— that Bertha was a liar, a cheat, and she hated her. Mort was astonished but did not reproach her. She then went on to talk about her anger at her father for letting her down even more after her marriage, when Bertha received large sums of money from him and persuaded him not to give her any. She was also angry because her husband had encouraged her father in thinking that he was successful and didn't need any financial help.

Mort and his mistress were present through the entire 111th session. Uncle Mort immediately took over, cracked jokes and ridiculed psychiatrists in a rather indirect way. The family made no attempt to deal with him and acted as though the therapists, who sat back passively and observed, were the hosts in the home. Uncle Mort presented himself as a man who had many problems but who faced them by saying things could be worse. Later in the session he admitted he frequently felt depressed and when that happened he drank a great deal. Initially he was reluctant to give his perspective on the family but, as the session progressed, he did say that he felt his father preferred him above the other children. He denied that his father had any special preference for Bertha; his father, he continued, had treated all the women in the home pretty much alike, ignoring them most of the time and lavishing all his affection upon him. Mrs. Island argued with her brother briefly at one point. As Uncle Mort talked further, it became clear that there was a strong paranoid flavor in his view of people. In reporting some aspects of his own business, he repeatedly mentioned that other people took advantage of him, robbed him and cheated him. When the police had ignored his story that he was being robbed by his associates, he felt that they were in cahoots with the people who were stealing from him. He spoke of his mother as a woman who was depressed most of the time and stayed mostly in the home, doing a lot of unnecessary tasks. However, he excused her by saying it was due mainly to her "ignorance."

In the following session we tried to get the family to react to their passivity in the previous session. They admitted that they had never really liked Uncle Mort but had never told him so. Father then went on to say he would like to have a reunion of his own side of the family, some of whom he hadn't seen in twenty or thirty years. Mother objected vehemently and at times almost pleaded with him not to carry out this plan. Cass and Harvey strongly supported their father, Harvey in particular trying to push his father into visiting his own father, whom he hadn't seen for many years. He did not succeed. Mr. Island said it was difficult for him to forgive his father for not having visited him since he had separated from his mother. Later on he admitted that whenever his father would try to come to town to visit, his mother would get a court order to put him in jail. Apparently the family was in some process of reassessing itself in its relationship to other members of the family on both sides. Harvey seemed to be more active in therapy at this point, and Cass continued to show considerable improvement in the areas of therapeutic involvement, personal appearance, social graces and attempts to move more into the outside world.

Session 114 had several interesting features. Therapist A was ill and Therapist B therefore went alone to the session that night. As Therapist B walked to the living room, he was surprised to see two strangers there drinking martinis. They introduced themselves to him by their last name and then Harvey, Mr. Island and Cass came into the room and introduced the strangers as Uncle Bill and Aunt Helen (the sister of Mr. Island). They had been visiting the family for the first time in over a year because of a funeral of Mr. Island's uncle which they had attended together. Mrs. Island came down to the session a few moments later. Mr. Island asked if his sister and brother-in-law could sit in on the session, and the whole family seemed to want this, particularly Cass, apparently because she wanted to visit with them after the session.

Helen and Bill seem markedly different from the Island family. They have an air of oversophistication about them. Helen drank two or three martinis during the session and both she and her husband became somewhat high. They left the session once or twice each to go to the bathroom; they were quite talkative and somewhat blasé, calling everyone "darling," "dear," or "sweetheart." Bill is a loquacious lawyer who tends to cross-examine everyone. He started this with the therapist about laws which prevent cousins from marrying. He indicated that he thought mental illness had a hereditary basis. He further went on to say that the whole Island family had emotional problems in all branches of the family and that his own son was sick because his wife was an Island. As Therapist B directed the conversation away from this topic and more toward the family and their relationships, Bill became somewhat obsequious, superficially flattering, and complimenting the therapist repeatedly for having performed a miracle with Cass; he then began to cross-examine Cass, particularly about the reasons for her illness but also at some length about her sexual life—whether she had sexual feelings, whether she was frigid, etc. At the same time he invited her out to have dinner with him. Cass handled all of this quite well and did not seem particularly embarrassed about the highly personal questions being asked of her. Mrs. Island looked quite morose through most of this.

Bill stated that he knew the cause of Cass's illness and then went into a detailed description of what the therapist had worked out dynamically as the father's contribution to Cass's illness. He told how the father's mother had been promiscuous and the father had left them at an early age. Mr. Island's youngest sister had been promiscuous as a teenager and the family got a notorious reputation from this. As a result, Bill and Helen had moved out of the neighborhood; however, Mr. and Mrs. Island had stayed there but vowed that they would never allow their daughter to go out with boys. Bill suggested that even today Mr. Island would not allow any kind of dating for Cass even if she eventually showed an interest in this. Mr. Island rather feebly tried to deny some of these things, particularly the part about his objecting to Cass's dating, but he did admit that he had always been overprotective and had become aware of it. Throughout all of this interaction, Bill and Helen were very supportive of Mrs. Island and tended to push the blame for Cass's illness directly on Mr. Island. The attempts of Therapist B to support Mr. Island seemed to have little effect.

Therapist B felt that this session was illustrative of some of the peculiar or difficult types of situations that arise from time to time in family therapy of schizophrenia. The family had not forewarned us that they would have guests at the session, nor that they had attended a funeral, nor that the guests would want to have martinis. In retrospect, it probably would have been best if the therapist had asked the guests to have their party afterward, if they wanted to attend the session. Therapist B did turn down an offer of martinis during the session, and the family did not drink either. Therapist B had a good deal of difficulty getting the session to focus around the relationships within the family. Instead, Bill and Helen tended to dominate and take over. If Therapist A had not been ill and had attended the session, he undoubtedly could have helped in neutralizing the two cocktail party guests. Despite these possibly negative considerations, some very interesting things happened. It seemed quite apparent that the mother, who came in last, had been active in inviting the guests to stay for the session. These guests then pushed all the blame for Cass's illness onto the father and his family. They rather directly took over and neutralized the therapist's role, and at the same time were quite effective in their ability to dominate and treat Cass as an incompetent child. From our hundreds of hours of contact with this family, it seemed clear to us that the mother was only too pleased to get someone into the therapy situation to break up some of the therapeutic relationship between Therapist B and Cass. In addition, Helen and Bill completely vindicated her as a causative agent in Cass's illness. Uncle Bill, furthermore, was able to vindicate himself and to blame the Island family, of whom his wife was a member, as the causative agent for the illness of his own son. At a future point in the therapy, Bill and Helen's son began to date Cass. Ostensibly he did this in order to help Cass but it was quite clear, almost from the beginning, that Cass gave more to him and was psychosexually the more mature one in her relationship with him.

Therapist A returned for the 115th session. The family greeted us warmly and seemed particularly pleased to have Therapist A back. Cass, representing the family, had sent a get-well card to him during his illness. Harvey started the session by stating how Cass had continued to make progress and that she had something quite unusual to report. He seemed quite enthusiastic about this but the other three members of the family looked blank. Harvey then stated that Cass had gone roller-skating but that she had become embarrassed when she could not stand up on the skates and after the first few minutes had done very little skating. He thought it was a landmark that Cass had gone skating with his friends, a married couple and himself. He then added that he wanted to throw a party at home and would like to have a foreign student there as a date for Cass. She kept commenting that she had nothing to say to people, and people did not like her because of this and that she was not yet ready for dating. Much of the session was spent in discussing the previous session, with the family being quite annoyed that Therapist B had not more actively restrained the activities of Bill and Helen. Throughout the session, both therapists repeatedly stated that the family would have to start to handle their own problems, both within and without the family; they also pointed out that the mother had invited Bill and Helen to stay for the session and had invited them to have martinis.

Session 116. When we entered the house that evening, the dog was barking furiously at us. For many months we had noticed that in this and other families the pet was the first family member to greet us at the door. We had also learned that a pet's behavior on any particular evening was a direct reflection of the feeling-tone of the family group. When we were received by the furiously barking dog, therefore, we both suspected immediately that this might be an angry session. We furthermore predicted that the most angry person would be the mother, which was just the way it turned out to be. Harvey was not at home; he had made a date for the evening to avoid coming to the session. The mother sat silent, looking pained and withdrawn and angry. After much questioning, she finally admitted that she was not feeling well, adding that that was none of our concern. It turned out that she had a headache which had lasted already for three days. She persisted throughout this session in stating that she just didn't feel well and that it had nothing to do with emotions. However, she had been quite angry with us and quite worried about Harvey who had taken a pre-induction physical examination for the Army three days before. As we continued the general theme of the mother's sickness, she became progressively more angry and both the father and Cass repeatedly tried to shift the conversation to something else; it was very apparent that they did not wish to make her angry with them. The mother was annoyed with us because we had been encouraging the father to bring friends and relatives into the home; she asked us if we would do such a thing to our wives, etc.

Session 117 began with Harvey being upstairs in bed, and Mr. and Mrs. Island stating that he was too ill to attend; however, a little later he came down and was present for most of the session. Much of the discussion of the evening centered around the animals in the family and their relationship with the human members. The dog, Candy, was lying close to the mother and everybody, except the mother, agreed that Candy is closest to the mother and belongs to her. The mother tended to give some offhand, casual reason for this—Candy is apt to go around the house checking up on everything and everyone, much as her husband does.

For several weeks, Cass has been raising a kitten which she had found near the house, deserted on its second day of life by the mother cat. This is a rather strange cat, quite withdrawn, and not as playful as kittens usually are; it also has something the matter with its back. The veterinarian told the family that it was some type of congenital arthritic condition. The kitten is quite rough and tends to jump at or scratch people. The father complained that the cat will not leave the house, and everyone agreed that the cat is very much like Cass in this regard. Harvey mentioned that both the cat and the dog were quite frightened about going out. Both parents were quite defensive and inclined to deny that anyone in the family had much difficulty in going out. The mother is able to go out to do some shopping and this is about all; the father goes out in order to work but hardly ever at other times. Harvey stays in the house a lot, more than the usual young college graduate would do. And, of course, Cass and the animals appear to have some specific fear connected with leaving the house.

Session 118. There were two main topics tonight. One concerned the fact that Harvey was absent again, and the other was a kind of duel between mother and Therapist A. The family discussed possible reasons for Harvey's absence; they eventually got around to mentioning that he had lost his job. After being generally angry for much of the session, the mother finally said that Therapist A reminded her of her brother Perry who had been her father's favorite.

Session 119. Therapist A was not present as he was ill. Both parents greeted Therapist B at the door and seemed quite concerned about the co-therapist's absence and asked repeated questions; Mr. Island, in particular, asked in hushed tones if it was Therapist A's heart. They were assured about this and told that Therapist A had had a recurrence of his previous illness (not a cardiac ailment), but were not given any specific details. Cass came down a few minutes late and when she arrived, Mr. Island immediately said that she should talk about herself and the events of the last two weeks. When Cass would not talk, Mr. Island stated that she had been depressed and had seemed to slip back, eat more and refuse to go out. She had been out of the house only twice in the last two weeks. Harvey then pointed out that although Mr. Island had not been feeling well, had been depressed and was overtired, he did not take the vacation due him and as a result had again lost his vacation time. Mr. Island talked as usual about the demands of his job and his lost vacation, at the same time talking rather pathetically about his fatigue, his great fears of a heart attack, loss of energy, "weakness," and his good intentions to change in the future. Mrs. Island had also been depressed over the past week. In fact, the entire session had a depressive tone to it. It did not come out clearly how the various depressions in the family had been brought about. In a way, it seemed that Cass's depression had touched off similar feelings in all other members of the family. She was unable to talk about the reasons for her depression but did tell of a dream in which she had twin babies and was quite annoyed at Harvey because he made up funny names for them and teased her about it.

Session 120. There was some discussion about a big party that Harvey had on the weekend with twenty-five people present. Cass seemed to enjoy herself at this party, as well as some other social functions. However, whenever Therapist A pointed this out to her, she became very angry and stated loudly that she had not enjoyed herself.

The following two sessions dealt with some improvement in relationships within the family and a rather marked increase in socialization for them. The family showed some pride in discussing this. The mother also told of her fantasy that if she were to argue with Therapist A he would get sick or hurt in some way, and she felt justified in this fantasy because after a previous angry session, Therapist A was in the hospital.

The next two sessions were characterized by a massive family resistance. They seemed bored, disinterested and followed up the therapy discussions with very little apparent clinical significance. Some of the resistance might have been due to the fact that the therapists had begun to focus more on the marital relationship, something the mother held to be sacred and which, she had declared, she would never discuss with anyone. Father abetted her in this. Although nothing had been said about this, the therapists were reasonably certain that the parents felt that any discussion of their marriage might further focus the blame upon them as causative factors in the genesis of Cass's schizophrenic illness.

In session 126 the entire family was present, and once again there was a rearrangement of chairs. The family felt that if they rearranged their chairs and the seating arrangements, they might be able to talk better. Mother sat in father's usual chair and Therapist B sat where Cass usually sat, with Therapist A and Cass sitting on the couch, and Harvey sitting between Therapist B and the mother. There was much discussion about a birthday party which Cass had wanted to attend, but would not go to unless her parents accompanied her. They had at first refused, but after Cass had had a temper tantrum, the father went with her. The father and Harvey had a rather heated discussion about how the father treats Harvey like a little kid, and how they are unable to converse because the father expects Harvey to talk to him. The only contribution the father makes to the conversation, according to Harvey, is to tell him to wear his overshoes, not to go out in the rain without a raincoat, etc.

The next couple of sessions dealt with further socializing by the family; e.g., one evening the parents went out together and the children separately. Cass had had a date with her cousin, the son of Bill and Helen whom we talked about earlier. The family had read an article on family therapy and stated that they did not realize that there were other families with similar problems. There was some discussion of Mrs. Island's dowdy appearance and how she was looking much as Cass had done in the early phases of therapy. Mr. Island had wanted to take her out to dinner to celebrate their wedding anniversary, but she had refused to do anything about her hair which was a mess; and she also had no suitable clothing because she had gained weight. We pointed out how similar this was to the time when Cass did not have suitable clothing. This, however, only served to make the mother very defensive.

By way of summary, the past fifteen sessions have dealt essentially with relationships within and without the family. There has been an increasing movement in the direction of social activity on the part of all family members. These sessions have focused primarily on the relationships between the therapists and the individual family members. The mother has remained somewhat depressed throughout these sessions and is quite angry and attacking of the therapists. Cass has tended to sit back a good deal through these sessions and vicariously enjoy the battle between the mother and the therapists. Harvey has missed several of the sessions, apparently in an effort to stay out of what is going on between the mother and the therapists. Cass has been making slow but steady improvement. This is manifested mainly in her ability to socialize, both inside and outside the home. Also, she is no longer so frightened of her mother. In addition, she has developed strong transference feelings about both therapists, but particularly about Therapist B who has been working to establish a closer relationship with her with the assistance of Therapist A, who has been preventing the mother from disrupting this therapeutic relationship.

In session 129 Therapist A was again ill and Therapist B saw the family alone. An interesting part of this session was the behavior of the animals. The dog sat in the center of the circle while the cat sat on the couch near Cass. It became very clear on several occasions that the cat was mimicking the dog's behavior. The cat was a young, male cat who had shown strange behavior almost from the beginning of its life when Cass began to nurse it and saved it from a certain death when it was deserted by its mother. It had none of the usual feline gracefulness in its movements but lumbered along like a dog. The cat would attempt to greet a human being much as a dog would, and display much of the same sniffing and, at times, licking behavior. However, the cat did not stay in the limelight, paralleling Cass who also stayed away from the center of attention. In later family therapy sessions this was to reverse itself. Early in this session the parents asked Harvey if he wanted to talk. Harvey joked that he was on the spot because he had announced to the family that he was moving in four days into an apartment with three boyfriends. The whole family was angry at him because of this decision. Mrs. Island acted hurt but had accepted the move. Mr. Island insisted that he could not understand this strange behavior, that Harvey had become a party boy and wanted more freedom to do things he would not be allowed to do at home. The implication was that Harvey's motivations for his move had a sexual basis. Cass said that now no one would come to the house, and it would be very difficult for her to meet people. She particularly stated that she wanted to meet men, and that Harvey was her means for doing this. She added that she had asked Harvey to get a date for her for a beatnik party he had given at the home last week, but he had seemed reluctant to do this, and she did not go to the party. Harvey finally invited Cass to a housewarming party at his new apartment, he told her how many girls would be there, when Cass exclaimed: "Harvey, you don't understand. I'm not interested in meeting the girls, I want to meet men." Harvey still seemed to ignore this. He said that he had signed a lease and had made up his mind, and the family was trying to make him feel guilty for leaving the home. We agreed that he had to go away for himself and get away from the atmosphere of the family for a while. The father expressed a great deal of concern that Harvey was not getting his rest because he was going to too many parties and would soon be exhausted. Harvey insisted, however, that he did not go out more than one or two nights a week. Mrs. Island said she was sick of doing things for Harvey, with nothing being done for her. Harvey invited his family up to the apartment for a dinner, but they refused and said he could not come back home if he went away. However, they then modified their position, and Harvey said that he would come home to visit if the family would let him. It was interesting to note how the family who had abetted him in his absences from the therapy sessions, obviously shifted their feelings at his moving out of the family altogether. It was as if they wanted him out of the family therapy so that further progress and change would not occur in the family, but they had not counted on his moving out of the family and, particularly, out of the parental sphere of influence.

In the next session Cass was rather depressed, and this was related to Harvey's leaving. She stated that she didn't realize until then how much of a pipeline to the outside world Harvey was, and she would miss the getting together at the house with his friends. Later in the session she suggested that she be hospitalized as a way to meet people. Although this did not sound too realistic, she said that this suggestion was motivated by the realities of her home life and that she was about ready to make some changes because if Harvey was gone, it would be very difficult for her to meet people and socialize. Harvey continued to come to the family sessions and also seemed quite depressed, although he was unable to talk about it.

In the next session the mother suggested that Cass go to the hospital. The therapists pointed out that the mother was reluctant to have Harvey leave the home but wanted to get rid of Cass. The mother denied this, although the facts were quite apparent. It was further pointed out that the parents seemed to need Cass and Harvey around in order to put meaning and purpose in their life. Both parents showed much evidence of boredom and lack of interests. They tended to deny that there was any significance in their concern about the children leaving the home.

The next several sessions dealt with Cass' fears of going outside and the strong fear which she has as soon as she leaves the house. By actually walking with her outside, the therapist found that her fear became over-powering when she got too far to see her own house. At that point she turned and ran home. It was as if the parental inhibitions which had been built into her were so strong that she could not trust herself out of their sight.

In session 135 Cass announced an interest in making a date with a certain dentist who was a bachelor and a friend of the family. He was about her father's age. The father pretended that he misunderstood whom she was talking about, and repeatedly suggested some people for her to consider dating. Both therapists encouraged her to speak back to her parents and to tell them what she felt about the father's misin-terpretations. She finally took command and became mildly assertive. In the next session this was discussed further, but there were massive family resistances.

In the following session Cass started by stating that she wanted to talk about dating. This was somewhat unusual for her although for some months she had been showing an increased communicativeness and willingness to discuss things which were bothering her. Following her mention of interest in the older dentist, her mother had spoken to a woman whose son was having severe difficulties in his relationships with girls. The mother had arranged for him to come around and see Cass. He was only twenty-one and quite effeminate. Cass was not attracted to him at all. The family, however, seemed to prefer that Cass choose an effeminate boy rather than an older man with a reputation for his prowess with women. When this was pointed out to them, both mother and father tended to deny it vehemently. Despite the fact that Cass repeatedly stated that she wanted to go out with the older dentist, both parents said that she had really no interest in this at all, and she merely wanted to invite the dentist to their home so that the family would have some social contact. The therapists pushed the family for their fantasies about what Cass might do if she went on a date with the dentist. The father repeatedly denied that he thought there would be any sex involved; he then mentioned that perhaps at one time in the past he had been concerned that Cass might end up as his sister had done, but that he does not feel this way anymore. However, Cass pointed out that the father monitors her television programs. If she is watching a program with Negro male dancers or any male who is quite sexy, the father will come into the room, calmly turn the switch to another channel and then walk out of the room again. The father denied that he does this, but both the mother and the brother agreed that he does it very frequently.

In the next session the family again discussed the effeminate young boy who had come to visit Cass a couple of times. Cass heatedly stated that she did not want to see him again, had no interest in him, but might be attracted to his father who had brought the boy over. This was rather shocking to the other family members. Cass then said that she had much less fear of going out of the house. It is interesting to note that once her fear of going out was related to the parental controls and the parents' fear that she might become promiscuous, Cass was able to feel less fearful about going out. Mrs. Island immediately and heatedly stated that Cass was not frightened of men and was not frightened of sex and that this had had absolutely nothing to do with her fear of leaving the house. Cass answered her by saying, "I think that Therapist B is correct when he states that I have to stay so close to home so that my parents will protect me from becoming promiscuous." She went on to say that she was a lonely person and had a great deal of need for physical contact, and that at the same time she was very frightened of this. Therapist B used this opportunity to try to get the family to discuss their opinions and feelings about morality in the present world. The parents immediately admitted that their ideas were much in keeping with the morality of thirty years ago. Both Cass and Harvey were quite interested in this discussion but seemed somewhat embarrassed by it. As the session progressed, the family seemed to focus the discussion onto Cass's distorted body image. Cass kept repeating that she is not attractive to men because she had abnormal thighs. Of course there is no evidence of this but she persisted in talking about it in a delusional way.

Session 139. The family arranged the seating so that Therapists A and B would have to sit side by side and apart from the rest of the family. Therapist A did not take his designated seat but sat between Cass and her mother on the couch. The session again was about Cass and her relationship to men and her feelings about sex. Father immediately raised the question about whether Cass was in a rut and should be in the hospital. This was interesting to note, as Cass was breaking through her fears about leaving the house and was in general feeling much better. However, both parents saw the hospital as a way of keeping Cass the way they wanted her to be. Although the parents persisted in trying to change the subject, the therapists were able to pursue the topic of Cass and her interest in dating. When Cass had reached puberty, the father had begun to show more interest in her as a person. However, at that time, when she had had one of her early dates, her father had slapped her face for no reason. He admits that he suspected something which had not occurred. The family seemed quite glum during all of this discussion, and the therapists repeatedly pointed out it was the first time in her adult life that Cass had shown any sexual interest, or for that matter, interest in men in general. Therapist B then raised the question about whether Cass might not be helped by getting a room in a hotel and moving out of the home for a few days. The whole family, except Cass, was quite upset about the sexual implications of this. The father admitted that his reaction previously had been extreme and that he had been very concerned that Cass might become as promiscuous as his sister; therefore, he had not trusted her.

Cass had had several offers of dates from various men but had turned them down after her parents had been so negative about her dating. It was quite clear that the parents were really not trying to persuade her to try to get out of the house. There was no feeling of elation because for the first time in her adult life, Cass really expressed interest in wanting to see someone. Therapist A then suggested that maybe Cass should stay out for several days and it might even be helpful for her to develop some type of sexual relationship. Both parents became very angry with this, particularly the father. He stated several times that he would rather have Cass remain schizophrenic than ever have a sexual relationship outside of marriage. For the first time, however, the family was able to discuss quite effectively their fears, concerns and fantasies about what Cass might do if she left the house. For the last ten minutes of the session, Therapist A held Cass's hand. Harvey blushed and turned away, and the mother and father were quite tense; however, Cass's hand was relaxed in Therapist A's hand, and she was quite comfortable. At the end of the session, she said that perhaps she might want to date her cousin or others who had called, and seemed quite reassured that the therapist did not see her dating as destructive or disruptive of the family situation as her parents saw it.

For several sessions there has been clear evidence that Cass is ready to take new steps in her emancipation from the parents. She has become quite interested in men and is about to begin dating. Most of this is over the very strong objections of the parents. They had made the very firm statement that they would rather she remain ill than run the risk of having sexual relationships and becoming promiscuous. Their attitude is so pathological and overprotective that whenever she begins to move definitely in a direction away from them and more towards independence and personal maturity, they even suggest that she should be hospitalized. Physical contact and walks with the patient were used to reassure her, and to convey to her that the therapists would go to extremes in assisting her in her emancipation.

The next couple of sessions were resistive ones, with the family unable to follow any topic and appearing depressed. The father and mother both continue to suggest that Cass should go to the hospital, that they are exhausted, and that Cass was slipping. Cass was angry and provocative with the other family members, at the same time agreeing that she should go to the hospital.

In session 142 the family dog was ill and the father did not show up. The dog was upstairs in the parents' bedroom in their bed, and the mother insisted that some member of the family be with the dog at all times. Therapist B suggested that the whole family and the therapists go up to the bedroom for the session but the mother felt that this would be too much for the dog who might get excited. Once the mother seemed to be able to talk somewhat more freely about her feelings, particularly about the dog, she went into great detail about the number of hours she was spending looking after the dog. She was very distrustful of the veterinarian and constantly questioned him about the medications he was giving and the reasons for these. Both Cass and Harvey were slightly depressed and somewhat reserved in this session. It was finally revealed that the mother was facing an operation and that she was concerned that she might have cancer of the breast. Throughout the session, the family cat assumed the previous position formerly held by the dog. In previous sessions the cat has always remained on the periphery of the family circle, but tonight it sat in the center of the group, repeatedly approaching the mother the way the dog had done. Because of the dog's serious illness, the father had taken his vacation and was spending his time looking after the dog. When the mother first took the dog to the veterinarian, he had thought the dog had a nervous illness; at this point, however, he had changed his diagnosis to distemper.

Session 143. Cass did not show up and the family tended to ignore this. When Therapist B asked directly where she was, they said, seemingly unconcerned, that they did not know. Therapist B then went outside and found Cass sitting in the garden. She immediately accused him of interfering with her and not helping her and ran away through the house and up the stairs to her room. Her mother then reported that the dog had died during the week; she was quite tearful about this. During the week, Cass had gone on a date with her cousin. She had become concerned because the cousin did not say that he would ask her out again.

In the following session Harvey was sick in bed and did not come down. Father's face was swollen, and he announced that he had had several teeth removed. These were the teeth that he had been talking about since we started coming to the family over two years ago, but had neglected because of a very strong phobia about seeing a dentist. He was able to get the teeth extracted when he got a letter from his boss instructing him to get them taken care of. Cass stated that she did not come to the last session because she knew that Candy's death would be discussed and this would upset her quite a bit. The mother stated that she had been comforted by this discussion. During this week, Cass had gone out a great deal. She had been on another date with her cousin, and she had gone downtown with her mother.

Before the next session the mother called Therapist A at his office to insist that Cass be admitted to a hospital. This request appeared to be related to Cass's increased dating and going out.

In the next few sessions the therapists worked primarily with Cass and her relationships on dates. They acted repeatedly in a way that interested parents might act toward a young adolescent who had not been out on dates before and did not know how to behave. This was done primarily in order to give Cass support and reassurance which she did not get from her parents.

Session 147. Harvey announced that he had moved out of his apartment and was returning to live with the family. This was unexpected news to us but for the past month or so he had been living mostly at home. He gave as his reason that one of the boys he was rooming with had been drafted into the Army, and the others did not feel like keeping up the apartment. Cass stated that she was feeling much better and would like to get some kind of job training. Arrangements were made for her to have some appointments with the Bureau of Vocational Rehabilitation. It did seem remarkable that Cass's increased moving out of the home seemed related to Harvey's moving back into the home again. The family conceded that this was so, but were totally unable to examine the meaning of this.

The next few sessions were spent with the parents trying to get Cass to accompany them to the shore for a vacation. It was clear that the parents, as in the past, would not be able to go away for a vacation unless Cass went with them. The therapists explored extensively the reasons for the parents' fear of leaving Cass alone. The parents felt that they would not be able to have a good time without her, and furthermore they feared that she would be terribly lonesome and might even make a suicidal attempt if they would leave her. She repeatedly reassured them that she was not interested in going and being under their supervision, and that she would not make a suicidal attempt in their absence. Cass was somewhat depressed in this session and again talked about her feelings of inferiority and how no men could ever be interested in her. Therapist B talked to her for two or three minutes about her vagina and about how desirable and attractive this would be to men. This had the effect of immediately relieving her depression, as had happened previously, and she felt quite relaxed and even somewhat proud of herself.

Session 150. When the therapists arrived, only Harvey and Cass were present. They mentioned that the parents had been down in Atlantic City for the past two days. They made use of this session to complain about certain things, particularly about the father's behavior. Father is unable to leave Cass alone. At times, he chases her around the house; if she is upstairs, he goes upstairs and calls her to see where she is, and if she goes into the basement, he follows her. The therapists pointed out that this might be increasing in frequency because of his anxiety about her leaving the house. Harvey pointed out, in addition, that the father never had had much self-confidence and that the therapy sessions seemed to be robbing him of the little he had. An interesting event occurred the day the parents left: they had Cass' cat castrated. The cat was now looking very ill and lying in a box. This unconscious act seemed to say to Cass and Harvey that they should be very careful about any type of sexual activity while their parents were away. During the session Cass acted as a very good hostess; she offered the therapists a drink of ginger ale, she got ash trays, etc., and in general seemed like a relaxed woman running her own home. She was doing very well and wanted to call her parents and encourage them to stay away a little longer.

Session 151. Cass recounted how her uncle's girl friend Christine, a young woman over thirty years younger than the uncle, had made open sexual references and connotations in talking to Cass' male cousin. The four of them had been out on a double date. Harvey mentioned that he often took out girls for other fellows to assess, so that he could then recommend them to his boyfriends. Cass did not feel that she could compete with a sexual woman like Christine, and launched into a long account about how abnormal she was and how distorted her body was. She has always stated that her thighs were abnormal, somewhat like those of a hippopotamus. The therapists had consistently denied that there was anything abnormal about her anatomy. This time Cass suddenly stood up in the middle of the session, announced that she would be willing to show us her thighs and immediately began taking off her clothes. She wore a very attractive, rather brief bathing suit and posed in that. Both therapists complimented her, looked at her thighs carefully and told her that there was nothing abnormal about them. Cass seemed quite surprised that they saw no abnormality in her figure. Her mother became very upset by this behavior and ordered her to put her clothes back on. Cass then put on a brief skirt that was part of a play suit, but left the top of the bathing suit exposed. As we left the house that evening, she seemed quite pleased that we had observed her and had approved of her anatomy. She seemed out of her depression. During the following sessions Harvey was absent and the father talked a great deal about his fears of water, of the dentist, of driving a car, etc. He came very close to admitting that these were true fears. Previously he had always maintained that there was nothing unusual in any of these symptoms. The family continued to discuss Cass' dating with her cousin. The parents were due to leave on another trip, their second in a very short period of time. Just as they were about to leave, Christine invited Cass to go to New York with her. A great deal of this and the following session was devoted to a discussion of Christine's promiscuity and the family's disapproval of Cass' accompanying such a promiscuous person out of town. Neither the mother nor father seemed at all pleased that Cass was about to take her first trip to New York. Cass, in a fairly mature and realistic way, handled her father's objections to the trip and was able to discuss her sexual impulses openly with him. She stated that he had trained her very well, and although she would like to have some kind of sexual contact, she knew that it would be impossible for her. At the same time, both the mother and father were complaining a great deal that Cass was much too stiff with boys, that she was not relaxed and could not talk to them.

In the next session the parents had left for the Midwest, and Harvey and Cass were home alone. Cass had taken her trip to New York with Christine; in addition, she had gone to a coffee house with her cousin. Cass was pleased that she could take the trip, but annoyed and irritable because she felt she did not get enough attention and could not compete with Christine. She felt alone and left out. The therapists spent a great deal of time telling her how women feel and act. Harvey participated in the discussion in a supportive way, but at times stated that he was fed up with her demands for constant reassurance. As the session closed Cass was discussing how her cousin gets upset whenever she gets close to him. She has been infatuated with him and has been attempting to get him to pay more attention to her. This tends to frighten him off, however. She was also upset because on a couple of occasions he would take her out on a brief date, then drop her off at home and ask Harvey to go out with him.

Session 155. The whole family was present for this session. The parents had returned from their trip and were quite pleased with their obvious enjoyment of it. The cat was ill with complications following the castration of about a month ago. While the parents had been away Cass had taken the cat to a veterinarian because of an obstructed urinary tract. The parents' trip was unique in that they had ceased to worry about Cass after they had called home in the middle of the week and found that everything was going well. Toward the end of the session, Cass was rather outspoken in her criticism of her father's overprotectiveness. Harvey stepped in immediately to tone down her comments. This had occurred before and gave the therapists the chance to point out how Harvey aids and abets the parents in maintaining Cass in a dependent, helpless, infantile condition. None of the family can tolerate seeing Cass take a mature, outspoken, self-assertive role in the family.

During the next four sessions Cass was somewhat depressed. The content of the sessions concerned the illness of her cat, her inability to go out during this illness because she was nursing the cat—at times almost night and day. Another, often repeated, theme was the father's overprotectiveness of Cass and his sexual fantasies about her. These mostly involved whether she might not be taken advantage of by some man if she went out into the world. He also had some fantasies that Negro men would be interested in her and that Cass would acquiesce to them. Much of this centered around Cass' trip to New York which still worried both parents. As the family became progressively more able to talk about sexual concerns, the father became quite outspoken about his views on sexuality. He stated very firmly and repeatedly that he would rather that his daughter remain schizophrenic than have a sexual affair with someone. During the following session we learned that the cat had had to be put away because of the hopelessness of its physical condition, apparently a chronic pyelonephritis precipitated originally by the castration. At one point in the session Cass got up and left the room, staying out for fifteen minutes because she could not tolerate discussing her feeling about the cat. She repeatedly requested that she be sent to a state hospital. Therapist B stated again and again that she was an attractive girl, that she had feelings and that she had something to offer men and the world. The discussion then switched to the father and his need to control every situation. The mother told how, if she and her husband were in a restaurant, he would suggest what she should eat without allowing her to choose what she wanted. Near the end of the session Cass again brought up the question of hospitalization although she seemed much more cheerful by this time and had participated well in the discussion.

During the following week, Mrs. Island called up saying that Cass was deeply depressed and needed to be hospitalized. This was handled by asking her what her thoughts were about the need for hospitalization, and when she hedged about this, it was decided to postpone discussion or evaluation until the next session. In session 163 Cass did not seem nearly as depressed. She had a little kitten with her which had been given to her by the veterinarian. Much of the discussion centered on Harvey's inability to keep his job and on Cass' inability to form a satisfactory relationship with her uncle's girlfriend. The latter has been seeing quite a bit of her, but Cass does not feel she has anything in common with her, and also feels unable to compete with her for men.

The next several sessions were spent with both therapists attempting to generate family interaction and work on some of the defenses and resistance. The constant defense has been a kind of denial of any type of latent content to the interaction among the family members. Both therapists felt that the family was quite frightened over the sexual content of many of the past sessions, and this seemed quite an emotionally laden area which had much to do with Cass' inability to leave the house.

In session 168 Cass appeared in a striking black outfit. The family mood as a whole was one of depression. The father stated he was depressed because of problems in his job but would not elaborate further on it. Harvey was having a return of a back condition and for the first time was seeing an orthopedic specialist. Cass said that she feels depressed and the mother stated that she is depressed because Cass is depressed. A family discussion ensued which brought out that the mother's brother has been having a long-time sexual affair with Christine, that Bill and Helen had had sexual relationships before marriage, and that their son was conceived out of wedlock. The mother further mentioned that Helen still has extra-marital affairs. The father stated that any woman who engages in sex outside of marriage is a prostitute. Therapist B was unable to attend session 169 because of a previous commitment, and the mother was ill in bed with a virus. Much of the session concerned Cass and her interaction with her father. She was quite openly hostile to him and complained strongly that he holds her in the house, doesn't want to let her get out—in fact the entire family wants to keep her home. She suggested that she would like to leave the house and live in a hotel room, and thought a nice busy hotel in the center of the city, where she could sit in the lobby and watch action going on, might be the place. The father said this was ridiculous, especially since Cass couldn't even walk out on the street, around the house. He then suggested that she move to a home for girls. Harvey also thought this would be a good idea. Cass also suggested that maybe she should go into a hospital.

In session 170 the same theme was continued. Cass almost held Christine up as a model. The father became very concerned that Cass would be picked up by some predatory male. Cass was expressing herself very well and voicing quite a few independent ideas. The mother was more accepting of these ideas than was the father.

During the next couple of sessions no further mention was made of Cass's moving out of the home. This was in part due to the fact that Mrs. Island's father had died, which had revived some of the feelings she had had regarding the death of the dog, Candy. The mother admitted that she felt much more upset about the death of the dog. Cass did not attend session 174 and remained upstairs in her room, with the door closed. The therapists decided to have Therapist A talk to her through the closed door. Cass talked freely about her fears of a coming meeting between the mother and the mother's sister. The mother admitted that she had had some angry words with her sister. During the preceding week Cass had expressed a lot of interest in going out and had painted a picture. It was a painting of a young girl holding a small child. The picture was stimulating and interesting and had a much more human quality than her previous paintings. The therapists interpreted to the family that whenever Cass begins to show improvement, the rest of the family become anxious or depressed.

At the next session the entire family was present. Harvey had been sleeping on the sofa, apparently surrounded by the family watching television. He was therefore quite sleepy throughout most of the session and again did not participate too much. Cass's latest painting was still on the wall and the early part of the session revolved around a discussion of it. Cass spoke in a rather animated way about the party that the family had had on the previous weekend for her mother's relatives. There had been a lot of people present, and although she had been somewhat anxious initially, she was able to relax and enjoy herself. The rest of the family were again very depressed and withdrawn. The father explained the family's lack of participation by saying that they were tired from the previous week's party. Cass began to attack her father for not giving her money to continue her painting. In addition, it was revealed that he spends about one-fifth of his annual income on various gifts for the employees of his office. This all comes out of his own pocket, and the company does not reimburse him for this. The family seemed surprised that he spent this much of his income for other people. In the following session it was again Cass who was the animated one, and the other members of the family were quiet and somewhat depressed.

In session 177 Harvey announced that he would be inducted into the army in a couple of weeks. Mother and Cass had been going out of the house more often. The other family members accused the father of keeping them in. They stated that if they stayed out past nine o'clock, he would become very worried about them and would get so upset that they would not be able to do it again. Cass reported a very interesting dream, the highlight of which was her leaving the home, going out by herself after being initially with her brother. She was in a store and she flirted with a fellow. She then disguised herself and was afraid that her father would come after her and send the police after her. In another part of the dream Cass is at home and wants to do something on her own and father comes over and grabs her hand and won't let go of her in a threatening way; she feels frightened and wakes up. This followed her mentioning that she and her mother were going out to a dinner-dance with the mother's brother and some of his friends. This was a very unusual event in this family. The therapists had to give both the mother and Cass a great deal of encouragement before they were able to do this. The rest of the session was spent in working on the father's need to control the other members and his complete lack of trust and approval whenever anyone steps out of his sight. Although Cass and the mother did go to the dance, they did not have a particularly good time. In session 179 Harvey asked the family if they would miss him when he went into the service. The entire family seemed hopeful that Harvey would be turned down for reasons of physical disability. The mother particularly was very angry at both therapists and felt that the Army doctors conducted inadequate physicals—otherwise, how could they have taken someone like Harvey.

Session 180 was the last one in which Harvey took part in the family therapy, since he was inducted a couple of days later. The mother, in this session, wanted to know how much longer the research project with the family was going to continue. The therapists indicated that the project would probably come to an end in a few months. There was no particular family reaction to this. Harvey several times suggested, as he had previously done, that the therapists use their influence to get him out of the Army. The therapists said they were unable to do this.

In session 181 only Cass and the mother were home. Harvey had left for the service, and the father was away for three days attending a convention. As we entered the home, the mother was visibly very tense. She was sitting in the corner of the couch and when Therapist B sat on the same couch about three feet away from her, she immediately asked him to sit somewhere else. He did not move, but instead asked her to discuss her request. She persisted in saying that she did not know why she was uncomfortable, and if the therapist wanted to sit there he could—but she looked quite uncomfortable for the next few minutes. The family had visited Harvey at the Army post about sixty miles away. This was unusual since they had rarely traveled anywhere together in the past.

The essential topic of the evening dealt with the father who was absent. Both the mother and Cass talked about his need to keep everyone in the home, and his keeping tabs on everyone even inside the home. The mother stated that for several years after the children were born she was quite depressed and agitated about this. She felt she wanted to go out and that her husband was holding her in. However, she finally resigned herself to the situation and it has been this way ever since. Although the mother strikes us as being depressed much of the time, she stated that she was much more depressed until Cass was sixteen or seventeen years of age. This was about the time that Cass became house-bound and psychotic. The mother stated that she sees her husband as the only decent person she has ever known. Her relationships with her siblings and parents were of such a traumatic nature, that when her husband came along and treated her kindly and wanted her, she felt that this was as much as she could expect from life. She views people in general as being hard, depriving, and hurting.

In the next few sessions the family told about what a difficult situation Harvey was in and how the Army was going to ruin him. They attacked the therapists for not doing something about it. For the next six sessions they continued to talk about how terrible the Army was, and told horrendous stories about how Harvey, when he was sick, had had to wait in line in front of a hospital for ten hours before being admitted. The family did not believe that he would live through the period of basic training. They said the food was so terrible that no one could survive that type of diet. When the therapists did not directly intervene with the Army, the mother particularly became very upset and angry, calling the therapists liars and inhuman.

In session 189 there was a great deal of family concern about Harvey's behavior toward the family when he had returned on leave. He had now finished basic training but seemed very angry. He was openly defiant of the father and at times threatened to strike Cass. The mother felt that she could no longer control him. The therapists attempted to reassure the family about Harvey's behavior and were partially successful. Therapist A mentioned at the end of the session that we would terminate therapy with the family at the end of another three months. The reaction to this announcement was the same as to many other events in the family's life—there were no questions about the future, or what we were going to do up to termination. It was accepted with the same kind of passive and somewhat depressed attitude that we had seen many times before.

The last three months of therapy continued with father, mother and Cass present. During this period Cass showed once again more interest in going out; the mother was becoming progressively more angry with the therapists. This seemed to revolve about her feeling that Cass may have gotten quite a bit of help from the therapy but that she was under attack and was made more tense by the therapy. The father was in a phase of increasing difficulties in his business. On several occasions people from company headquarters had investigated his business and been very critical of his methods of office management. Interestingly enough, whenever the company insisted that he make changes, he was at least able to make an attempt in this direction. The very same things had been discussed in the family therapy over many months and he had been unable to do anything. Some of the final therapy sessions were conducted in a hospital out-patient setting. The family, however, much preferred the home. They were suspicious about the purposes of coming to a clinic and particularly the mother and Cass felt quite confined in a room, and complained a great deal about feelings of tension because the door was closed. Both requested, and were given permission, to explore the out-patient building to reassure themselves that the room was not wired, people were not watching, etc. (This seemed further evidence of the fact that paranoid trends are an illness of the whole family.) A good deal of time was spent in discussing future plans for the family and for Cass. Cass was encouraged to continue to go out, to seek a job and perhaps eventually to leave home. The parents were encouraged to bring people into the home, to develop their own interests, and particularly to form a more real relationship between each other instead of clinging to Cass.

About two months after the termination of therapy, Cass called Therapist A to request an individual appointment. This was granted and she came to a hospital clinic alone. She looked very attractive and not nearly as self-conscious as she had in the past. She stated that almost coincidental with the termination of therapy, she had been going out much more than ever before. She had met a young man and had been dating him. She was very satisfied with this relationship but was developing concern that it might lead into a sexual relationship and wanted the therapist to tell her how to conduct herself properly. She stated that Harvey had gotten out of the service and was looking for a job. She added that she had lost most of her fear of leaving the house and that although she did not feel that her parents were making the changes which had been recommended for them, she felt much better and was looking forward to her future. She thought that she might be able to use an individual therapist, but was not ready to undertake this as yet.

Summary

The Island family treatment has been presented chronologically and in more detail than the other case histories in this book. We feel that it illustrates well the concept of a socially shared psychopathology. It involved constant attempts to get various family members to make changes so as to allow for change in others. Mr. and Mrs. Island are, of course, products of their parents and grandparents; both suffered severe object losses in their own families of origin. Their children represented to them not only a reparative process for the original loneliness, emptiness and object loss, but a continuing and permanent restitution. To allow Harvey and Cass to separate themselves and become true individuals with their own individual lives brought about acute anxiety, depression, and a reliving of the breakup that had occurred in their families; stated another way, Harvey and Cass represented new parents, security and stability. The records of this family's treatment show how homeostasis is maintained within a family and how a seemingly devoted father can state and maintain that he would prefer his daughter to remain schizophrenic rather than have her involved in an extra-marital sexual relationship.

Despite the marked improvement in Cass, which has been maintained over the past four years, Mrs. Island is more paranoid and depressed than before, and stays even closer to home. This case also proves that it is frequently easier to reach and understand the schizophrenic patient in a family than it is to deal with and help some of the other family members.

The Rituell family

Jerome E. Jungreis and Ross V. Speck

This family, consisting of mother and father in their late fifties and their schizophrenic son in his twenties, has been treated in their home in weekly one and one-half hour sessions for the past two and one-half years. The therapy team consisted of a psychiatric case worker and a psychiatrist, one of the members of the team having been chosen by virtue of his interest and belief in Orthodox Judaism. Much of the life of this family centers around religious ritual, and the schizophrenic son's symptoms are, to a great extent, involved with perversions, accentuations, and caricatures of extreme Jewish orthodoxy. Prior to family therapy the symptomatic patient had seen about a dozen different psychiatrists, always terminating the treatment because he did not feel that he had any problems.

This presentation of the Rituell family is structured so that the section headings reflect the important areas of family functioning as they were revealed during the course of the observation and therapy of the family unit. The sub-headings are chosen to reflect the most cogent areas but are not necessarily arranged in order of significance, although an effort has been made to present the family life in such a structured form.

Religion

Jewish orthodoxy of a peculiar variety is a central theme of this family. The mother professes no interest in religion but has carefully kept a kosher home throughout her married life.

Equally carefully, she has managed to deliberately interfere with the religious practices in the family. The father observes much of the ritual of his religion, but never lets this interfere with his business. He is not averse to working on Saturday, but he is very careful to hang the mezuzahs properly in his house. He constantly quotes the holy scriptures in a pious way, but usually to justify his view of life.

The schizophrenic son says the father and mother are not religious enough, and as if to make up for this, he spends much of his time flamboyantly practicing various religious rituals or perversions of these rituals. For instance, there must be a set of Chanukah candles for each family member and these have to be placed in the room in such a way that no two sets can be seen from the same place; prayers must be said so loudly that they interfere with any activity within the home, and he insists that his father say "Amen" to each of these prayers. Morning prayers take several hours because each word must be pronounced and understood by the person praying. One can easily run through a number of rituals which the patient has built up to take up most of his available time.

It is also interesting to note that the family has a veritable string of rabbis in its religious stable. They turn to them for advice in various matters and if not satisfied with one, will call another. There was almost nothing of a spiritual quality in the religious practices of any member of the family. The one coming closest to it is the one who practices the least: the mother.

The Grandparents

Mr. Rituell's father was a very orthodox Jew of Russian birth. He would not work on the Sabbath and is reported by his son to have once lost $40,000 in a business deal because of it. He was hard-working but minimally successful. The paternal grandmother was a more influential figure in Mr. Rituell's life and was idolized by him. Mr. Rituell still becomes angry if anyone makes a critical remark about her. "She was an angel and a perfect mother," he says, yet she was depressed a good deal of her life and domineered the family. He excuses the fact that she never loved her husband. After Mr. Rituell had married, he had to call her daily on the telephone, and frequently contributed to her support; this behavior, despite his wife's objections, persisted during her lifetime. She died one month after therapy was initiated, and her son was so crushed by this that he had a heart attack on his way home from the funeral.

Of eight children, Mr. Rituell is the only one to hold to Jewish orthodoxy. He feels that he caused his father's death by not being religious enough, and has since then tried to practice the orthodox religion.

Mrs. Rituell's mother wore the pants in the home. She constantly made derogatory allusions about men; she was very outspoken and Mrs. Rituell said that people looked up to her mother because of it. The grandmother was full of adages and advice about how women had to be self-sufficient. "You can never count on a man, so always learn a trade for a rainy day," or "busy hands keep the devil away." At the same time she never gave her daughter any sexual education.

By contrast, Mrs. Rituell scarcely was impressed with her father who had a very inferior role in the household. She always felt that men were weak and had to be treated like helpless or unruly children.

The Physical Home

The Rituells live in a row home in a lower middle-class neighborhood. Both parents are penurious and hard-working and have accumulated a good deal of wealth from their small business. Although adequately furnished, and in good repair, the home does not reflect this wealth. The basement of the home contains stock from the family business. Both parents work at this business with much disharmony but mutual effort. Their schizophrenic son uses the business as a convenient rationalization for not working elsewhere, and as a way of practicing full-time religion and very part-time work.

The first floor of the home contains a living room, a dining room and a kitchen. The living room is a lounging area for the men and an activity area for the mother. She enjoys playing the piano, but this is forbidden her by her husband. The dining room is their work room for the paper work and record-keeping part of the business, and is also the room where family gatherings are held. Social contacts of the family are largely limited to relatives. The family therapy sessions are held in the dining room which is the usual place for this family's arguments or intrafamily communications. The kitchen is an eating and food preparation area, contains the telephone, and is a hotbed of family religious arguments.

Upstairs are three bedrooms and a bathroom. Each family member has a bedroom, and the bathroom has some shared aspects between the son and the mother, the father attending to his toilet functions alone. There is about 20' x 15' piece of land in front of the house which the parents use in good weather to sit outside—although usually not together. When they do, loud arguments are a frequent occurrence.

Lethal Factors

Certain of our observations would suggest a lethal factor operating in schizophrenic families. This would confirm the work cited by V. Sanua[96] that the incidence of sibling death in schizophrenic families is double that in non-schizophrenic families. In the Rituell family, the younger sibling, a daughter, died of leukemia at age three.

Soon after initiation of family therapy—during the fourth week—the father had a heart attack. Psychodynamic factors undoubtedly were present, as there was much tension in the family. The father had a paranoid attitude about family therapy and was under much emotional stress during and in the interval between sessions. His mother had died suddenly and he was greatly saddened and upset by this. On the way home from her funeral one of his fingers was crushed in a door of the funeral car and while getting this treated in a hospital emergency room, he developed substernal pain and a coronary attack. During his recovery in the hospital and afterwards at home, both his wife and his son openly baited him, said he was malingering and almost openly and consciously tried to yank out all his supports.

Themes and Communications During Therapy Sessions

A fair approximation of how the family spent the time during therapy session looks as follows:

Bickering between mother and father		65%
The son, Martin, baiting parents; parents responding to it and vice versa		15%
Meaningful interaction on a therapeutic level		14%
Between spouses	1%	
Between therapists and parents	8%	
Between therapists and boy	5%	
Other		6%
		100%

The arguments between the parents revolve around the joint business enterprise and the handling of Martin in the ratio of two to one. The basic business argument consists essentially, as do all parental arguments, of mother aggressively accusing father of some failing, with the accompanying theme of her exemplary behavior and his need to emulate her. Father responds initially with defensive maneuvers in which he points out in many ways that mother is not respecting him as head of the house or of the business, that in this respect she is unlike all the wives of other business colleagues. When father seizes the offensive, as he occasionally does, he recalls examples, going back to the beginning of their marriage, of how she publicly humiliated him and in other ways tended to castrate him. Following this, both appeal to the therapists for confirmation of their attitudes, convinced that any right-minded person would agree with their reasonable position. This scene is constantly reenacted as are others, without profit or resolution—endlessly, and always with the same fervor and intensity. This charade has been going on during all the twenty-nine years of their marriage, and is as bitter and charged today as it was on their wedding day when Mrs. Rituell spit in her husband's face. This overwhelming rigidity and compulsive repetition reminds us of the ancient tragedies that were played each year in Greece, where the dialogue was known to all but was reenacted with great religious fervor, in the belief that some primal anxiety can be assuaged temporarily by its expressive reproduction.

The second theme, similar in its endless intensity and mutuality is the struggle around the parental need for Martin to conform to external social norms, and his need for the parents to conform to his version of social norms. His version consists of having the parents externally enact stylized religious forms in the most minute degree. Neither the parents nor Martin are at all interested in psychic investment, only in external representations by acts and deeds. The parents insist on non-bizarre behavior on Martin's part—no rolling of eyes, head scratching, going to sleep in the sessions, odd postures and flabby verbal responses—and on his getting a job. They want him "to act like a normal human being." They exhibit little genuine interest in his psychotic ideations, however bizarre. In the same way, Martin is not concerned with his parents becoming religious with a sense of personal commitment to a deity, he only wants them to conform to religious practices.

Typically, one of the parents would call attention to Martin's posture or unconventional behavior. He would respond by either ignoring this attention in a sweeping, dramatic, provocative way or by feebly suggesting that he didn't understand them. Both parents insisted that Martin was not affectively reacting to them with anger, hate or provocation. At times Martin would look at one of his parents with an intense stare of murderous hate; the signal, the non-verbal obvious communication, would find no recognition. At other times he would respond to any family problem, however unrelated, by exhorting either or both parents to practice their religion with greater assiduousness, calling attention to deeds left undone by father, and suggesting more careful attention to choice or preparation of food by mother. He would open the "Code of Jewish Laws" and read from it aloud, knowing very well that this would infuriate his parents, particularly his father. Father had already disposed of five of six copies of this book only to have his son purchase new ones. Father would then start arguing with Martin as to his lack of Jewish scholarship and his misinterpretation of the law. Martin's responses would be a caricature of his father's approach to problems: sure of the righteousness of his cause he will ask people in a carefully skewed way as to who is right. These family compulsions in their endless, intense repetition provide an interesting correspondence to and parallel with comparable compulsive mechanisms of ritual of each family member. The individual compulsions are also vehicles for the control of others in the family, the endless arguments work as a control of the therapy, and also seem to keep the family relatively static.

An interwoven theme is that of Dr. O., the absent member. This gentleman was never present, is in no way a part of the family, and probably would be quite surprised to find himself the object of so much family discussion. Martin met him shortly after being discharged from service, for reasons other than honorable. Martin then had been teetering on the edge of acute psychosis, looking for a father substitute with stability or a defensive system that he could copy in strength. Dr. O. filled this bill. He had achieved considerable recognition in the orthodox Jewish community. Martin has copied his mannerisms, constantly refers to him, knowing fully well that this infuriates his parents, particularly his father, and uses this man as a model to further indoctrinate himself in the Jewish ritual.

The themes in the communication patterns as described above have been the overt ones. Concurrently the communications between those members of the family operate on other levels, non-verbal, unconscious or with implications. For instance, communications between the Mother and Martin are that he is not sick, just needs instruction in proper social customs, which she handles by telling him not to scratch his head, not to roll his eyes, to speak up, etcetera. On another level she is saying, "I don't care whether or not you are sick, just act normal, don't shame your parents." On still another level she is saying, "I care more about you than your father does," and on again another level she is saying, "You are a child and I must treat you like one." Another theme is each family member's insistence that his interpretation of events is correct, regardless of what the other person has to say about it. This particularly relates to mother's interpreting an action or thought of Father's or Martin's. It is equally true of the others. Father, for instance, may come home from a hard day's work, being quite tired and tell his wife how tired he is. This means to her that he wants her back in the business and in a much more active role. When she verbalizes this, he insists he does not mean this at all, he is simply talking about his tiredness and wants to get it off his chest. Mother says that nothing he could say or do would change her mind as to why he is talking about being tired. Father attempts to demonstrate his sincerity by giving her less work in the business and by verbally reassuring her that he does not intend to have her work any harder. This means nothing to mother. On one level, she is saying that she understands Father even if he doesn't understand himself, and again is tending to treat him like a child; on another level she is also saying that she wants to keep her hand in the business but that he is forcing her out and he is the strong parent. On yet another level, she is telling him there can be no communication between them of a mutual give and take variety. Another pattern again relates to her insisting that things only mean what she wants them to mean, regardless of whatever obvious meanings they may have. For instance, she comes into the bathroom when Martin is actually in the process of having a bowel movement. Martin says that this is embarrassing, he doesn't want her to come in, and so on. Mother insists this doesn't mean anything, or she may say, "You really don't mind at all, you simply somehow feel you have to say this," or "I am always right and you are usually wrong." Invariably there is an association with father who gets mentioned in a derogatory fashion when she and Martin are attempting to work something out. The implication always is that "I care about you, but father is out to hurt you." An example of Mother's saying one thing and meaning another is that she will often tell Martin that she wants him to enjoy life, have girls, get married, get a job and so on, but in other ways tells him that he really can't do anything without her help; in addition, she is constantly telling him how to do things and do them better, and never really giving him credit for whatever efforts he may make. She always has a rationalization for this, using Martin to prove her point because he isn't doing things as well as she can do them. This is similar in some respects to the way she acts with her husband where she always feels that whatever he does she could have done much better. A good example of this deals with the fact that Martin is a substitute teacher. Mother says, "Even though you are a college graduate and have been trained as a teacher, and I am not even a high school graduate and have never taught," there is much that she can teach him about teaching. Another theme of hers is that she is self-sufficient and needs no one, but at the same time she also says that she would miss her husband or Martin quite a bit.

All of the communication patterns and relationships have to do with a series of dyads that exist in the family. The dyad is usually directed against the third person. In the dyad with mother and Martin, mother is always telling him that essentially his father is bad for him and she is there to protect him. For instance, father may lose his temper, start to yell and scream, and she tries to shush him. However, she also yells at Martin. Sometimes she will even agree with father, but if he then gets into an argument with Martin over the issue on which she had previously agreed with him, she will back Martin up.

Another favorite theme, implicit, is that "Father doesn't understand you, Martin, I do . . . Father's family is no good; my family is a very fine family. . . . Even though I am openly more against religion than father, I sympathize more with you and your religious aspirations than your father does."

The following sentences, directed at Martin, are another example of mother's deliberately misperceiving reality and further helping to distort Martin's reality perceptions: "You say you are angry at me, but really you aren't. You close your eyes, you mean you are sleepy, not angry. You read the code of Jewish laws at these family meetings, but this is just bad manners, not resistance. Martin, you should really model yourself after me, not after your father, because I am the man of the house. I am prompt, swift, efficient, industrious and you should be like that."

In the dyad between father and Martin, the following communications take place with the accent on excluding mother. Father says that "When mother is not around, somehow Martin and I get along much better." He gives various examples of this, such as when he takes Martin with him in his car and they do some business together. He tells Martin that he is too extreme in his religious behavior, but then says that he and Martin understand religion and can quote the scriptures to each other. Mother is excluded from this. Father tells Martin too that mother doesn't take proper care of either one of them; she doesn't have the meals ready, they are not properly prepared, and so on. Martin, in response and on his own, mentions that father is frequently much more helpful than mother; he uses the code of Jewish laws to back father up in asserting his authority over mother. When the issue of Martin's leaving the home and living elsewhere came up, it was the father and Martin who banded together and tried to keep him in the home as long as possible. They excluded mother from this and tried to set her up as the bad one who wanted Martin out of the house, even though that suggestion had been a professional recommendation.

The dyad of mother and father excludes Martin. They will argue over how to handle him without including him in their deliberations. It is particularly worthy of note that the dyadic relationship between the parents excludes the son and deals with their interpersonal arguments. Such arguments center around who is going to be in control of the business, and sometimes Martin will feebly interject that he hopes he will get a greater share of the business, and that perhaps some day father will turn the business over to him. He is excluded from this kind of discussion by the parents' interactions. They also argue a great deal about sex and being unloved, with each partner accusing the other of not giving him or her enough love and again excluding Martin. In fact, what looms largest in these sessions, in terms of time spent, is the amount of interaction between mother and father from which Martin is excluded.

In order to understand this family, from the communication's point of view, one has to realize that their openly expressed dissatisfaction with each other is a cover-up for mother's wanting to be masculine and domineering and for father's ambivalent acceptance of this. Martin's ambivalence is to grow up or to stay a child; to have the fun of irresponsibility or to strive toward masculinity and maturity. His argument with his parents again is a cover-up for his ambivalence, and their arguments with him cover-up for their mixed feelings about this and their unconscious acceptance of his childlike role.

Family Resistances

The family resistance to therapy must be seen as part of an ongoing family resistance to change, to moving the family dynamics from a static level to a dynamic one. This resistance may be categorized under several headings. The first is acting out; the second is the use of dyads; the third is undermining; the fourth projection; the fifth refusal to accept responsibility; the sixth refusal to see patterns and dynamic interplay; the seventh somatic symptoms; and the eighth is the unconscious fear of the destruction of the family should any one person change.

The acting out of the family assumes various poses. In the acting-out phase mother moves in and out of the business sufficiently to cause the family to be constantly unsettled. She does this on her own initiative and will persist, if father tries to be strong, until he finally gives in. Both parents move in and out of the bedroom; they will not have relations with each other and then will move back together again for a while. Martin's use of religion for himself as well as with the parents is an acting-out kind of behavior to prevent an awareness of what is really bothering him. The family's use of consultants outside of the therapy team (and this is a pattern that has been going on for many years) is again a means of refusing to face each other and to change a static situation into a dynamic one. The people who are consulted are rabbis, relatives, customers of the family and friends. Each family member will shop around among these people until they find one who is in agreement with them. This then is used as a rationalization and as support to maintain a fixed position. Finally, the various battles that go on on a verbal level between the parents are a persistent means of maintaining the family pathological homeostasis and preventing any emerging maturity and change.

The use of dyads is another mechanism for preventing family growth and development. The dyads in themselves are static mechanisms which by their very nature tend to prevent growth and change. The use of three people in a relationship tends to promote instability and hence some change, whereas the fixation on dyadic relationships tends to promote a permanence and rigidity in the family structure. As long as father and mother can exclude Martin or Martin and father can exclude mother, or mother and Martin can exclude father, there is no real family. The concept, therefore, of a developmental relationship, ever-changing and related both to the reality of the immediate situation as well as to the normal progression of a family from a couple to a couple with children, to the growing up of children, to their moving away from the intense family interaction and forming separate family units, is defeated by the use of dyads.

Another mechanism of resistance is the undermining of change by either one of the parents or Martin in order to maintain the family homeostasis. For instance, if one parent gives in to the other on a point, this does not bring them closer together but only serves to increase the demands of the person who has won the point. If one family member finally decides to really talk about his feelings, it is not accepted by the other members but instead is used to attack that person and thus stop the flow of feelings and fantasies. The one exception to this may be feelings of anger and hostility which are acceptable because they tend to maintain the family homeostasis on a fixed level.

The theme of projection is another mechanism the family uses to prevent growth and change. No one will assume responsibility for anything that turns out to be difficult or unhealthy. For instance, Martin was not supposed to be in the home anymore, but the family had invited him for Friday dinner. It was extremely difficult for the therapy team to find out who actually had invited him, with each parent accusing the other. Not only did Martin remain that evening, but he slept over and remained all day Saturday, slept over again and only left Sunday evening. When the therapy team made attempts to find out why he had stayed so long, it was impossible to learn anything, because every member of the family accused everyone else of permitting Martin to stay, or of encouraging him to do so. Martin himself also projected that he hadn't wanted to stay but that his father in some way, even indirectly, had suggested that he remain. There has yet to be a single theme raised in the family therapy sessions where one of the three members of this family has assumed responsibility for an action, unless that action turned out to be objectively considered good. Thus, the themes—seen in relation to the therapy by arguments between the parents and Martin and by complaints of how they are being mistreated by the other—are handled by trying to set us up as judges in much the same way they go shopping around to their relatives, friends and customers. Yet, each family member is absolutely convinced that he is right and turns to us only to confirm what he believes is really so. The theme of projection is seen with each one constantly feeling that if the other person would change all would be well, that it is the other person who is disturbed and needs help, and that the therapists should tell that person what to do. No effort is made to even try to understand the other person. In regard to the religious theme, both parents feel that Martin should stop his excessive religious practices, which they relate to social conventions rather than to psychotic thinking. Another theme is that everyone in the family is really normal. Both parents insist that their marriage is a typical one, Martin only needs instruction in social graces, that once he relaxes a little bit in his religious practices, all will be well.

The parents and Martin refuse to see patterns and dynamic interplay; they absolutely refuse to see—in spite of their obvious manifestation— continued patterns that repeat themselves endlessly. They sometimes will give lip service to understanding and accepting an interpretation but actually do neither. A good example of this is the father's tentative acceptance of the fact that his wife perhaps has some kind of neurosis and irrational feelings in regard to money; that he should understand therefore that when he wants to give money to charity or work less hard or go into a semi-retired state, she will object. After working on this throughout an entire session and attempting to interpret his wife's behavior to him on this simple level, he tentatively agreed. When we came in the next time Mrs. Rituell told us how furious her husband had become with her the following day—again over the question of money. This time he backtracked completely and said that although he understood, he saw no reason why his wife had to act this way.

Another dilution of the therapy is father's physical condition. He implies, and sometimes states directly, that we must not get things upset and must not change the static pattern of the family, for if we do, he will get sick, have heart failure and die, and then it will be our fault. Martin dilutes the therapy by reading from the holy books during the sessions, by praying loudly, by reading from a school and engaging in other similar practices that are designed to infuriate both his parents and perhaps us; in addition they serve to exclude him from the therapeutic experience.

Finally, there is the fear of destruction of the family, should any one person change. If we look at the family dynamics from the point of view of only one person changing, we can see how homeostasis can be destroyed. If the father, for instance, became more masculine and mother or Martin did not really change, one could expect increased competitiveness on the father's part with an effort to assume more direct control of the family; this would lead to mother's becoming more depressed, expressing more somatic symptoms, being unable to continue to act out, and having increased feelings of inadequacy. Father would perhaps start to run around, or just simply leave her if she did not change. Martin would in one way like and admire his father for assuming a more masculine role, but would also become very guilty about the increased depression and conflict in the family; he would be increasingly unable to resolve his ambivalence about his identification, and the result would be a more acute exacerbation of symptoms.

If only mother changed and became more feminine and father and Martin did not change we would find father becoming increasingly anxious, paranoid and acting out further in the home, with an intensification of symptoms that might even kill him; Martin would feel quite threatened by this, a heightened Oedipal situation would ensue and he might well break out into outright psychosis; he also might be further encouraged in his dependency feelings. If Martin alone got well, he would leave home; the parents then would fight more and there would be an intensification of symptoms for both of them; they would have less of a possibility of working out a dyad which excludes the son (since he has already excluded himself); mother would probably become depressed and start ruminating on what might have been, and both would make attempts to suck Martin back into the home. If he were to get married, they would interfere with his marriage in many different subtle ways; mother would become increasingly seductive with Martin and father would probably feel more and more threatened by his son's masculinity, a condition he may perhaps resolve by attempting to be more dependent on him.

Each of the above actually has a possible positive corollary too. For instance, if father alone became more masculine, it is quite possible that mother might eventually accept him and identify with his masculinity, and that Martin would get a great deal of support from his father's more masculine role which would help him to resolve his own sexual ambivalence. The problem, though, is that much of this is buried intrapsychically in Martin, and while it may have been valid to work it out when he was four or five years of age, it would be difficult to resolve at this point. If mother alone became more feminine, it might possibly lead to father's acting more masculine and moving closer to her, thus giving Martin a great deal of Oedipal reassurance. However, what is more probable is that the father could not tolerate his wife's increasing femininity since he would then be forced into an independent masculine role which is quite frightening to him. If Martin alone were to get well, it is possible that the parents would get a great deal of satisfaction from their offspring's success in the business world; this satisfaction might tend to bring them together but this is much too threatening to them because of their fears about themselves, and their highly ambivalent sexual identifications.

Siblings of the Parents

Both parents have had a number of siblings. Mr. Rituell is the oldest of five sons and Mrs. Rituell is the oldest of several sisters and brothers. She does not speak particularly warmly about any of her siblings, but claims she has always gotten along with them. She tends to idealize them somewhat but the reality situation is that none of them are really doing very well. Her sister is always used to point out her inadequacies, and is considered by Mr. Rituell as the ideal wife who gives in to her husband and is sympathetic and understanding. Mr. Rituell also idealizes his siblings in a general kind of way, but when discussed individually, it turns out that there has been a great deal of disturbance among them. He has been the only one to continue the religious practices taught them by their parents, but he refuses to get involved in meaningful discussions of how this relates to his feelings about his siblings, or whether or not they have even discussed it among themselves. The only way the siblings come into the discussion in the family therapy session is in terms of specific business transactions such as buying or selling to them, lending them things, or making outright donations of money to a less well-off sibling. Mrs. Rituell always makes derogatory remarks about her husband's siblings. She almost never brings up the subject of her own siblings and only reacts to it when he mentions the one sister he favors. He also will make cracks about her other siblings, pointing out the number of divorces in the family, the incidence of mental disturbance and other things. To this Mrs. Rituell makes some sharp rejoinders or tries to change the subject. In no way does one get the feeling that, on a reality level, they are warm and friendly toward their siblings, or that they see much of each other, or that these are really significant people in their current life.

The Female Role

This is an all-male household in that the mother psychologically relinquishes most of her claim to femininity. Although feminine in appearance, she is very dominant and aggressive. As early as during the honeymoon, she spat in her husband's face when he suggested that she should help support the family by working. Actually, she has always wanted to work and has had her own business; throughout her marriage she has run her husband's business.

The mother takes responsibility for keeping a kosher home and doing the housework. However, she insists—without much success—that the males follow her household schedule.

Both marital members use sex as a weapon and a lever for control. There had been no intercourse between the parents for five years prior to the onset of therapy because they had had a fight. Mother complains about her husband's less frequent interest in sex, but at the same time is rather pleased about it. Father typically sees sex and affection together, feeling that his wife denies him affection, interest and concern, and ties this in with her using sex as a weapon.

Both Mr. Rituell and his son are somewhat effeminate. Mr. Rituell has a lisp, and is too weak to do many things. He complains that he is not as strong as his wife, and identifies with his mother. The son identifies with this weak, feminine father. Mr. Rituell also complains bitterly that his wife belittles him, pushes him around, and doesn't take care of him.

The Male Role

Superficially, there is a division of male and female role function in this family. Most household chores are done by the mother. The men take care of the cars, take out the trash, mow the lawn, etc. However, the father constantly turns to his wife for all decisions, including business ones. This is done under the guise of "talking things over." The son emulates his father, essentially getting the mother's approval before undertaking even a trivial task. The father often complains about the lack of approval he gets from his wife in contrast to the constant approval that mother gave him.

Both men covertly hand over authority, decisions, and responsibility to the woman in the family. They agree that she plays an important role and at the same time insist that she is forcibly taking their role away from them. She triumphantly accepts her superior role and is disdainful of the weakness of men.

The father is more maternal than the mother in his attitude toward the son; he is also a much more sensitive person but is suspicious and guarded and at times shows marked paranoid trends.

Children

Children represent a gratification of the mother's or father's narcissistic needs. A child is someone to manipulate to gain strength over the marital partner. The father seems to have some genuine mothering feelings which are most likely based on his identification with his mother. Mrs. Rituell can be quite callous in her attitude toward children. She kept working in her business, for instance, when her young daughter was dying of cancer and she has never shown any remorse or genuine evidence of emotion regarding the daughter's death. The patient is quite forthright in stating that he was pleased when his sister died. The mother smiled whenever her son said this. Mr. Rituell becomes tearful at any mention of his daughter's death; he also was most upset when his son moved out of the home during the terminal phase of the therapy.

The parents are unable to allow their son to mature and individuate. Their needs to control each other find ready expression through first dominating him and then using him as an ally. Their son is a tool of their own neurotic complementary marital interaction.

A child is someone who will obey the parents and be a willing and devoted slave or servant. Independence on the son's part produces anxiety in both parents, partially because it leaves them in their unholy dyad. A child in this kind of family acts as an anxiety reducer for the parents. He allows the marriage to go on in name although he becomes emotionally married to the mother, and also to the father. He is the mother's lover and the father's homosexual object. This arrangement is more acceptable and less anxiety provoking than extra-marital affairs or alliances.

Family Myths

Every family has its own mythology which is passed on and added to by each generation. In the Rituell family we notice a number of such myths, several of them associated with platitudes going back over the centuries. For instance, the family has the myth that to keep busy means to keep out of mischief. Seldom is a reason or explanation given or accepted why a member of the family may not be able to keep busy. Just the act of not being busy is sufficient to cause fear and anxiety. Another myth is contained in the saying, "Those who work together, stay together." Thus, mother and father and son form a triad in which not one member can work effectively with the other. There are constant shifts in this system which usually amount to at least one member not functioning in the family business at any one time. Therapy has shifted this so that father has assumed a greater role as head of the business, and mother and son have increasingly dropped out. However, father is unable to tolerate this situation very long and forces his wife or son to come back and help him, but puts it on the basis that this decision was forced on him.

This also relates to the myth that each member of the family is in-dependent, though in actual fact neither one will work or play without the others, either separately, or together. This myth places considerable value on independence and self sufficiency, and constantly denies inter-dependence.

Another myth is that marital discord is the norm. We see here a family in which the husband and wife have been fighting since the onset of their marriage, and who show very little evidence of tenderness or affection or for positive feelings towards one another; yet they are amazed to think that they are not the typical American middle-class family and married couple.

A reaction which approaches distortions and projections in other areas, but generally seems to be rather prevalent, is to accept responsibility for anything positive that comes out of the family but to consider anything that doesn't turn out well as having been forced upon them. This reaction is so instantaneous and so much a part of this family, that it is included here as a myth—aside from the fact that it represents distortions in com-munications and immaturity.

Health and Illness

Mrs. Rituell tends to deny illness. She has worked constantly through-out her life, even when seriously ill physically. She has stated that she has no time to be sick. She regards illness as infantile and regressed, and does not feel that a person who is ill should have sympathy or be looked after, as this will tend to affix the infantile behavior. Illness is, to her, a demand for affection and attention which she deeply resents. To her husband it is an acceptable sign of regression and he always is extremely hurt when his illness does not result in any more positive feeling on her part. He himself, on the other hand, is quite concerned about his health and always has been so. He has had numerous symptoms and physical illnesses throughout his life. He has consulted physicians on many occasions. At such consulta-tions his wife is apt to suggest that he also present her symptoms and get the doctor to prescribe for her, partially because she has little faith in medical care, but mainly because she feels that maybe she could get free treatment this way.

Mrs. Rituell showed a peculiar coldness, lack of involvement, and possibly denial when her young daughter became ill and died of leukemia. The schizophrenic son has openly said that he was quite happy when his little sister died, because subsequently all the attention centered on him. The father was very upset, and becomes emotional whenever his daughter's death is mentioned; he tends to blame his wife for her lack of care and feeling for her.

As in many families who have become part of our study, emotional illness is not recognized as such. It is seen as a violation of the social graces, as a result of something which the patient refuses to do but should do, or that he does and should not do. Consequently, the patient in this family is constantly being told such things as "Stop making a face like that or people will think you're nuts," or "Speak up in a firm voice or people will think you're nuts"; "Sit up straight"; "Get a job"; etc. Emotional illness is something which is to be greatly feared and which, of course, occurs only in somebody else's family. The advice of any lay person is always worth more than that of any expert, which is probably due to the fact that the expert calls a spade a spade.

The parents are apt to recognize emotional sickness in their partner, yet they label it with the same term they use to label the signs of illness in their schizophrenic son.

Dr. O.

Probably one of the most difficult problems in this case, from the inception of therapy, was the presence of Dr. O., an outside figure with whom Martin had a delusional transference relationship. There is considerable indirect evidence that this physician in his youth had had problems very similar to Martin's. Dr. O. had had a problem with passivity, schizoid personality trends, latent homosexuality and in relationships with women. When Martin was slipping into an overt psychosis, he fortuitously met and became involved with this physician who solved his problems by helping him to become fanatically religious. This doctor subsequently sealed off the patient's psychosis by helping him build up a compulsive-delusional system. Dr. O. has been successful in his practice; in addition he has taught at a local university in a totally unrelated field and has devoted all his spare time to a study of the Jewish orthodox religion. He is a most bizarre individual, with many peculiar mannerisms. Since a sort of imitative identification has occurred in the primary patient, to see Dr. O. is to see Martin. An attempt was made early in the therapy to enlist the doctor's aid, but it was obvious that he was allied with the patient and against us. This remained consistently so throughout the therapy. He has repeatedly told the patient that there is nothing the matter with him, that if he follows Jewish orthodoxy in a sincere and devoted way he will have a happy and complete life. To him, Martin is a chance acquaintance, but to Martin, Dr. O. is a strong, reliant father figure.

Social Life

The Rituell family is a little unusual in comparison with other psychotic families we have studied, because there is somewhat more interaction with the outside world. The parents are able to take a vacation together away from the schizophrenic son, although they experience a great deal of guilt and concern about his welfare. The social life in the home centers around the dining room; it is always accompanied by food, from the beginning of the social contact until the end. The family and their guests sit around the table and argue with each other. Mother and father will frequently quarrel openly and directly when they are in social gatherings. Typically, mother will insult father, followed either by a brooding silence on his part or by an immediate rejoinder. When Mr. Rituell is insulted this way, he will brood about it for weeks and probably not forget it for the rest of his life.

The family is also a little unusual in that there is a great deal of animated liveliness, most of it aggressive and hostile but some of it filled with genuine enjoyment of a good argument. We often get the feeling that this family does not want us to leave after a session, even if there is violent anger. There seems to be a certain type of humor and obvious enjoyment of the situation, and we almost have a sense of the family's being able to make interpersonal contact on that level.

Much of this family's social life is related to their customers. They visit them in their homes, and apparently there is a lot of personal interaction, with relating of personal events and wanting sympathy and support—in general, quite an unusual business relationship. Father's fantasies about his customers and his way of relating his business life to us almost border on his seeing his customers as maternal objects.

When Mother is not involved in the business she is very active in various charitable organizations where she takes over in a short time and is asked to become an executive officer. Father's social activities seem to center essentially around his wife's siblings and his customers. The son's social life, if it may be called that, is completely taken up by the synagogue and other Jewish affairs. However, the word "social" has to be taken out of its usual context and used here more to relate to his interest in affairs outside the family. There is very little interpersonal contact or relationship in his synagogue activities, except for Dr. O. whom we mentioned previously.

By and large, the family appears to have few close personal friends. Mother will occasionally see a few of her childhood friends to whom she pours out her heart, or ask for advice and solutions to problems from people with whom she has only a nodding acquaintance. Mostly, the social system involves members of the extended family.

Money

This family is penurious and penny-pinching, a character trait that is particularly exaggerated in mother. Father is careful with his money but does give to charities willingly. Mother, however, gets very anxious, upset and demanding if she finds out that her husband has given any money to charity. She can become very vindictive about it and has at times drawn the same amount that her husband has given to charity out of their joint account and deposited it in her own account. She rails at him for his donations, knowing that he will get angry at her miserliness. He gives to charity, knowing that it will make her furious.

Despite the modest appearance of their home, the family has over $60,000 in assets. Yet, the mother worries incessantly that they will be poor and not able to support themselves in their old age. She also feels that people who do not work hard want to live off people who do and since there are various relatives who are waiting in the wings to pounce upon their money she has to keep a sharp eye on her husband's charitable spendings.

She objects much less to spending money on vacations or on things that she and her husband can use themselves. She would not give ten cents to charity, but would not hesitate to go on a cruise. If her husband suggested this, she would probably turn him down and would not want to go because it is too expensive.

The schizophrenic son gives away or lends as much as 20% of his limited income. He seems mostly amused by the consternation which this produces in the mother and father.

Both mother and father seem completely unable to turn business customers down. Where a dollar is to be made, mother particularly will go out of her way to make it. She will, however, refuse to take responsibility for this, putting the blame on the customer, stating that he insisted upon her services and that she is powerless to turn them down. Father continues to work very hard in the business despite the fact that he has had a coronary attack a few years ago and almost daily comes home completely exhausted. Before he and his wife set up their joint business—they had been married ten years and he suddenly lost his job—he had worked many years for a stationer, and before that had had various jobs in different cities. Despite the fact that he had been able to support the family during the ten years he had worked for another company, his wife had opened up a store while raising the children. This again was a source of complaint to him, saying that she wasn't giving the children sufficient attention. Mother denied this vehemently and insisted that she had been helping out the family financially—in spite of its having been proven unnecessary.

There was a subtle interaction with regard to the family business. The father clearly states that his son will not inherit the business because he has shown little capacity for it. On a non-verbal level, he has indicated that the son should stick around because possibly he may obtain the business. Both parents tend to deny the effectiveness of the other in the family business.

Food

In one aspect of their life the mother has respected the father's wishes: she has always kept a kosher home, even though her own home was not a kosher one. However, she is not above dominating the men in the family even in this area. She insists that they eat when she is ready, not when they are. There is much interaction between the mother and the son, and between the mother and the father around the preparation and serving of meals. The son insists that the mother is not careful enough in her kosher preparations. There is little evidence to suggest that she is not extremely careful, but he goes into terrifically petty details about every item which is served. Many times he will refuse bread because one Rabbi out of five whom he called said that a certain bakery was not kosher. The father is satisfied with the quality and preparation of the food but would like to eat when he feels like eating.

Meal preparation and eating is a hostile and angry experience for all, yet strangely satisfying. The son's eating habits annoy the father, as he goes through numerous extraneous rituals to which the father objects; the mother tends to support the son with the result that the father becomes angry at both the mother and the son.

Most of the social interaction in this family is accompanied by the serving of food. This is the only family, for instance, in which it seemed unnatural to have a conversation and not to eat at the same time.

Sex

The Rituell family is unusual in another way: they can discuss their sexual lives quite openly. Prior to our starting the therapy, the father and mother had not slept together for five years. This meant that there was almost no sexual life. This state of affairs existed not because either partner did not desire the sexual life, but because they were so violently angry with each other that each was withholding this pleasure from the other.

It has been indicated previously that there is a sexual role reversal within the family. The father is somewhat effeminate in speech and mannerisms; the mother, on the other hand, is aggressive, dominant, vivacious and readily admits that she thinks like a man; and the son tends to identify with the father and is quite passive and also effeminate. As mentioned before, the mother is frequently seductive with her son, though she denies the implications of this. The son has openly requested several times that she not touch him on the buttocks or the genital region. She tends to consider this behavior as playful and maternal. She has on numerous occasions undressed her adult son when he has fallen asleep fully clothed on his bed. Similarly, she thinks nothing of walking into the bathroom to attend to a toilet function while he is there. But for convention, she freely admits, she would walk around the house in the nude.

In a less seductive manner, the father has some limited physical contact with his son. He likes to have his son around him at work or at home, although there is always some fighting, bickering and complaining.

The son has had overt homosexual relationships with a friend while in adolescence. Following this he had some heterosexual relationships which were apparently satisfying but also upsetting. The mother was interested to hear the son during the therapy relate some of his sexual affairs while in service. She was pleased to find out about it but expressed shock that this should have happened. She said she was shocked because she had always thought that her son was "pure," yet at other times she maintained that she would love to have her son enjoy women, premaritally or in any other way. Both parents encourage the son towards heterosexuality and apparently sincerely mean this. However, on another level they keep him and treat him as a small child within their home.

Father insisted that a great deal of the hostility in the family is related to the first few weeks of his marriage. Mother apparently had had an affair prior to her marriage; she insisted that this affair was a chaste one. The man was crippled but it seems that he had certain ways about him which she found very attractive. Her own mother, however, had objected to that marriage and favored Mr. Rituell. But when she told her husband two weeks after their wedding that this man had a bigger penis than he, he became extremely upset and has not stopped talking about it ever since. Mother now denies that she has ever said this to him.

At the present time their sexual life is fairly limited, with father almost always taking the initiative in general affection as well as in whatever sex life there is. Mother generally submits, claiming that she is passive in the matter and has been taught that a woman has no choice. This is in stark contrast to the fact that she is extremely aggressive when she wants to be. It also ties in with the family myth that nobody takes responsibility for things he doesn't like but always projects them on to the other person.

Recreational Life

Essentially this family does not do much in the way of recreation. There are occasional automobile rides on a Sunday which frequently involve members of the extended family. Mother and father do occasionally take vacations together and seem to enjoy this quite a bit. Mother talks about her love of good music and the theater, but almost never goes to hear either unless it is a benefit of one of her organizations, or she is not active in the business. She plays both the violin and the piano, but can only enjoy these instruments when her husband is home. He hates to hear her play, and this is always a source of friction between them. The son used to have some recreational outlets such as bird watching, nature study and similar pursuits, and also belonged to the Boy Scouts. However, since the onset of his psychosis he has lost almost all of them. It may be possible to consider some of his religious activities as recreational outlets, but there is a deep sense of compulsion about them that tends to rule that out.

Genesis of Schizophrenic Symptoms

These parents were not particularly oriented to the values of sharing in the relationship to each other and their child. Each parent saw the child as an ally against the other parent; each was in competition with the other for work and for what might amount to the male role in the family. The father was rather ambivalent about whether he wanted the male role. Despite having small children the parents continued to work throughout most of their marriage. Father probably wished the mother to stay in the home but he was powerless to keep her there, and also ambivalent about this. The son was really never raised by either parent, he just grew up. There is little in early childhood to suggest the future psychotic type of reaction. However, one senses something which John Rosen has called "a perversion of the maternal instinct present in the mother's relationship with children." It is questionable whether the mother was ever truly maternal. The son probably represented a narcissistic extension of herself, such as her desired penis. Even at this date, when Martin is almost thirty years old, she still treats him as a toy or a small child to do her every bidding. She seems to delight in correcting him, telling him to wash behind his ears, take a bath, et cetera. A further example of this perverse maternal attitude is her previously mentioned lack of feeling in discussing the death of the daughter. This was not an isolated episode. When the father was hospitalized after his heart attack, she tended to pooh-pooh the seriousness of the illness, saying openly that he was malingering, and that he could be back in the home and working. The father correctly perceived this as an attempt on her part to kill him. She did not deny this very vehemently; she did state, though, that she did not believe a heart attack to be a very serious thing, particularly not in her husband. It is interesting that the son identified with her in this, and voiced the same kinds of opinions about his father's illness as his mother had.

Following puberty, the son first became enamored of other boys his age, and in particular one neighborhood boy. He was apparently seduced by this boy into homosexual activities and sexual play. This provoked a good deal of guilt in him. As a result, of these experiences he turned away from all forms of sexuality and became markedly interested in biology and nature. He became a bird watcher, botanical and biological student, and in fact became very expert in these occupations. He received much encouragement and laudatory comments from his teachers to the point of being recommended for the job of a junior-type curator in a museum and being urged to make the biological sciences his career.

While avidly engaged in bird watching and visiting arboreta, etc., the patient made the acquaintance of a psychiatrist. He enjoyed this relationship and was quite flattered that an older man (he was actually a young man in his late twenties) would show interest in him and appreciation of his communion with nature. It was a great shock when the patient discovered one day that the psychiatrist had hanged himself. (This was corroborated by the therapy team.) Around this time he began to take courses in biology at a local university. Coincident with this phase of his life there was a return of heterosexual interest, and he resumed some dating, dancing and even won prizes as a dancer. He also showed overt heterosexual interest and had a few affairs. However, while in college he began to have some awareness of emotional illness. He was dissatisfied with his relations with his parents, felt that he was put upon, that too much was demanded of him, and that he was treated like a child; he was increasingly aware of his loneliness and was greatly concerned about the homosexual activities of adolescence and masturbation. He tried therapy but never stayed with it, tending to shop around and go from psychiatrist to psychiatrist. He was too competitive and was extremely aggressive in the interviews. He would tend to use a great deal of projection and treat the psychiatrist as a patient, thus reversing the therapeutic roles. On one occasion he even visited a rabbi who was a psychiatrist and who threw him out of the office as being impertinent. Before graduation from college he was inducted into military service, a most unhappy and unfortunate time in his life. He was sent overseas. He could not identify with his buddies; they singled him out as being different, made fun of him, chided him about not being interested in women, and about his religion. He could not have kosher food to which he had been used in the past, and there was a marked increase in his religious interest in this period. He also had some sexual affairs which were upsetting to him in terms of his morality, although he enjoyed the actual affairs. With his increasing resentment of the Army, its regimentation and forced group living, his defenses began to break down. The anxiety connected with latent homosexuality and having to live in army barracks were undoubtedly factors in the impending breakdown. Following a traumatic experience in which a sergeant beat him up viciously, he became totally unable to function in the army situation and was discharged administratively after twenty months of service.

On return to his home he was in a markedly agitated condition, verging on acute panic and psychosis. At this point in his life he met Dr. O. The two seemed to find each other and were markedly similar in their orientation to life, their personality structure and probable mutual latent homosexuality which was controlled under the guise of religious observances and practices. The compulsive religious practices rigidly adhered to by Dr. O., and the extreme orthodoxy rescued the patient from a flamboyant psychosis. In fact, it made so much of an impression on him that any challenge to the religious obsessive compulsive defense was met with vigorous opposition, and viewed as an attempt to make him crazy. On various occasions the patient went back into therapy with a variety of psychiatrists and psychologists, but he never persisted in the therapy and dropped out after attempting to reverse the roles—a standard maneuver of his.

Therapeutic Techniques

Initially, a passive approach was used in which the family who interacted extremely vocally and exuberantly most of the time, were allowed to talk it out with the idea that eventually they would get down to meaningful interaction. However, as with other families, the time came when both therapists agreed that this could go on forever as it had, in fact, for the twenty-nine years of the parents' married life. There was a general intensification of acting out and of all other defense systems used by the family. Simultaneously, attempts were made to establish with each family member the nature of his communications with the others. These were unsuccessful too, since there was a tremendous amount of denial and projection. No member of the family helped the therapists by pointing out the reality of the communication patterns.

Quite vigorous attacks were then made on the mother, as both therapists agreed she was the strongest member of the family, the most motivated for therapy and the one who held many of the keys to the therapy's success. Although both the schizophrenic son and the father seemed to enjoy this phase, it was obvious that the mother's defenses were such that this technique was doomed to failure also; she was completely able to project, deny, and isolate; she asked numerous professional and lay people outside the family for contrary opinions and—in short—was extremely effective at holding her own in any argument.

The next technique was what one of the therapists has called direct intervention. The parents were ordered to begin sleeping together and having sexual relations again, and the therapists explained to the family, the mother in particular, that unless they agreed with this and carried out these instructions, therapy would be terminated. This was the first technique which showed any significant results. The mother did as she was told, and the family seemed to interact more positively, at least for a time. The mother was also ordered to assume a more feminine role and to abide by her husband's bidding. For a time she complied with this very well, but later on she showed varying degrees of covert and overt resistance.

This technique was also used with the primary patient but with much more limited success. He ran to Dr. O. for support and reassurance, and it is quite obvious that through much of the therapy he was able to effectively fight the therapists by getting a contrary opinion from him.

At an earlier phase in the therapy when the symptomatic patient claimed that he could not talk back to his parents for religious reasons, the therapists had obtained rabbinical sanction for this. Another striking evidence of direct intervention occurred early in the therapy when Martin suddenly announced that he was getting married. The therapists accepted the family's wish that the fiancee come to the sessions, and it is interesting to note that either love is blind or the girl was not too bright, or there was a combination of both factors operating or the girl was simply desperate—at any rate, she had not noticed that Martin was ill in any way. It took about three sessions for this to demonstrate itself to her, at which point she broke the engagement. We would like to emphasize that at no point, however, did we advise the family or the fiancee to break the engagement, nor did we invite her to attend the sessions. When the family suggested that she be allowed to come, we agreed to it. In addition, a rabbi was once invited to the sessions. Probably and partially because we did not sufficiently orient him as to his role in the session, or possibly for personal reasons of his own, he did not give us any degree of firm support; he tended rather to hedge or overtly support the primary patient.

Another technique was to shift the dominant therapist role. As one of the therapists was a follower of the Jewish orthodox religion, his role was made a more dominant one. One reason for making this switch was the potent use which the entire family, but particularly the father and son, made of the religion as a resistance. Also we hoped that we could wean the patient away from Dr. O. However, this technique had only limited results.

Later in the therapy one of the therapists decided to use a technique somewhat like Lindner's;[72] he crowded the patient in a psychosis by adopting the psychotic symptoms and going along with him. This technique initially showed some promise in that the patient became "real" and in addition more anxious than he had been. The mother, however, felt that the therapist had become overtly psychotic and wanted to call another psychiatrist in to examine him. This technique was abandoned when it became obvious that it would require from us a tremendous amount of active participation in psychosis and in the study of religion, Judaism, etc. It was also a difficult role to maintain without anxiety over a long period of time. Incidentally, the technique did little to our relationship with the family, except perhaps to develop some increased transference relationship between the patient and the therapist who played the psychotic role.

Another technique, probably also best classified as direct intervention, was to get the mother out of the business. This was successful, but there have been many vicissitudes through the mother's actively interjecting herself back into the business, and the father's pulling her back in.

A more recent technique which we have used and which has met with marked difficulty, is to get the symptomatic patient out of his home and to live in another home. This technique showed promise, and provoked marked anxiety in both of the parents and the patient. The entire family showed acute distress in dealing with the separation of the son from his parents. There was marked overt and covert sabotage of this, with the parents and the son finally indicating the various symptoms related to separation. The parents complained of stomach upsets, inability to sleep and general free-floating anxiety. The son, as though to defy the recommendations, showed greater signs of regression which also was pointed toward making the parents sorry that they had agreed to the separation. This last technique seems to have resulted in the most outstanding shift that had taken place in therapy with this family for over three-and-a-half years. It has caused more shift of symptom, more expression of fantasy material, and has exposed the family more to therapy than any of the previous techniques attempted.

The removal of Martin from the home, eventually successful, unhinged the homeostasis; the homeostasis representing the primary family defense against the anxiety of change. Only with this change in the spatial relationship could therapeutic leverage be obtained. Therapy with the entire family successfully continued after Martin went to live elsewhere.

Follow-up on Rituell Family

A follow-up visit one year later revealed that the son had moved to another city, had been working steadily for nine months and had just recently married a girl with similar interests and religious connections. The parents were more comfortable with each other. There was still friction over business matters, but the disagreements lacked the intensity and perseverence of the earlier period.

The Oralcle family

Ivan Boszormenyi-Nagy and George Spivack

Chapter
6

Joe, the primary patient, was seventeen years of age when he and his family came to the attention of the project team. He, his fifteen-year-old sister, mother and father had moved about a year before to a new home in the suburbs, an area of neatly kept new homes owned mainly by young couples of reasonable income and apparent stability.

Joe had initially come to the out-patient clinic because his parents had exerted pressure on him to get some help. He expressed no interest in therapy himself, had in fact lost interest in general, had failed all his subjects in his senior year of high school, and had dropped out of school. He was reluctant to give his time to therapy, appeared quite unmotivated. He said that he did not go to school because he "felt funny," but at the same time he engaged in gross rationalizations and denial of any problems. At times he was inaudible and incoherent, and assumed odd postures during the interview.

Hospitalization was recommended after evaluation in the clinic, on the basis of his resistance to psychotherapy and his apparent lack of insight. But the parents could not decide to hospitalize him, and a brief attempt at out-patient individual psychotherapy was made. After four such resistive, hostile sessions, Joe was refusing to continue, and hospitalization was again recommended. Joe's father made an ambivalent attempt to take him forcefully by the arm and lead him through the hospital door. When the father came to report that his attempt had failed and he was unable to cope with Joe's resistiveness to the clinic, it was decided to offer the family a trial of family treatment to be conducted in their home.

Joe was tall and well proportioned, but somewhat overweight and "soft" in appearance. He walked with his head thrust forward and a slight bend to his shoulders. Although intelligent, he had a "dull," though not affectless, expression. His hair was unusually disheveled, and his clothing unkempt. He seemed indifferent to his body as well as to his appearance, and how these might impress others.

Though bright, Joe had not attended school regularly for four years. At times he would read books far beyond his academic level for hours. In recent years his behavior was reported as quite regressed, he had little social contact outside the family, and his speech was frequently "symbolic" and non-communicative. He often ate large quantities of food, and for long stretches of time would ride around aimlessly in the family car. His sleeping habits were quite irregular. Severe disturbance began with the onset of adolescence when he became suspicious of others, entertained omnipotent thoughts, and expressed magical thoughts regarding material he read. Prior to adolescence he is described as an obedient youngster, showing great scholastic promise.

Doris, Joe's sister, had a stocky, squarish build, and a roundish pubertal face which usually expressed little emotion. Her movements lacked grace and smoothness, and her walk was ungainly. One gained the impression that she could be much more attractive looking were it not for her unkempt hair, and her indifference to or lack of taste about clothing and physical appearance.

Doris was attending high school with passing, though at times borderline, grades. She was not socially active, rarely having friends who visited her home. She seemed to move through both her school and social life without marked success but, on the other hand, without serious difficulties.

Father was a man in his forties, slightly shorter than Joe, but above average in size. He had a typical "middle-age" corporation, but this was somewhat accentuated by his bent-over posture. Physically, he carried himself as though his body were a burden to him, and his face usually had a serious, worried expression. Both his carriage and clothing suggested a lack of pride in appearance, although no particular article of clothing was in poor taste or unattended to. He and his parents had migrated to this country when he was a small boy. He had a high school education and presently managed a small concession. His business was reasonably successful, and he looked forward to expansion.

Mother was the only family member who exhibited obvious concern with her physical appearance. Her clothing was stylish and well kept, though somewhat exhibitionistic. Her hair was dyed blond, and her use of cosmetics, though oriented to make her appear younger, gave her a "hard" looking facial expression. Though small in stature, she had a good figure which she carried with assertive pride. Her total appearance seemed to say: "Flatter and attend to me, but don't cross swords with me!" At the time of contact with the family, she was a housewife, although on occasion she had assisted her husband in his business. She was born in this country. She and her husband had been married twenty years.

The furnishings very much reflected mother's tastes and character, and the house was neat and compulsively kept. It had all the modern conveniences and modern furniture, but the latter lacked subtlety of taste and sophistication of style. Though not cheap or overtly colorful, certain items were close to being garish.

In general, the family—aside from Joe—exhibited no obvious symptoms of psychiatric disturbance. Although not socially active in the community, they reportedly maintained contact with the larger family unit in the area; father regularly attended synagogue and a social club, and the family was on friendly terms with neighbors. At the time of contact, the parents were becoming increasingly concerned over the effect of their son's behavior upon the family relations with neighbors.

Initial Perception of Family Members and their Interaction, "Old Style"

Initial contacts with the family in their home quickly revealed many facets of their individual personalities, their conceptions of each other, and the problems they faced. The spotless, though somewhat tasteless, style of bourgeois living reflected the mother's compulsive and cold temperament. She described herself as being blunt and frank, and respected by her friends for this. Her femininity was "hard" and phallic, and her demeanor suggested that her relationships were most satisfying when involving primitive emotions. Her sexual identity was conveyed through her tight-fitting clothing, sexy in an adolescent way. She prided herself on being a "fighter," able to tolerate the hardship inflicted upon the family by her son, though this was masked by a need to present herself also as a person willing to sacrifice and suffer through the present situation.

Father presented himself as a hard-working, serious man. He was friendly and reasonable, offering himself as a "humble" man who tried to understand his son and never lost hope. He spoke of religion and various books and articles he had read, his tone of voice softer and less piercing than mother's. He worked long hours, and liked to come home to relax, watch TV, perhaps fall asleep at the TV set. He offered all the truisms about people, yet quickly revealed himself as a "hungry child" wanting care and attention.

Doris remained on the periphery of events, making brief appearances and then disappearing. Her immaturity (for a girl her age) was obvious in her walk and ungainly physique. She presented herself as a "good" and fragile thing, without much inner drive.

During the initial sessions the manifest family image was one of parents suffering the heartbreak of a sick son. Joe, the patient, was seldom present, remaining in his bedroom despite parental coaxing. The parents described Joe's "arrogance," his peculiar looks directed toward mother, his clinging to her in such a way that she feared leaving him alone. They also described his outbursts of anger and excitement, inattention to cleanliness, overeating, and their general inability to control him. Joe was a sick person, and the other "normal" family members were struggling to cope with the situation. Father repeatedly commented that if Joe would only attend the session, he knew "the doctors" could help Joe. The parents early raised the question of the therapists giving Joe drugs, almost convincing them of the wisdom of this. That Joe "played" this sick "role" was clear during the initial session when he made a brief appearance in the living room. He lay on the sofa in a fetal-like position, his speech largely incoherent, and said he would only talk alone with the therapists. The rest of the family was willing, if not eager, to leave Joe alone with the therapists, once again pointing the finger at Joe as the "sick" member and the only one needing contact with the therapists.

For some months sessions were held twice a week in the physical absence of Joe. The parents generally began each session with a report of Joe's behavior the prior week. As the therapists attempted to focus on family interaction, the parents repeated that if only Joe would join the group, then *he* could get some help. During this period the therapists formed impressions of certain family relationships. Father insisted on keeping his business affairs separated from his "home," and mother complained of this. Actually, there seemed to be little active relating between mother and father, except while discussing Joe. One or the other might express an opinion, but there was never a heated interchange or a genuinely "personal" conversation. Father insisted on maintaining an image of his wife as the perfect cook and mother, almost blatantly denying her non-maternal traits and her own verbalized objection to this image. He seemed in awe of Joe's "brightness," responding as though accepting even bizarre statements as indicative of a magical, omnipotent power in the relationship between father and son. Though superficially the most "reasonable" person in the family, his weakness was immediately clear in his essentially "oral" level of functioning.

Mother seemed the stronger or "harder" in the marriage relationship, at least superficially. It was obvious, however, that she could not relate maturely and felt satisfied in a relationship only insofar as impulsive emotions were expressed. Her home was compulsively clean and she cooked as a maternal chore, but was totally unable to give affection. While father seemed to fear Joe's outbursts of anger, mother, complaining of them, seemed to come alive when describing her counter-aggression. Occasional Oedipal-like manifestations between mother and son were almost too obvious, just as father's apparent unconcern was puzzling. Mother might report Joe's sexual curiosity and "closeness" to her or his desire for her to kiss him. In one session mother reported how she had told Joe that father, and not he, was the head of the family, but had then committed a slip of the tongue revealing the contrary. Father would listen to all this without responding, at one point suggesting that perhaps mother and Joe should take a vacation in Florida together. Doris remained on the periphery, saying little but listening. Mother repeatedly emphasized how she had to help Doris with school work and keep tabs on her because Doris was unable or unwilling to "do" for herself. While mother paid lip service to the need for Doris to grow more independent, it was clear that she also wished to keep her immature and under her control. Mother frequently expressed fear of leaving Doris alone with Joe and worried that Doris heard the "kind of language" Joe used at times. Doris neither complained nor seemed very upset or fearful about Joe's behavior. She very soon began to challenge mother in subtle ways. After three sessions mother reported that Doris had attended the Dick Clark (bandstand) show, contrary to her expressed wishes. Doris responded that mother had at various times suggested that attending this show was not a good idea but had not explicitly forbidden her to attend the day she went.

Inconsistencies During Initial Treatment Period

During this initial period many dynamic hypotheses were formed. Though Joe was usually absent, sporadic contacts with him in his room, and comments by other family members indicated he was clearly schizophrenic. Our own observations revealed certain pathological relationships between pairs of family members.

Yet the picture seemed incomplete, as though an entire dimension of family interaction was being missed. While initially Joe was described as withdrawn, without good judgment, or even "dangerous" to himself and others, he was not hospitalized by the parents, and in fact had free use of the family car in which he drove long distances. While "admitting" that Joe was "sick," the father suggested that it might help if Joe got his nose fixed. On another occasion father reported that perhaps he might offer to take Joe to a "smoker" where he could meet some girls, learn the "facts of life," and develop some outside "interest." There were contradictory stories as to just how "sick" Joe's behavior was. Despite considering him "crazy" and admitting that his behavior and his demands were unreasonable, the parents listened to his ramblings as though meaningful at their manifest level. While expressing the opinion that finishing high school would be a great achievement, the family experienced more rather than less tension when Joe actually did pass his last two courses. And despite complaints of Joe's overeating, father on one occasion brought home a "special" lobster salad, almost insisting Joe eat it, even after mother said she had just served him a large meal.

The most dramatic events occurred within the context of the treatment itself. The parents reported repeatedly that Joe did not want the therapists to visit the home. Yet frequently Joe would be in the living room when the therapists arrived, and after his departure the parents would report that an emotional "scene" had occurred just prior to arrival. During the session Joe could be heard leaving his room upstairs and approaching the stairway leading down into the living room, at which time father would begin to whisper as though not wanting Joe to hear what was being said. The parents might report that after the last session Joe was worse, suggesting that therapy was not working (even though they reported events indicating Joe was less withdrawn). In one session, when one of the therapists rose to go upstairs to talk with Joe, father jumped up from his seat, quite tense, and—almost blocking the therapist's path—implied that going upstairs might get Joe upset and even be dangerous to the therapist. On another occasion father, while purportedly going to the garage to encourage Joe to join the group (Joe having returned "early" from a ride), essentially chased Joe back into the garage.

Although, as indicated above, the picture of Joe as given by the parents was far from consistent, there was little question that Joe continued to function essentially on a psychotic level. However, there was also little doubt that the parents, despite statements to the contrary, actively sought to keep him away from the sessions and the therapists. In spite of the above there were many indications, during the initial phase of treatment, of relaxation in Joe.

A Transition Phase to Perception of Family Interaction, "New Style"

As suggested earlier, the initial months of treatment contained numerous instances wherein manifest behavior was markedly inconsistent with the professed beliefs or opinions of individual family members. This was particularly true of both parents.

One often-professed belief or family myth—to use Wynne's term[117]—conspicuous during the first half year of family therapy in the home, was the frequently explicit and constantly implicit belief of the parents that they were intensely frustrated by Joe's physical absence from the therapy sessions. Before describing in some detail how this myth became "punctured," it is of interest to reconstruct its deeper significance in the family members retrospectively. The fact that the parents ostensibly were rather unhappy about Joe's absence would imply parental concern and love. Thus, this myth was a variation of a major theme: are these parents' attitudes really parental?

While the parents' interest in Joe was intense, it was not clearly of a parental kind. They did admire him, but their rigid type of admiration suggested a desire to possess someone as a gratifier of their own dependent needs. Their dual expectation of affection and superiority added up to a double bind and a rejection of Joe's infantile needs. Mother expected Joe to be a source of security through his support of her feminine self-esteem, and also demanded warm, accepting attitudes without realizing that she used her son as a main object of her own needs for possessing both a father and a mother. She may not have consciously realized that her major libidinal responses were evoked by her son's comments, e.g., "Mother you look so young you shouldn't stay home where no one can see you." Yet she often blamed herself for her own lack of warm affection towards her son and for her cold mothering attitudes in his early years. Even her seemingly motherly ministrations (preparing and serving breakfast, etc.) were, for some reason, perceived by Joe as teasing which filled him with even more frustration. Although this mother displayed considerable conscious self-blame, her unfulfilled personal demands were channeled towards Joe, seeing an ungrateful child in him. It is likely that, unconsciously, she salvaged her marital relationship at the expense of her relationship with her son. It seemed that Joe was able to provide many of those infantile satisfactions which the often absent, hard-working husband was not able to furnish. Guilt over the "use" of her son as a parent substitute, as well as guilt over the gratification aspects of having regular visits from the "two doctors," may have contributed to her need for repeated statements of frustration over Joe's absence from therapy. It was only on rare occasions that she expressed deep frustration over her husband's habitually long working hours.

It appears that emotionally Joe gave more to his father than he received from him. In a way he was expected to fulfill the father's needs (by being pious, respectful, and learned) while he could not receive personal gratification from his always rational and impersonal father in return. Apparently the father's main contribution to the family was limited in the main to areas of financial stability and cliché-like maxims of reasonable living. Many of Joe's awkward, psychotic statements appear, retrospectively, to be attempts at proving the lack of a true parental attitude on his father's part. He often implied that he had missed being disciplined and controlled by his father while in school. The father usually defended himself against accusations of this type by claiming that Joe had not needed discipline because he used to be so "good" in school. This type of statement, on the other hand, infuriated Joe invariably, because of its symbolic repudiation of a parental concern on the father's part.

It is reasonable to assume that just as Joe's desperate struggle for parental care was transposed onto a psychotic level of demanding and blame (e.g., that his bones are soft because mother's milk failed to deposit enough calcium), the parents' care took the form of concern about Joe's illness and his therapy. But was the parents' interest in the continuation of family therapy an expression of genuine concern for Joe? Their overt statements certainly sounded so. If only Joe could decide to join the sessions! There was no reason to doubt that many exhortations were in fact given Joe about attending the sessions. Yet the suspicion was mounting in the therapists that the parents' deeper motivations aimed at Joe's exclusion. Why would they otherwise shame him for his timid attempts at listening at the top of the stairs? Why the many non-verbal messages to the contrary of the parents' stated intention of having Joe join the sessions?

The change from the "old style" came about in a gradual fashion, and when manifest, probably caught the members of the family unaware of the deep underlying paradoxes of their motivations. The main dynamic factor in the change must have been Joe's own autonomous "better half" which motivated him to engage first one and then both therapists in personal contact. However, many other dynamically significant events started to take place at about the same time, the seventh month of the family therapy.

The following is a chronological account of a few of the more striking details as they were revealed in family sessions.

Through this particular session one could hear Joe pacing up and down in his room on the second floor. Mother reported that he had asked the therapist's first name presumably for the purpose of calling him on the phone. She then reported that for the first time in years, she and her husband had gone out to see a movie. Then the father, in complete disregard for Joe's apparently serious and new interest in the therapists, asked whether they would advise that Joe go to Florida for a three-week visit. During the same session, almost to document improvement, Doris too displayed an unusual degree of assertiveness. She demonstrated the correct feminine ways of sitting and walking as she had learned them at a charm school. She changed her hairdo in the session, as if she wanted to demonstrate her ability to play the role of the appearance-conscious young girl.

Ten days later the parents reported again that Joe had not been in a bad mood recently. Father displayed an unusually outgoing and seemingly interested attitude towards Doris. He discussed her schoolwork with her in a rarely seen animated fashion. Mother seemingly approved of the closeness between father and daughter but appeared to infantilize her daughter.

After about a week, to the therapists' surprise, Joe was in the living room when they arrived. This had not happened for over six months. One of the therapists asked him how his shoulder was (the parents had reported that he had been complaining about pains in that area). Before he could speak, the father answered, whereupon Joe slowly withdrew from the room and did not return for the rest of the session. Later on, father insisted on talking at length about a book he had read about the psychological preparation for accepting death.

Two weeks later the mother reported that Joe had been hesitating about whether to stay, and had left the room shortly before the therapists' arrival. Yet, unexpectedly, she poured out a great deal of despair, concluding that Joe would have to be hospitalized unless he improved significantly within weeks. Father reported that on the previous day he had had a good hour's discussion with Joe and that Joe had seemed to be strongly considering to accept treatment. Yet the morning of the session Joe upset his father very considerably. In essence, he reported to him that his mother was having an intimate relation with the next-door neighbor. Both parents seemed rather tense and anxious during this discussion. The therapist offered to go upstairs and see Joe in person. This meant leaving the parents and Doris alone since the other therapist was absent in this session. The parents' reaction to the suggestion was completely disorganized. The mother's warning, "He may throw you out if he is in a bad mood," was coupled with a statement that they have no hope if Joe is unwilling "to talk with the therapists." When the therapist went upstairs, he found Joe hiding near the stairs. He soon invited the therapist into his room. A formally very psychotic yet deeply meaningful conversation followed in which Joe made every effort to encourage the therapist to help him. At the end of the conversation he offered to walk downstairs to join the family together with the therapist. Curiously, the parents seemed more baffled than relieved upon his arrival. When the therapist left, the father did not get up from his chair. Mother walked him to the door and made a few skeptical comments about the prospects of the therapy. There was no encouragement, recognition, or hope shown by anybody except Joe. The therapist left more puzzled after this session than after any one before or after. In the following session father openly expressed his concern about whether talking to the psychiatrist might not upset Joe, in which case he might display an increased tension as far as the family interaction was concerned. In retrospect, it is rather obvious that already at that time the parents and Joe were competing for the therapists.

From here on for several weeks the family therapy sessions took on a new form. One of the therapists spent most of the hour in Joe's room while the other therapist stayed with the rest of the family. On the whole, Joe seemed to progress gradually toward joining the sessions. He actually did so a few weeks later.

Finally the time arrived to test the family's reaction to the long awaited joint session with Joe. The father reported at the beginning that Joe had been "wonderful" during the past week; he had not been "arrogant" and looked happier. It seemed that this, if any, was the right moment for an attempt to invite Joe downstairs. After father's initial remarks, it was even more surprising to see what happened when Joe actually joined the meeting for the first time in over seven months. Joe sat down on the sofa right next to his father, whereupon the latter instantaneously got up and walked to Doris, kissed her and whispered something in her ear. Doris immediately got up, left and never returned the entire evening. Father then sat down in Doris' chair, leaving Joe to sit alone on the sofa. A tense and anxious silence followed. Nobody volunteered to act as a mediator. In the face of such brutal rejection, Joe got up and started back to his room. The therapists then insisted on a conversation with him, and he sat down again. Throughout the session the parents did not offer a single spontaneous comment, and were satisfied with the role of listeners to Joe's disjointed schizophrenic communications to the therapists.

Although Joe began to attend the sessions regularly, there were unmistakable signs of increasing tension in the family. Probably it was true that Joe became more expressive of his anger toward his parents during this period. However, the nature of the parents' complaints about his symptoms were essentially similar to the ones that were tolerated prior to his decision to join the meetings. Why was there less tolerance for his actions now that he was able to give explanations for them? For instance, the mother related that Joe had cursed her so badly that it had made her cry, although, she added, he had been nice to her ever since. Joe explained that he had hurt her so that she would know how much he was suffering. It is worth noting that not once did the parents comment on the fact that Joe had started attending the meetings as a positive element that could possibly counterbalance the concurrently intensified symptomatic manifestations. Even when the therapists asked how the parents felt about his changed attitude, they usually gave evasive answers.

The inconsistency of the parents' thinking about Joe's condition can be seen from a comparison of two consecutive sessions. In one meeting the parents reported that Joe had been more cheerful during the past week. Mother commented on the fact that he is very eager to chauffeur her to town for shopping rounds. The day previous to the session the entire family went to the movies together and had dinner out. Joe seemed to enjoy it. However, in a marked contrast to this session, a few weeks later, the parents began the session by stating that they were at the break of their tolerance for Joe at home.

Though various evidences of Joe's disturbances were reported, they did not seem to explain the sudden change in the parents' thinking. They said that Joe drives the car for long periods, a behavior that certainly was not new. The father commented that Joe has a mocking or sneering expression that he dislikes. They stated that the fact that Doris has itches at various parts of her body was due to her nervousness caused by Joe. The mother reported that she had recently started to work at her husband's store, partly because Joe's behavior had been going on far too long without any improvement and that he ought to be hospitalized. When the therapists inquired for more specific reasons, father stated that both parents had made a resolution that Joe would be hospitalized "and that is that." Although there was no reason to question the veracity of the parents' complaints, viewed realistically they seemed to be signs of a habitual disturbed functioning on Joe's part rather than horrifying, new danger signals. One of the main complaints on that day was that

Joe had failed to pick mother up at the beauty shop. The parents showed no relief when, after an initial angry withdrawal, Joe changed his mind, came down to join the session and was even able to compliment the therapists for their persistent willingness to help.

Several days thereafter, the parents judged Joe to be sick enough to be in need of hospitalization. The father modified his position so overtly as to block one of the therapists in his effort to see Joe—because, as he said, Joe had asked him to do so. It is perhaps significant that the mother asked the therapists whether they could come twice a week instead of once. She also stated in that session that she would not want to have Joe hospitalized.

The struggle and doubts went on for a few more weeks until Joe was suddenly hospitalized with the help of tranquilization. The family had contacted an outside doctor on their own. Doubtless, Joe was having manifest signs of strain prior to hospitalization, and so did his father. It was reported that the father was having sleep disturbances, that his interest in marital life had stopped, and that he was "depressed" due to Joe's illness. However, the therapists were not certain as to the causes of his "depression." He had operated his first independent store for only a few months, and it had already been "invaded" by his wife. In the past he used to point out the necessity for isolating business from family life, more specifically from his wife's critical attacks. In the first session following Joe's hospitalization, the mother complained about missing Joe and having trouble in eating, while the father talked about plans for a new summer job which would take him out of the home even on weekends. Generally, a tense atmosphere of hunger and guilt pervaded the parents for many weeks after Joe's hospitalization.

In retrospect we are aware of the complex set of forces at work during this transition period, in particular the shift in the nature of family living soon after Joe "joined" the sessions as an active member. These shifts and rearrangements, while consciously an attempt to improve family living with professional help, also reflected much unconscious resistance by the parents. It was obvious that certain rearrangements (e.g., the parents' first evening out for years by themselves; mother's returning to work in father's business) were interpreted by Joe as discouraging rather than rewarding messages, subsequent to his having attained the parents' avowed goal of "family therapy in the presence of Joe." There were reasons to assume the presence of some competitiveness between Joe and his parents for the therapists as transference parental figures. Joe himself interpreted his parents' interest in family therapy as a competitive situation. It was also during this period that the parents' resistance took on an overt expression with an inquiry into the therapists' status with the hospital. They also established contact with another psychiatrist without consulting the family therapists.

This first of a series of hospitalizations revealed, as did subsequent family maneuvers, the complex of family-game-playing, and the strategies and counterstrategies that typified this family unit. They necessitated the application of a new frame of reference regarding human dynamics and interplay, a "new style" of description appropriate to the ebb and flow of this small, "sick" human grouping. The new frame of reference had to discard the validity of the family myth according to which the parents were anxiously waiting for Joe to avail himself of the opportunity to share family therapy in the interest of his own recovery. The therapists became aware of a complex, confusing group dynamic of which the patient's illness was a meaningful part but by no means the entire picture.

Interaction, "New Style"

Manifestations of total family functioning, which we have labeled "interaction, new style" merely for the sake of presentation, was evident throughout the remaining contact with this family. One aspect of this phase was a shift from therapy of individuals to a unitary family framework. To exemplify family functioning we have chosen examples representative of the two main qualities of these sessions. One quality was the active, complex, ever-shifting system of family resistances against dealing with core family pathology. The other quality involved intense transference feelings toward one or both therapists. Family members functioned as a unit, through the resistances as well as the transference involvement, serving one another while serving (or misusing) themselves. Throughout there was manifest an essential facet of this family's pathology—the unyielding and rigidly held primitive ties, ties that were challenged by any move toward independence on the part of the children, and by jealousy of any relationship wherein one member gave evidence of relating to someone to the exclusion of someone else.

One manifestation of family resistance took the form of threats of hospitalization by the parents or the patient, or of actual hospitalization. In the latter case the patient acted "crazy" and disruptive, and the parents behaved as though hospitalization were the only tolerable solution. Although at different times the threat to the family varied, it was clear that hospitalization or mention of it was a family maneuver to reduce intrafamilial anxiety or the threat of revelation of a core family problem. At other times hospitalization appeared to be determined by complex secondary gains within the therapy relationship, e.g., regulation of competitiveness, etc.

One example of this maneuver is revealed in highlights of a series of sessions covering a period of one and one-half months. At first the patient began by dominating the discussion. When this was pointed out, he said he felt like a child who wants to be a baby yet wants to break away and be an individual too. He added that when he feels like breaking away, he feels "treacherous."

There immediately followed an interchange between mother and Doris, the latter challenging mother's implication that she was afraid to be without her. In an outspoken fashion, unusual for her, Doris said if the whole family took a vacation she would "manage."

As soon as the therapists arrived for the following session Doris picked up her purse, said good-bye and left. After this Joe talked of not having an identity of his own, and the therapists supported him, noting his guilt when he talked of independence. Mother reported that Joe also said the therapists were his only friends. Tension in both parents was noted, and the progress notes reveal the suspicion on the part of the therapists of parental fear that both children may attempt to break symbiotic ties with both parents. During this session the issue of hospitalization was mentioned, significantly even though tangentially.

At the beginning of the ensuing session mother commented, as though merely to impart information, that she did not see Doris on weekends because she had a summer job. When pressed, she expressed ambivalence. Doris said she "loved" to have her parents go away so she could be by herself, the mother laughed uneasily, and Doris giggled as though she enjoyed teasing her mother. When father made a passing comment, Joe angrily said, "What do you want from me?" Following this Joe associated being arrogant with being independent. The progress report of this session comments of a suspected though not clarified parental resistance, as well as anxiety regarding a pending vacation period (i.e., separation) of one of the therapists.

The next session revealed the same theme of ambivalent independence but with increased tension on Joe's part, and particularly when both parents manifestly encouraged independence on his part. The therapists sensed the subtle resistance of the parents as actual destructive undercutting of independence wishes in both children. When attention focused on mother's need to have the children close to her, she vehemently denied this. When instances were mentioned indicating this in her relationship with Doris, mother put Doris on the spot with a direct question which forced her to retreat and agree with mother that the latter encouraged independence.

In the following session both parents put great, though inappropriate, pressure on Joe to shave, get a haircut, and get out to meet people. Joe could only respond with "oh, keep quiet," or "that's enough" or "that's unimportant." While manifestly positive, this destructive pressure created a generally depressed atmosphere. Family resistance was apparent in the form of parental superficial encouragement, which was actually rejection and excessively destructive of reasonable strides to independence. Similarly, while Joe "teased" both parents with talk of independence, he too showed signs of unwillingness to give up the close ties within the family.

The following session mother commented: "Doesn't Joe look nice with a haircut?" Father entered late, sat next to his wife (not the usual seating arrangement), and immediately made "innocent" comments about Joe getting out of the house and meeting people. Such comments increasingly upset Joe who openly accused his father of being dishonest, trying to get him upset, and finally exploded with "Are you trying to make me crazy!!" The cold "factual" response of both parents further raised the tension level, so that Joe struck his father and went to his room. When the therapist entered Joe's room, he poured forth deep feelings, including the comment, "My father wants me to stay crazy!"

In the interim between sessions one of the therapists received two telephone calls from the father, describing in anxious tones Joe's "sick" and angry behavior and expressing the hope that the therapists would suggest hospitalization. During the subsequent session Doris was sick in bed. When mother said that if such angry and destructive behavior occurred again with Joe, he would be hospitalized, Joe shouted threateningly, "O.K.—that's it—hospitalize me!" Mother retreated. At the end of the session she said that she could not stay at home with Joe all the time, and Joe threatened that if he were to show outside interest, "things would no longer be the same as far as affection between mother and him was concerned." The following week Joe was hospitalized.

What has been presented are only certain elements of a complex system of interactions during this period. The main forces are nevertheless clear, and were repeated more than once during contact with this family. "Sick" behavior and/or hospitalization became a family maneuver whenever there appeared a threat to symbiotic family living (e.g., the children indicated independence wishes). While this family resistance was manifested mainly through the patient, the sister also gave expression to this defense (i.e., she became physically ill). Just as both siblings could threaten the parents and arouse their guilt (and frighten themselves) with moves toward independence, both parents could destructively threaten rejection or arouse guilt in the children. Having a "crazy" son not only maintained the pathological family unit, but also maintained the son in a primitively satisfying role, satisfying in its way to everyone concerned. Joe was the "sick" one, not the family—and exploration of the total family would lose meaning if this premise were acted out and accepted. The pressure would be further supported by the cultural view that hospitalization is for the "sick." The rest of the family—the supposed "healthy" part—could visit and try to "help"; anyway, they could do the right thing for the "sick" person. Thus hospitalization itself, though separation in a physical sense, meant a "freezing" of change. This limited view was clearly revealed for what it is, and sense could be made out of hospitalization only when conceived of as a total family resistance maneuver. While in one sense the parents would actually "drive" Joe "crazy," he accepted and played this "role" as an expression of the total family pathology, at times seeming to rebel against it but never totally.

An even more subtle form of resistance was manifest in ever-shifting dyadic ties which were acted out from session to session. Whenever the therapists approached the meaning of a particular maneuver, relationships shifted: one or both members might deny any underlying significance or another member might be brought into the picture to cloud the issue, and shift the focus in the subsequent session. This is exemplified in highlights from a series of sessions covering a five-month period wherein the family's oral and affectional needs, frustration, and mutual jealousy were the essential theme.

The first of these series of sessions consisted of individual contacts with each parent separately, followed by a joint session in the absence of the children. This session was in addition to the usual complete family session, the therapists attempting at the time to stimulate discussion of the marital relationship. One highlight of this session was the extent of mutual distrust revealed. Mother openly accused father of doing things outside of the home that were not "kosher," alluding to his relationships with another woman. Father, on the other hand, related an instance wherein mother had "gone out" with other men. The validity of these accusations was not obvious. The final statement in the progress notes reads: "It is as though neither completely trusts the other's capacity to 'give,' so as a consequence cannot give freely."

Joe began the subsequent family session by expressing concern lest others expect him to give too much. Doris acted quite infantile. The parents remained silent. When the therapists directed attention to Doris, she was pleased, and Joe expressed jealousy by commenting that he did not want to share his "boyfriends" with her. Both parents were relatively inactive, but at the close of the session, the children were reminded of "something," whereupon Joe rose and presented the therapists with a holiday gift.

The following session mother related Joe's feelings of frustration to her own as a child, but the focus then shifted to father's sources of satisfaction and his own family history. When a connection became apparent between father's feelings and Joe's, mother and Doris became close, with mother being solicitous of Doris' chest cold. During the following session Joe exhibited close feelings toward one of the therapists, leading father to compete for Joe's interest in competition with the therapist. Mother seemed jealous of father's cathexis of Joe. Subsequently, mother accused father of not giving enough time to Joe, at the same time "signaling" for Doris to sit next to her and Doris complying.

The following session mother changed from her previous self, becoming more aggressive and seductive toward Joe. She rearranged her skirt and sat on the sofa, rather suggestively. Joe responded with playful suggestiveness, saying in another context: ". . . so all that remains now is to sit back and enjoy." Father then entered the picture, obviously made jealous by this mother-son interchange, and engaged Joe in a heated debate on a senseless topic.

The next session showed another shift wherein Joe became jealous of a discussion that focused on his sister, and he moved closer to his father. After this session the father became jealous of the therapists' questions of Joe, implying that unsatisfied needs are not limited to "younger people." This was followed by Joe teasing both parents with his fantasies of returning to the hospital, associating this with having his needs taken care of by others (i.e., the "doctors"). When Doris corrected him on a point of information, both parents retaliated against his threat of rejection by supporting Doris and encouraging her to hold to her opinions against Joe.

During the session that followed the parents mentioned that they were going to have the first weekend vacation alone (without the children) in ten years. The focus then moved to the close father-son relationship, and when mother tried to engage herself in the discussion, she was excluded. This father-son closeness remained the focus for the two subsequent sessions but in the next session mother immediately made a few remarks about Doris' "careless" way of sitting, with her skirt so high that it exposed a considerable portion of her thigh, and adding that she was not going to take her top coat off that day because she had a very short skirt on. This move to draw attention to herself and away from the father-son relationship was blatant, considering the fact that, in the past, she had generally been considerably exhibitionistic without commenting. The following session marked another shift. Although the discussion began with comments regarding father and son, there soon evolved an intense emotional interchange between Joe and mother, with father getting increasingly tense. When father attempted to interfere, Joe told him to "mind his business," and a heated exchange began between father and Joe. When the therapists pointed out that mother was smiling while the two "men" in the family were arguing (over her?!) an intense interchange followed between mother and father, to the exclusion of Joe. Father finally left the room but could not remain away for more than ten minutes. Then Joe left the room. Feelings of jealousy, hunger and rage were again dramatically evident.

The shifting family ties were obvious in subsequent sessions when mother implicitly blamed Joe for the loss of her husband's attention, when she told of paired driving arrangements wherein she and Joe would travel in one car and father and Doris in another, and in the final session of this series when Joe attacked mother, father stepped in, and Joe and father argued. Then mother cried, turning attention onto herself again—and so it went with little attempt or apparent ability on anyone's part to see or consider the meaning of the interactions.

Certainly, there were varying dynamic forces at work during these sessions, and other material of importance was expressed and acted out. However, despite certain significant shifts in affects and manifest adjustments outside of the sessions, there persisted a style of resistance difficult to grapple with, and typical of this family throughout the therapy experience. As soon as one relationship or facet of family life came into focus for analysis, the family shifted the focus to a new relationship. Seldom did any member fully grasp the significance of an interchange because another member, or members, would intervene, drawing attention to himself or another relationship. The manifest content of an interchange completely masked the more meaningful emotional undercurrent. Beyond individual defenses and resistances (e.g., denial, projection, intellectualization), different members at different times acted so as to block exploration of others' relationships. The essential themes could thus be avoided or, if approached, dealt with briefly or superficially.

A third form of family resistance was evident whenever an attempt was made to explore the marital relationship. While the therapists believed this to be a central issue, it was strikingly difficult to focus discussion for any length of time on the parental pair. Initially the focus of both parents had been on Joe as the "sick" member. Later it became apparent that both parents seemed to relate meaningfully only to and through Joe, placing him "in the middle." The therapists finally decided to make a concerted effort to focus on the marriage.

At this point Joe began to function so as to "protect" the marriage relationship from exposure. One maneuver was simply to dominate the discussion and not allow others to speak. Another maneuver was to talk in a psychotic fashion, as though attempting to seduce the therapists into making intrapsychic interpretations that would have "deep" and "significant" meaning. At times Joe would engage father in a heated interchange, senseless on the surface but with potential importance in its own right. At other times he would complain that he was the "sick" person, implying that to pay attention to the parental relationship was beside the essential purpose of the sessions.

The subtle quality of this resistance lay in the fact that the content varied from one instance to another; only the timing of the maneuver defined its purpose. An added difficulty in handling this form of resistance was the willingness of both parents to allow interruption whenever the marital relationship was being approached, since it allowed them to maintain their superficial congeniality. Furthermore, when they participated with Joe in his interruption, they not only avoided the issue, but could repetitiously "act out" primitive dyadic ties which afforded them "pleasure." That this resistance involved the parents as well as Joe was indicated by subtle, and at times not so subtle, invitations on the part of one or both to have Joe make a comment or enter into the parental discussion. More frequently than not, the " invitation" took the form of a nonverbal communication to Joe to intrude himself or engage one or both parents in an argument.

The second main quality of these "new style" sessions—the intense transference feelings to one or both therapists—is difficult to document specifically since it manifested itself more as a constant background than as a focus of discussion. It was evident, however, that for about half a year both the stable adjustment of the patient as well as the content of the sessions was predicated upon a dependent transference relationship between family and therapists.

Session content dealt in large part with the affectional needs of family members, the symbiotic dyadic relationships, and the frustrations each member felt with the others in not being able to satisfy these dependency and/or symbiotic needs. It was during these sessions that the likely role of Doris within the total family constellation was discovered. In everyone's eye's, she was the member who acted like a child and got satisfaction.

Just as in prior sessions jealousy was revealed when one family member was excluded by another, the sessions during this period revealed instances of jealousy between family members for attention and "affection" from the therapists. During one session mother approached her own affectional needs by discussing her relationship with her husband. Joe read a newspaper during her discussion, as though indifferent to his mother's expression of need. She showed genuine anger at Joe for this. The following session she was more communicative than usual, and the notes of this session reveal: ". . . she was pleased that she could talk about herself." She connected this with the help she was getting from the therapists. Joe interfered and began to talk about himself, acting disturbed and as though he were the one who needed attention, and mentioned his possible need for hospitalization.

Much of the subsequent session focused on father's affectional needs, in a fashion more natural than was usual for him. He seemed genuinely relieved by the attention now being shown him by the therapists. Interestingly enough, Joe and mother at this point held hands, as though attending to each other, or expressing jealousy of father in the momentary absence of attention from the therapists. The therapists hypothesized from this session that the entire family viewed them as "mother figures," and that this might serve to minimize family tension outside of the sessions. (This in fact proved to be the case.)

Overt evidence of jealous desire for therapeutic attention occurred two sessions later when Doris was the center of discussion. Joe was blatantly annoyed and mother acted seductive with the therapists. Father, also annoyed by the discussion, tended to fall asleep, but denied his annoyance when this was pointed out to him.

During the subsequent session mother questioned the therapists as to the possible "emotional" meaning of Doris' colitis. Joe interrupted, saying that discussion of sickness should center on him and that no one was listening to what he had to say. When he complained that what he needed was "closer friends outside the home" (i.e., the therapists), mother implied that he could have no outside friends until he found satisfaction inside the home.

Subsequent sessions revealed the same type of evidence of dependent transference feelings. At times one or another family member would feel excluded from the attention of the therapeutic discussion (i.e., the therapists' attention), and do or say something to gain the center of the stage. Each would reveal his frustration differently—mother might act seductively or baldly introduce a new topic; father might act depressed and beaten or sit silently; Joe might intrude himself, demanding the conversation focus on him.

Whatever the specific form, this dependent-transference phase of treatment was intense, more intense than perhaps even the therapists realized. Of interest, nevertheless, is the fact that during this period the family enjoyed a less tumultuous life than they had during many years previously.

Termination Phase

The question of terminating the therapy became the third main phase of therapy with this family. The first phase was that of incomplete family sessions, with Joe being absent; the second phase was characterized by the "new style," i.e., the adaptation of the family to sharing the sessions and, to some extent, the patient role. The question of termination arose from the necessities of project organization, specifically budget considerations. The termination phase turned out to be the most important phase of the entire course of therapy, especially as far as technique is concerned.

Termination plans were announced approximately six months prior to the projected actual date in order to give the family an opportunity to work through their feelings concerning the loss of the therapists as transference parental figures. By this time the therapists had learned that the spontaneous growth capacities of this family were limited, and that their main use of therapy was to obtain a feeling of dependent gratification from the therapists. This enabled the family members to somewhat diminish the pressure of their demands on each other. There was a certain regularity in the periodic appearance of strongly competitive attention-seeking by various family members during the family sessions. In fact, this hungry, rivalrous attention-seeking became the continuous texture of family therapy in which the various individual dynamic threads seemed to have lost significance. Furthermore, it was evident that the family members did not want to miss any of the therapy sessions.

The timing of the announcement of termination was such that it followed a five-to-six-month period of relatively non-psychotic behavior on Joe's part. There was no evidence of any significant change in the parent's marital relationship, but there seemed to be growing willingness on their part to display more genuine feeling, especially since it was usually gratified by the therapists' attention during the hour. Doris was about to finish high school. She certainly became considerably freer in feminine expressiveness. Joe's symptomatic flare-ups seemed to be essentially limited to occasions of temporarily needed additional attention, or to apparent efforts at masking the parent's exploration of their own feelings and relationships.

In the session previous to the one in which the plan for termination was first announced the father had made flattering remarks about the results of the family therapy, and implied that the family were planning to send the therapists some gifts on the occasion of the coming holidays. Then Joe asked us directly whether we could tell how long the project would last. (It is possible that the family, through their hospital connections, had heard of some rumor regarding the approaching end of the project's work.) When we announced that it would probably end in June of next year, he became rather silent and expressionless. The mother was the only one who could respond in any direct fashion; she said that the family hoped the therapists would make the necessary arrangements for some therapy to continue after termination. The therapists made no concrete promises on the subject. The father looked somber and sad. At the end of the session the mother brought up the issue of Joe's medication, which was not usually handled in the family therapy session.

The new, terminal phase soon began to take shape in the next few sessions and it reached a marked climax within a few months. The parents gradually became more subdued, and countered interpretations of their obvious disappointment over separation with evasive answers. Joe, on the other hand, became increasingly agitated and overtly aggressive, ostensibly toward his father. He did not accept the interpretation that he is actually angry at the therapists and that he displaced this feeling upon his father. Thus Joe became spokesman for the family's grief over "parental" rejection (in the transference). A few brief sketches will illustrate the issues of what had come to be the termination period.

The family started a new pattern: they began coming late to sessions. After an initial silence, followed by a markedly "crazy" rambling on Joe's part, the therapists explored the question of the family's feelings about the approaching termination. Joe admitted that he has to "swallow up" the therapists while they are available. Doris acknowledged some gains from family therapy but added that she would prefer watching television. Usually, both parents denied any feelings concerning separation, and gave rational lip service to the value of family therapy for Joe and the rest of the family.

An increased tension appeared in the family when the initial, apparently hostile silence was interpreted as the family's anger at the therapists. Joe soon worked himself up to an overtly angry state. He stated that he had been "good" and controlled for six months, and that his father preferred to push him back into psychosis. The incident he was referring to, presumably some argument over the use of the car, remained obscure, especially since the father chose not to describe it from his vantage point. As tension was mounting, the therapists pointed out to the father that they wanted him to express his own feelings on this matter. But, not only was he reluctant to do so but his wife instructed him, contrary to the therapists' advice, to "shut up" in order not to "upset" Joe any further, and then started to cry. This turn of events did upset Joe, and he made an attempt to interrupt his mother, whereupon she also told him to "shut up." Joe at this point spat at his mother and threatened to leave. Locked up in his helpless rage he became verbally abusive to which the parents replied with a regained composure. As the therapists learned the next day, the family had him hospitalized the night of this session.

It is probable that the family's desperate efforts to make the therapists change their minds about termination took the form of a complicated unconscious plot, consisting of renewed psychotic-like behavior on Joe's part, and a "reasonable" and understanding withdrawal on the parents' part. In the following few sessions the parents took up again the issue of the impossibility of "living with Joe when he breaks things at home." It seemed, therefore, that the whole "new style" picture hinged on the "transference-cure" dimensions of the therapeutic dependency, and a complete reversal to the early symptomatic behavior patterns was threatened.

A few weeks later a new theme began to take shape: Joe started to talk persistently about a need for independence. He claimed that he did not want his parents to visit him again. He stated that he can talk better to his resident physician in the hospital than to the family therapists and, as it turned out later, he began to show a romantic interest in a young female patient. Much of this can certainly be characterized as pseudo-autonomous behavior, but it would be difficult to exclude the possibility of a genuine search for independence.

The subsequent session brought the family's play more clearly into the open. The mother was active and pointed out that she would not want Joe back in the home unless he changed radically. Joe angrily stated that he might have to be transferred to the area state hospital if his mother thought that way. This statement provoked a prompt reaction from her by announcing: "You are not going to Byberry." The father confirmed Joe's contention that for several months prior to his hospitalization his behavior had been more peaceful. At the end of the session the mother felt compelled to state her deeper feelings about the therapists' attitude: "They are only interested in Joe and are not concerned with the other family members." In a way this statement was rather inappropriate, since the therapists had made efforts to explore the parents' feelings. However, the mother's statement represented a rare and direct admission of the parents' feelings of competition in the therapy situation.

A desperate attempt to test the involvement of the therapists was made in a later session. A few minutes before the beginning of the family session, the father, in an urgent telephone call, notified the therapists of Joe's automobile escapade to western Pennsylvania where he had run out of gas on the turnpike and had been detained by the state police for not carrying a driver's license and behaving strangely. Later on during the session, the father for the first time became capable of expressing his fears about the pending loss of the therapists. In describing his feelings he talked about being left to drift along, half drowning. He asked whether the family could see the therapists on a private basis, outside the project. When he was informed that the therapists were not planning to see them privately but were interested in exploring the family members' feelings, the father produced some overtly primary process-type thinking. He discovered a disquieting and yet potentially promising sparkle in one of the therapists' eyes. While he was manifesting this amount of separation anxiety, the mother remained hard and tightly controlled. Joe, though released from the hospital, had not been attending the sessions for several weeks.

The next session was characterized by further even more desperate elements. Joe had been admitted to the state hospital as a result of his "breaking things" in the home. Mother had contacted "someone with influence" who would give Joe a chance to be hospitalized at a "good" hospital. There were statements from both parents to the effect that they had suffered enough, but only a minimal amount of blame was directed at the project or the therapists. As the therapists pursued the parents' feelings, father's acknowledgement of his "hatred" for Joe, and mother's fantasies that Joe would be killed came out eventually in a rarely seen pure picture.

This session left the therapists with an uneasy feeling. Even when the expression of the parents' long repressed ambivalent feelings towards rejecting parental figures was almost openly dealt with in the transference, the parents were only able to turn these feelings toward their intrapsychic representatives, or towards Joe's "bad" illness. The therapists were doubtful whether the available time would permit the therapeutic exploration of this difficult area. Would the members of the family have to channel their stress into acting-out?

The session following was shorter because the family was forty-five minutes late. Again, the parents showed no willingness to blame the therapists for termination. Instead, the mother described the state hospital in all its pitiful aspects. We learned that Joe had actually asked to be brought to the family meeting but the mother had preferred not to ask the doctor for permission to take him out of the hospital. Father looked very depressed but when questioned, could attribute his bad mood only to his feelings about Joe's condition. When he was asked whether he would prefer to have his son hospitalized for a long time in a state hospital, or to have him lead a socially unattractive living far away from the family, he preferred Joe's being in a hospital. Gradually he backed out of this position, with considerable expressions of guilt over what seemed to be a wish to "put Joe away." Towards the end the mother became more explicit about her doubts concerning the entire treatment of the family project. This time she did not put it in such personal terms as she had done a few weeks ago. She did not blame the therapists any more for their preference for helping Joe rather than the other family members. Her ideation was back where it was at the beginning of the therapy: the only problem that she could see was that Joe was ill, and we did not help.

This was the last time the mother came. The next session was the last one, and the father came alone. He obviously would have been interested in continuing but was powerless against his wife's hurt pride and her need to reject the therapists before the set date of termination.

Several weeks after the end of the therapeutic contact, it was learned by the project that Joe was soon discharged from the state hospital, and was able to live at home with the family. Plans were being explored by the family for individual out-patient therapy for Joe.

The termination phase and its problems hold especial significance in view of the central pathology assumed to exist in this and other families with schizophrenic offspring. Periodic relational movements between closeness and separation underlie the phenomena of rejection, over-protection, symbiosis, etc., often described by various observers as characteristic of these families. We have assumed that the parents brought into this family their own problems of unresolved separation from their parents, and that these problems colored their parental attitudes. We have often in their various behaviors witnessed evidences of their attribution of parental roles to their son.

It is reasonable to assume that the abrupt hospitalizations, which always seemed to follow ambivalent, aggressive outbursts of great intensity, were unconscious attempts at partial and temporary separation from the "bad" parental image on the part of all three members. On the other hand, discussions of the possibility of, or realistic planning for separation have been invariably blocked by any or all members of the parents-son triad throughout the more than three years of therapy. Even interpretations of intimate or shameful aspects of any individual's life had considerably more chance of exploration with this family than interpretations of separation fears. The latter, at best, were answered with short general statements of the type: "Of course we want our children to have their own life."

As the final phase of family therapy has demonstrated, the therapists' termination threats were too real to be denied and too painful to be dealt with. The threat of termination turned out to be the most powerful means of exploring the main dynamics of this family.

The Ichabod family

John C. Sonne and Geraldine Lincoln

Chapter

7

In our work with schizophrenic families, we were often distressed by working with a seriously disturbed family which was also handicapped by a low level of sophistication and a lack of ability to conceptualize. We therefore sought a family in which at least one member, preferably two, had had psychoanalysis or psychotherapy. We felt such a family might be able to teach us; we also thought that we might learn how the intrapsychic changes occurring in individual treatment had or had not gone into solution in the matrix of family relationships.

The family to be described here is one in which the father had completed a psychoanalysis and the mother and two children had all had psychotherapy. We will attempt to describe the individual members, their pathology, and their patterns of relating within the family with some illustrations from the first 40 therapy sessions. Particularly to be noted in the description of these sessions are the dyadic latent homosexual relationships, the dyadic latent incestuous relationships, the latent divorce, and the composition of these psychopathological dyads within the framework of a family lacking a family image. (*See* Chapter 19 for a discussion of these terms.) Noteworthy also in these sessions were certain shifts in who played the paramount role as patient. The son, who we thought was to have been the primary patient, only fleetingly remained primary. Also noteworthy is the importance of the non-verbal interaction in providing clues to and confirmation of the meaning of family interaction.

The role of the father seemed to have great bearing on the form in which the family struggled with their problems. When he took charge, conflict occurred with its opportunities for insight; when he was vapid, chaos reigned. The mother's concept of herself as relatively healthy was just beginning to fragment toward the end of the forty sessions.

In addition to describing the family and some of its relationship patterns, and their examination in the first 40 sessions, this chapter deals with certain superficial mechanisms of defense and the techniques used to handle them. Noteworthy here is the denial of feeling and projection. In addition, we have outlined one particular family psychodynamic around the role of Ginger as family penis.

Family Constellation

This is a family of four, composed of father, thirty-seven; mother, thirty-five; Robert, fourteen; and Ginger, ten. The family is a middle-class, Jewish, educated and cultured family, living in a fashionable suburban neighborhood. The father is an extremely bright engineer who works for a chain store as a maintenance supervisor, a job that is beneath his talents. He had completed an analysis of eighteen months' duration, three years prior to being in family treatment. His chief complaint in analysis has been passivity. He still was having a problem being effective in his work and in his marriage, and with his children; he had tended to be an island unto himself in the intervening three years, unable to follow through on the apparent growth made in analysis and, in some respects, had regressed. Significant in his childhood history were a preoccupation with sexual curiosity, bed wetting and intense rivalry with his younger brother. He had never been able to please his intellectually teasing father and was indulged by his mother. Upon reaching maturity, he viewed the world cynically as an unsatisfying place which denied him the pleasures he wanted. He tended to have spurts of aggressiveness which were soon extinguished.

The mother is a thin, bony, gloomy-faced, bleak looking woman who frequently is dressed in a bobby-sox style. She is highly verbal and has almost no affective display. In addition to being a "housewife" she has been working part-time in a bank for the past seven years. She enjoys her work and feels that it is necessary for her to work in order that the family be economically secure. Economic security and the finer things in life are uppermost in her mind and she rationalizes this as due to her father's lack of financial success during the depression years. She sees in her husband the same poor and undependable provider her father was. She encourages her husband to be more aggressive, but on a crest of an idea she brings up various conditions which take the wind out of his sails. Her behavior thus fits hand in glove with her husband's neurotic tendency to inhibit his aggression and defeat himself. She thinks of her childhood as a very unhappy one and feels that she could never please her mother. She also feels that her mother tried to make a boy out of her but that she resisted these attempts; she consciously sees herself as feminine. She had the symptom of pica as a child, was very lonesome and always on the fringe of a group rather than part of it. She regards her father as having been one of two people in her life by whom she felt loved, the other one being her daughter Ginger. There is some evidence on the psychological tests that she never felt loved. Prior to her marriage she was an art student, and her home is tastefully decorated with many of her paintings and sketches. Her husband married her partly because he was attracted by her being different from other women, being talented and creative. She herself, however, depreciated her talents, gave up art school very willingly to marry and hasn't painted since.

The mother's experience with psychiatry began nine years ago when she first took Robert to a child guidance clinic because of his passivity. She was counseled in three different such clinics and then saw two therapists privately on a once or twice a week basis. Her last experience ended at the onset of family therapy. Her therapist and consultants over this period considered that only minimal progress had been made.

Their marriage has not been a very happy one. The parents' sexual relationship seemed to be characterized by reward, revenge and post-ponement under the guise of concern for the fact that Robert might still be awake.

Robert, the older child resembles his father but is a bit heavier. He has very shifty, darty eyes that tend at times to go out of focus. Although he, too, is quite bright he is not doing well in junior high school. He is isolated socially and spends most of his time watching TV, reading comics, or teasing his sister. He has had treatment episodically since the age of five, his family being concerned about his passivity and poor intellectual and social performance. His last therapist was seriously concerned that he might murder his sister in response to her seductive and hostile teasing of him. Treatment once a week was considered insufficient but the family never followed through on a recommendation of analysis. Robert feels unloved by his mother who quite obviously prefers his sister to him. She ignores his complaints and is quick to take Ginger's part in an argument without taking the time to learn the pertinent facts; nor does she have any awareness of his feelings. Consequently, Robert has turned to his father for consolation and receives some sporadic help from him. Their relation-ship, however, is influenced by Mr. Ichabod's tendency to vacillate so that at times he supports Robert but, at other times, derides and under-cuts him. Robert, being unable to express his feelings, is tending to de-velop psychosomatic symptoms. These, rather than gaining him the sym-pathy of his parents, only provoke them to anger and scorn.

Ginger, the ten-year-old daughter, is an attractive but fractious "little girl." She behaves in the oppositional, provocative manner of a three-year-old, yet is sexually precocious, acting at times like a seductive teen-ager. She was originally brought for treatment by her mother at age five with the problem of severe enuresis. She was seen once a week for a two-year period and was discharged, considered much improved. How-ever, upon evaluation for family treatment, it was learned that the symp-toms had recurred. She was a social outcast at school and regarded as a somewhat "freakish kid." She is hyperactive and overtalkative and, in the evaluative sessions, was a veritable itch. She and her brother are engaged in a running battle with sexual overtones, involving stealing of comic books, pencils, looking and intruding into each other's privacy which is facilitated by the fact that they share a bathroom with no exits except into the bedrooms.

The family treatment team consisted of a male psychiatrist and a female psychologist who saw the family jointly. For the first three interviews, due to accidental factors, the psychologist had not yet joined the team, and the psychiatrist saw the family by himself. We felt somewhat handicapped because we had not known each other initially and had worked in different settings. We both had a deep interest in the concept of shared psychopathology in families, and were both psychoanalytically oriented. We were both married and parents.

Treatment sessions, with the exception of two visits to the home, took place weekly in the Philadelphia Psychiatric Center Research Building in a small 12′ x 15′ room, with the family and the therapists sitting around in a circle. A one-way mirror was at one end of the room and behind this our group sat as observers. All sessions were taped with a visible recorder. No sessions were held in the absence of any family or co-therapy team member. No drugs or physical restraints were ever used, nor did hospitalization occur. Sessions were ninety minutes in duration. At the time of termination, after three and one-half years of treatment, all participants gave evidence of marked improvement in total family and individual family member functioning; a fact that was also born out by independent psychological testing.

This account represents a highly condensed and economical selection and description of our data. We have simplified the data to its essence and placed them in context and in sequence, thus attempting to reveal their significance by means of presentation rather than analysis.

History of First Forty Sessions of Therapy

In the first interview father was concerned that the treatment might expose some of the marital problems and cause a lowering of his status in the eyes of the children. His wife, on the other hand, felt that it would be better to have all problems brought out into the open. Robert said he noted a pattern: Ginger gets grouchy, mother gets grouchy, then father takes it out on him. The apparent beginning of this pattern was a teasing and rivalrous relationship between Robert and Ginger which was freely talked about by the entire family. Robert would go into Ginger's room, look around and touch things. Ginger said, "He doesn't know what he's looking for, he pokes me and one time he pulled down my bathing suit top." She in turn steals pencils and comic books from Robert's room because "it's so junky." In these early sessions, in discussing this teasing, Robert was generally blamed for these incidents and attacked by father, mother and Ginger. More was expected of him because he was the older of the children and a boy. Despite this focus on Robert, Ginger seemed to dominate the interviews—sitting close to her mother, rubbing her, speaking up without restraint against all. This behavior was not only tolerated but enjoyed by her parents. The father acknowledged an interpretation that possibly he enjoyed her behavior as a hostile instrument against his wife, and the mother defended her leniency with Ginger on the basis that she didn't want to repress Ginger as her mother had repressed her. Ginger, in her anger against Robert, said she wanted to take a nice juicy bite out of him.

In the fifth session a chair grabbing and switching took place which was initiated by Ginger and ended at father's behest with Robert switching to the least comfortable seat. The therapists pointed out that Robert often gets the worst of the situation. Mother seemed more tender to Robert and asked Ginger what she would do if she always got into trouble with her as Robert seemed to do. Ginger said, "Then I'd go to Daddy." When mother asked her, "What would you do if Daddy always said you were wrong too," Ginger replied, "I'd go mad." Ginger seemed uncomfortable at this point and started to tease Robert by calling him Roberta. Ginger during this session played with a long scarf, first making it into a necktie, later bandaging her left arm and then putting her right arm in a sling. She also played with a detachable long braid, repeatedly attaching it to her head and then taking it off. This pantomime seemed to be a response to mother's threatening remark. Its dynamic meaning is discussed in the later section on psychodynamics.

Father missed the next session. We chose not to meet without him and the family was overheard in the hall as they were leaving. Ginger said, "Why don't we meet without Daddy?", and mother answered, "Because he's part of the family." The team speculated that father, for his own needs, enjoyed Ginger as being a little boy in order to tease his wife, and he was threatened by the exposure of this defense. In the next several sessions Ginger continued to be increasingly hyperactive, blowing up balloons, shooting rubber bands, playing with her scarf, covering her head with her coat, wetting her pants and being generally irrepressible and unrestrained. During this period she tried to stay very close to her mother who tended to defend her behavior as reasonable. Father, after some backing and filling, finally pulled Ginger away from mother and held her still, with Ginger kicking, clawing and hitting him in an animal-like way. During this period also the father made a statement that the whole family had difficulty with their roles. Ginger wants a penis, Robert acts feminine, mother is not sure of herself insofar as her home or an outside career is concerned, and he is not sure of how assertive he should be. In the 10th session father did control Ginger. There was a lot of discussion around Ginger's wetting. In answering her parents' question as to how she felt when she wet her pants, she retorted by asking her mother how she felt when she was smoking and when she was driving. Instead of answering the question, mother switched the subject to reporting an incident when the children stole some candy which the father had locked away. Father saw this theft mostly as symbolizing Robert's wish to take the mother away from him; he then objected to his wife's marching around partially clothed in a sexy manner in front of Robert. He also saw himself as cuddling Ginger when he was angry at mother, but became so anxious when the therapists speculated that Ginger's wish for power and candy represented a wish for mother that he terminated the session fifteen minutes early. Robert became so anxious at his father's talk about Oedipal competition that his eyes went out of focus. The next five sessions were rather turbulent. There was a great deal of inappropriate humor, hostility and complaints. The complaints were mainly about lack of romance between the parents and lack of privacy between the children. Robert complained about his mother walking around in panties and bra.

Ginger stepped on a nail just prior to the next session and the family, arriving shortly after, treated the incident lightly and humorously, denying an implication of an unconscious wish on Ginger's part to hurt herself. In the ensuing session the parents discussed their in-laws and a salient point came out, namely, that Mother consciously determined at Ginger's birth to give her extra love because her mother-in-law preferred boys to girls. Mr. Ichabod revealed an unusually close relationship with his father and expressed resentment about receiving money from Mrs. Ichabod's parents. Over this period the parents seemed to be increasingly interested in the marital relationship. In the 15th session Mr. Ichabod was late. When he arrived, the family, especially Ginger, chastized him for his domineering behavior of the evening before. He took this for a while and then explosively laid down the law, saying that he planned to continue his present behavior until his family acted in a more satisfactory manner. Although this seemed to be a first appearance of strength on the part of Mr. Ichabod, his vulnerability to his wife's criticism was revealed in his crushed look when she stated that he was "all talk and no performance." In the next session, when mother was deaf to Robert's plea for protection from Ginger's intolerable kicking of Robert's seat in the car, Mr. Ichabod challenged her on her overprotectiveness of Ginger and asked who she thought were better, men or women. He went on to say he felt mother was not contented with her role as a woman and had transmitted this attitude to Ginger. He pointed out both her depreciation of Robert and her low expectations of Ginger. Over the next three sessions he wavered, and after promising Robert that he would keep Ginger out of his bedroom, began to attack him for not doing his homework; he then proposed that the kids solve their own problems, suggesting a "hands off" policy. At the low point of his passivity during this five-week downward swing from his aggressive stand, the father challenged the male therapist by accusing him of being bored and putting on a blasé pose for the observers. He said that psychiatry was a woman's business. He was able to accept the suggestion that his remarks represented a projection of his own feeling of boredom and impotency in relationship to his family.

During session 19 Mrs. Ichabod came forward with her own complaints and stated that for the past sixteen years her husband had vacillated, refusing to make any kind of decision. She has to make all the decisions and he then calls her bossy. At the close of the meeting father said, "I don't want much—a good relationship with my kids, a wife to go to bed with—I don't have either so I don't give a shit." Robert, during this period, showed an increase in inappropriate grimacing and smiling; Ginger was relatively quiet. Mr. Ichabod's comments about the male therapist represented the first show of strong feeling about the therapists by a family member. Despite his apparent resignation he was more genuinely involved in the subsequent sessions and strongly challenged his wife on her remote, cool manner, saying she acted as if she were not part of the family. With this show of more genuine feeling on the part of the father, the therapists were able to elicit from Mrs. Ichabod a feeling that, at times, she hated all members of the family. At the end of the session she cried and then stated that what made her so unhappy was that Mr. Ichabod did not treat her as or make her feel like a woman.

Over the next few weeks there was a development of sexual topics by the family in various relationships. Ginger complained of social ostracism by her girl friends, and mother speculated that her ostracism was a result of her telling dirty jokes which she had learned from a boy friend of questionable repute. The therapists were able to draw from the mother a parallel situation during her adolescence in which she regained favor with her girl friends by abandoning a boy friend. The father overlooked Ginger's sexuality and changed the subject by accusing her of having just wet her pants.

During this period the father had an operation for varicose veins and a hernia, and the therapists visited the family at home. The father reacted to this as an intrusion and resented the therapists' inspecting the bedroom arrangement; he also complained that his wife used sexual deprivation as a weapon against him. Mrs. Ichabod again complained of lack of romance. The female therapist was rejected by Mr. Ichabod, he being unable to attribute to her any warm or friendly feelings, especially in reference to the therapists' visit to the home during his convalescence. He was able to see that his inability to envision women as having something to offer was a problem of his. He seemed genuinely perplexed by this new insight and said he had never thought of himself this way before. In this discussion he revealed considerable interest in the female therapist, and Mrs. Ichabod reacted somewhat jealously by frequently injecting herself into the discussion.

The next five sessions centered around the theme of Mrs. Ichabod's difficulty in expressing her feelings, and her inability to give to and accept her family. There was a great deal of competitive struggle by the father, son and daughter for her affection. In regard to Mrs. Ichabod's difficulty in expressing herself, she said that she had been stoical as a child and had not felt free to show her feelings or express them verbally. She added that she had attempted to express her feelings in her paintings. The therapists remarked that they had been struck by the warmth expressed in her paintings in her home in contrast to the lack of warmth in her personality. She gave up art school to marry and has not painted since. She felt that part of her holding back in art was a rebellion against her mother's wish for her to be aggressive, i.e., masculine. Father expressed keen disappointment at mother's abandonment of painting, complimented her and wished that she would resume it. He bemoaned her inability to give of herself to the family and complained that he felt uncomfortable when Robert came to him for affection instead of to his mother. He related Robert's behavior to his father's telling him recently that he was now impotent and that Mr. Ichabod would probably inherit this weakness. Mr. Ichabod made an indirect reference to his mother by saying that she had made a nasty remark about his father's impotency. Ginger was very curious to know all the details. Mrs. Ichabod's reaction to this discussion was to talk of her pride in Robert's strength, and her pleasure in being whirled off her feet by him. Robert acknowledged that he was sexually excited when near his mother, and she complained that he shies away from her when she tries to show him affection.

In the interview following the discussion of mother's difficulty in expressing her feelings, Ginger began the session by throwing up. Her upset stomach was related to her feeling upset because of an argument she had had with Robert just before the session, in which he had threatened to throw her down the steps. He was angry with her because she had tattled to her mother that he had pilfered some Ritz crackers. A great deal of feeling centered about Mrs. Ichabod's withholding of food from both children, but mainly from Ginger because of her fear that she would become overly fat. While making sucking noises with her lips, Ginger complained she was always hungry and then added that she wanted to be married to her mother and be with her twenty-four hours a day. Mrs. Ichabod, in discussing her fantasies and her experiences at the time the children were born, said she could envision Robert prenatally as exactly the blond-haired, blue-eyed boy he turned out to be. Although she consciously wished for a girl before Ginger's birth, she was so afraid she wouldn't get one that she wouldn't fantasy the kind of girl she wanted. When Ginger was born, Mrs. Ichabod realized that she had wanted a girl that would look similar to Robert, but instead found Ginger dark-haired and homely. She felt sorry for her. She felt she had to make it up to her because Robert was the favorite of her mother-in-law. In response to her husband's question she said that during adolescence she had wished she were a boy. Despite her conscious wish to protect Ginger, she was unable to breast-feed her; bottle-feeding took hours, and she was confined to bed with infected stitches for a month during which Mr. Ichabod handled the making of the formula and the night feeding. He expressed ambivalence about this "messy business" of infant care. All of this was expressed with Ginger listening attentively.

Robert was very quiet in this session but in the next one he began to protest that his mother preferred Ginger and ignored him. Mrs. Ichabod was so unresponsive to Robert's anguish that the male therapist wondered if she loved Robert. Mrs. Ichabod responded that if she didn't love Robert, she loved no one, and if this were true she might as well kill herself. She said that she herself had only felt loved by her father and Ginger. At this point Ginger tried to comfort her, and father reassured Robert that his mother's problems were not a result of his words but had been in existance long before he was born. In the next session Mrs. Ichabod painfully dealt with a recognition that Robert and Mr. Ichabod strongly felt that she had offered them very little. She expressed a wish to leave home with Ginger.

In the next sessions the father turned somewhat against Robert. For example, he undercut Robert's relationship with mother by criticizing her for going along with Robert's request to stay home from school one day with a vague stomach complaint. The father was also critical of the male therapist, calling him namby-pamby because the therapist suggested that they read a book rather than commanding them to do so. Despite his attempts to establish himself as the boss, Mr. Ichabod weakly allowed his wife to ignore his wishes. While father was struggling to define the male roles in the family, mother revealed that she withheld comic books and candy from Robert as a means of distinguishing her husband from her son.

Although Mr. Ichabod stated that he felt sure of his position as leader, it was evident that neither his wife nor his son acknowledged his preeminence. They both challenged his judgment when he invested $75.00 in a patent search for an invention. His wife had repeatedly complained of his lack of initiative. When he did show some, she squashed it. Robert seemed to be in conflict between wanting to be proud of his father and contemptuously siding with mother against him. He complained of chronic stomach aches. Robert further showed his contempt of father one evening by passing wind arrogantly as he left their bedroom. Father came back after this insult, broke down the bathroom door, and cornered Robert in the bathroom to again affirm himself as the strongest man in the house.

In the therapy session following the door-breaking episode, Mr. Ichabod turned against the male therapist. He resisted the passive position which he felt had been imposed upon him in the family treatment situation. He was able to see his passivity as originating within himself, as a defense to protect himself against his fear of castration, as well as a weapon with which to castrate the therapists. He acknowledged this defense as being a determining factor in his prematurely terminating his analysis. He told of using this defense against his father's efforts to belittle him and admitted using the same belittling tactics against Robert, who in turn used passive resistance against his father. Father said to the male therapist that he felt exposed and ashamed, reminiscent of a time when, as a child, he'd had a leg operation.

Following these four interviews, Mr. Ichabod seemed to have achieved an improved capacity to be comfortably aggressive in his relationships. There was a conspicuous improvement in the way he handled his relationship with his wife.

With the shifting of Mr. Ichabod's attitude and the improvement of the marital relationship, we observed a change in the relationship between mother and Ginger. Formerly, Ginger had said she wanted to marry her mother and would sit close to her, pawing her, fondling her, playing with her jewelry and pocketbook, pulling her hair, rubbing her legs and in general making what would ordinarily be considered a nuisance of herself. Mother had condoned this behavior, only rarely uttering a feeble "not now, later."

Ginger expressed her new mood by becoming demanding, jealous, hyperactive and overtly hostile toward her mother. Mother, in turn started to scream at Ginger, punish her, and freely expressed her annoyance toward her in the sessions. Over the next few weeks Ginger's expression of jealousy, unhappiness and hunger for affection became more pronounced, and eventually became the central theme of the therapy. She begged for a bra and silk stockings, tearfully told her mother that she had ruined her life, accused her of being weak, of not feeding her enough and of not understanding her. She defiantly threatened her mother that she would go and meet an older boy who had told her, "come back when you're older and we'll have intercourse." She openly flirted with her father. Father asked her if she thought he had the same kind of love for her as he had for mother. Ginger whispered playfully to him that if he did they'd be having intercourse right now. One of the reasons she gave for not having intercourse with him was that his penis would be too big and her vagina would be too small. The father said that size would not be a problem but there were strong taboos against incest. Ginger said that she felt mother was jealous of her but she in turn regarded mother, with her dyed hair, wrinkly face and glasses as not worthy of jealousy. Although ostensibly father and mother had moved closer by the 40th session, there was a strong element of flirtation going on in the dyads between mother and Robert, and father and Ginger.

Superficial Defense Mechanisms

In our early work with the family we noted several superficial defense mechanisms which interfered with the uncovering of deeper dynamics, the expression of genuine feeling in the family interaction, and seemed to preserve the stereotyped relationship patterns. These defenses were seen more frequently in the earlier sessions and tended to diminish as time went on.

Questioning, perfected to an art, constitutes a major defense mechanism. One family member would tend to avoid expressing his own feelings and instead subject another member to intensive interrogation and cross-examination. At one time Ginger said her father was giving Robert a quiz, and father later admitted to playing prosecuting attorney. For example, he would ask Robert: "Do you think mother and father love each other?"; "Are you jealous of your sister?"; "Do you hate me?"; "Do you think you can take mother away from me?" We would handle this by pointing out the defense and then asking the member how he felt about his own question. A question could also be used as a way of signaling a person to retract a statement. For example, Robert once tearfully said that he felt his mother preferred Ginger to him, and she said, "Is that how you really feel?" And he answered "No." They would often ask a barrage of "whys" without waiting for an answer. The "why" represented an indictment rather than a sincere question. Multiple choice questions including no acceptable choice were frequently thrown at the children by the father.

Reporting, describing and self-righteous judging were common. We would turn these defenses into an exploration of the situation and its antecedents. In much of the above, the members rationalized their role as therapeutic, playing the role of a helpful therapist. Although at times this was true, such tactics were more often than not non-therapeutic.

Condoning inappropriate behavior was prominent. Mother particularly used this, calling Ginger's atrocious behavior reasonable. Switching of the subject was used by all. Inexplicably, while listening to the parents discussing their marriage, we would become aware that the subject had been changed to father's hounding Robert about his homework. Once, when Ginger was complaining about lack of love from mother, father then wanted to know why Robert didn't obey his mother. A much less subtle defense, which we called the "you too" defense, involved the switching of an attack by the victim to his accuser. For example, when Robert criticized his mother for obviously not listening to him, she responded by saying that he did not listen either. We were quick to point out the use of this defense and focus back on the feelings of the original accuser and the accused in this dyad. We at times called these tactics unfair. Name calling and inappropriate levity were also seen but to a lesser degree.

A Family Psychodynamic

A major dynamic in this family which seemed to be operating with impetus from every family member was portrayed by Ginger. Although she was not the primary patient, after the first few sessions she took the center of the stage and most of the interaction centered about her. She seemed to be symptomatically acting out a shared, unconscious family fantasy, multidetermined by unconscious wishes from every family member. She behaved generally in a flamboyant, overactive, overtalkative, disruptive way with a great deal of pantomime involving the use of scarves, pigtails, pencils, purses, chairs, hypodermic syringes, coats, caps, rubber bands and orthodontic braces. She frequently wet herself and indulged in disguised masturbation by rubbing her thighs and rocking. We began to think of her as "the family penis"—a symbolic role which, as time went on, it became even clearer she had both chosen for herself and had been assigned to play by the family. She was both victim and culprit. We saw partial evidence of her wish for her brother's penis in reports of her continuous invasion of her brother's room to steal pencils and comics. Robert, tuned in to this symbolic behavior, said, "She thinks she's missing out on something because I had it and she didn't." A few weeks later Ginger expressed a wish to take a "nice juicy bite" out of her brother. She aggressively preempted his chair and feminized him by calling him Roberta. Coincident with the family discussion of her apparent castration assaults on Robert which were connected with a feeling of being threatened in her relationship with mother, she pantomimed injury, castration and restitution. First she faked a broken left arm, using a scarf as a sling. Then she detached and re-attached two long artificial pigtails. She also used the scarf as a necktie which she put on and took off repeatedly. Her penis wish was revealed in the early weeks of treatment mainly in symbolic behavior, but was not explicitly verbalized until later.

Despite Robert's occasional protest to his parents about Ginger's phallic behavior, he seemed to have an interest in maintaining it whenever it was disturbing his parents and not directly harming him. When it was directed toward him he appealed to his parents in a whining, passive, helpless way to rescue him. Much of the time he seemed to be reasonably comfortable in a non-expressive, quiet, buddy-buddy, ambivalent relationship with his father. Both males, the victims of phallic onslaughts from women, commiserated with one another. In a sense Robert says that if he were father he would not handle Ginger's phallic attacks impotently as his father did. When Father did become more forceful, Robert undercut him by defending Ginger's behavior, reducing him again to a castrated state.

Ginger attempted to get father's penis by usurping father's position of authority by taking his chair, by procrastinating, and by incessant evasions of disciplinary action. She succeeded in dodging every disciplinary action by turning it into a joke—and only after her father had made a fool of himself might she comply with a smirk. When the situation was reversed and her father's behavior was in question, she was tyrannical in berating him for any minor misdemeanor with accusations painful enough to make him hang his head. She giggled when he related a dream in which he saw himself as a castrated jester. When this giggling was explored, she said she'd laugh if she saw a man without a penis. She said she thought a penis was an obstacle. She then recounted a dream of her own in which a girl was lying on the ground. First some boys danced around her, then some dogs came and licked her because she had steak juice on her; finally someone came and cut all her fat off and took it away. Both parents interpreted this dream to mean that Ginger thought she had once had a penis which had been cut off. Despite her earlier remark that a penis was an obstacle, Ginger herself said at this point that she'd like to have a penis or at least to try having one for a while. She said a crazy man might think he could eat a penis and when he'd urinate it would come out again. Although Ginger could not see this remark as her own projected fantasy, everyone else saw it as additional evidence not only of a castration fantasy, but of a fantasy of restitution by eating and urinating. This latter fantasy was especially relevant to her symptoms of hunger and enuresis.

While talking of castration, she was also expressing her anxiety non-verbally by trying to pull off the arm of her father's chair, by playing with his finger and his pencil. We commented on some of this synchronous non-verbal behavior involving the pencil and the finger. Her father, hep to the situation and not to be outdone by the therapists or his daughter, managed to salvage a scrap of his penis by noting her attack on his chair.

Father utilized Ginger as a phallic weapon of attack on mother. He obviously enjoyed her capricious antics and allowed her to flagellate him with verbal castigation. He ineffectively disciplined her, repeatedly behaving in an impotent manner toward her until he began to change in therapy. This manner was reminiscent of his current manner toward his mother. He encouraged Ginger's lesbian-like behavior, saying, "Don't you think it's all right for girls to kiss girls?"

Ginger acted out her "penis role" in relating to mother. In the 27th session she said explicitly that she felt hungry constantly, that she wanted to be with her mother twenty-four hours a day, and that she'd like to marry her. Since the early meetings she had continued to act out this wish by sitting close to her mother, rubbing mother's arms and legs in a romantic way, and playing with mother's jewelry. She kissed her mother's fingers and played with her hands. Her intent seemed to be to excite and stimulate mother. Much of Ginger's overactive behavior, mentioned above, seemed to be a performance for mother's admitted enjoyment. She also functioned as her mother's right arm in assaulting father or Robert.

Mother's wish that Ginger be a boy and have a penis was reflected in the fact that she did little to curtail her daughter's inappropriate behavior. She said she enjoyed Ginger's closeness and excused her bizarre, overactive and phallic behavior as normal feminine expressiveness. She said her mother had inhibited her as a child and she didn't want to do the same thing to Ginger. Her overprotectiveness of Ginger served as a defense for her hostility toward her own mother. Despite Robert's complaints that Ginger had the upper hand, the mother continued to allow Ginger to be bossy, to call Robert Roberta and to shift the blame constantly on to Robert. She refused to allow Robert to assert himself. She continually overprotected Ginger and, as has been mentioned in the description of the course of therapy, revealed that she felt sorry for Ginger from the time she was born because she wasn't a beautiful blond-haired boy like Robert; and because her mother-in-law preferred boys to girls. Mrs. Ichabod used this as a reason to deprecate Robert and to favor Ginger. We felt that the influence Mrs. Ichabod's mother and mother-in-law had on her attitude toward Ginger indicated that Mrs. Ichabod's desire for Ginger to be masculine was an unconscious wish to satisfy her own mother who, she felt, had wanted her to be masculine. Despite Mrs. Ichabod's conscious desire for Ginger to be feminine, it was interesting to note that as the sessions continued and Ginger showed an increased inclination to express herself as a girl, mother stalled. Ginger asked to be allowed to wear stockings and a bra, and related some stories and a dream about a boyfriend. In one session she sat with a hypodermic needle in her hand and a purse between her legs. In this session, as in others, Mrs. Ichabod tried to block her feminine strivings by denying her the bra and stockings and belittling her stories. The team pointed out that whereas Ginger was now showing signs of shifting from her phallic position, Mrs. Ichabod was not encouraging her to be feminine. Eventually Ginger was allowed to wear the stockings and bra. She then became increasingly competitive with mother for father and Mrs. Ichabod was crushed under the onslaught. She was unable to hold her own as a woman and admitted that Ginger's seductiveness with her husband was more than she could take. She blamed her difficulty in this feminine role on the men close to her and expressed resentment to her husband for not supporting her properly, for not being aggressive or romantic. She claimed her husband squelched her as a woman and failed to support her in disciplining Ginger. She herself reinforced Ginger's provocative behavior in turn to spite her husband. He claims he likes a soft quiet woman—quite the opposite of Ginger. Mother, in her frustration with her husband because he refuses to give her romantic love, turns to Ginger as a lover instead of as a daughter.

Our findings may be summarized as follows:

1. The above elucidation of the family members' unconscious feelings and thoughts about Ginger is significant in that it reveals a cluster of largely unconscious fantasies that—although from various origins and needs, and existing in the unconscious mind of separate family members—interlocked to facilitate multidetermined pathologic thinking, feeling and action on the part of Ginger.

2. A further point of significance is the fact that Ginger's role assignment is useless, since she is assigned to be a single instrument from clashing parental motives for clashing purposes. She is not symbolized by the family as a person with any qualities of unity and integrity.

3. A third significant finding concerns the possible unique value of family treatment in that it reveals the hidden process by which a family has been unconsciously maintaining a pathology which may hitherto not have been manifestly observable by therapists treating the individual members.

The degree of severity of Ginger's illness was not revealed prior to family therapy because of her role in the family emotional economy. When therapy took the heat off her brother Robert, the role she was playing became insupportable. She fell apart and in her psychotic behavior she and the rest of the family gave a more genuine cry for help.

Retrospectively we could say that the uncovered material in the course of family therapy validated Robert's early complaint of being the scapegoat in a patterned cyclical sequence of family functioning. As he observed: "Ginger gets grouchy, then mother gets grouchy, then father gets grouchy and takes it out on me."

III

RESULTS OF TREATMENT

This section contains an evaluation of the effectiveness of our demonstration and treatment method. Four general factors will be considered in assessing change: 1) degree of psychopathology and symptomatology of individual family members; 2) adequacy of social functioning of individual family members; 3) improvement in family relationships; and 4) level of effective-functioning of the family as a unit in the community. First, we shall report some of the results obtained by the quantitative family evaluation measures that we employed. Secondly, we shall report a study of observations of therapeutic process and movement made by our experienced clinicians, based on a structured rating scale. We shall also report some examples of the social and clinical improvement which has occurred in the families we have treated, based on our clinical observations and on reports which the families themselves have written.

Quantitative family evaluation measures

Alfred S. Friedman and Geraldine Lincoln

Chapter 8

The quantitative instruments which adequately measure total family functioning, or even some of the more meaningful variables in family relationships and functioning, have not yet been developed. We can only hope that a major breakthrough will occur in this area in the next few years, following the success of conceptualizing family system psychodynamics, psychopathology and treatment. In the meantime we have some tools, such as rating scales, adjective check lists, codings of joint discussions and joint projective test responses, etc., by means of which certain discrete aspects of family functioning, phenotypic rather than genotypic, can be measured.

From the latter available instruments, we have selected for our evaluation the Family Participation Index, the Family Disagreement Check List, the Leary Interpersonal Check List, which we have briefly described in Chapter 3, and such psychological projective techniques as the Rorschach test.

We will describe in some detail how these instruments were applied in evaluating a particular family before treatment, and how we measured the changes which occurred in this family after treatment. This will be followed by a summary of some of the quantitative results obtained on a small group of families.

Measuring the Ichabod Family

We have chosen the Ichabod family for a detailed quantitative analysis, since the reader will be most familiar with this particular family due to the several levels of analysis of the treatment process with this family which are presented in this book, (*see* Chapters 7, 9, 14, 15). The four members of this family were, at the time the treatment started, the thirty-seven-year-old father, the thirty-five-year-old mother, the fourteen-year-old schizophrenic son and his ten-year-old younger sister.

146

The Leary Interpersonal Check List (ICL)

Each family member rated himself and other family members, before and after treatment, on this list, which consists of 128 personality trait items. These percepts have been scored on the two main axes of this system of interacting personality variables: "dominance-submission" and "love-hate." (*See* Tables 8-1 and 8-2.)

Table 8-1 FAMILY MEMBERS' SELF-PERCEPTIONS AND OTHER-PERCEPTIONS, PRE- AND POST-TREATMENT. THE RANK ORDER OF THE FAMILY MEMBERS ACCORDING TO THE DOMINANCE–SUBMISSION AND LOVE–HATE SCORES OF THE LEARY INTERPERSONAL CHECK LIST

("F" denotes father, "M" denotes mother, "S" denotes son, and "D" denotes daughter)

DOMINANCE–SUBMISSION SCORES				LOVE–HATE SCORES			
Father's Perceptions				Father's Perceptions			
Pre		Post		Pre		Post	
M	− 61	F	− 61	D	− 47	F	− 46
F	− 45	S	− 59	S	− 40	D	− 44
D	− 41	D	− 44	M	− 39	S	− 38
S	− 36	M	− 42	F	− 34	M	− 36
Mother's Perceptions				Mother's Perceptions			
Pre		Post		Pre		Post	
M	− 65	M	− 64	D	− 53	S	− 52
F	− 56	F	− 59	M	− 47	F	− 48
S	− 48	S	− 56	S	− 47	M	− 48
D	− 47	D	− 51	F	− 42	D	− 43
Son's Perceptions				Son's Perceptions			
Pre		Post		Pre		Post	
F	− 68	M	− 61	F	− 46	F	− 45
M	− 63	F	− 61	S	− 45	M	− 44
S	− 45	S	− 54	D	− 44	S	− 42
D	− 40	D	− 50	M	− 43	D	− 37
Daughter's Perceptions				Daughter's Perceptions			
Pre		Post		Pre		Post	
M	− 66	F	− 62	D	− 50	M	− 57
F	− 64	S	− 60	M	− 45	D	− 52
S	− 57	M	− 58	S	− 45	F	− 46
D	− 52	D	− 58	F	− 43	S	− 45

Table 8-1 lists the scores, in rank order, which are derived from each family member's perceptions of himself and of every other family member. Looking, for example, at father's pre-treatment perceptions on dominance, we see that he ranks mother the highest by far on dominance, and then himself, his daughter and his son—in that order. The pre-treatment scores obtained by this family may be compared with the standard scores derived by Leary from the self-ratings of a large psychiatric out-patient sample: The mean dominance-submission scores for adult patient males is 51, with a standard deviation of 7.9 points; for adult patient females the mean is 49, with a standard deviation of 7.8 points. The mean love-hate scores for patient males is 48, with a standard deviation of 8.5 points; for patient females the mean is 52, with a standard deviation of 8.9 points. We would expect that normal subjects would show a greater differentiation between the sexes on these scores than the above psychiatric patients did, with normal males higher on dominance than psychiatric males, and normal females higher on love than psychiatric females.

In comparing the psychiatric out-patient norms with the pre-treatment scores of the two adult members of this family, as shown in Table 8-1, we note that 1) the father rated himself as lower than the norm on dominance-submission, and rated his wife as higher than the norm; 2) the father rated both himself and his wife as considerably lower than the norm on the love-hate scale; 3) the mother rated herself as extremely higher than the norm on dominance-submission, and rated her husband as somewhat higher than the norm; and 4) the mother rated both herself and her husband as lower than the norm on the love-hate scale. It is also of interest to note that of the sixteen self and other ratings on the love-hate scale, made by the whole family, all except two are lower than the norms. These two are the mother's rating of the daughter, and the daughter's rating of herself. This points to the low love image within this family, or conversely to the high perception of hostility within this family, especially by the male members.

This particular family had a wide range of scores on the two scales—36 points on the dominance-submission scale and 20 points on the love-hate scale. This wide range of scores might be taken as a positive indication, provided there is a relatively high degree of congruence or agreement between members in the way they rated each other. If this had been the fact it might have indicated a relatively high degree of differentiation of roles, and a multiplicity of roles within the family. However, what actually occurred was that there was a great amount of discrepancy or lack of congruence in the way family members rated each other on the two scales. As a result, the wide range of scores can only be taken as a negative indication. In fact, when we look at Part B of Table 8-2, we see clear evidence of a lack of differentiation in the role of the father and the mother in the family: each spouse obtains exactly the same score on dominance, 63 points, in the pre-treatment modal perception of him or her by the other family members. The father and mother are also perceived as very much alike to each other on the love-hate scale, on which the father obtains a score of 44 points and the mother 42 points. These pre-treatment scores, showing the lack of differentiation in the roles of the parents, defined one of the goals of therapy as that of achieving a healthier differentiation of roles between the mother and father.

Part A of Table 8-2 shows the modal perceptions of each family member, obtained by computing the mean value of his rating by all four family members including his own self-rating. In these pooled family perceptions we see that the mother is perceived to be the most dominant family member, and the daughter the least. On the love-hate scale, the daughter was perceived to be highest in love. This may have related to the fact that as the youngest child she was assigned the role of pleasure, id expression and acting out, by the family.

We have used the same dominance-submission and love-hate scores to measure change in perception within the family, resulting from treatment and uncontrolled concurrent factors. Our first hypothesis regarding the effects of treatment was that the self-perceptions, as well as the perceptions of each member by the other family members, would change in the direction of the self and other perceptions of the ideal or normal family. The main shifts noticed in the family's perceptions of each other on the two scales are shown on Table 8-2.

Table 8-2 MODAL FAMILY PERCEPTIONS OF EACH FAMILY MEMBER, IN RANK ORDER, PRE- AND POST-TREATMENT ON THE LEARY INTERPERSONAL CHECK LIST

A. Each score represents the mean value of the four family members' ratings of the individual, including his self-rating.

DOMINANCE–SUBMISSION SCORES				LOVE–HATE SCORES			
Pre		Post		Pre		Post	
M	− 64	F	− 61	D	− 47	M	− 46
F	− 58	S	− 57	S	− 44	F	− 46
S	− 47	M	− 56	M	− 43	D	− 44
D	− 45	D	− 51	F	− 41	S	− 44

B. Each score represents the mean value of the other three family members' ratings of the individual, not including his self-rating.

DOMINANCE–SUBMISSION SCORES				LOVE–HATE SCORES			
Pre		Post		Pre		Post	
M	− 63	F	− 61	D	− 46	M	− 46
F	− 63	S	− 58	F	− 44	F	− 46
S	− 47	M	− 54	S	− 44	S	− 45
D	− 43	D	− 48	M	− 42	D	− 41

The father's shift in rank-order position on the dominance-submission axis was quite striking, since he was rated in the pre-treatment ratings as the most dominant member of the family by only one of the members, the son; in the post-treatment ratings he was rated as the most dominant member by three of the four members—himself, his son and his daughter, but not his wife.

Originally the father rated himself 16 points below his wife in dominance; after treatment he reversed the positions and rated himself 19 points above her. It is of interest to analyze the specific items and traits on which the father improved his self-rating, and which contributed to his increased dominance score. The items fell mostly in the quadrant of of the grid which included "self-effacing," "modest," "skeptical," "distrustful," and "dependent" traits. He no longer described himself as "self-punishing," "shy," "modest," "apologetic," "obedient," "usually giving in," "frequently disappointed," "bitter," "complaining," "slow to forgive a wrong," "very anxious to be approved of," "very respectful to authority," and "trusting and eager to please."

When we consider the absolute values of the dominance-submission scores rather than the rank-order ratings, we find that the son was perceived, by the family as a whole, as having made the largest absolute increase in dominance; the four members of the family accorded him increases of 23, 8, 9 and 3 points, respectively, resulting in an impressive mean increase of 10.7 points. The son made a greater absolute increase in dominance than did the father, due to the fact that he started from a much lower base line. Also, three members each perceived the family as a whole to have gained in dominance. The fourth, the daughter, saw relatively little change in the whole family as far as dominance was concerned.

As regards the love-hate scores, the most interesting change occurred in the children's perception of their mother. The daughter moved the mother up 12 points, from a rank-order position of a three-way tie for second place into first place. The son moved the mother up from fourth to second place. When we consider this shift in the mother's position on the love-hate axis, together with the father's striking shift upward on the dominance-submission axis, we observe that the family has moved in that direction of the model of the ideal family: the father is now perceived to be the most dominant member of the family—the acknowledged leader—and the mother somewhat more as the source of love. The shift in the children's perception of love in the mother is not, however, very marked. Also, the father still ranks the mother as low in love, and has in fact moved her to the lowest position in the family which was where he had placed himself before treatment. The father's perception of himself now, following treatment, has improved strikingly in regard to the love-hate score as well as to the previously mentioned dominance-submission score. He has increased his score of himself on this latter scale by 12 points.

The fact that the father did not move the mother up on the love-hate axis is surprising to us. It does not support our independent evidence from treatment and projective testing that there is an improved heterosexual relationship between the two of them.

The second major hypothesis which we were testing with the Leary Interpersonal Check List was that better self-understanding and communication should result in a reduction in discrepancies between self-image and the modal picture of the person held by other family members. In regard to this hypothesis, the father is again seen to make the most impressive improvement. In the pre-treatment testing the father's perception of himself, combining both scales, totaled 17 points of distance or discrepancy from the family's perception of him. Now, on post-treatment, the father's perception of himself is exactly the same as the family's perception of him. The pre- and post-perceptions of the father are shown on Figure 8-1. His initial self-perception is indicated on the diagnostic grid by a point (F_1) which is determined by his scores on the two main axes. (The dominance-submission score is plotted on the ordinate, or Y-axis, of the grid, and the love-hate score is plotted on the abcissa, or X-axis, of the grid.) The initial modal perception of him by the other three family members is indicated by a point (f_1) on the same grid which was obtained by computing the mean of their pooled perceptions of him. The post perceptions are indicated, correspondingly, as F_2 and f_2 on the same diagnostic grid. The distance between points F_1 and F_2, shown by the broken line, indicates change in the father's perception of himself over the course of treatment.

Similarly, Figures 8-2, 8-3, and 8-4 illustrate the perceptions by self and others of mother, son, and daughter, respectively. The son was the family member who showed the best congruence, and the least amount of discrepancy between his self-perceptions and the others' perception of him. (See Figure 8-3.) It is interesting to note that it was this schizophrenic member, manifestly and symptomologically the sickest one in the family, whose perception of himself was the most consistent with the way others perceived him. We have often observed that the sick member of a family may be the most insightful, or has the most accurate picture of the family relationships at a "deep" or psychodynamic level. Since there was so little discrepancy in the self to other ratings of the son to begin with, there was very little room for improvement in post treatment. In fact, there was a larger discrepancy because the family now perceives him as considerably more dominant than he perceives himself.

Noteworthy discrepancies occurred in the pre-treatment perceptions of the two female members of the family, and continued undiminished in the post-treatment ratings. This was due to the fact that the mother con-

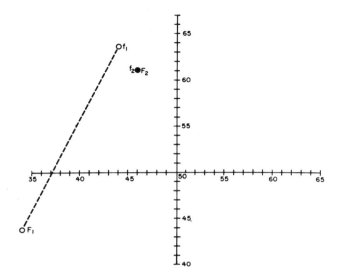

Figure 8-1 Discrepancy (distance) between the father's perception of himself pre-treatment (F_1) and the modal perception of him by the family (f_1), compared to the corresponding post-treatment discrepany (F_2 and f_2).

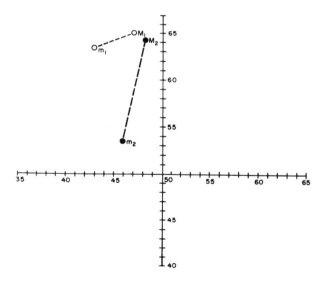

Figure 8-2 Discrepancy (distance) between the mother's perception of herself pre-treatment (M_1) and the modal perception of her by the family (m_1), compared to the corresponding post-treatment discrepancy (M_2 and m_2).

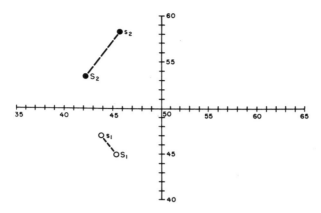

Figure 8-3 Discrepancy (distance) between the son's perception of himself pre-treatment (S_1) and the modal perception of him by the family (s_1), compared to the corresponding post-treatment discrepancy (S_2 and s_2).

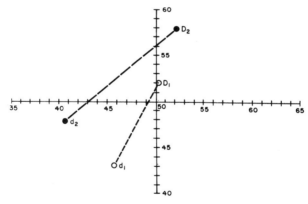

Figure 8-4 Discrepancy (distance) beween the daughter's perception of herself pre-treatment (D_1) and the modal perception of her by the family (d_1), compared to the corresponding post-treatment discrepancy (D_2 and d_2).

tinued to rate herself high on dominance, 11 points higher than the other members rated her. The discrepancy, on the love-hate scale, though, decreased a little in that the other members of the family now saw the mother as being almost as loving as she originally perceived herself to be, and still does. In the pre-treatment testing the other members of the family had seen the mother as much less loving than she at that time had perceived herself to be. This finding could be interpreted in one of two ways—either that she knew she had the basic capacity to be more loving, a capacity which was blocked in expression and which the other family members therefore did not get from her or perceive in her; or, that it was so important to her image of herself to appear as a loving mother and wife, that she had to deny in the beginning that she was not actually loving and not fulfilling her role properly.

A comparison of Figure 8-1 illustrating the father perceptions, with Figure 8-2, illustrating the mother perceptions, reveals how differently the parents have responded to the first phase of the family treatment. The father, who worked most with his feelings and his intrapsychic conflicts in this phase of treatment, changed his perception of himself markedly in the direction of the image that the family had of him originally, and still holds of him. (See Figure 8-1.) The mother, on the other hand, retained the same image of herself that she had originally, regardless of the different way the family perceived her. (See Figure 8-2.) In fact, the family now perceived her as considerably less dominant than they had originally, which resulted in an increased discrepancy between her self-perception and their model perception of her. This contrast between the way the father's and mother's perceptions changed is partially explained by the different defense operations and mechanisms in the treatment process found to be characteristic of them as individuals. The father defends himself by being open, by obsessively ruminating, confessing, messing up the situation, etc. The mother, on the other hand, has more closed and guarded defenses, and uses denial to a greater degree. This results in her appearing to be more unyielding, and thus holding on to her original perception of herself. Due to these patterns of hers, the children, in the first phase of treatment, may have been somewhat less free to communicate to her their reactions and feelings towards her than they were with their father, resulting in less free communication which in turn resulted in less change in her perception of herself.

The daughter had the largest discrepancy between her self-description and the perception of her by the others, a total of 26 points on both scales in the post-treatment ratings. This discrepancy is now even greater than the marked discrepancy which occurred in the pre-treatment ratings. She perceives herself to an extreme degree as more loving and more dominant than the others perceive her. We would question the authenticity of this description of herself, if only because the rest of the family markedly disagrees with it. In addition, it is not in accord with the impression of the therapy team, and must be considered as a denial or an unrealistic attitude on her part.

The parents now perceive their daughter as being considerably less loving and positive than they perceived her to be in the beginning. The therapy uncovered her internal conflicts and the hostile-aggressive feelings associated with them, which the parents had not wanted to see before. In the pre-treatment phase the parents were prone to see her as the cute, acting-up little girl and to ignore the amount of aggression and hostility implicit in her behavior and attitudes; in a sense, she got away with murder. Now, in the post-treatment phase, the parents see her as she actually is and more consonant with the way the therapists see her.

We are reminded here of the psychodynamic formulation that the therapy team developed regarding the shared unconscious family fantasy in which the daughter symbolized the family penis. This might be considered consistent with her viewing herself as the most dominant in the family, as the family's source of power. In the post-treatment rating she rated herself highest on both scales, as did the father. This might suggest that a competition had developed between the two for leadership and power in the family. The father had begun during the treatment to discipline and control her in a direct and decisive manner and to a much greater extent than he had done previously. She was apparently not yet capitulating, or accepting this, in her mind, even if she found it necessary to submit in superficial behavior.

If, however, the family still perceives the daughter unconsciously as the family penis, or family id—in the event that this intrapsychic distortion is not yet sufficiently uncovered and worked through—then her description of herself on the ICL is in one sense valid. The parents may have changed their conscious attitudes towards her behavior, and may even criticize and try to control her overt aggressive and libidinized actions, but they still need her to some extent to act out their own repressed wishes. This method of conceptualizing our data follows the formulation of Johnson and Szurek[59] in which superego lacunae in the parents permit and encourage the child's acting out.

Family's Perception of Therapists

The family members rated each member of the co-therapy team pre- and post-treatment on the same 128 ICL trait items on which they rated each other. These initial ratings were made after the family had had two sessions with the therapists, and obviously could not be based on adequate observation or much objective data. In a sense the ratings were like a projective test in which the family members were required to guess at the personalities of the therapists. Several changes of interest occurred in the family members' perceptions of the therapists: the father originally saw the female co-therapist as more dominant than the male co-therapist, but in the post-testing he saw the male therapist as more dominant. This change paralleled the changes in his perception of himself, and the changes he saw in his marital relationship between himself and his wife. Similarly, the son's perception of the change in the female therapist paralleled his perception of the change in his mother. He saw a large increase on the love scale for the female therapist, just as he saw a smaller increase for his mother.

It follows from the principle of neurotic transference distortion that the therapists are not seen realistically at all in the beginning phase of treatment, but as the transference distortions become gradually corrected during treatment, the patient's perception of the therapists approximates their real personalities more closely. These results may be considered to represent one of the first quantified documentations of the transference phenomenon on record.

Family Participation Index

This index lists 20 types of activities and the respondent indicates the frequency with which he engages in them, and if so, whether alone or with other family members or friends whom he designates by use of appropriate symbols.

In our original plan of using the Family Participation Index as a measure of change in family relationships, we had two general hypotheses: 1) that there would be an increase in the number of activities in which family members participated together; and 2) that following treatment there would be more congruent perception by the various family members of what kind of activity actually occurred in the family, and which family members participated together. The changes that occurred in the Ichabod family were in general consistent with these two hypotheses, although with some minor variations. The father showed the greatest increase in activities with all members of the family. One of the frequent complaints by the family in the beginning of treatment had been that father had removed himself from the family. Mother reported herself as somewhat more involved in activities with father towards the end of treatment, and to have become less involved in activities with both children. This too was consistent with what we had seen in treatment: that she became less involved with the children as she became more involved libidinally, and in activities with her husband. There was also marked lessening of involvement between the siblings. This was also reflected in the T.A.T. story of the son, and was considered a positive development since their initial involvement was seen by all to be excessive, conflictual and pathological.

According to father's perception there was an increase of 33% in his activities. There was an increase of 23% in the activities in which he engaged with his wife, 19% in those with his daughter, and 33% in those with his son. The total of these latter three increases of participation is 75%. It is greater than the 33% recorded as increase in his activities because it reflects not only the different activities, but also the increased number of family members involved with him in these new activities.

Mother reported herself on post-treatment as engaging in the same number of activities with her daughter; she also listed a decrease of 16% in activities she shared with her son, and a small increase in activities with her husband. The daughter saw herself as engaging in about the same number of activities with both father and brother as she had previously, and reported a decrease of 16% in activities with her mother. The son saw himself participating in about the same number of activities with mother and father, but noted a decrease of 22% in activities with his sister. It appeared that father and daughter were the most isolated when treatment of the family began, and that father made the greatest change, going from 23% of the activities listed to 57%. The daughter remained relatively isolated. This is consistent with the observation during treatment that she had gained the least from the treatment process.

In reference to the second hypothesis pertaining to the discrepancies between family members in their reporting of family activity, the hypothesis stated that following treatment there would be less discrepancies in the perception of activities shared with one another than at the beginning of treatment. At pre-treatment there were four discrepancies noted in the number of activities reported to be engaged in jointly by dyads (between father and mother, father and daughter, father and son, and son and daughter.) At the end of treatment there was only one such discrepancy, and that was between mother and daughter. This was now the only dyadic combination in which one member reported participating in an activity with the other, and the other did not independently corroborate this participation. The relationship between mother and daughter was, of all the dyadic relationships in the family, the one least worked on in treatment and considered to be least improved by the team. Thus, our second hypothesis regarding family change as measured by the Family Participation Index has received a moderate degree of support.

Projective Test Responses

There was a comprehensive projective testing of each family member before treatment started. There has however been only a limited amount of projctive testing of this family at this post-treatment stage. Card III of Rorschach and Card 10 of the T.A.T. are among the few test stimulus materials which have been readministered. We are pleased to find that the responses of the family members to just these two test stimuli contain some substantial data relevant to our purpose.

We shall first list the pre-treatment and post-treatment responses to Card III of the Rorschach, and then make some observations on the changes in response which have occurred. The post-treatment responses are briefer, since they were written by the subject in a family group-test procedure, while the pre-treatment tests were individually administered.

We observed from the aforegoing protocols that three of the four members of the family showed a definite change in the quality of their human responses to Card III of the Rorschach, in that they gave responses on post-testing of two persons spontaneously doing something, in an

Rorschach Card III Responses

Father's Pre-Treatment

1) Couple of marionettes—two figures made out of connected pieces of wood —like those things they use to teach sculpture
2) The couple of red splotches or curves look like blotched monkeys or parrot or something
3) A rumpled up bow tie in the middle, that's about all.

Father's Post-Treatment

1) This shows two girls dancing back to back
2) A view in a microscope of a tissue section.
3) A look down an animal's throat
4) Inverted (V) two dancers face to face

Mother's Pre-Treatment

1) Two people facing each other over something. Women—but lower portion looks like part of a back bone and two kidneys
2) (V) Like an optical illusion—like a heavy man, fat stomach with arms up
3) (V) Two grey portions look like some sort of animals, with mouths open. Would almost be natives—Ubangi's with bracelets; mouth and eye, very elongated heads
4) These look like arms—pointing—just by selves
5) These two red are similar to two sea horses—I can't find definite sex symbol

Mother's Post-Treatment

1) Two women facing each other
2) Large skeleton-like grinning face
3) Upside down it looks like a giant bug

Son's Pre-Treatment

1) . . . . two people holding on to a crab—crab is in the middle—that's all . . .

Son's Post-Treatment

1) Two people playing bongo drums
2) Two girls pulling at the legs of a crab
3) A big bug
4) A crab with his hands in front of him

Daughter's Pre-Treatment

1) Oh, I see two people holding on to something—each half is a separate person

Daughter's Post-Treatment

1) Two people taking bowling balls
2) Two girls

2) This looks like sea horse—2 red blotches

3) Middle looks like bow tie

4) Upside down looks like two other people with feet tied to a wheel. They have feet in a wheel and could roll down hill.

3) A girl stirring something

4) A dribbly inkblot

active rather than passive position. In two of these three cases the responses were of two persons acting together or cooperatively, which is considered to be the ideal response. These post-testing human responses were different from the original pre-testing responses in which the human figures were either lifeless, such as "wooden marionettes," or were just two persons facing each other, without spontaneous action; or as in the remaining two cases where there had been life and action but the persons were in the passive role. These latter two responses were those of the children in the family. The daughter's pre-testing response of "persons holding on to each other" is a passive, clinging, dependent response which she then followed by the statement "they are two separate persons," emphasizing the effort required to achieve an adequate differentiation of self and to relate on a mature, independent basis. The son also gave a human response which was passive and dependent, i.e., "persons holding on to a crab." This response became more active in the post-testing and appeared in the following form: "two girls pulling on the leg of a crab."

The daughter gave an additional passive-dependent response involving two human figures which disappeared on post-testing. This response was "upside down it looks like two other people with feet tied to a wheel— they have feet in a wheel and could roll down hill." The symbiotic, hopeless bind in which the two family members were trapped together could hardly have been better characterized than by this response.

Thus, the human responses to Card III of three of the four members of the family improved on post-testing, according to usually accepted criteria. In the case of the fourth member of the family, the mother, the human responses on post-testing remained essentially the same as on pre-testing, that is "two women facing each other." But even in this case there was a slight improvement in the post-testing in that she spontaneously identified the sex of the two human figures as "two women," whereas in the pre-testing she first responded "two people facing each other," and somewhat later identified them as "two women."

As an example of the improvement reflected in the T.A.T. productions we shall present the stories to Card 10 as told by the father and the son, pre- and post-treatment. (Card 10 shows a woman's and a man's head, with the woman's head against the man's shoulder.) In a number of ways these stories show a striking improvement in their perception of heterosexual relationships:

T.A.T. Card 10

Father's Pre-Treatment

"A lovey-dovey scene—I mean, I can build a story around it. They're in a railroad station and he's been drafted and they're embracing before he has to leave."

Father's Post-Treatment

"This picture shows a man comforting his wife. Something troubled her during the day and when her husband came home, she told him of her problem. He is holding her close to let her feel she is not alone. She is drawing comfort from the sharing of the trouble and the calm reassurance her husband offers. Together they can stand much more than each alone."

Son's Pre-Treatment

"A notorious gangster had a very beautiful sister. When he attended parties he always took his sister with him. At one party he was shot by a rival. She looked away in horror, and cried on her fiance's shoulder. After the gangster's funeral, he was forgotten and put out of everyone's mind."

Son's Post-Treatment

"The boy and girl were sweethearts all through college; when they finally graduated they were so joyful they celebrated and had a party. When everyone left they were alone and he took her for a walk in the moonlight, then he took her in his arms and kissed her and asked her to marry him. She did and they lived happily ever after. They were very happy together."

We note that the father's early story is devoid of feeling and implies a sneering attitude when he says that this is a "lovey-dovey scene." He doesn't state who the characters are in the story, but just that "they're in a railroad station and he has been drafted, and they are embracing before he has to leave." In the later story there are many verbs expressing feelings between a man and a wife. For example, "there is a man comforting his wife," "something troubled her," "he is holding her close to let her feel she is not alone," "she is drawing comfort from the sharing of the trouble," and "together they can stand much more than each alone." Not only is there a much greater degree of feeling involved in this story, but there is a stress on the mutuality of the relationship in which he sees a husband as one who can comfort and reassure his wife.

The theme of the son's pre-treatment story does not come as a surprise to us, in that his pathological incestuous involvement with his sister was considered one of the main problems in this family. The "hero" of this story is a gangster which in itself is not too wholesome. His incestuous relationship with his sister could only end disastrously, as it does in the story, and prevent him from going on to lead a more normal satisfying life.

In the son's post-treatment story the theme of violence, horror and death drops out, and the relationship instead of being between brother and sister is between a boy and girl who are sweethearts, who have graduated from college and anticipate being married and living happily together. The incestuous theme is gone, allowing the son to enjoy a more normal, heterosexual relationship which instead of ending disastrously, ends in anticipation of a future which he can share with a woman. Whereas the first story revealed a great deal of pathology insofar as possible anti-social behavior and more morbid anticipation of disaster is concerned, the second story is a healthy one, implying the ability to enjoy a heterosexual relationship.

Family Therapy Observation Rating Scale

In a systematic study of the process of the therapy conducted with this family, six staff members observed the weekly sessions through a one-way screen. Immediately after each session, all eight staff members, including the two members of the therapy team, independently completed structured rating scales relating to various process features of the therapy session. (*See* "Family Therapy Observation Rating Scale" in the Appendix.) These features are the emotional climate of a session; principal lines of verbal and non-verbal communication; cliques and alliances between family members and therapists; order of liking of the family members by the observers; degree of emotional involvement of each family member in the therapy; and the selection of the most positive and most negative critical therapeutic incident of the session.

We shall report here an analysis of the ratings made on two of the features: the order of liking of the family members by the observers, and the principle lines of communication in the family interaction. This report is based on 80 ratings, completed by the eight observers for each of ten therapy sessions conducted early during the first few months of treatment.

Therapists' Ranking of Family Members

We consider the real feelings of the therapists a factor not to be ignored, but to be used properly in the conduct of family therapy. We have therefore included in our rating scales a ranking of the members of the family after each session, according to the order in which the observers and therapists found them to be likeable. An interesting finding here is that the male therapist gave the mother in the family a higher ranking than did any of the other seven raters. He was the only one who rated her, over the sessions, as the most likeable of the four members of the family. This may be a fortuitous circumstance. In all too many of our schizophrenic families the mother is the least liked member, the least supported, and most confronted and challenged by the therapists. Perhaps for these reasons she is often likely to block or terminate the family therapy. As it is difficult to support someone you do not like, it is good that the male therapist finds the mother likeable. In complementary fashion, the female therapist finds the father to be most likeable. This should add a balanced healthy heterosexual tone to the therapeutic transference complex. All six observers agree that the father is most likeable. There is general agreement that the two children are less likeable than the two parents. (This has been partially explained in the previous section as related to the fact that they verbalize less and contribute less to the therapy sessions.) The schizophrenic male patient and his younger sister were ranked as about equal in likeability by the six observers. The therapy team however, ranked the male patient as somewhat less likeable than his sister; perhaps because he did not respond to their very strenuous efforts to get him to express his feelings.

Lines of Communication

There was a very high degree of agreement (95%) on the person who was the main center of focus of the communication in any particular session. This indicates that although a dyadic or total family relationship was being explored, one member usually took the lead in exploring the problem, or had the central role in the problem assigned to him by the consensus. In this family, it was usually father or mother, sometimes daughter, but never the primary patient who took the central or leading role.

There was also a rather high degree of agreement (87%) on the composition of cliques and alliances which were observed in the family, in spite of the fact that the alignments shifted from session to session. The therapists were frequently included in these alignments as supporting one family member against another. The mother significantly more often than anyone else had two or more family members or therapists aligned against her. While she occasionally had her daughter or a therapist allied with her, she never had her husband or son allied with her sufficiently long for this to be rated as one of the main alignments during a session.

In the early sessions the daughter was allied with the mother and there was a split in the family between the male and female members. As the father began to assert himself more during the course of therapy, and take more of an interest in the children, his little daughter moved closer to him. This apparently left the mother more isolated, except for the fact that she and her husband were beginning to move close to each other.

While many other measures and tests were employed in this study, we believe that the above analysis—probably the most detailed and comprehensive one of this type that has been reported to date—will suffice to demonstrate the potentialities as well as the limitations of such a quantitative family analysis.

Quantitative Data on a Group of Families

As one example of how our quantitative evaluative data is employed on a group basis, we shall present here conclusions from the results of the Family Participation Index with the first seven families treated.

In Table 8-3 we have computed the percentages of the 20 types of activities which each member of Family A indicated he engaged in alone

Table 8-3 PERCENTAGE OF CHANGE REPORTED IN PARTICIPATION IN 20 ACTIVITY AREAS BY FAMILY MEMBERS INITIALLY AND IN FOLLOW-UP

	Percentage of 20 Activities		
	Initial	Follow-Up 1st	2nd
1. Report by *Father* with:			
a. self alone	55	70	＊
b. daughter (primary patient)	35	35	50
c. wife	50	60	55
d. son	55	75	60
e. other relatives	0	0	20
f. friends	0	0	15
2. Report by *Mother* with:			
a. self alone	35	10	40
b. daughter	25	20	35
c. husband	40	35	50
d. son	30	30	40
e. other relatives	0	0	0
f. friends	0	0	5
3. Report by *Daughter* (primary patient) with:			
a. self alone	15	40	40
b. mother	20	40	40
c. father	30	25	50
d. brother	55	35	55
e. other relatives	5	0	0
f. friends	45	0	35
4. Report by *Brother* with:			
a. self alone	90	85	95
b. mother	15	30	35
c. father	30	30	45
d. sister	55	30	55
e. other relatives	5	5	0
f. friends	70	50	60

＊No information given

or with other family members. For example, the father initially checked 7 of 20 activities (35%) in which he engaged with his daughter (the primary patient). Column 2 shows that at the initial follow-up, nine months later, he still checked 7 of the 20 activities (35%). At the time of the second follow-up, another eight months later, he reported an increase in activity with the primary patient (50%).

Our conclusions, based on this type of analysis of the changes in the self-reported activities of the first seven families, are as follows. 1) Some families are considerably more active initially within the home, both in regard to individual activity and in regard to shared activity, than are others. 2) The greatest changes appear to relate to a person's individual activity rather than to interpersonal relationship between family members. 3) Most active are siblings other than the primary patient in the three families. 4) Most of the parents when initially tested did not even indicate that they were participating in any activities at all with other relatives, or with friends. This is consistent with the clinical experience with many of these families indicating the extreme isolation of the parents from associates outside the family. 5) There was no clear trend to support the hypothesis that a decrease would occur after treatment, in the discrepancies between the various family members' perceptions of their shared activities. This hoped for decrease in discrepancies occurred in the ratings of most of the families, but not in the others.

The above conclusions are to be considered as preliminary observations or trends in the data rather than as hard research data, since they are not all based on tests of statistical significance.

The Clinician's views regarding therapeutic

movement, and the reliability of his observations

regarding communication

George Spivack

Chapter
9

As is true of most relatively new treatment approaches, initial experience and insights derive from intense clinical observation of cases. From such experience there evolves not only theory, but specific hypotheses that attempt to define the significant parameters at work. Research methodology then becomes necessary in order to solidify and reliably articulate what is happening and what one should do to achieve certain ends.

During the initial stages of the project no attempt was made to structure rigidly our therapeutic methods or our means of observation. We felt it more appropriate to explore freely and speculate, to inform ourselves of the work of others and actively to exchange our views and share our experiences regarding families in treatment during (and frequently in between) weekly project conferences.

In retrospect, this approach has proved fruitful on many grounds. Our views shifted, initial biases in approach to therapy were challenged if not drastically revamped, and project members felt free to criticize, formulate and discard habits developed in other therapeutic contexts. At the same time, however, it became obvious that case discussions repeatedly focused much attention on communication patterns. Involved in intense family interchange, therapists reflected upon their feelings towards one or more family members. Questions and differences of opinion arose among team members as to significant positive therapeutic events during a session and the nature of family resistances.

These consistencies led to an initial attempt to study ourselves in operation. Since we discussed and debated whether this or that approach to a specific family during a specific session was productive of "positive" therapeutic movement, we had to ask ourselves what was positive therapeutic movement in our eyes and what events seemed to precipitate such movement? Similarly, what events during a session were taken as indicative of "locked" movement, and what events precipitated these?

How reliable were our observations of what transpired during a session?
During the usual weekly project meeting co-therapists would "present"
a family for discussion, but only they had seen the family in action.
Would the other project members have made the same observations as
to the significance of what transpired?

An opportunity arose to attempt at least a pilot exploration of these
questions during the third year of the project. The decision to compare
family treatment in the home and in the clinic provided the opportunity
to have the sessions of one family carried out in a one-way observation
room in the research institute. Thus, not only could a series of sessions
be taped for other purposes, but all project team members could observe
sessions in progress through the one-way glass and make judgments
regarding the session along with the family's therapists. For feasibility
reasons it was necessary to construct techniques that would be brief and
easy to use, and yet provide answers to questions of interest. Following
some discussion, it was decided to focus mainly on two questions:
1) What do reasonably experienced clinicians see as indicative of positive
therapeutic movement during a family session, what do they see as
indicative of interference or blocking of therapeutic movement, and what
do they see as precipitating such events; and 2) how reliable are the
observations of reasonably experienced clinicians as to the principal lines
of communication during a session.

To answer the first question it was decided to employ a "critical incidents" approach. This would afford maximum latitude of expression of
opinion, and avoid premature structuring of our thinking. Following each
observed session, both family therapists and all observing project members independently responded to the following statements: 1) Describe
in some detail the incident in this session that was most indicative of
positive therapeutic movement; 2) describe what you think precipitated
or facilitated this positive movement, and check on the line below the
confidence you feel in this judgment (these ratings were made on a
5-point scale of confidence); 3) describe in some detail the incident in
this session that seemed to block or interfere with positive therapeutic
movement (e.g., main resistance); 4) describe what you think precipitated or facilitated this blocking or interference, and check on the line
below the confidence you feel in this judgment.

To assess the reliability of observations after each session observed,
two questions were asked of each observer regarding communication
during the session. They were: 1) to indicate the principal lines of verbal
communication among the participants (family members and co-therapists) observed during the session; and 2) to indicate the principal lines
of non-verbal communication (i.e., all levels of behavior exclusive of
actual verbal communication) among the participants (family members
and co-therapists) observed during the session. Each observer also

ranked the family members in terms of how much the observer "liked" them upon observing their behavior during the session.

The family observed consisted of parents, a teen-age son (the primary patient) and a latency age daughter. Fortunately, both parents were verbal individuals, with the son being somewhat reticent though quite capable of self-expression, and the daughter a physically active and bright youngster. Observations were made of ten family sessions over a six-month period during initial stages of therapy. From six to eight observers rated each session, including the co-therapists. All questions for each session were answered immediately following the session, prior to a discussion of the session. The analyses below are, then, specific to this particular family and the period during which the observations were made. These two factors, among others, must be considered as serious limits to any generalization one might wish to make but the results are suggestive and at least in part encouraging of further work along these lines.

CRITICAL INCIDENTS

Nature of Incidents Indicative of Positive Therapeutic Movement

The most frequent incident noted was one wherein one family member expressed a feeling (need) or opinion regarding current family inter-action, or admitted to feeling or was willing to explore an area of family interaction, and this member's activity implicated other family members (46% of instances). There appeared to be as much chance that all family members were implicated in the expression of feeling or opinion as two or three, and during the series of sessions considered there was no ten-dency through time for dyadic, triadic, or total family interactions to become more or less significant. Interestingly, seldom was a family mem-ber's "insight," as distinct from feeling or opinion, regarding current family interaction specified, although in a few instances (5%) a family member's insight into family interaction was noted. Clearly, the observers focused mainly on active interactional expression of feeling and desire as the most crucial factor to explore in the family setting.

The second most frequent gauge of positive movement was the will-ingness or attempt of a family member (i.e., parent) to assume a "posi-tive" family role (14%). In this family it related mainly to father, and interestingly there was more than usual agreement between observers as to what was "positive" when this issue became the focus in the therapy. It would appear that father's assuming a dominant role, even though it may have been out of "unhealthy" or unresolved intrapsychic issues, was judged as "good."

In less than 1% of instances was a "general family atmosphere" or emotional "outburst" noted as indicating positive movement. Possibly, emotional "outbursts" rarely occurred in this family, and the one instance when it was noted also involved the father's assuming a leadership role. It was rare for the observers to articulate family interaction at the conceptual level of "atmosphere," focusing instead on individual expression and interaction.

In 15% of instances noted, a non-verbal communication was noted as part of a positive incident. However, such communication was never noted alone as indicative of positive movement. Considering the frequent mention of such communication in other parts of the rating schedule and during team meetings, the possibility arises that whereas such communication allows for interpretation of family dynamics, it itself is seldom judged as "good" in the sense of family therapy movement. At least with this family, *verbal* expression which implicated other family members was most highly valued by observers as indicative of positive movement.

In only 27% of incidents was expression of feeling about or willingness to explore intrapsychic issues noted as a "positive" incident, and seldom independent of issues pertaining to current family interaction. Of great interest is the fact that in the two sessions where intrapsychic issues in one or more family members were noted in connection with positive movement, one or both therapists entered into the picture more dramatically than usual. In one instance, the therapists were involved in a significant interaction (as transference objects), and in the other a therapist's interpretation was noted as a significant ingredient of the positive incident. What this may mean is not clear. Perhaps the observers were more able to articulate or are more confident in their perceptions of the relationship between the therapists' role and intrapsychic phenomena in a family member, than between therapist role and family interactional phenomena.

Factors That Precipitate or Facilitate the Positive Incident

The experts most frequently viewed positive movement as resulting directly from the activity of one or both therapists (66% of instances). In 15% of these instances, the positive incident followed upon a therapist's interpretation; in 17% it followed upon the therapists' support of one or more members; in another 17% it followed upon the therapists' persistence in focusing upon an issue or actively confronting the family or a family member. In 10% of instances, the therapists' assuming a role or roles and their having paid a previous visit to the family's home were seen as precipitating positive movement. The remaining 7% consisted of instances wherein a therapist's feelings facilitated movement, or a question was asked or observation made at the right moment.

RELIABILITY OF OBSERVATIONS REGARDING
PRINCIPAL LINES OF COMMUNICATION

Verbal Communication

Since there were four family members and two therapists present in each session, and verbal communications observed were most frequently expressed in dyadic terms, reliability of the observations had to take into account the fact that fifteen communication pairs were possible. For each session, tabulation was made of the percent of observers specifying each possible pair of individuals as engaged in a principal verbal communication link. For each of the ten sessions, these percentages ranged from zero to 100 (both of these considered as perfect or 100% agreement). The percent agreement over the ten sessions ranged from 50% to 100%, the median being 87%.

Although this percent of agreement seemed encouraging, the question arose as to whether it may be dependent upon the number of principal verbal communications noted by the various observers during a session. Under the "open" write-in procedure employed, an observer might judge that two, three, or more principal lines of verbal communication were manifest. One might argue that, at least up to a certain point, the greater the number of communication pairs noted, the greater the likelihood of agreement on one or more pairs. Taken to its extreme, if every observer judged all fifteen communication pairs as important, there would be perfect agreement!

Analysis of the number of principal communication pairs noted by each observer for each session indicated that usually far fewer than fifteen pairs were felt important. The median number noted over the ten sessions was three, with a range from one to eight. However, to check on the possibility of such an artifact in operation, a rank order correlation was calculated between agreement percentage for each session and the median number of principal verbal communication pairs noted by the observers. The rho was insignificant, indicating that the observed reliability of observations regarding principal lines of verbal communication was not dependent upon the number of communications submitted by the observers. (The obtained rho of —.36 did not approach statistical significance, and is probably inflated since no correction was made for tied ranks.)

Non-Verbal Communication

A similar analysis of percent agreement among observers was made for non-verbal dyadic communications. A median of 100% agreement for the ten sessions suggested an artifact at work, and further analysis revealed that observers noted fewer non-verbal than verbal principal lines of communication (a median of two in contrast to three for verbal communications). In this instance, agreement more frequently took the form of a consensus that *no* principal non-verbal communications occurred between *most* pairs of participants. It was further noted that in approximately two-thirds of the principal non-verbal communications, one family member— the daughter—was most actively engaged. It would seem that while non-verbal communication may be an important facet of interaction, this finding supports the critical incident findings, suggesting greater appreciation of verbal than non-verbal modes of interpersonal expression. It is also possible that the family being observed did not "emit" the frequency of non-verbal cues that one might find in other families. One at least can say, from the present data, that all observers agreed on the *absence* of principal non-verbal communication, and were in reasonable agreement as to who was the focus of such communication when it occurred.

Considering the importance of reliability of observation, a further check was made. An analysis, similar to that described above, was made of eight sessions during the four-month period following the previously mentioned observation period. Again, tabulation was made of the percent of observers specifying each of the possible fifteen pairs of individuals as involved in a principal verbal interchange. The median percent agreement over these eight sessions was 100. It was also noted that in seven of the eight sessions, there was agreement among *all* observers on at least one dyad as involved in a principal line of verbal communication. A check back indicated this was true in only four of the ten sessions examined earlier, suggesting possible improvement in reliability with the passage of time and/or experience with the observation procedures.

A new item to be filled out by all observers had been added to the observation forms for these eight sessions, and tabulation of the responses to this item further spells out the reliability data. Each observer was asked to "indicate the person or persons about whom the communication network appeared to revolve during this session . . . communication network is defined here to include both verbal and non-verbal behavioral observations." Only one individual, dyad, or triad, etc. was asked of each observer for each session. Clearly, the number of possible combinations, statistically speaking, is large. Considering only individuals, dyadic and triadic combinations, there were 61 possible focuses of communication. The nature of agreement between judges can best be presented by giving the actual results. In the first session of this series (seven observers), five observers noted father, and two observers the father-male therapist interaction; in the second session (eight observers), four observers noted the daughter, two the daughter-mother interaction, one the daughter-father interaction, and one the father alone; in the third session (seven observers), five observers noted the mother-daughter interaction, and two the daughter alone; in the fourth session (eight observers), four noted the mother-father-daughter interaction, three noted the mother alone, and one the mother-daughter interaction; in the fifth session (eight observers), seven observers noted the father, and one noted the father-mother interaction; in the sixth session (seven observers), all observers noted the mother alone; in the seventh session (seven observers), six observers noted father, and one noted the father-mother-both therapists interchange; and in the eighth session (six observers), four observers noted the mother-father interchange, one the father, and one the mother. Considering the number of choices possible, agreement among observers seems quite reasonable. In seven of the eight sessions, the same family member is mentioned by all observers as involved in a focus of verbal and/or non-verbal communication.

No analysis was made of non-verbal communication since initial observation of the data suggested a repetition of the earlier findings, indicating that the daughter, either alone or with one other family member, dominated the instances noted.

Concluding Remarks

As has been suggested earlier, the data obtained must be considered in the light of limitations in sampling, and as merely suggestive. The sampling of observations derived from an interest in self-observation and a pilot attempt to obtain some objective data as to our mode of operation. It is offered as one element in a total report rather than as evidence for assuming one or another therapeutic posture. Nevertheless, the data reflect the opinions and operation of a group of experienced clinicians who had worked together over a long period of time and shared experiences with a particular technique. For these reasons the data may be of interest.

The data suggest that active verbal interaction at a feeling level among family members, the willingness or ability to interact emotionally, is highly valued by therapists and is construed as an encouraging sign as far as therapeutic progress is concerned. Apparently, while one might conceptualize a family structure in other terms, the therapeutic enterprise itself is seen in the "flesh and bones" context of interweaving emotions and fantasies that are shared by family members. Just as one family member may precipitate or act as a catalyst to therapeutic movement, one member also may block movement, for the family moves as an interacting system wherein one element may affect all other elements. Most striking is the suggestion that active engagement by the therapists in the therapeutic enterprise is crucial. Frequently this may take a form which would be considered overinvolved or overdirective in other therapeutic contexts. In the present instance, such engagement is felt to lead to positive results as well as blockage of movement. In both cases, its potency is clear as far as judged family response is concerned. As "closed" as the family system may at first appear, the therapist soon finds himself included, whether he likes it or not.

Yet despite the complex interpersonal system at work, the data suggest that observation of what goes on may be objectified and shared. The least that can be said is that experienced clinicians, after working together, can reasonably agree on certain important therapeutic transactions and apply the same labels to them. To what extent this is true, and whether or not this is mere consensus about an illusion, must await more exacting data collection.

Clinical assessment of improvement

Alfred S. Friedman

Changes in Family Functioning

Members of our family therapy staff group have treated well over a hundred families by now, most of whom had an adolescent or young adult schizophrenic member. This would have been a sufficient sample from which to draw some meaningful statistical conclusions, if we had been able to establish the necessary scientific controls by evaluating a sample of comparable schizophrenic families who either had received no treatment or some other form of treatment. We have not been able, however, to achieve such a controlled assessment of the effects of family treatment, nor, to our knowledge, has anyone else. We shall resort therefore, to our clinical impressions and to reports made by the families themselves, in an attempt to appraise the results of our therapeutic endeavor with the families.

We shall present some examples of clinical and social improvement which have occurred. These are not presented as strictly representative; and having occurred without the benefit of experimental controls, they cannot be demonstrated to be the result of family treatment alone. A follow-up evaluation of the families at six months and at a year after termination of therapy could well give us a clearer impression of the results of the therapy than we have today. The families at that point also may be better able to see themselves in perspective.

It is our subjective impression that all the families who were in treatment gained something of importance from the therapeutic enterprise. Excluded from this generalization would be only those families who terminated after one or several sessions, and who never really accepted the idea of family treatment in the first place. These were usually families where one of the parents came to the family sessions in order to maneuver some other member into treatment, or to try to get the therapy team to make that other member behave in a certain way. As soon as it became clear that the therapy team would not play such a game and could not be readily controlled, the controlling parent would terminate the family treatment. Usually this decision to terminate was not expressed directly and openly; instead, the more dominant, controlling parent would maneuver the spouse who may have been ambivalent about the treatment to make the first move to terminate.

When we say all the other families gained something of importance in our subjective impression, we are not speaking of so-called "cures," or implying that the family no longer has any serious problems, or even that a basic structural change has occurred in the family system. We usually saw a type of improvement that was less basic or global, and sometimes an improvement that was not very dramatic or obvious. Nevertheless, a few families did experience fundamental and dramatic change. The foregoing case histories of family treatment show clearly that the improvements in the family were hard to come by and that they occurred in slow, arduous steps. These case histories incidentally were not selected to show only examples of good results, but are rather fairly representative of the kind of progress, and also of lack of progress, which we made with the schizophrenic families in our sample.

The types of results we are referring to here are for example: the return to school of an adolescent member who had dropped out of school; improvement in vocational and social functioning; relief from anxiety, internal discomfort, hostile tension and depression; giving up delusional ideas and somatic preoccupations; experiencing new insights; understanding pathological family patterns; changes in intrafamily role relationships and task assignments; improvement in the family emotional relationship and communication; and an attitude of hopefulness in place of earlier resignation.

Our experience indicates that any family member—whether a parent, a sibling, or the patient—is as likely as any other to change or to profit from the family therapy. Any family member may be the first to begin changing and improving his pattern of interaction, his role relationships. Most often it has appeared to us that the first to change is the one who in our opinion is the strongest member, the one with the best ego assets, the least rigid defenses, and who is most flexible. This member would at the same time be the one most likely to develop a positive transference to the therapist. After one member has changed, it is easier for other members to change their patterns. However, if a second member does not soon begin to respond and make a real effort to change, the first one who already showed some progress is liable to relapse back to the original pattern.

We have also observed that changes in general family function and interaction are as likely to occur as is improvement in the independent social adjustment of the individual members outside the home. The family changes that we have had the best opportunity to observe are those that occurred in their behavior in the therapy sessions. These have been changes specifically from sterile, indirect forms of interaction, characterized in the beginning by gross denial, to a more direct, open and genuine affective interaction; and from vague, meaningless and contradictory communications to clearer and more effective communications. We have often, in the early phase of treatment, seen family members change from a state of passive withdrawal, indifference and resignation in their relationship to each other to one where they express anger, disagreement, and complaints, as well as the desires and the frustrations in their efforts to reach each other. Sometimes anger and disagreement that had been suppressed in the family for many years, and had been prohibited and denied by mechanisms of pseudo-mutuality and brain washing, now became released. There then ensued a second phase of treatment in which the primitive rage, the destructive impulses and fantasies were expressed in a series of chaotic family sessions until they were worked through and brought under control. The families did not quit treatment during these disturbed painful periods as long as they were helped to work on their frustrated desires and anger toward each other, and not permitted to project these onto the therapists.

Sometimes these changes in quality and quantity of affect and communication, which we consider indicative of movement and improvement in family relationship, occurred rather quickly and with quite dramatic, extreme shifts in the interaction pattern; sometimes they were slow, almost imperceptible or minor in degree. It is our observation however, that some degree of such change in the quality of affective communication has occurred in all families that have been in treatment for more than a few sessions.

In some families, the most obvious significant development was a closer and more satisfactory marriage relationship between the parental pairs. This was usually followed by an increase in genuine affective interaction and communication between all family members. As the schism in the marriage was repaired, and the distant relationship of the parents gave way to some affectional, emotional and sexual contact, the children were also able to express their feelings more directly and spontaneously. The children, on one level, liked to see more love between their parents; but on another level—particularly if there had been an excessively close bond between a child and the mother which had excluded the father—that child now became fearful of losing his mother to the father. The child now either tried to sabotage the development of the new marital relationship, or withdrew and regressed into illness. This new phase in the family relationship had to be dealt with in the family therapy. If the parents held firm to the gains of their new-found marriage relationship, the child was reassured that the change was good for him too. In families where we could not alter the basic quality of the marriage relationship, overall family improvement was less substantial.

Following are several examples of the types of social and clinical improvement which have occurred. They are taken from families *other* than those whose case histories have already been presented.

The treatment of one of our earliest families was terminated after nine months of weekly therapy sessions, when three of the four family members had shown clear evidence of progress, and when reasonable goals of treatment appeared to have been achieved. The eighteen-year-old schizophrenic younger son had originally engaged in the bizarre behavior of phoning the Fire Department to report that his older brother was having sex relations with a girl friend; and he had the delusional idea that a fly had flown into his mouth and had eaten out vital parts of his insides. After nine months this patient became a more assertive, confident member of the family and spoke for himself and his family in stating that they felt ready to see how they would do on their own without therapy. He had started on a job, liked it and the people he worked with, and was able to make decisions. He laughed off the fantasy about the fly as a ridiculous notion he had. The father reported for himself that he was less tense, slept better, and no longer dwelled excessively on his daughter who had died many years ago, as he had previously been doing. The mother agreed to this and added that he yelled a lot less than he used to do. Father was going out socially now with the two boys and doing things for them. Mother had shown a lesser amount of change, but felt that she was expressing herself somewhat more freely (she had been quite unresponsive), was taking more of an interest in the others, and giving more. All members agreed that they were now able to communicate more readily and were more willing to listen to each other. They also agreed on each member's evaluation of the way he had changed. The home, which had been very neglected and had deteriorated, underwent a striking improvement in decoration and maintenance.

The therapy team felt that the four members of this quite dependent family were now able to give each other more love and support, and to get more of their satisfactions from outside the home. Perhaps a dependency "transference cure" had occurred in the therapy.

The older son showed the least improvement. In the face of the striking, rapid improvement in the patient, he now appeared to be the focus of the remaining family weakness and problem. He no longer had as frequent hypochondriacal exacerbations, which occurred with such anxiety that he demanded immediate hospitalization, but he still had anxiety reactions, and he contacted the team in an effort to get more help a year after the termination of the family therapy.

The changes in the ratings on the Family Participation Index independently reflected this significant movement of the family in a positive direction. Both of the sons, and particularly the patient, now rated themselves as considerably more active in the community. The whole family had maintained only the minimum necessary social contact before therapy. In the pre-rating Interpersonal Check List, the father had perceived both of his sons as more authoritative and dominant than himself. In the therapy he worked through his unrealistic fears that his sons might become threateningly aggressive and challenging to him. The sons were able to reassure him on this score. They, in turn, had perceived the father as more dominant than themselves. In the post-ratings, their perceptions of the other reflected more accurately the others' self-images.

Also in our first group of cases was the family in which a fifteen-year-old schizophrenic girl was given emergency treatment in the home for an acute schizophrenic break at the same time that family treatment was initiated. The girl had apparently been acutely psychotic for two weeks, was hallucinating and clearly in a regressed state, saying "I need mommy," sucking her thumb and other objects, and trying to swallow pins. The mother, who was a nurse, had not taken action on hospitalizing the girl. As an experiment, we sent one of our more experienced and maternal psychiatric nurses to stay in the home with the girl and feed her over the weekend while the mother was out working. A tranquilizer was prescribed. In the meantime we met with the family in the evening in the home and persuaded the career-oriented mother to give up her job temporarily, and to stay home with the girl. The acute psychosis subsided, and the girl could be observed to come back into contact with reality during the dramatic second family session when the therapists took a very strong stand and insisted that the family pull themselves together, recognize the seriousness of the girl's situation and attempt to control some of their chaotic and aggressive acting out. Due to the crisis situation one of the therapists decided temporarily to adopt the role of an authoritative superego figure, to represent society to the family, and to lecture them about their uncontrolled aggressive acting-out behavior, in an effort to neutralize the excess of aggression and to bring order out of chaos. Many problems remained in this family; the father, for example, was found to be alcoholic and with signs of brain impairment, but the acute crisis was passed and the girl returned to school and completed the year successfully.

In another family, of Jewish background and middle-class socio-economic status, the sixteen-year-old only daughter was a frightened, withdrawn girl in a borderline schizophrenic state, who had been out of school for a period of months. She lived in a large, old three-story house, together with her maternal grandparents, her maternal uncle and aunt, and her parents. The therapy unit included all the members of this three-generation household throughout the course of therapy. The rather likeable, but strong-willed and paranoid maternal grandmother ruled over the household; she owned the house and another property. The others, and particularly the son-in-law (the primary patient's father), were afraid to stand up to her and tell her what they thought.

Within ten months after the start of treatment, the girl started in and graduated from a beautician's school, got a job, became engaged, and became less fractious and intractible with her parents. The mother became somewhat less bossy toward the daughter, and simultaneously did not permit the domineering tendencies of her own mother—the grandmatriarchal ruler of the home—to upset her as much as before.

Statements by Families

At the conclusion of therapy, each member of the family was asked independently, to respond in writing to the following two questions: 1. "What did you, personally, and the family gain from the family therapy sessions?" 2. "In what way did you think the therapy was limited, or what was wrong with the way it was conducted?" The members of the three-generation family referred to above, for instance, with the only daughter as the patient, wrote the following:

Family X

Mother: "I am very pleased at the present time with the condition of my daughter. I myself am more calm and am able to cope with the situations as they arise. I can say that there is a great change in G. (daughter), so they must have done the cure. I am grateful for everything."

Daughter (primary patient): "A better understanding of myself and family; and different subjects that would touch people in different ways, such as bitterness, sad feelings, and happy feelings."

Uncle: "A decided change can be seen. It has been beneficial to the entire family, and has helped G. It has also taken the fear out of her parents about G. doing herself bodily harm."

Aunt 1: "Dr. S. and Mr. F. were a good team. I would like to say how grateful we all are that when help was needed in this family, we were able to obtain such competent help. Thank you.

"M (mother) seemed to change considerably. She became closer to G. and gained her confidence, F (father) did the same. There seems to be more harmony in the family. I do not know whether G. has overcome her main inner difficulties, but she has progressed greatly, with the people and in the business world."

Aunt 2: "As far as I am concerned, what I learned from the sessions was: 1) to listen, then speak; 2) to be more tolerant of others' mistakes (in my opinion); 3) to inquire—why? what for?"

Father: Did not return the questionnaire.

Following are the statements of the four family members of one of our most successful cases. The seventeen-year-old schizophrenic girl was referred for hospitalization but was not hospitalized. The case was mutually terminated after one year of weekly family therapy sessions.

Family Y

Father: "I personally gained everything that I lacked in being a good husband, father and a better man. I received the gift of understanding, patience, and consideration. I am now the master of my home and family. My family have gained understanding also. We can now converse with each other as a unit. We are trying to better ourselves daily. This was a priceless experience.

"I think the therapy was excellent and in no way limited. It is just miraculous, and approximately 95% of the people that I observe should have this type of therapy. I also think that this therapy should be a requirement for newlyweds to better their future relations, etc."

Mother: "I feel that for myself, I gained a feeling of freedom and independence, also, I think I see things more realistically than before. I learned not to interfere with my husband when he speaks to the children, which has helped my family's relationship greatly. My family has gained from the therapy sessions by not being afraid to express themselves to their father, and he has learned to try to understand them better without losing his temper.

"After giving this question a good bit of thought, I cannot seem to find anything wrong. From the way the therapists conducted the meetings, we learned a great deal and I felt most comfortable to express my feelings and feel that I have gained two wonderful friends.

Daughter (seventeen years of age—designated patient): "I learned which of the things in life are of most importance. I learned how to project my feelings so as to make others take an interest in me. I am not afraid to argue a point until I win the other's consideration and until I become considerate of the other. My family is not so quick to blame others for their misconceptions. They are more willing to ask the opinions of others.

"My honest opinion is that the therapy was not limited. It was conducted in such a manner as to provide effectiveness."

Son (fourteen years of age): "I gained a better understanding of myself and my family. I can now look at myself and see what is wrong with me. I now understand the relationship I am supposed to have with my family and people in general. The sessions have given me an understanding of people and normal feelings people have. In short I have learned how to deal with life and people.

"I think the therapy was as good as possible. The only thing one might find wrong with it is that it takes a lot of time. This cannot be said in reference to these circumstances because dealing with human qualities takes a long time."

Family Z

Father: "Satisfaction of opening up the lines of communication between members of my family so we could discuss our mutual problems and bring these problems out in the open so we could resolve them and cope with them. It brought out many areas we were not aware of, for example, my own overprotectiveness . . . an understanding of ourselves. I was being overprotective of whole family . . . all three—I didn't realize family resented it. It was one big thing that came out.

"Of course big satisfaction was seeing the improvement in Cass—not cured —but a lot. Has actually gone out on a few dates in recent weeks.

Frankly I don't know what we would have done with Cass in beginning— at end of rope. It is a wonderful feeling. I would say that this 'experiment' was quite successful. Something happened—I don't think Cass would have changed without it—with thought of helping others I do compliment the team."

Mother: "I feel that Cass was helped. The consistent weekly meetings were helpful. We knew that whatever problems came up could be discussed. It made us remember our problems and try to do something about them instead of accepting the situation and feeling hopeless. We were all helped to become more assertive. Son is more or less unchanged. He didn't involve himself in the discussions.

"Still, daughter is better than she was and even if only because of that we are a great deal better off than we were before."

Daughter: "I learned to accept criticism. I became much less sensitive. I learned to control my temper. After being a recluse for so many years I now enjoy seeing people and being in different social situations. Even though I still have difficulties, I have improved considerably.

"My parents became aware that they were often using me as an excuse for not doing things. Even now that I am more independent they still do not have enough social activities.

"I think that the meetings were very hard on all of us at one time or another. But I think that they were most difficult for my father and really not of much help to him.

"I think that too many times an insignificant matter was picked up and discussed through an entire meeting instead of talking about more important things."

Son: Was away in the Army at time of this evaluation.

Family Treatment in the Home In Lieu of Hospitalization

Our experience has been quite conclusive in demonstrating to our own satisfaction that it is possible to maintain in the home, by means of an intensive ongoing family treatment, many schizophrenic patients who would otherwise require hospitalization. Only two of the first twenty-five schizophrenic families we worked with, found it necessary to resort to hospitalizing their adolescent schizophrenic member during the course of treatment. In both instances the duration of hospitalization was fairly brief: one week in one case, and somewhat longer in the other. The latter instance has already been reported in the case history of the Oralcle Family in Chapter 6: the parents felt they had to hospitalize their son when he started to push furniture around, and came into their bedroom in the middle of the night threatening them with a knife. In the former instance, the patient was a twenty-year-old boy, the elder of two sons, who had been in the hospital for an acute episode at the time the family treatment was initiated. He had achieved only a very tenuous social and clinical adjustment outside the hospital during the first six months of family treatment. The family had made some progress in separating from the excessive influence of the maternal grandparents who had interfered in the training of the two boys, and had seduced them with money and gifts. Then, when it looked as if the parents might get closer together in their marital relationship, and the mother was coming out of the depression she had been in, the patient regressed into an overt psychotic state. He began to hug and kiss his mother frequently, and to fondle objects sensuously in her presence, something he had not done in his more controlled state. The parents could not tolerate this behavior, and he was rehospitalized for a week. The family treatment continued for approximately six more months, and the patient has now been out of hospital for a period of one and a half years.

The fact that the therapists came to the home weekly, maintained contact with and reasonable control of the patient, and did not appear to be anxious about the possibility of violence, was usually sufficient reassurance for the parents that hospitalization was not necessary. Most of the instances in which it did become an issue were situations where the parents were unable to handle the threat of violence, sometimes combined with a libidinal threat from their schizophrenic offspring. They felt this threat coming directly to themselves, although they would often rationalize it as a threat to the community, or a concern that their offspring would get in trouble. In such a crisis situation, hospitalization is more likely to occur if the therapist is unwilling, or considers it inappropriate, to reassure the parents explicitly about the danger, or to state that hospitalization is not necessary. This is not to deny that situations of sufficient danger to warrant hospitalization may occur, regardless of what approach or effort is made by the therapy team. We did observe however, that our more active and controlling therapists seemed less likely to have such crises occur during the course of the family treatment. They might, for example, challenge the father in the family more directly, push him harder to stand up to the acting out of the children and to do more to maintain control in the family. The gradual establishment of such proper role function and control in the family would, when it succeeded, make hospitalization less necessary in the future.

Another observation we made was that the need to hospitalize, or not to hospitalize, appeared to be a part of the family system. It had its roots in the family dynamic structure and often was not easily influenced by professional opinion. Some parents felt they had to hospitalize to survive, even when the problem and threat they saw in their adolescent was mostly of their own projection—a "narcissistic externalization" of their personal intrapsychic conflicts—and clearly did not warrant hospitalization. Other parents, perhaps, used hospitalization as a way to avoid separation on a deeper level which they could not tolerate, as, for example, when their child made a move toward a flight for independence as a way of breaking out of the pathological family system. To hospitalize in this instance would serve the purpose of holding on to the child who is now obviously and formally labeled "sick" by the community, and therefore should not try to leave his parents and emancipate himself.

Still other parents absolutely refused to hospitalize in the face of very definite recommendations to do so by our treatment team, and also by other psychiatrists whom they had previously consulted. They apparently needed their sick child in the home so desperately in order not to upset the balance of the pathological family system that they could not trust to let him out of their control even temporarily. Such families are perhaps the sickest of all, and their children are victims who are trapped and incarcerated as securely as if they were behind iron bars. In one such paranoid schizophrenic family, the risk of homicide and suicide became intensified at the point the therapy team decided to pressure the parents to hospitalize their boy. The parents had participated in isolating this twenty-year-old boy permanently from the outside world and had entombed him in a bizarre and highly ritualized environment, consisting of many non-human objects, gadgets and paraphernalia. Both the boy and his father threatened serious violence when hospitalization was urged on them. The threat was taken seriously and the plan was dropped.

IV

THERAPEUTIC TECHNIQUES

In the beginning sections of this volume we described our initial rationale, our plans and methods, and our immediate experience in visiting the families in their homes in the form of chronological and global clinical reports. It now remains for us to extract and abstract certain segments from these organic global experiences for further elaboration and analysis.

Originally we had hoped that the project would come up with what could be considered an emerging conceptual framework for family therapy. As we went along, however, it seemed more appropriate to select only conceptual issues that stood out clearly as distinctive features of the family therapy approach. Whereas at the beginning project members were discussing and analyzing anxieties and doubts concerning their new enterprise, in the fifth year, having acquired the identity of the family therapist, they found that their chief difficulty was how to communicate an experience without an adequate conceptual framework. Just as the therapeutic team proved to be the proper authorship team for empirically describing the shared clinical experience, the individual therapist, in most instances, turned out to be the natural author for the emerging theoretical issues. Actually, most individual contributions reflect the combined thinking of the entire project, since there was continuous interplay and feedback of ideas and each author submitted the rough draft of his paper for group discussion.

This section, then, contains chapters that deal with selected aspects of our experience, as regards therapeutic techniques, the therapeutic process, and related problems. Moving from concrete topics toward broader, more abstract issues, these chapters encompass questions of family therapy as a method, as well as the relevance of this method of treatment to the family disorder to be treated. They reflect the efforts of the therapists to shift from their traditional orientation with individual therapeutic techniques, to the position of family therapists, employing newly-developed, family-centered techniques. While several other family-therapy groups, in addition to ours, are presently working on developing these new techniques, we still have a long way to go in making this shift in our therapeutic approach.

The active role of the family therapist

Jerome E. Jungreis

Jerome E. Jungreis

Chapter
11

In this chapter we shall discuss some very specific family therapy techniques that have been used with schizophrenic patients and their families. Some of these techniques have been specifically used by the author and other research associates of this demonstration project. Before discussing these specific techniques, however, it might be well to provide a brief background of general observations, concepts and therapeutic goals which have been found useful in family therapy. These general concepts of the family will be those which we have found to be working models, from the point of view of family therapy, rather than "global" concepts of "the family." From this frame of reference we hope to lead into general therapeutic goals and finally to our main point of discussing the specific techniques used to carry out these goals.

One of the most impressive observations of those working with families with a clinically identifiable schizophrenic member is the intensity, tenacity and strength of the family homeostatic patterns. Our thinking has been guided by work done elsewhere with the concept of homeostasis in the family.[56] Specifically in these families the patterns are essentially static and serve the purpose of keeping the family in the situation that is rather than in a situation that might be. We have also been impressed with the fact, as have other observers, that the pathology is socially shared.[46] We have noted the rather unusual communicative quality of these families. Their messages to each other are frequently vague and confusing, or there is simultaneous contradiction of the verbal and nonverbal transmission.[115] We sense that these poor communications are used to keep the family in a regressed state. Other observers have been impressed, as we have, with the number of "pseudo-qualities"[117] which are unconscious, and which again serve the purpose of keeping the family from being more aware of what messages are going on in the family, and the nature of the intrafamily relationships. These too serve the purpose, as in individuals, of creating unconscious conflicting feelings that are too threatening.

In family therapy part of the problem is to make these feelings conscious, so that the healthy part of the family can deal with them. We have been impressed clinically by the fact, which has also been confirmed by psychological testing, that almost every member of the family of our treatment caseload is seriously disturbed, although some may function very well in limited areas. Furthermore, we have been concerned with the fact that without therapeutic intervention, and frequently with, the symptom picture may shift from one member of the family to another. We have found that individuals in these families are unable to effectively discharge family-generated tensions outside the home. The quality of the usual sublimation in work, school, social and community activities is such that it does little to diminish the intensity of the family relations. What follows from this is that the patterns of the family, deep-seated and tenacious, are patterns which result in the family consistently handling their internal and external pressures through various mechanisms used and discharged within the family. These are non-maturational, non-problem solving, static and endlessly repetitious. The changes that do take place within this family are changes designed only to maintain this homeostasis, as described in Chapter 23.

The daily life of a family, normal or clinical, affords each member the opportunity to act and react, satisfy or frustrate reality demands of other members. For example, families expect fathers to provide financial support, mothers to provide daily meals, children to learn to grow up. The family also provides a means for the living out of sublimations and other healthy defense mechanisms, for resolving conflict, and for fostering utilization of the community for such purposes. At the same time, the family provides the most easily available opportunity to build up fantasies, and perpetrate distortions to reconstruct unresolved conflict and trauma from the past. We term the typical operations of any family, its constant interaction with each other and with the world outside the family, as "ongoing family life transactions." All the factors just mentioned—reality needs and demands; creation and/or resolution of fantasies and conflicts; recreation of unresolved conflict from the past—go on simultaneously, with every ongoing family life transaction having a potential bearing on each or all of these.

In the schizophrenic family the ongoing family life transactions are used to build up a wall against family growth and maturation. In the normal family, mechanisms somehow exist, though only partially known, which permit members of the family to resolve their conflict-laden fantasies against the reality of the family's life situation and community experiences on a day to day basis; whereas in these sick families the mechanisms are such as to prevent such resolution. There exists in sick families some unconscious communication that to strive towards dynamism and change is of tremendous danger and destructiveness to the family as a whole. Thus, the therapeutic view of the schizophrenic family is one of an extremely narrow, restricted family adjustment to growth and change. The families demonstrate a series of static, binding relationships, with almost all of the affective discharge of the fantasy life being worked out within the nexus of the family. Although one person may show the symptoms, the psychopathology is shared among various members of the family.[19] Characteristically, this kind of family prevents any kind of dynamism, and hence any kind of maturation or change or growth. In the normal family, the family of procreation starts out with two persons, then children are added who grow and mature within the intense relationships of the family. As they get older these ties are loosened and bound more and more elsewhere, until the children are finally able to leave the home and set up their own family of procreation. In the schizophrenic family, the fixations remain on the early binding, intense family interaction without an opportunity for outlets to gradual withdrawal from the family, gradual sublimations elsewhere, and on the prevention of independent living.

From this concept of the schizophrenic family, it becomes clear that one of the prime therapeutic goals is to assist this kind of family to shift from a series of static relationships to dynamic ones. It means that destructive patterns in the relationships within the family have to be altered. Mostly it means that the view of the sickness is not of the individual or individuals, but of the family as a whole. The schizophrenic family is a family in which parents cannot permit the children to grow up; in fact, the children are afraid to grow up. The socially shared psychopathology hardens into a faulty "family image,"[105] an image of static relationships and transactions, perceived by every member of the family. Because the family is engaging in ongoing family life transactions, it becomes clear that self-awareness of the individual members of the family as the initial therapeutic goal in itself would be difficult to attain. These families are similar to individual character-disordered persons who are constantly acting out to dissipate anxiety and deny to themselves inner conflicts. "Analysts noted that some patients, instead of remembering and verbalizing the traumatic situations of their childhood, would unconsciously 'act out' these early situations outside the analytic hour."[53] There is much gain, satisfaction and some sense of mastery of discomfort in the ongoing family life transactions. The family members have unconsciously chosen these transactions as the preferred way of dealing with problems. Hence, we typically find the family giving lip service to their being in treatment. They rarely have full recognition of the limited degree of acceptance they have given to therapy for *each* member. Each family member maintains an awareness or wish that therapy is for the "sick" one.

We would like for a moment to contrast the problem of the family transactions in family therapy with individual transactions in individual therapy. One could argue that a person is living a daily life where there is a considerable amount of acting out in the sense of various attempts at restitution and of dealing with internal pressures. The big difference is that in individual therapy attempts are made to narrow the focus of the problem area in the interpersonal relationship with patient and therapist. The therapist does not permit the patient to act out, as it were, in the therapeutic hour. Also, transference elements can be strongly utilized as an instrument of self-awareness, and of limiting the acting out to its strictly therapeutic application in the treatment session. However, in the family there are many ongoing relationships during therapy. In addition, therapeutic transference relationships would call for the therapist to be neutral, so that the individual members of the family or the family as a whole could then see themselves in their irrational attitudes or behavior, because the therapist had done nothing to provoke them. But when the family meets with the therapy team, they are in the process of transacting with each other and cannot be restricted to the relationship with the therapy team. As J. E. Bell[11] has noted: "The therapy hour is a continuation of a family life." However, we do feel that self-awareness is very much a part of therapy, particularly as it sets the stage for the family to try to look at themselves more objectively and not to be caught up as much in the intensity of shared feelings. For instance, when one member of the family sees how similar his own pattern is to that of another, he can create some distance in the relationship and become more reflective on what is going on in the family. It creates a stage before the family, helping them to realize that they have problems, and to look to each other and to the therapist for help. Thus, it is both a preliminary as well as a parallel process occurring together with other therapeutic techniques of greater significance. The parents might see how their own childhood is related to the current family life, and might be able in time to start to question the family functioning and relationships and then be open to real therapy. In other words, helping the family to see patterns; to be aware of what they're doing and what they're like; and to point out the distortion in communication patterns, conscious and unconscious, and how these may affect other members of the family—all these are valuable and useful initial adjuncts in family therapy with a schizophrenic member.

As mentioned above, the essence of change in family therapy must be preceded by actual transactional change, which means a disruption in the usual family patterns of operating, of relating to each other, and a disruption in the performance of any of the ongoing family life transactions which have been handled in a stereotyped, fixed pattern. The main purpose, therefore, is to disrupt the fixed pattern. Hopefully, this disruption—however mild it may be in the initial phase of treatment—will then lead to anxiety, and to concern with the very limited useful potential range of action that the family possesses. It will give the family something tangible to struggle with and will fix them more on family interaction and problems than on insisting that the sick person is the problem. It will show them that they all have a problem with change. It has been our experience with almost every family that we have dealt with, that a suggestion of even the mildest kind of change meets with considerable resistance. Even though there is initial resistance to the awareness that change is a family problem, it certainly does structure an environment and create a situation in which the family can struggle tangibly with something more concrete than abstract discussions of problems, which may be projected or displaced or denied—typical operations of these kinds of families. Finally, we are convinced that schizophrenic families are prepared to talk or not to talk *ad nauseam*, but not to change.

To have the family deal with a family problem that is directly related to the ongoing therapy is the most useful technique in family therapy of schizophrenia in the family. It points up problems that the family is having at the moment, making it relevant to all. It encourages meaningful and affect-laden interaction, involving the therapists who precipitated it and hence prevents the family from excluding them. It permits the therapists to observe, interpret, hold up, and point out patterns that are immediately and emotionally relevant to the family; and gives them access to therapeutic intervention.

To encourage expression of each member's feelings is very important because it is directly connected with setting ego boundaries for each member of the family, helping them to be aware of themselves as unique individuals and helping them find self-identification within the loosening bonds of the family. Such expression is particularly important in schizophrenic familes because the ego boundaries of the individual family members are somewhat more tenuous, with each member attempting in part to borrow the ego of other members of the family, and/or to withhold it from them for fear that any change in the relationship would mean family and individual disintegration. The persistence of the therapist in insisting on some change, within a kindly and understanding framework, and his refusal to be drawn into the family's attempts at accomodation and adjustment to the therapist on their terms, are the basic levers both in making family therapy truly meaningful to each member of the family and in assisting the family in seeing the pathology that exists. The family then has to struggle with its inability to make change and its anxiety about being unable to incorporate the therapist into the ongoing family life transactions that they have been spending their lives structuring. This is a difficult and indeed a painful experience for them. If the timing and dosage have been correctly estimated, the relationship with the therapist, their sensing his strength and comfort, their guilt over not letting each other down, their discomfort with the identified patient, and their own individual and collective desire for a better life, will see them through.

The family's attempts at incorporating the therapists into their ongoing transactions may be likened to the non-individuated free-floating trans-ference phenomena of character-disordered patients. The patient or family attempts to put the therapist into a frame of reference that he or they have known and to involve him in things they have been doing all their lives to each other and to others. It has been unconscious, harmful to the patient, and persistent. The family members tend to reinforce each other in structuring the therapist's role. There is much more to be said about family transference which cannot adequately be dealt with in this chapter.

These joint processes, of recommending and insisting on change in the ongoing family life transactions as well as the refusal of the therapist to be incorporated into the family's typical adjustment to his presence, lead eventually to their seeing their life transactions as being ego-alien, pa-thological, and in need of change. Their concern and anxiety leads to discussion of fantasies, exposure of dyads, receptivity to noting the faulty communication and the pseudo-quality of their roles. Each falls into place as they individually and collectively examine themselves and their relation to each other. (We would consider a family member's dwelling upon his individual fantasies or early life experiences as being resistance and seduction of the therapist by attempting to establish another dyad, one with the therapist—except where the fantasies relate to the other family members or evoke an affective response from the others.)

By exposing fantasies and dyads and the need for their existence to the light of day the way for healthy triadic, hence dynamic family life is paved. A family's ability to survive the tension and anxiety of this therapeutic phase and a realization that they have not been destroyed as a unit or have acted out incestuous or murderous impulses encourages the family members to face a life of change, growth and maturation. This then is the ideal we strive for in family therapy.

The case-history chapters of this book contain numerous instances in which the therapists recommended specific changes in family life trans-actions. In the Island family, for example, consistent pressure was placed upon the parents to live a life of their own, independent of their sick daughter. They were frequently impressed with the need to have some social life outside of the family living room. This denied them the scape-goating mechanism of blaming Cass for their social isolation. It assisted in pointing out that they were expecting more of Cass than they them-selves could accomplish, indicating that they had a serious problem of maladaptation of their own. It opened the way for them to discuss their own internal pressures, fears and anxieties; it exposed the father-daughter dyad and the hidden, shared incest fantasy, revealing the conflicting messages from parents to daughter and vice versa. The reader may recall that all this took many months, due partially to the therapists' learning and caution, and partially to the great rigidity of the life transactions.

The behavior of the Rituell family changed only after the therapists insisted that the son no longer live at home. The mother then started to talk with considerable affect of her fantasies about her twenty-seven-year-old son, seeing him as an infant unable to care for himself; the father revealed his dependence upon his son, and the son accepted his role as both father's crutch and mother's little child. Only then did the flood of parent verbalization signify affect-laden concern and anxiety. Prior to that, they were prepared to fight with each other, calling upon the therapists or others to mediate between them, much as they had done all through the thirty years of their married lives. Significantly, after berating each other all through the session, they were smiling and relaxed as the therapists left. They had been exploiting the therapy to perpetuate their ongoing family life transactions.

It is sometimes easier for the therapist to refuse the role the family tries to impose on him than it is to detect the subtle attempts at such an imposition. As one therapist remarked, "I don't understand myself why, but I instinctively want to oppose any action or theme the family proposes." She was right. Sometimes it is obvious, as when there is a denial of the therapist's role as healer; at other times, it can be difficult to ascertain. In one family, the eighteen-year-old son was able to get involved with a number of girls whereby somehow the parents of both parties got deeply involved with each other. It all seemed accidental and left the son feeling that everyone was interfering and that, if he could only manage things on his own, he would manage quite satisfactorily. In one session during which the current girl friend was being discussed, the therapist found himself caught up in considerable discussion with the parents around the interference. The son seemed detached and at times almost asleep. The parents and therapist were hotly involved. The therapist suddenly realized that he had somehow been sucked into a role that was really a continuation of the family pattern. He attempted to understand both how this happened, and how this perpetuated the homeostasis. He then refused to accept this role and worked towards the son dealing with his parents in the matter. Simultaneously, he insisted that the parents desist from communicating with the girl's parents. Only then did the affect-charged fantasies come out in part, with the son no longer able to maintain the fiction that he could manage on his own, and stating that he was quite anxious in relating to the girl and somehow needed his parents involved, for he was dependent upon them. His mother was very upset about letting her son grow up and manage his own affairs and was competitive with the girl friend; the father was threatened, in his unconscious homosexual need for his son, by the possibility of the son's heterosexual expression. Instead of taking the role of another adult, the therapist chose the more therapeutic one of catalyzing family interaction on a *meaningful* level. "Meaningful" must be emphasised because what seems at first to be much family interaction in therapy is not really mean-

ingful but only an extension of the ongoing pathologic family life transaction. It should be noted, in this example, that the therapist ba~'
to accept the role in which the family had subtly cast
insisted on a change in the ongoing transaction.

The following small segment of a case illustrates
where the therapist refused to accept the family-assigi
family of parents with a sixteen-year-old girl and a thirt
the father and son were quiet, with most of the interac
between mother and daughter. The mother's role was
co-therapist; she read a lot, thought long and deeply a
during the week, and was the force for therapy. Th
extremely provocative and hostile to the mother and the
it became clear that these poses were essential to the fan
transactions, the therapist started to change his role. Wh
open the session with long reports of her ruminations c
week's therapy and challenge the rest of the family to
therapist pointed out a number of times that she was sa[.]
the good one in this family, that she cared about the
others didn't. She also was saying that she and the thera·
relationship of understanding and concern. When thi
effect, mother became angry at the therapist and simult
of the family became very active. Numerous fantasies
clearly indicating how each one in the family was rel
way, unmastered previous family experiences. The moth
had banded together against her mother. The father rep·
ignored in his family, neglected, and had always felt
didn't want any children. The daughter reported that t
operated in cliques against the others and she resented
she could have a whole family. The son reported that h
that discussion was good for the family but that she
device of domination and control. Because the therapi
the role assigned to him, overtly by the mother but
family, a major realignment was possible with emphas·
creation of triads as well as total family units. There was
in this family. It should be noted that it would have b·
the therapist to be sucked in, to accept the mother's ob·
help, her insistence that she cared and was trying to
come regularly and work on their problems, to see the f<
as resistive.

In this context, the exposure of communication diffict
the family can be seen, not as ends in themselves, b·
disrupt the sick ongoing transactions, paving the way
and to having the family see what purposes they serv
mechanisms forces the family to readjust and in their

the hidden motives, feelings and fantasies come to light. Thus, we see the therapist in his role as clarifier of what is being said—verbally and non-verbally—helping all to understand why they act as they do and, through the realignment of the family forces in the living situation of the therapy, to experience other ways of reality. The exposure of communication distortions does not possess the quality of an interpretation. Asking a family to react to such exposure in a reflective way is, as we see it, nowhere near as effective as the exposure and denial of such mechanisms to the family as a prelude to having the family struggle with a change in the ongoing communication patterns in the living experience of the moment. "A moment of concretely felt living in interaction contains many potential meanings—and resolution of problems—and not all of these can or need be conceptually insightfully symbolized."[42]

One of the main things the active family therapist has to guard against is being sucked into the family pattern of behaving, into their typical attitudes and their typical defenses. In the case of the Rituell family, for instance, mother and father had constantly been arguing with each other, accusing each other of various failings. They had always turned to others to indicate who was right and who was wrong, and for many months attempted to use the therapist precisely the same way. In the Island family, it was their passivity and inability to mobilize themselves in any direction. In various subtle ways they got across to the therapists that they would be passive and would want them to be passive, too. They indicated that anything other than this on the part of the therapists would be fraught with considerable anxiety for the family, and projected in a sado-masochistic way that the therapists were attempting to upset and hurt the family. In another family, where there was considerable acting out, the sense of the initial family therapy sessions was that the therapist should do something extremely active, and "action" was their attempt to deal radically with the situation, a radical situation the family had been living with for many years. Where the family feels apathetic and hopeless, the therapists must not accept this; where the family feels overenthu-siastic and optimistic, it is important that the therapists temper it with their own true realization and assessment of the family situation. The range of activity on the part of the family therapists seems to vary, as the literature notes, from Ackerman's[2] taking sides with various members of the family from time to time to some of the milder suggestions for shifting family patterns which have been made by Jackson and Weak-land.[58] We are convinced that activity is mandatory. In the Rituell family, to use this example again, it was only after the family therapists became more active and refused to accept the role that the family had assigned them, that some things started to happen and change in the family. We realized, too, that the arguments between mother and father, and their wanting to use the therapists against one another, could continue

easily for another fifty years without pause or reflection
there was active intervention by the therapists.

There is one final point that should be mentioned w
activity of the therapists, and this relates itself to the rol
the home. There is no doubt that the therapists' taking
instrumental leadership of the family is quite threateni
On the surface many fathers seem to accept this, almos
this; in fact, they seem glad to have another male take o
attempt in part then to identify with the therapist almost
a parent. This would seem to subvert the father's ro
within limits, it is a risk. The therapeutic attitude is
therapists' activity is due to default by the father.
assertion by the father are greeted with seriousness and
by the therapists. Their family role also changes. What fre
is that other members of the family, once the therapists
up the father's role for discussion, will take over from tl
challenge the father to act as the father in the home. Tl
be from the therapists to the members of the family
change in the father while the therapists sit back, re
different role with changing circumstances. One of the
that so many a father is so very passive and indicates n
therapists' activity although from time to time, as they
family better and the family become more comfortable
blings come back to them of father having made disp
after they were gone. Frequently the father is challenge
to assume more leadership and is encouraged in various
even very small projects indicating an assertion of his p
family. This too is part of what is meant by insisting o
changes in the family, in this particular case, in the role
due time it does get across to the father that the therap
no way going to be a permanent one, that therapy is g
even more important, that their role is merely due to hi
that there is no intrinsic desire on the part of the therapi
the family.

:cific therapeutic techniques with

renic families

Ross V. Speck

Encounter With the Family

The atmosphere in the first session with the schizo-phrenic family is exciting. The therapists must be pre-pared to engage the family at whatever level the family presents itself; they must be flexible and not use a standardized or rigid approach. A power struggle be-tween the therapists and the family is in the immediate offing. The ground rules to the family therapy are set by the therapists. The time and duration of the session as well as frequency and fees are discussed. The reasons for the family therapy are talked about as a family problem, with the therapists asking themselves, "What is this family's problem?"

Deliberate attempts are made by the therapists to avoid having one family member accept the role of scapegoat. They are particularly careful to avoid setting up an alliance with the person or persons who have made the telephone contact or who have initiated the family referral, or to allow this person or persons to structure the session, or to play the role of a third therapist. If the person who makes the initial contact attempts to play a "helping" role, the therapists openly interpret this as part of this particular person's problem in the family. Family members are directed very early to talk to each other rather than to talk to the therapists. Strong and repeated attempts are made to involve all family members in the ongoing therapeutic process. The family is told that no communication between any member of the family and the therapists will be respected as private or confidential but that it will be revealed by the therapists to the other family members. Furthermore, the family is told that most families have secrets and that these family secrets will have to be exposed to the entire family once their existence has been revealed.

The Island family (Chapter 4) began their therapy with Cass upstairs and barricaded in the bathroom. She thus was volunteering herself as the scapegoat of the family, the one responsible for the family problems. The rest of the family were quite willing to accept this arrangement. When after several sessions the therapists started up the stairs to try to talk to Cass, mother became panicky and physically prevented their coming any closer to Cass. The therapists had to make an issue on the spot of their insistence to involve Cass directly and physically in the family therapy sessions. Had they backed down, it might have taken several months to get Cass to come to the sessions.

Enthusiasm, Vivacity and Optimism of the Therapist

As pointed out by Jungreis in the preceding section, when the family meets with the therapy team they are in the process of transacting with each other. Transactions of the schizophrenic family are disordered, disorganized, primary process, usually stereotyped and non-goal directed. The therapist's job is to bring some order out of this chaos. He uses his own personality to confront the family with the fact that he is a definite personality and a factor to be reckoned with. In more conventional individual therapy the therapist is more or less neutral and purposely does not reveal his own personality; in family therapy with a schizophrenic family, therapists will often present the vibrant, alive, involved, challenging and exploring aspects of their own personalities for the families to deal with.

The use of various techniques, of course, depends on the personality of the therapist and his own ability to engage the families on a constantly changing series of affective and experiential levels.

Becoming Part of the Family

As therapists observe the family patterns and the family way of life, they attempt to become a member of the family system. The process of becoming part of the family does not occur immediately and often takes many months. Our group has felt that it is generally desirable for the therapists to get inside the family system and work from within, rather than remain an outsider, having to work from without. When therapists become a member of the family system, they are much more sensitive to the nuances of feelings and relationships within the family. The depression and boredom in some schizophrenic families will at times become almost unbearable to the therapists. At the same time they may experience more of the spirit of cooperation and desire to change in the various family members when they have become a member of the system.

The following clinical example illustrates how becoming part of the family system can become a potent resistance to change as well. A sixteen-year-old boy became psychotic on the day his older sister was leaving to become a nun. Another older sister had married a short time before. The mother and father were grieving over the loss of their children, although they were not able to admit this consciously. The mother assumed a martyred role and the father professed to have no interest in any of them, although underneath the surface he was intensely dependent on all of his children. Family therapy started as the sister in the convent was due to leave Philadelphia for a distant area to continue her training as a nun. The family reacted rather enthusiastically to our initiation of family therapy, and we began to feel very comfortable with them and to feel that we had become part of the family system. It was not until much later however, that we realized that the mother, father, brother and sister saw us as a replacement for the sister who was training to be a nun in an order which did social work. Eventually, the family was able to verbalize that they regarded us as responsible for allowing that sister to continue in her work. Since we did not try to get her home to look after the rest of the family, we were in a way volunteering ourselves to take her place in the family. This delusion was clung to tenaciously by all family members, and functioned effectively to prevent and obstruct our efforts to work towards individuation and maturity in the various members of the family.

The Power Struggle

As noted earlier, a power struggle between the therapists and the family members is the rule rather than the exception. Most schizophrenic families seem ready to challenge and test the therapists almost from the outset of therapy. Schizophrenic families are often leaderless and without clearly defined authority invested in any one family member. Rather typically, fathers are passive and weak. The therapists take over the leadership role, and it is not uncommon for the father to identify with the aggressive, masculine role of the male therapist, and to borrow from him until he can function as the authority figure of the family.

In one of the first families we treated, the mother was the undisputed family leader. As the only adult female among five adult males, she was able to split them off one by one in such a fashion that she retained all the controls. (This is Family B, described in the section on the absent-member maneuver.) The mother also managed to induce the various males to leave the family treatment, one by one, until finally only she, her husband and her schizophrenic son were attending the sessions. She exerted complete control over her husband, and the only male in the family who was able to stand up to her effectively was her schizophrenic son. When the therapists finally confronted her with her role in the family pathology, she terminated the treatment and would not allow them to return to the home.

The therapists were fortunate to have the family power struggle so blatantly demonstrated in one of their early family therapy cases. Both therapists felt that if they had had this case later, they would have been able to take the control away from the mother, and continue further treatment of this family. At the same time it should be noted that the therapists did persist in the treatment of this family for many sessions after the mother had obtained family consensus that they did not wish further treatment. In "schizophrenic" families persistence by the therapists sometimes overcomes potent family resistances. This family still, from time to time, contacts the therapists by telephone.

Doing the Opposite

Our teams have come to recognize that a fundamental rule in the treatment of the schizophrenic family is to reverse the family request into its opposite.

In one family, for instance, both parents had had severe poliomyelitis involving the lower extremities. Despite their severe handicaps they showed an unusual desire to be successful as self-supporting citizens. They complained repeatedly that their schizophrenic son did not organize his activities. They felt that he was rather lazy, remained in bed a good part of the day, and had no schedule. This was at complete variance with the overly organized rituals and schedules of their lives. At an earlier period of the mother's life—when she was in a period of crisis, however—she had just sat around being depressed and not assuming responsibility for the care of her young son. The parents repeatedly requested the therapists to order their son to get busy and to organize his life. They persisted in complaining that he did not have enough to do, that he never spent any time looking for a job, and that he just lay around reading a book. The therapists, instead of aligning with the parents, instructed the son to do nothing for the next week. In fact, they went further and stated, "If you do anything we want you to come back next week and explain in detail what you did and why you did it." The therapists' handling of the situation was crucial and helped the schizophrenic, but physically normal, son to maintain an identity separate from the severely polio-crippled parents. The week following the one in which he had been instructed to do nothing, the son made his first serious effort to find a job, something he had not done for two years.

In another family, the therapist persisted in calling the father a prude. The father maintained that this was not so because he was an artist, and had had much exposure to nudity in his art subjects. To prove his point, he stated that his twenty-year-old daughter walked around nude in front of him and that it never bothered him. The therapist immediately responded, "well, it bothers me." This response illustrates both: doing the opposite of what the family wishes, and executing a maneuver whereby the therapist maintains control of the family encounter. In doing the opposite of what the family wishes, the therapist places himself in control. This also heightens the family's awareness that he expects changes to occur within the family pattern.

Redirecting Communication Within the Family

A common pattern in schizophrenic families is that one member acts as the spokesman, communicator, and channelor of information for the family. This pattern allows the family to maintain a fixed, often delusional situation, where the will or power of one family member, often the mother, completely overrides that of the remaining members.

In one family the mother monopolized practically all of the time in the session. The therapists quickly noted that she often spoke of how her husband, her son, and her schizophrenic daughter were feeling or thinking, when they had made no statement at all. When they were asked about their feelings, they merely shrugged and turned to the mother. When the therapists persisted in asking their real feelings, it became very apparent that all family members resented the mother's speaking for them, but did not have the faintest idea of how to challenge her. As therapy developed further, it became evident that the other family members encouraged the mother to state opinions for them. It was only when the therapists ordered the mother to be silent and also ordered the others to speak for themselves, that the resentment and contrary feelings of the father and the schizophrenic daughter became particularly obvious. The son persisted in his old behavior which reinforced the position of the mother. It was aptly demonstrated during the therapy that the son was in alliance with the mother in order to maintain the homeostasis within the family unit, at the same time that he covertly enjoyed an unconscious homosexual alliance with his father. He had a concept of himself and of his father as passive allies in a struggle against his mother and his sister. As therapy progressed, this particular defense of the son was seen to be stronger and more impervious than the schizophrenic defenses of his sister. It seemed as if the son could only function in a non-psychotic way when he felt a passive homosexual alliance with his father.

When the therapists forced the father, the son and the daughter to speak for themselves and not to use the mother as a spokesman, the daughter showed remarkable improvement from her previous symptomatic schizophrenic state, but both the father and son were revealed to have reluctance to dissolve their unconscious, passive, homosexual alliance.

The Physical Struggle

Our work with schizophrenic families has shown us that the power balance in the family is as disordered as the channels of communcation are. It is not uncommon to find that the father has relinquished his authority to the psychotic member of the household, who may consciously or unconsciously be abetted by the mother.

Earlier in our work with schizophrenic families, the therapists attempted to control a schizophrenic member of the family by physical means. This occurred when a disturbed young boy spit at a therapist as well as at his father. The rest of the family simply sat back and watched this. It soon became evident that it should be the father who, as head of the household, should control an unruly family member. Thus we began encouraging the father to physically control another family member if this were needed. However, fathers in general have been reluctant to do this. When we have been able to get them to firmly stand their ground, the fathers have usually won the struggle and this has been a distinct therapeutic advantage. The following clinical examples are illustrative of such a situation.

A sixteen-year-old girl, who is slightly taller than her parents, was overtly contemptuous of her father from the very outset of family treatment. She was provocative, sarcastic, belittling, and even felt that she could beat him up physically. In rages she would break furniture, and show all kinds of capricious behavior in the family therapy sessions. Although she completely disrupted the family therapy at times, the father would do nothing about it. After several months of work with him, during which the therapists pointed out that the daughter really believed she could beat him up, and that she was in control of the family rather than he, he began to indicate that he would not tolerate any further abuse from the daughter. He said that part of his fear in having a struggle with the daughter, was that he might kill her. Finally, a session came when the father ordered the daughter to control herself; after she continued to disrupt the session, he got up and began to chase her. A violent struggle ensued in which the therapists acted like passive referees; after about five minutes the father was able to sit the daughter in a chair with her arms pinned behind her back. After another five minutes she agreed that he had beaten her, and that further physical force was not necessary. The daughter came to the next session saying that she was amazed she could not take on her father. She also stated that for the first time in her life she had some respect for him. Following that session she obeyed him for a couple of months but then again began testing him. The first time he backed down and lost face; the second time he was again able to control her. From that point on there was no further physical violence between the father and daughter.

In another family, the seventeen-year-old schizophrenic son had been violent and broken pieces of furniture on several occasions. His blind father and his mother insisted that they were not frightened of him, and the father felt that he could control him if he wanted to. However, he stated that he felt sorry for him therefore was not controlling him physically. In reality, the son was a good deal taller and stronger than the father. This father also expressed the fear that if he should ever struggle physically with his son that he would kill him. One day when the son refused to do some trivial task which the father asked him to do, the father became enraged, shoved the son against a wall and began to choke him. To break the hold, the son pushed the father away who tripped and fell, breaking some ribs and lacerating his head. The boy's brother-in-law was nearby and ran up and punched the boy, knocking him down. Following this episode of physical violence, the schizophrenic boy no longer felt in control of the entire family, and no further physical violence occurred during the remainder of the therapy. The family had been told by the therapists that they must control his behavior if he got too far out of line, and although they chose an inappropriate way to do this, the end result was a satisfactory one.

Direct Intervention in the Family System

Sometimes the most effective way to change a schizophrenic family is to insist upon it. This can be done in many different ways. We do not assume that ordering the family to change their eating or sleeping habits, etc., will produce anything startling. However, such insistence does place the therapist firmly in a position of power. The Rituell case is probably the best example for this technique. (*See* Chapter 5.) The therapists ordered the mother to begin sleeping with the father again and having sexual relations with him. The mother actually followed these instructions. At times we have requested a wife not to have sexual relations with her husband or to divorce herself emotionally from him for a period of time; or we have asked a husband to get his wife out of the family business when it was obvious that her presence was a destructive influence upon the family life and functioning. At times we have invited the family physician, the family rabbi, priest or minister, aunts and uncles and other relatives to participate in the family treatment sessions. In the Rituell case the patient's fiancee, who apparently had no inkling that he was psychotic, was invited to take part in the therapy sessions.

Revealing Family Secrets

Schizophrenic families frequently distort information which is given to various family members or withhold information, and both maneuvers produce bizarre and distorted communication in the family. We decided in the beginning of our work to tell all family members that we would maintain no secrets or keep confidential material; that one of our goals was to reveal all family secrets. Although this becomes very emotionally laden at times, there are obvious advantages in breaking up faulty habits of communication. In one family, the wife had not told her jealous husband that she had had an affair prior to marriage and had become illegitimately pregnant and had an abortion. The husband acted uninvolved in the family therapy until the therapists encouraged the wife to tell him about this episode. She did so but told her schizophrenic daughter about it first.

In another family the wife had not told her husband about her joint deposit box which he imagined contained his life's earnings. The wife however, had this deposit box in safekeeping with her sister.

Use of Family Pets

Since much of our work with schizophrenic families has been done in the home, we have had frequent experiences with families who have pets. Behavior of these pets has often been revealing as an extension or indicator of human psychopathology. In one family the pet dog was acquired by the father after the death of his favorite daughter. The dog was practically inseparable from him, and when he became anxious he would hold and fondle the dog. He showed very little interest in his two sons, belittled them, and treated them as less than human. When the therapists asked the family to fill out the Leary Interpersonal Check List, the father insisted that they fill out a form on the family dog. Later on in the therapy, when the same check list was being used again, he thought it was ridiculous to fill out a form on the dog, having now a more realistic and human relationship with his sons. The father's attitude toward the family dog could be observed and discussed in the family sessions and contrasted with his behavior towards his sons. Therapists should not hesitate to discuss the family's relationships to their pets. Anecdotes of deep significance to the family are often revealed. Families also are less guarded and defensive when talking about their animals, probably because humans are more tolerant of instinctual drives in animals than in humans. In the author's experience, drawing attention to the behavior of family pets is highly productive of useful psychotherapeutic material.

We have often noted that when tensions in a schizophrenic family rise, and the fears of sexual and aggressive drives become paralyzing, a family member may fall ill. In families that have pets, the pet may become ill—either in conjunction with another family member or members, or as a substitute for illness in one of the human members. At such times of duress the pet may die. The author has observed a pet's death in a schizophrenic family at a time of crisis on seven occasions. The family then grieves over the pet and in the mourning process channels off their intense destructive forces. At times we have advised that a family acquire a pet when we feared that a human member of the family may be injured or killed.

The above techniques are mutually overlapping at times, and it is difficult to sort them out as distinct and separate techniques. Furthermore, the techniques discussed here are by no means the only ones that have been used in our family treatment project. They are all intimately related to resistances and are frequently used in the attempted resolution of a particular family resistance.

The demands upon the therapist

George Spivack

It is perhaps natural that, in describing a new treatment approach, the emphasis be placed upon therapeutic technique, course of treatment, and what is learned about the object of the treatment—in this case the schizophrenic family. The project team had been aware almost from the outset, however, of certain unique parameters of their work with those families. One of these was the fact that the work could—on occasion—be extremely demanding of the therapists, at times arousing anxiety or intense feelings of discomfort and uneasiness.

At least two reasons present themselves for attempting a cursory exposition of reflections of the team regarding this issue. As therapeutic "agents" we may at times too easily bypass the rather obvious fact that we are also human beings attempting to use *ourselves* in a somewhat unique social situation. It is a relatively unexplored though frequently admitted truism that our effectiveness in this taxing enterprise of family treatment depends in large part upon *who* we are—on our own character, and our unique personal experiences. It also depends greatly upon the current climate of relationships within our own personal families.

In recent years there has been increasing interest in countertransference (and other) feelings of the therapist in individual therapy with neurotics, not merely as something indicative of unresolved therapist neurotic needs but as inevitable and perhaps even useful responses in the therapeutic relationship (Searles,[101] Szasz[108]). To date, however, little research data is available relating the therapist's personality to his behavior in the therapeutic relationship (Snyder[104]). The necessity of exploring the demands of the therapy situation and the therapists' response is accentuated in the treatment of the schizophrenic. In considering therapist feelings while treating the schizophrenic, Malone[78] emphasizes that many factors ". . . assure a more intense personal participation by the therapist . . . his personal feelings become critical factors in treatment." In discussing his particular treatment approach, Rosen[94] states: "Therapeutic experience in direct analysis is so intense and the involvement with the patient so extreme that one is just about completely absorbed in it while it takes place." According to Arieti[7]: "When the patient is very sick, his requirements are immense and the help of a therapeutic assistant may be necessary." Searles[100] claims that one ingredient in the therapy of the schizophrenic is the latter's attempt to drive the therapist "crazy." In discussing family psychotherapy, Ackerman[2] states: "The responsibilities of the therapist are multiple, complex, and require the most flexible, open, and undefensive use of the therapist's own self . . . he permits himself to be drawn into the family processes as a kind of chemical reagent, a catalyst or hormone." The stresses felt by the therapists in the present project were all the more interesting in light of the fact that all team members were experienced therapists, used to the more usual demands imposed upon them by a therapeutic relationship. All had had experience with psychotics and their families in the more usual settings.

The material presented below was not collected as part of a standardized, ongoing data-collection procedure. Although comments were made frequently during our weekly team discussion periods, the decision to report on this topic was made at the end of the second year. Once it was agreed that such reflections might be useful and important to others interested in this approach to schizophrenic families, an entire session was given over to discussion of the topic. The session was taped, and the material organized and subsequently enriched by further reflections. The product is not intended as a definitive statement, but rather as an indication of the importance of the issue in the eyes of the project team and the advisability of more careful exploration in the future.

Initial Family Contacts

As the project got under way, the therapy teams started to discuss their personal reactions to treating families in their homes. Everyone sensed some personal anxiety at leaving the "security" of his office or institution —the home territory with its familiar props—to do treatment in the home. We became aware that one facet of this uneasiness involved a subtle threat of loss of professional status in relationship to the family. In more than its obvious sense, the family was not coming to the office for help from "the doctors." We were impressed with the fact that our own sense of well-being, at least in part, hinged upon the concrete supports of our usual work setting. Though visiting the home presented an exciting challenge, there was also the initial anxiety of facing the unknown and unfamiliar.

Expectations of facing an unfamiliar setting were reinforced in many initial contacts. Inexperience in this type of work accentuated the absence of a single and clear frame of reference for the therapists. They were unconventional guests in the house, yet they were "doctors" with a purpose. Were they also friends? How does the family see the therapist—as a helper, an intruder, a magician? Though he might attempt to fall back upon the more orthodox role of the semi-detached, psychic expert, he soon felt uneasy and sensed the inappropriateness of the role.

The home also had an imposing and unexpected "reality" about it, yet therapists at times sensed it reflected a strange and unique "*Familien-geist*"—a pathological setting that was not only a challenge but in some cases forbidding. Frequently the homes were unusual in their special and living arrangements. One family, consisting of father, mother and schizophrenic teen-aged son, lived in a small three-room apartment. Both mother and father worked, while the son never left the apartment. The living room had a sofa which opened into a bed at night for the parents to sleep in, while the son used the double bed in the bedroom. Besides the usual—though exceptionally drab—living room chairs, the living room also contained a large bird cage, folded bedding (always left in one chair during the day), a small book case for the son's coin collection and some reading matter, a pinball machine, and a variety of games designed to maintain a strange world within a world that had a Charles Addams quality. In all instances the therapists were confronted with individuals who knew the arrangements in their home and could use them to their own advantage in the therapeutic process. Should the therapist freely move about in the home and examine its contents? Should he accept an evening snack when offered?

While many of these questions were eventually answered through experience, with a subsequent reduction in the therapists' initial anxiety, other issues remained as real ones throughout our experiences in the home. When engaged in this type of treatment, one is actually, at times, in "enemy" territory. The home and its contents are used as a means not only of communicating changes but also of fending off the therapist-intruder, of keeping him off balance, of blocking therapeutic movement. On one occasion a therapist was offered a chair he knew might collapse under him if he sat down; on another, the primary patient locked herself in the bathroom and refused to join the session, while the mother physically blocked the therapist from ascending the stairs. On yet another occasion, the primary patient evaded the therapists by using another door of the house to get to the garage, and then drove off.

Multiplicity of Observable Events

A very taxing element of our work at times was to keep track of the quantity and variability of communications passing between family members and therapists. Within any one session emotional tones might vary, the focus of conversation shift innumerable times, two discussions be held simultaneously, and yet all the talk may merely serve as a decoy for a meaningful nonverbal maneuver or to protect one family member who says nothing, but by so doing is "sending" the major message of the session! The therapist has to follow the "flow" carefully, but can never hope to catch all that is going on. Although having two therapists in a session made the situation more manageable—one therapist could "check" the observations of the other—it was not unusual for the therapists to hold quite different views as to what constituted the most significant interactions during a session.

Confronted with such a situation, the therapist must not only be capable of selective scanning of fast changing events, but tolerate at least brief periods of not knowing what is going on and/or the ambiguities of what seem like infinite possibilities.

Heightened Affective Charge

The experience of all therapy teams indicated that perhaps the most taxing facet of this work is the requirement that the therapist tolerate and become engaged in intense family emotions. On occasion the stress involved a challenge to the therapist's own conventional cultural or family values. A mother tells her daughter she does not love her; a father must face the fact he is not the "man" of the house in front of his own children. In contrast to individual therapy or the more usual group work, the therapist must tolerate the exposure of feelings in an intense family relationship when all family members are present and looking on.

At times painful family scenes occur, when no family member is responding with equanimity or there is a cold yet deadly affective tone. Following one session, a therapist had the feeling he had been experiencing a "murder" in the family. It reminded him of the play, "The Visit," where a murder plot moves through its ultimate course, accepted by everyone as inevitable. Lest this sound unduly dramatic, it is worth noting that serious physical illness in the family was not unusual (particularly among fathers), and at least two therapists noted that they had suffered more frequent physical illness during the project period than was usual for them! In more than one weekly project meeting, the question was raised as to the risk of continuing in a particular fashion because of the possibility that the father may suffer a heart attack.

Intense feelings were sometimes directed toward the therapists. In the home setting they could be attacked by the entire family, organized to drive them away. Some families openly threatened them in a paranoid fashion. One father told a therapist that if he came back for the next session he (the father) and other relatives would be waiting to beat him up.

Yet the emotional demands inherent in the families treated were not limited to hostile affect. Not infrequently therapists left a session feeling as though they had been "sucked dry," or in some way "seduced" into a pathological interplay. Neither experience nor lengthy team discussions completely eliminated the feeling that a therapist in family sessions is personally more vulnerable to the primitive interplay of group members. One therapist commented on how one's own need to be included in a "family" could be triggered off by the therapy, while another related how on at least one occasion he had not wanted to be included into a particular "sick" family and its destructive interactions, and had had to grapple with a strong aversive feeling toward the family and its pathological themes.

Therapeutic Use of the Therapist's Feelings

Of great importance in a therapeutic setting where the therapist must tolerate intense affect in others are his own feelings—countertransference and otherwise—and how they may be used for therapeutic ends lest they add to the family anxiety and chaos. Experience suggests that the therapist must be able to face and deal with his own emotions "on the spot." While it was apparent that the more usual, detached *tabula rasa* role was inappropriate, as well as unfeasible under conditions of emotional bombardment, therapists did not always find it easy to estimate the relatedness of their own feelings to the family interaction, and to use them productively. Needless to say, indecision, hesitation, or conflict as to whether to express a feeling or not could sap the therapist's energies, attentive powers, and objectivity. Emotional spontaneity is at times indispensable in a treatment session, but therapists also related experiences where they had been afraid of being "swallowed up," "overwhelmed," or left "defenseless" had they allowed their own feelings free expression. While one could conceive of the therapist being completely spontaneous in expressing the feelings aroused in him by a particular family interaction, most of the project team felt it was necessary to maintain some limited detachment. There was general agreement, however, that the therapist frequently had to be willing and able to respond with his own feelings, and to tolerate the possibility of revealing himself as a real person, neurosis and all.

Active engagement can take many forms, depending on the therapist and the particular family. On occasion the therapist may hold up his feelings before the family as a mirror wherein the family or one of its members can see himself or what he arouses in others. He may support or reprimand the family as though he were a representative of society who is involved and concerned with them. He may feel on occasion that a particular family member needs protection from the others and will communicate supportive affection to him, or restraint to the others. In all these and other situations, however, he is rarely, in the family's perception, completely realistic or totally a transference object. What is needed is for him to discriminate between his own feelings, to be at home with them, and to admit to them within the family session when necessary.

In discussing this issue perhaps more than another, the personalities of the project team members were manifest. It was apparent that the attitude toward frequency of use and manner of expression of the therapist's feeling as an active therapeutic ingredient would depend upon the character and habit structure of the therapist himself. The need for him to know, tolerate and use himself is clear.

Unlearning and Relearning

For most members of the project team, to engage in this therapeutic approach demanded some shifts in orientation. This involved both the unlearning of therapeutic habits not appropriate to this form of therapy and the incorporating of a new repertoire of responses, at first alien or even strange to one's concept of the therapeutic role. It would be a mistake to underestimate how taxing this can be in view of the years of training and experience that had taught us to think along more conventional therapeutic lines. Our theoretical orientation was either totally inappropriate or required translation and incorporation into a new set of conceptions.

In contrast to individual office or institutional work, therapy teams had to "set" themselves to be alert to complex interactions between two, three, or even more individuals, often moving about their homes and communicating as much if not more through non-verbal than verbal symbols. The "natural" tendency to listen to what was said frequently masked the significant communication via an exchange of glances, seating arrangements, physical postures of family members, and the myriad of stimuli of potential communication value. It was necessary for the therapist not only to be attentive to many levels of reactivity but himself to respond at more than one level.

Where previous training in individual work had focused on intrapsychic defenses, this approach required also a sensitivity to defensive maneuvers shared by two or more family members. Whereas habit would lead one to deal with one family member's fantasy productions in terms of his individual history and dynamics, their significance in family sessions often lay in revealing alliances or cliques between two family members, expressing a family theme for the session, or revealing a fantasy shared by all family members.

Perhaps the most obvious new demand for all members of the project team was to become more fully acquainted with a literature in areas that had previously been perceived as outside, or merely peripheral, to their professional work. Research and theory on family and social roles, communication, small-group dynamics, and the sociology of family-culture interaction became directly pertinent to any discussion of family movement in therapy and the goals of family work.

In discussing what he feels are difficulties in doing "conjoint" family therapy, Jackson[55] states: "Our language for small-group interaction is inadequate and conventional dyadic frames of reference do not suffice. When one is dealing with present and past, the hopes and expectations, the verbal and nonverbal behavior, and the immediate on-going interactions of at least four people, it seems doubtful that it can ever be encased within a framework smaller than a circus tent." Which framework(s) will eventually prove most useful must await further experience. In the project's case it became necessary for all of us to begin to question our own values regarding our conceptions of "mental health" and the limits we had previously imposed upon ourselves as professionals.

Conclusion

In dealing with a new technique it is perhaps best to avoid concluding statements lest they suggest that all issues are closed or resolved. But a few words seem appropriate. As noted earlier, the comments above are offered in the belief that the therapist as a person is an issue in therapy with schizophrenic families in the home, and warrants more detailed consideration than the present data allows.

Our experience indicates that this type of work is not for the meek at heart, those "sold" on a particular intrapsychic approach, those who by nature are ill at ease with intense affect, or those who for whatever reason prefer not to become emotionally involved with their "patients." If our work has supplied in any way a representative sample of experience, it suggests that the therapist must have a fair supply of physical as well as emotional stamina, a flexibility of mind, and a willingness to travel in rain and snow.

Previous experience with psychotics would seem essential, and any experience in work with families (e.g., child guidance clinic, functioning home-visit case work) extremely helpful. Whether therapy for the therapist himself is crucial may be debated, but there is little doubt that self-awareness—awareness of one's own emotional tendencies and character structure—is crucial.

Heterosexual co-therapy relationship and its

significance in family therapy

John C. Sonne and Geraldine Lincoln

This chapter represents an attempt to make a contribution toward an appreciation of the problems of technique in family therapy. It represents an examination of the co-therapy relationship in the early and late phase of family treatment with a schizophrenogenic family; it describes the working-out of our particular relationship in working with a particular family, the Ichabod family. (The Ichabod family and the first 40 weeks of their therapy have been described in detail in Chapter 7.) The therapists met with this family once a week for an hour and a half for a period of three and a half years, and no meetings were held unless both therapists and all four family members were present. At the time of termination, all participants and independent psychological testing gave evidence of marked improvement in total family and individual family member functioning. We have chosen this method because we feel that something would be lost if we presented our concepts without that setting. We hope the reader will be able to grasp the essence of the examination in this form and to use the concepts more universally.

Early Phase

We feel that an examination of the therapeutic process in any family is incomplete without considering the thoughts and feelings of the co-therapists, not only about the family, but about each other. One initial consideration in this area had to do with the fact that the male therapist had great expectations from this particular family in that he felt that it might make a unique contribution towards increased knowledge and conceptualizations concerning the dynamics of schizophrenia. He had specifically sought a referral of a family in which both parents had been analyzed, and in which there was also a schizophrenic offspring. In this family, only the father had been analyzed, but all of the other members had had considerable psychotherapy. The male therapist expected that—despite their resistances—this family, with its capacity for conceptualization, its sophistication, its high level of intelligence, and its obvious painful search for help individually, would in this search for help also make a contribution to psychiatric knowledge. He had seen the family alone for three sessions before being joined by the female therapist, and part of the initial development of the co-therapist relationship involved telling the female therapist why he had selected this family and his enthusiasm for working with them.

Despite our reservoir of enthusiasm, we found ourselves experiencing a growing sense of futility in the initial phase of treatment. It became more and more obvious that the family members had no respect for the feelings of each other or for our feelings. Frequently, when one member of the family was able to express genuine feeling, another member would vitiate the expression, attempt to get a retraction, or counterattack. We felt we were witnessing and becoming involved in the inexorable progress of a powerful process devoted to the destruction of all vitality and creativity. This experience became very stressful to us, and we saw both in the family and in ourselves many of the phenomena described by Schaffer et al.[97] We also noted in this atmosphere the development of a heightened awareness of each other and our co-therapy relationship, which we felt was significant and which we wish to describe.

By contrast to the family, we were appreciative of each other's sensitivity, vitality, and appropriateness in a situation where the family members were flat, stiff, surly, hopeless, inappropriate and generally unresponsive to their own or to our thoughts and feelings. We felt an increasing need within ourselves to clarify for each other our co-therapist relationship in the areas of respect for feelings, honest expression of feeling, dependency, trust and work—areas which were being eroded in the family. The area with which we struggled, and which was perhaps the most important of all, involved the definition of man, woman and the important aspects of a man-woman relationship; again, an area being eroded in the family. We found ourselves communicating with each other about these areas in the family sessions, interwoven with, pertinent to, and reactive with the family interaction. In order to be able to help the family we needed to clearly understand each other. And in helping the family, we clarified our positions for each other. For example, in a session in which Mrs. Ichabod undercut her husband for spending $75 on a patent search for an invention, and Mr. Ichabod failed to defend himself, the female therapist expressed amazement that Mrs. Ichabod wouldn't gamble on her husband. The male therapist questioned the husband's readiness to take this lack of support lying down. In the face of this destructive family interaction which in this instance weakened the father, we helped each other, in our remarks and attitude, maintain our own sexual identities, and survived as an effective voice of reality which challenged family role distortion. The family division was unable to distort the co-therapy shared sense of reality.

An additional stress factor involved in the development of our co-therapist relationship came from being observed by our research group via a one-way screen, and having our relationship scrutinized and discussed in post-therapy session reviews. This was particularly difficult in that the observers looked for smooth team functioning while we were struggling not only with the family, but with the fact that we had come from different settings, had known each other only a few months, and that the female therapist had had no prior experience in family treatment. The female therapist felt this stress differently than did her male co-therapist, who, although he wanted the criticism and had in fact suggested the observation, had a partial subjective feeling of intrusiveness by the observers. The observers at that time were all men, and tended to lean toward being protective of the female therapist. The latter minded the intrusiveness less by virtue of her enjoyment of the protective attitude she received from the observers. We have had subsequent sessions in which the observation group contained both men and women and in this group the reactions to the therapists were mixed and did not have the skew mentioned above. We feel this may be significant in terms of the dramatic, exhibitionistic aspects of being observed and the voyeuristic and competitive aspects involved in observing. The observers' comments, although they might have had a divisive effect, in actuality motivated us—as did the family stress—toward achieving a greater sense of unity.

We realized that relating within the context of the family therapy room left us with many questions unanswered. We adopted a plan of bi-weekly co-therapy conferences in which we found time to talk of many diverse things. For example, we found ourselves, in addition to discussing psychodynamics, talking about such seemingly mundane matters as whether the man or the woman of the house goes to get a new bar of soap when it wears down to a sliver in the bathroom. Although the subject matter on the surface seemed trivial, the latent content was important. On this and many other matters we were working metaphorically on the definition and appreciation of the male and female points of view, as well as on the vital importance of appreciation of feeling. These two areas were major problem areas in this family. By working through various misunderstandings and difficulties of communication between them we arrived at an agreement, which colored the therapy, that being loved to a woman is most important, and that it is only when she feels she is not loved that she places undue stress on such things as status and responsibility. Moreover, she feels happiest when her husband is the winner even though she may fight hard to beat him in an argument. As therapists we worked out our feelings with each other in terms of the questions of dominance of the male over the female, acceptance by the female therapist of aggressiveness on the part of the male, and much mutual acceptance of feeling. In the co-therapy relationship operating in this treatment situation, the male therapist learned that he could be aggressive and strong and feel supported by the female therapist without fear of her undercutting him or mistaking aggression for cruelty. She, in turn, felt free to express herself openly without fear of hurting or being hurt by the male therapist, or to be quiet and passive if she so chose.

In working out our relationship we saw an analogy to the family situation as if we were the parents and the family represented our children, and compared our interest in each other with our interest in the family. Along these lines we talked to each other a great deal about parent-child relationships; who comes first, the parents or the children; who comes first, the therapists or the family; and who comes first, the man or the woman. The theme of appreciation seemed to pervade the working out of all the above mentioned areas.

Having described to some extent the therapeutic homework, let us now discuss its function in the family treatment. First, at the outermost operational level we felt that there were three derivatives from our therapeutic homework. a) We were able in a variety of situations to give the family a clear, unified and unambivalent presentation of reality. For example, in one situation, the mother described her insulation from the family by withdrawing at an early hour to her bed where she comforted herself with a hot-water bottle, TV, her knitting, and candy. She was simultaneously protesting that her husband was inattentive. The female therapist's agreement with the male therapist's emphasis on Mrs. Ichabod's insulation rather than allowing herself to be used by the mother to support her charge of husbandly neglect, was the crucial factor in helping the mother to genuinely examine and question her defensive behavior. This therapeutic unity prevented the use of a man-woman argument as a defense and thereby precluded the continuation of the incessant paranoid projection which had marked the disunity in the family marriage. b) Through our discussions with each other, we maintained a clear and up-to-date understanding of the family which enabled us to present to them essentially similar concepts of the ever-changing family dynamics. Neither one of us seemed to be lagging behind or out of tune with the other. c) A third operational derivative was that, having taken the time necessary to communicate with each other in our co-therapy conferences, we were not preoccupied with each other in the family therapy sessions and could be more occupied in attending to the family. Bowen[20, 21] has mentioned that at times parents are so close that they exclude their children from an appropriate parent-child experience with them. (In amplifying this point, Bowen[21] speaks of a pathological overcloseness of the parents as a phase of the "emotional divorce," harmful to the children. With a healthy closeness there is no fear of harming the children by exclusion; as a matter of fact, they can benefit from such an exclusion.) We have considered this same possible danger in terms of the therapists' communication with each other possibly blocking communication to and from the family. We believe, however, that the co-therapist unity was therapeutic and not exclusive. We might add that at times, without this unity, it would have been impossible to make certain painful and difficult interpretations. For example, at one point in treatment the male therapist knew that he was required to interpret explicitly to the mother that, after months of observation, he had to conclude from the evidence of her thoughts, feelings and way of interacting, that she did not truly love her son, nor did she ever listen to him. This confrontation greatly disturbed her. She wept for the first time, and subsequently threatened suicide and separation. The family, although aware of the truth of the confrontation, had a need to perpetuate denial and compromise. Partly verbally, but mainly non-verbally or implicitly, they conveyed their feelings that they wished the confrontation had not taken place. The male therapist felt the presence of the female therapist enabled him to endure the burden of having revealed a painful truth and to face the powerful reaction with courage. The therapists felt that their unity gave the family less of an opportunity for unconscious reasons to refute the confrontation as cruel and unkind, and in so doing fortify their defenses. On a manifest level the credibility and benevolent intent associated with the confrontation were increased by its validation by the female therapist. By virtue of their secure unity they kept their attention on what the family needed and did not escape or let themselves be diverted by the family from the hard work of dealing with, in this instance, an inescapable, painful reality.

The disastrous consequences of a lack of co-therapist unity were observed in the initial phase of the treatment of another family. The referring female social worker had had a long relationship with the mother in the family before family treatment was begun. She was allowed to participate as a trainee co-therapist with a male therapist during the first several family therapy sessions. The exposure in the family setting of some of the mother's hostility toward her daughter so disturbed this female social worker that she became intensely anxious, was unable to function in the therapy, and became estranged in her relationship with her co-therapist.

She identified with the mother and became so overly involved with the family that against the co-therapist's wishes she allowed herself to be driven home by the family in their car. Ultimately, this co-therapist relationship became so difficult that the female therapist dropped out of the family treatment.

Second, at a level deeper than the three surface derivatives from the co-therapy relationship mentioned above—namely, a clear understanding, lack of ambivalence, and freedom of attention—we felt that the actual experiential process taking place in our relationship was in itself therapeutic to the family. It was as if we had imbibed the family problems and embodied them as a partial element in the composition of our relationship, thus creating stress in us which demanded resolution. Out of this process taking place in the co-therapy relationship came an acting back on the family in which all messages had evidence of having been through a period of symbolic gestation in our "marriage." Our messages to the family, in addition to their explicit content, all bore implicit evidence of having been through the mill of the co-therapist relationship. Beyond this, the interpretations were additionally enriched by an implicit nascent element of creative heterosexual potential. This quality is difficult to express, but we felt that the total capacity for perception and expression was greater than the sum of each of our individual capacities. The fact that this implicit message had reached the family became evident when they began to display a new quality or hopefulness in their demeanor.

Third, we would like to consider the question of the neurotic aspects of our relationship. The therapeutic homework described so far has assumed the therapists to be idealized and healthy. Naturally, since the material touched on primitive areas, much took place in us at an unconscious level; hence, some of our thinking and functioning must of necessity have been colored by residual unconscious conflicts. For example, after a certain home visit, we compared notes on our reactions. The male therapist said that he had enjoyed seeing the home and felt as though he would have liked to have been offered a cup of coffee, whereas the female therapist recalled feeling uncomfortable and having had the impulse to leave. In discussing this, the female therapist recalled that she had felt most uneasy when Mrs. Ichabod had taken the therapists for a tour of the bedrooms. The male therapist speculated that men may feel more comfortable with their sexual curiosity than women, whereupon the female therapist had a flashback of her mother saying, "never look."

The next home visit was far more comfortable for her to the point where she easily complimented Mrs. Ichabod on the graciousness of her home. We also learned gradually that it was important to use as much of our conference time as was necessary to deal with whatever neurotic areas we perceived in each other; sometimes a dream gave us insight; at other times we were helped by observations from our research group. In addition to the three dimensions of the co-therapy relationship outlined above—the operational functioning in the family therapy, the embodiment of the family's problems in our relationship experience, and the resolution of our own residual neurotic conflicts—there is a fourth dimension, and that is the real relationship which prevails throughout and is implicit in all of the foregoing.

Although our relationship began with our common interest in understanding and helping the Ichabod family, we have come to realize as we look back over the past 3½ years, that our development into an effective co-therapy team stemmed from the fact that we expected a great deal from ourselves and from the other. It seemed false to expect the family to communicate directly with one another on a feeling level without applying the same standards to ourselves. In experiencing the stress of the indirect communication of the family and seeking for more honest and direct communication, we found it impossible to tolerate any vagueness in our relationship. We expected no difficulties to remain unresolved. When we were appreciative of each other we said so; when we didn't like something the other had said or done, we also said so. We allowed little time to pass before eliminating any static, and each of us felt free to take the initiative. This required a degree of trust that took some time to develop but increased with each successful clarification. This development of trust required that we both reach out and dare to risk the exposure of our feelings and ideas in order to fully communicate our thoughts.

Through this basic, implicit commitment to direct expression of feeling, we were able to experience a process involving several derivatives: 1) It enabled us to explore a broader area of thought and feeling than would ordinarily have been possible. We experienced the pleasure of free discussion and exchange of ideas which we related not only to the therapy situation, but to our lives in general. In doing so, it seemed natural to include personal experiences pertaining to both our present families and our families of origin. We discussed the degree to which we saw some of our personal family problems revealed in bolder type in this grossly sick family. New ideas derived from working with this family found their way into our family relationships at home. 2) We experienced both the pain of intense argument and the reward of satisfaction for having worked out our difficulties. 3) We each clarified our own thoughts and feelings. This required patience from both of us in that in the process of clarification one or the other might thrash through many tentative thoughts before arriving at an unambivalent position on an issue. 4) We noticed two major changes in our personalities: the female therapist acquired more directness, and the male therapist more tact. 5) By virtue of clear communication we enjoyed the male and female points of view, and found no need for sexual role distortion and its accompanying element of competition for recognition. We felt and enjoyed the support we gave each other when under stress. 6) Having struggled with our own difficulties in communication in our co-therapy relationship, we found we approached our relationships with colleagues and other co-therapists with whom we worked with an increased capacity and willingness to reach out, to seek and expect resolution of difficulties. The knowledge and capacity derived from our own co-therapy experience found its way into other co-therapy experiences in which we were involved or became involved, and was also used in teaching our students the importance of clear communication in their work as co-therapists. At times we experienced prolonged and turbulent stress with our team colleagues before resolution occurred. The stress involved fear of disapproval, of being misunderstood, of hurting and of precipitating a permanent rift. On a few occasions, our seeking clear communication between therapists led us to the sudden and painful awareness that we were almost at an impasse with co-therapists who did not have an approach similar to ours. For example, working with another co-therapist we once became involved in a discussion about schizophrenia. He said he didn't dislike the illness, that he thought schizophrenics couldn't be cured but that they were interesting people, and it was interesting to hear what they thought. We told him that it was all very well to be detached and unrelated, but what business did he have working in therapy with schizophrenics, and furthermore, what did he think was going on in his co-therapy relationship? (At the time of this writing, this discussion seemed like giving a speech to an empty hall, a speech quite likely destined to failure. As it turned out, we were rewarded in that the confrontation validated our thesis on the importance of direct communication between co-therapists. Facing this impasse was the beginning of growth in our relationship. This growth was demonstrated when the co-therapist expressed appreciation for the confrontation and initiated further exploration of the co-therapy relationship.) We regard the increased dedication to the importance of direct communication of feeling between co-therapists, something we arrived at through a theoretical consideration of our co-therapy experience, as a valuable development. 7) The co-therapy experience has led us to an even greater sense of conviction of the importance of the direct communication of feelings in therapy.

Late Phase

After working with the Ichabod family for two years, we became aware over a period of six months that we were at a point of impasse. Father had worked through many transference feelings with both the male and female therapist. The mother, on the other hand, seemed to stop the relationship at a level involving superficial appreciation of the attention she was receiving, particularly from the male therapist. For example, she would say in a somewhat coquettish and slightly praising manner that one of the main reasons she liked to come to the meetings was because she enjoyed hearing the male therapist tell her she looked pretty. She limited the closeness to the male therapist to this; she avoided relating to the female therapist in a manner reminiscent of her treatment of Ginger. When confronted with her apparent lack of deep involvement, she would respond with a ready list of platitudinous disclaimers. She would say, for example that she thought the therapists were very nice people, and that it was wonderful that they were able to do this very difficult work so easily.

Over this period of time we were aware of a difference between us. The male therapist was much more discouraged than the female therapist, with the latter having to remind him of some of his earlier enthusiasm about the family and his argument for time and patience in their treatment. Despite this, his dissatisfaction reached such proportions that, in one session, he expressed himself strongly, initiating an engagement which profoundly altered the family and involved much working-out of feelings in the co-therapy relationship.

At the beginning of this particular session the mother was asked how she felt about three things: the female therapist's efforts in the previous session to reach Ginger; the fact that Ginger, despite having gained her mother's permission in the previous session to wear lipstick, was not wearing it; and her husband's suffering from a respiratory infection during the intervening week. She gave a blasé, bland, unfeeling response to all three questions. At this point, the male therapist—with a sense of utter futility— picked up a newspaper and began to read it. He then turned to the female therapist and initiated a conversation on items of general news interest, including the description of a new painting which he had brought home and hung on the wall near the kitchen, and anecdotes about one of the children's hobby of rock collecting. Mrs. Ichabod quipped, "Isn't hanging pictures woman's work?"

The female therapist, although surprised and feeling temporarily out of tune with the male therapist's behavior, responded to this engagement with interest and added some ideas of her own as regards to aspects of everyday life. She felt secure enough in the co-therapy relationship to respond to what seemed, at the moment, to be a crazy swing, trusting that clarity would ultimately appear. What resulted turned out to be a free discussion on creativity between the therapists, with Mr. Ichabod joining in. Mrs. Ichabod, feeling ignored, wanted to leave but was ordered to stay by her husband. A critical point in the discussion came when the female therapist related a story about an artist who, in order to please a prospective buyer, had agreed to move the position of the sun in one of the paintings. Both therapists saw eye to eye in agreeing that they would never do such a thing. Mr. Ichabod hesitantly called them naive and unworldly. The male therapist proceeded along these lines to complain in unequivocal terms about the lack of appreciation for him and the female co-therapist.

The next two months were taken up with a great struggle in the co-therapy relationship. The male therapist plagued the female therapist with his discouragement about family treatment, complaining that they had repeatedly arrived at a point where they were unable to effect fundamental change in the mothers. He contrasted the limited information this mother had given about herself with cases in his experience where the deep dynamics had unfolded. The female therapist agreed intellectually but on an emotional level did not identify with him. There was a marked difference in the level of feeling. The male therapist felt he was a fake and that family therapy would be written off the books in a few years, whereas the female therapist tended to be less angry and pessimistic, functioning as the spokesman for moderation and patience. She tempered the atmosphere with reminders of how much worse the family had been at the beginning of the treatment.

The male therapist was particularly angry at the mother's lack of appreciation of what he felt were the mothering qualities of the female therapist, and was resentful of her not appreciating what he felt were marked differences between the male and female therapist. The mother seemed to regard both therapists as of similar service to her, indiscriminate of what he felt were sharp qualitative differences in the way each therapist might be able to give. The male therapist felt that in some way she was asking him to be a mother; that what she really wanted was a castrated man and not a woman with breasts. She made him feel impotent. He insisted to the female therapist that she should feel more unrecognized and unfulfilled than she did. The female therapist wondered why she didn't feel this way. She had doubts as to whether her or her co-therapist's perception of the family was accurate; she was bewildered as to why he reacted so differently at this phase in therapy. Both therapists spent a great deal of time struggling to define and understand the significance of their difference. They speculated that it might be caused by the fact that the male therapist's role was being distorted whereas the female therapist was being under-used, though without any role distortion.

The male therapist felt that if the family, and particularly the mother, were not going to make better use of the female therapist, he fantasied that he'd go off fishing and meet her later for dinner. He definitely did not intend to be a mother himself. The female therapist reacted to the intensity of her co-therapist's feelings by becoming concerned about him. She wondered at first if this were a neurotic problem of his or whether his feelings were an appropriate index of what was going on in the therapy. She had a mixture of concern for his feelings, a wish to take care of him and a fear that unless he felt more satisfied he might leave the therapy situation. She didn't want to take care of the family alone. The male therapist became increasingly irritable with Mrs. Ichabod, anticipating what she was going to say when a sentence was half out of her mouth. He also became increasingly disinterested and withdrawn.

When the problem of dealing with the mothers of schizophrenogenic families was being discussed by our research group one day, with a fair amount of introspection on the part of the group members, it turned out that many of them felt they had not sufficiently dealt with the problem of their own mothers and that this might be causing a problem in their work. A colleague had half jokingly suggested that he write a book about himself and his own family, with particular interest centering on his mother, rather than write a book on family therapy. At this point the male therapist described the problems of getting to the mother in the schizophrenogenic family and the importance of the female co-therapist in this matter. He said, "I finally got them a mother and they won't use her. I'd like her to take care of them while I go fishing." The female therapist laughed and answered: "I'll take care of them but only if you'll stick with me." Some group members then reminisced about their mothers, and there was a considerable loosening up of feelings accompanied by increased comfort.

In the family session immediately following this staff conference the female therapist revealed to the family a dream she had had about the male co-therapist. In this dream she had seen him as old and beaten down apparently from years of unavailing, hard work. She said that she felt the dream represented her concern for him, and that she shared his frustration at the mother's lack of involvement and her lack of engagement in reciprocal relationships. Mr. Ichabod was very moved by the dream and said he thought it was very loving. He felt sufficiently encouraged by this openness to reveal some closely-guarded, secret feelings of inadequacy and weakness in regard to his work. Mrs. Ichabod, appearing imperturbable, delivered a perfunctory apology, "I'm sorry if I've hurt you." Her response was so grossly inappropriate that the male therapist left the room. Mr. Ichabod, alarmed, dashed after him and called him back, saying, "You scared me. I don't want you to leave." This was quite in contrast to his earlier protective attitude of wanting to rescue his wife from confrontations. We resumed the session along the theme of a crescendo of demands by all that mother expose herself. She promised to bring in her dreams and fantasies the following week.

Following are the notes of the subsequent session, written by the female therapist:

After an initial exchange of pleasantries, Mrs. Ichabod reached into her pocketbook and brought out a stack of papers on which she had written down her dreams this week, many from the night following the preceding session. In the first dream, she saw a box containing many shoes and was delighted with the feeling that she had the choice of any pair she wished. In a second dream, she saw the female therapist as a witch, in a family meeting with everyone present except the male therapist and Robert. The group was waiting for them to come in. When they did arrive, everyone went in two cars out to the country, where the male therapist said the meeting would be held. Mrs. Ichabod said she had felt better in the latter part of the dream, with the shift in scene from a very small, dark closed room, to a bright open country landscape. She felt in the dream that not only was the female therapist a witch, but that she was a representation of her mother as well. In a third dream, Mrs. Ichabod saw herself in her mother's house, watching her mother dress for a party, full of resentment because she had not informed her in advance about this party. In associating to this dream, Mrs. Ichabod told us that a few weeks ago her mother had invited Ginger over to her house, but had neglected to inform Mrs. Ichabod that she was having a cocktail party. Mrs. Ichabod had arrived with Ginger, dressed in slacks and shirt, and had felt taken aback, trapped and humiliated by her mother's, "How could you do this to me" attitude. On her way to her next appointment she had gradually become aware of a burning anger toward her mother, had stopped the car and called Robert to pick up Ginger and bring her right home. When Robert arrived, however, Ginger was enjoying herself, and both children stayed for the rest of the afternoon. On hearing this, the mother had shifts in feeling from anger to rage to numb indifference. A fourth dream was of a scene of rabbits and children in the country. This dream had occurred a few days prior to the session being described, and was remembered by Mrs. Ichabod as a pleasant and enjoyable dream.

The female therapist asked Mrs. Ichabod if she noted any theme running throughout the dreams, and Mrs. Ichabod responded that she was aware that her mother was in many of her dreams, but minimized this as nothing new. The male therapist noted and commented on a subtle tone of anger in Mrs. Ichabod's reply and wondered if her "nothing new" answer might represent an attempt to ward off the female therapist. Mrs. Ichabod reflected that she was aware of having felt angry towards the female therapist after last week's meeting, and also when she dreamt of her as a witch, but she was not aware of feeling angry with her at the present time. After the male therapist pointed out how different her tone of voice was when she spoke to him and when she spoke to the female therapist, she went on to say that she couldn't even look at the female therapist, that she had always had a difficult time looking at other women and that she was sure that she saw her mother in the female therapist. She said that try as she might, she couldn't differentiate too well in this respect, that at times, when she looked at the female therapist, she recognized her true identity but nevertheless she hated her as she hated her mother.

The male therapist repeatedly and strongly instructed Mrs. Ichabod to talk about her mother and how she had felt toward her when she was a little girl; whenever she faltered, he prodded her on. He also insisted that she talk to the female therapist. Mrs. Ichabod responded by saying that she had never gotten from her mother what she wanted, that she wasn't even able to touch her as she had desperately wanted to do, that she had wanted her mother to look at her but her mother had always been too busy or not at home. She had felt unloved and uncared for, and had retaliated by being such a "nasty little brat" that her mother had lost every maid she'd ever hired. She recognized and related many of these ambivalent feelings to the female therapist. At this point the male therapist asked Mrs. Ichabod what she wanted today from the female therapist. She blandly supposed that she wanted mothering. In an effort to more specifically draw the mother out, the female therapist asked her if she really did want help, and if so, in what way did she want the female therapist to help her. It was very difficult for Mrs. Ichabod to admit that she did want help, but with her husband and the male therapist encouraging her, she finally turned to the female therapist and said that she did want mothering, that she did want her to help her, and asked if the female therapist could help her. The female therapist then asked Mrs. Ichabod how she felt at the moment. Mrs. Ichabod responded that she'd just like to cry on her shoulder. The female therapist suggested to Mr. Ichabod that they change seats so she could sit next to his wife. Mrs. Ichabod put her head on the female therapist's shoulder and cried for several minutes. After some time she looked up to say that she was now able to feel feelings of love for the female therapist. She then turned to the male therapist and said that now she knew what he had meant when he had said to her that if she let herself go she could probably cry for days on end, adding that that was exactly what she wanted to do. When Mrs. Ichabod was crying, Ginger also cried.

Impression

We felt this was a major breakthrough in the family; Mrs. Ichabod had been helped to really persevere in a major piece of work, involving her ambivalent feelings toward both her mother and the female therapist. She had been able to let go of her defenses to ask for what she needed, and to cry. Significant in this session also was her statement that she had been helped by the fact that her husband had talked to her and explained what the therapists had meant when they said they wanted her to give them something to work with. This had helped her to bring in her dreams and to give them to the therapists.

The above themes were further developed in ensuing sessions. Three episodes are noteworthy in that they illustrate the mother's relationship to her mother, to the female therapist and to her daughter. In one session the male therapist asked Mrs. Ichabod what she felt the female co-therapist wanted from her, and Mrs. Ichabod responded with alarm and genuine misunderstanding, "Don't go away yet." The second episode came up a few weeks later when she related how absolutely terrified she had been, both as a child and an adult, of having a pet for fear that she would never be able to care for such a helpless creature. She was able to see this as her perception of her mother's attitude toward herself, with herself as the pet. As a result of further work on this over the next few months she told us, in association to a dream in which she was shopping for a layette for her third child, a baby girl, that she felt she had grown enough so that she had room to love another person; she felt this time she could be a good mother and take good care of the baby. In the dream she felt she knew just the right things to buy because she was experienced, having had two other children.

The third point illustrating both her sensitivity and newly acquired fluidity occurred in a session following one canceled by the therapists. (The reason for the cancellation was the birthday celebration of the female therapist's son but the family had not been told this.) Mrs. Ichabod appeared flat. Ginger complained that her mother had not attended her school play the preceding evening. Mother laconically reported occupying herself with trivialities the evening of the play, in a manner of indifference to her daughter's hurt feelings. The therapists were surprised. The female therapist could not understand Mrs. Ichabod's behavior because she was so firmly convinced that a permanent shift had taken place in her character; she wondered what could have gone wrong in their relationship. Mrs. Ichabod volunteered no clues other than her coolness which she herself found incomprehensible. The female therapist thought to herself, "Could it really be that this reaction is a result of our having missed last week's session?" As soon as the question popped into her mind she knew that that was it and verbalized the question to Mrs. Ichabod. The latter answered that she thought about the therapists constantly. Further exploration brought tears and surprise to Mrs. Ichabod as she realized how fully devastated she had been at the cancellation, how much feeling she had for the therapists, and how unaware of her feelings she had learned to be.

We feel that the development of therapy in the late phase of family treatment is dependent upon dealing with and introducing the concept of mothering into the therapy; this cannot take place until the concept is clarified and has become an integral part of the team relationship. The stress within the family around mothering created stress in the co-therapy relationship which demanded resolution. Some of the working-out of this has been mentioned above. Whereas in the early phase of treatment the co-therapy relationship primarily involved a definition of the male-female points of view—with special emphasis on the prominence of the male and support of his aggressiveness—the emphasis in the late phase seemed to be on the male and female points of view with special emphasis on the pre-eminence of mothering. To say that the early phase involved a delineation of the father function both in the co-therapy relationship and in the family, and the late phase a delineation of the mother function both in the co-therapy relationship and in the family, would be a gross oversimplification. It would have been impossible to define the father function in the early phase without the help of the female therapist and it would have been equally impossible to define the mother function in the late phase without the male therapist's help. In each phase there was a symbolic marriage of the co-therapists.

In arriving at a mutually agreeable definition of the concept of mothering, we realized that, although we saw eye to eye intellectually, we reacted quite differently emotionally. This at times created an impression that we were at odds. When we analyzed this, we became aware of the fact that we often approached this area with markedly different moods. In accepting these differences as natural, we actually achieved a sense of unity.

Mothering, as we conceived of it, involved the following functions:

1) tolerance; 2) nurturing; 3) expectations that the child will be expressive, responsive and sexual; and 4) the maintenance of an image by the mother of her marriage, simultaneously with caring for her child. Using this concept in treatment involved some gratifying of the "child" in the mother, primarily as an avenue toward resolving the negative mother transference. This role of the female therapist was also needed as a model against which to contrast the original negative mother-child relationship which had apparently been so depriving that very little, if any, concept of adequate mothering was even known or understood by the "child." Actual teaching and limited gratification had to precede analysis.

In order for the female therapist to feel comfortable in dealing with areas involving the concept of mothering in the therapy, she needed to feel secure in her relationship with the co-therapist, and in order to function seemingly separated from him, she needed to feel that he completely supported her and would not abandon her even when he had temporarily "gone fishing." The male therapist in turn had to know that his co-therapist, in dealing with deep levels of mother-baby pathology, would continue to maintain an awareness of her relatedness to him. The female therapist had to know that the male therapist was not resentful of a "mother-baby" reciprocal closeness and mutuality between her and the mother, and that he was available to intrude if a psychopathological dyadic alliance appeared to be developing. The degree of trust required in the late phase exceeded that of the early phase of therapy, since the therapists now proceeded along lines which were somewhat more separate and distinct—lines they weren't so sure would complement or validate each other.

We saw that the female point of view was characterized by a marked degree of tolerance while the male point of view, in its concern for order and change, was characterized at times by intolerance and impatience. The ability of the co-therapists to maintain a creative symbolic "marriage," encompassing at times divergent but nevertheless complementary points of view, presents the family with an opportunity to deal with a relationship which can facilitate the construction of a family image,[105] to supplant the dyadic relationships so prevalent in the schizophrenogenic family.

Ideas harmonious with the co-therapists' thinking about male and female points of view, both in the early and late phases of therapy may be found in a paper by Ludwig B. Lefebre.[69] Helpful also to an understanding of the heterosexual co-therapy team functioning in the course of family treatment are the discussions of the male and female roles by Parsons and Bales.[86]

Open discussion of sexual material in family therapy

John C. Sonne and Geraldine Lincoln

Chapter
15

One of the questions frequently asked by our associates, students, referral sources and by ourselves is whether one does, can or should discuss sexual matters openly in the family. Initially, we found ourselves reticent to approach an open discussion of intimate sexual matters, particularly concerning the marital sexual relationship, with the total family present. On the manifest level we were aware that the "sitting face to face in a family group" was not the usual situation for a discussion of intimate sexual matters, in fact it was a situation in which one is ordinarily inhibited from sexual discussion. We had to get beyond the barrier of the seemingly "social" setting of the family interviews and consciously remind ourselves of the professional reason for our meeting.

Furthermore, even realizing the professional nature of our meetings, we still wondered on an intellectual level whether an open discussion of sexual material might not be harmful to the family. Perhaps the closed state of affairs existed for a good cause. Was it not possible that we, though being serious investigators, acting in a professional capacity, might impair the line of parental authority, foster acting out, increase unconscious resistance to treatment and provide the family with openings for consciously depreciating the therapy on moral grounds?

Beyond the social inhibition and the professional caution, we had to deal with our possible unconscious reluctance to deal with sexual material in the family, i.e., to witness the primal scene. The fact that we did have some unconscious resistance was revealed in our exaggerated annoyance when some referral sources displayed a skeptical attitude about discussing sexual material in the presence of children, and in our feeling of comfort and absence of anxiety when we considered obtaining sexual material in a more indirect way, for instance, through questionnaires or private sessions with the parents.

In our research group, several possible approaches to dealing with the sexual relationship of the parents were suggested, such as seeing mother and father separately, obtaining the information by questionnaire, or discussing the sexual material openly in the family. The degree to which varied psychological research studies are colored by unconscious or social factors is difficult to assess. In the case of the Ichabod family (*see* Chapter 7), for example, we elected to do what we were somewhat reluctant to do, i.e., to conduct no interviews unless every family member was present and encourage open discussion of sexual material when timely.

We reasoned that there were latent incestuous and homosexual dyads in the family, involving unconscious fantasies of a sexual nature. To resolve these pathological relationships seemed to us to be impossible without bringing into consciousness the unconscious fantasies about sexual feelings and anatomy. We reasoned as Freud[38] had done in the case of Dora: "*Pour faire une omelette il faut casser des oeufs.*" He stated further: "There is no necessity for feeling any compunction at discussing the facts of normal or abnormal sexual life with them (patients); with the exercise of a little caution all that is done is to translate into conscious ideas what was already known in the unconscious; and after all, the whole effectiveness of the treatment is based upon our knowledge that the affect attached to an unconscious idea operates more strongly and, since it cannot be inhibited, more injuriously than the affect attached to a conscious one. There is never any danger of corrupting an inexperienced girl. For where there is no knowledge of sexual processes even in the unconscious, no hysterical symptom will arise: and where hysteria is found, there can no longer be any question of innocence of mind in the sense in which parents and educators use the phrase. With children of ten, of twelve or of fourteen, with boys and girls alike, I have satisfied myself that the truth of this statement can invariably be relied upon."

We realize that we are extending this reasoning, here applied to an individual hysteric, to formulate a hypothesis that open discussion of sexual matters in a *schizophrenogenic* family (including small children) is equally necessary. We have worked with families who had children aged five or six and have found that these children have already incorporated the family's problem and are preoccupied with fantasies involving sex, anatomy and pregnancy. The work of Lidz[71] and his co-workers would suggest that since the schizophrenogenic family's members are already too close or intimate, discussions of sexual matters might best be held separately to achieve greater distance.

Some members of another family therapy group were opposed to open discussion of sexual material on the grounds that the primary patient had achieved too much gratification from hearing accounts of her parents' poor sexual adjustment. (In that family, we learned later, there had been actual incest.)

Much of the material illustrating the open discussion of sexual matters is interspersed in the previous descriptions of family therapy and psychodynamics. Returning to the Ichabods once more, the father's reluctance to speak of his partial impotence and his lack of deriving sexual pleasure from his wife, turned out to be connected with his closeness to his daughter and her pseudo triumph over the "wrinkle-faced, hair-dyed, bespectacled" mother. The daughter had a storehouse of "dirty stories" and was involved in sexual teasing and exhibitionism with her brother. The daughter's penis envy as a defense against her hostility to her mother led quite naturally to talk of sex. Mother's insulation and frigidity could not remain a secret, and led to further talk about sex. Most important, these discussions about sex in no way seemed to disturb or alarm any family member, parent or child, or cause any adverse reaction. To the contrary they led to greater clarity in comprehending the family roles and to a reduction of abnormal behavior. The sexual relationship between the parents improved and the children, surprisingly enough, seemed to be more relaxed and, although somewhat jealous, to show a greater capacity to identify with the parent of the same sex; this was illustrated by Ginger's suggesting to father that he buy perfume for mother, and Robert's joining the school crew. This was Robert's first participation in a team sport. In this particular family, no objection was raised to the discussion of sexual material after the first three sessions.

The value of exploring marital sexual behavior in depth was illustrated in a series of developments occurring in the latter half of the second year of therapy with the Ichabods. The sequence of events began with an exploration of the mother's attitudes about sex. She felt disgusted using a diaphragm or having intercourse during her menses. Through many family discussions and the reading of several books on sex which we gave to her and her husband, she became much more relaxed and less inhibited. They both reported a "second honeymoon" which was followed by a three-month period of withdrawal by Mr. Ichabod. During this interim we administered to every member of the family the sexual adjustment forms used by the Marriage Council, which we had been planning to give at an appropriate time. We asked the children to guess what their parents might say by filling out the forms themselves. Both children accurately guessed their parents' attitudes and conduct with one exception—Ginger fantasied that the parents had anal play which in fact they did not have. The parents' answers revealed their sexual practices to be ultra-conservative. They also reported that although they felt free to talk about sex and that they understood each others feelings, they really did not understand each others feelings nor did they care to. Further exploration of their sexual attitudes and conduct led the husband to reveal a fear that his penis would be caught and bitten off by his wife's vagina during intercourse. His three-month withdrawal period started when his wife, much to her surprise, began to experience vaginal orgastic spasms that grasped the husband's penis and both delighted and terrified him.

Discussion of sexual matters by no means constituted the main body of our therapy. We do not mean to imply that discussion of sex à la "wild analysis" [39] is in itself therapeutic. Discussion of sexual matters must be integrated in terms of shared unconscious fantasies and family interrelationships. However, we do feel that the discussion of the families and their relationships would be incomplete if disconnected from their sexual elements. Our experience with this family has supported our hypothesis. Experience with other families has so far given us no cause to lean in the opposite direction. The matter remains an unsettled scientific question. We feel that in considering this question it is always important to remember that the argument that "one does not do this" which is frequently heard in normal families is irrelevant, for these are extremely sick families and the way to healthy repression is by lifting temporarily a pathological repression. Families seem to be able to tolerate sexual discussions if the therapists feel free to let them.

The single therapist in family therapy

Jerome E. Jungreis

There is almost no discussion in the family therapy literature on the relative advantage of one therapist vs. co-
therapists. The reports by Ackerman,[3] Bell,[12] and others
on their work with families seem to indicate that each
conducted the therapy alone and apparently did not
experiment with the use of a co-therapist. Our project
group has worked with schizophrenic families almost
exclusively by using co-therapist teams as part of the
demonstration design. These teams have been composed
of same sex and opposite sex members. MacGregor's[76]
successful use of multiple therapists was originally designed to meet specific practical problems in providing
intensive family therapy in as compressed a time as possible. Sonne and Lincoln found, as described in Chapter
14, that the overwhelming destructiveness and sickness
in the schizophrenic family requires a male and female
co-therapist to draw from each other a reinforcement of
their sex role in the face of the family's onslaught against
their identity and integrity. They also felt that heterosexual co-therapists can supply much-needed balanced
fathering and mothering. Thus, the number of therapists
to be employed would appear to depend in part on the
degree of pathology in the family to be treated, and the
particular issues which are considered crucial to the
treatment.

The literature dealing with group therapy, however, discusses the issue of
the single therapist vs. co-therapists at considerable length. Robert Gans[41]
debates this question rather fully, concluding that co-therapists are not
necessary except that where "greater distribution of authority is needed,
co-therapists fit the need." To make use of the opinion of group therapists
on the relative value of the single therapist vs. two or more would involve
elaboration on the similarities and differences between group and family
therapy. Such elaboration would not be germane here. I need only point
to one very essential difference, and that is that the family is a system that
operates continuously—before, during, and after the therapy. Therapy
groups, on the other hand, are an artificial creation whose life begins and
ends with the therapy session.

There are many factors involved, in the determination of whether one or two therapists will treat a family. For example: the need of some therapists to work alone; the therapeutic freedom and creativity that therapists experience when they are responsive only to the family and not to the co-therapist; the therapist's experience with family therapy; his previous training and orientation; the use of staff-time; the requirements of a family therapy training program; the nature of the family system of the family to be treated, and its relative accessibility to therapeutic intervention.

I have worked with schizophrenic families alone and with co-therapists and there is no question in my mind that co-therapy adds team operation, division and re-enforcement of roles, mutual consultation, and planning—all valuable features, especially in the case of very sick and difficult families as already noted by Friedman in Chapter 3. However, I have found that there is one technique that is more effective with a single family therapist, and that requires the active participation and involvement of the therapist in the family transactions and his becoming a member of the family. In other words, the therapist permits himself to become incorporated into the family system. This becoming a part of the family adds one more dimension to the different roles a family therapist can play.

There are varying concepts concerning the therapist's relationship to the family. Ackerman[2] permits himself to be drawn into the family processes as a kind of catalyst. Such a position is in contrast to Bell's[11] therapeutic role, who states that "The therapist relates *to* the family, not within the family." However, in some schizophrenic families the resistance to change is so great that special techniques must be seriously considered, some of which call for a particular relationship with the family. Intentionally entering the family system, becoming part of the family is one such relationship. If the therapist can successfully become a member of the family, his presence will overload the closed family system and cause it to break down. He is then in a position to help the family reconstitute itself in a dynamic, growth-oriented way. I have found the single therapist most easily able to get "tuned into" the family system and become incorporated into it. The single therapist can feel in an almost physical sense the various family forces at work on him. His empathy with various family members is heightened, and because he is not committed to the system—although he is tuned in—his intuitive capacity is sharpened. There is a considerably greater awareness of the family mood. Even more important, a family with one therapist can more easily probe from whence this mood comes, what sustains it, what distortions and fears hold the system in rigid suspension. The therapist can thus convey to the members of the family his understanding of their problems and tensions in terms that are meaningfully relevant to them.

It is difficult to describe the process of tuning into the family system, of becoming sensitized to its nuances and emotional envelopment. I have experimented with entering the system by partially ignoring my role of observer, helper, and clarifier and reacting spontaneously with the family as though I *was* a member. I may be aroused to annoyance, anger, compassion, frustration; be sucked into dyads; be clobbered by single binds, double binds, desire dependence; revolt against it all and feel helpless or omnipotent but I attempt to participate as fully as I comfortably can. This comfort depends on the degree to which I can maintain an awareness of the process while it is going on, knowing its irrationality, the family's readiness to accept me as one of them, being sure of my own sense of reality and finally, being able to handle the intensity of the emotional impact that this technique imparts. Part of my security too lies in the knowledge that, though I may have become part of the system, I am not committed to it.

This method is somewhat analogous to a technique that is used in individual therapy, where the therapist, when he senses strong feelings in himself that are provoked by the patient, points this out to him as a step in helping the patient understand himself. An individual therapist with an acutely ill schizophrenic patient may go further and enter into the delusional system together with the patient—as Lindner[72] did—and then fight his way out of it, bringing the patient along with him; or leaving no room in the system for the patient. The individual patient's delusional system is analogous to the pathological family system of our abnormal families.

At the point where I feel myself emotionally aroused by the interplay of feelings in the family, I feel tuned into the family system. This is the phase that is most difficult to get into in the presence of a co-therapist. (At least this was so for me; some of the other project therapists were not so sure that the presence of a co-therapist made that much difference in their use of this technique.) Where I have tried this technique with a co-therapist, I have found myself at moments of family tension looking at him, seeking relief by moving emotionally closer to him and thus away from the family system. The co-therapist acts for me as the guardian of reality who protects me from emotional excess, and from being sucked into the swirling storm center before us. The stronger temptation is to avoid the psychopathology and take refuge in mental health. However, this temptation serves to keep me outside the family system. For the family too, the presence of two therapists may provide too much sense of reality, too much awareness of social conventions and need to maintain an outward posture of normalcy for full arousal of their primitive transactions. I therefore have found that even where two therapists enter the family system, the intensity of the family's reaction is nowhere near as great as it is with a single therapist. At best too, it appears to be only a partial entry. It is difficult enough for the family to swallow one addi-tional member—two become almost undigestible. Hence, if I am at all convinced that a particular family requires entry into its pattern, I can most easily and successfully accomplish this if I work alone rather than with a co-therapist. It is to be noted that entry into the family system, feeling the emotional charges and tension, also helps the therapist to understand more clearly what these tensions are, preparatory to following them to their source. In this sense, I am not really absorbed by the family. Through entry into the family, I can quickly move to the locus of the problems, define them, and at the appropriate time call upon the family health to deal with them.

This process needs to be contrasted with the second technique which I described in Chapter 11, entitled "The Active Role of the Family Thera-pist." There I noted how the family attempts to incorporate the therapist into their ongoing transactions. That is, the family attempts to assign the therapist a role which would be compatible with their system, i.e., leave the system untouched. The therapist may relate to the family, as have other non-family members, but the family has structured the role of the non-member in such a way that will leave the family system, on a meaningful level, undisturbed. I observed that the purpose of the family in assigning the therapist a role was to *maintain* their static transactions by working out a conscious or unconscious accomodation on their terms. Only by refusing the role assigned to him by the family and by assuming an active role himself can the therapist hope to bring about a change—a technique that can be used as effectively by co-therapists as it can by a single therapist. What I am suggesting in this chapter, however, is a technique that—while still aimed at bringing about change in the family transactions—is more effective when it is used by a single therapist. Again, the therapist does not accept the role designed by the family to enable it to continue its static pattern. Instead, he enters a family system that has no place for him as currently operating. The single therapist can join the family because he has shared with them the experience of being caught up in the pathology, and has established a common bond with their confusion, anger, depression, guilt, or whatever feelings were aroused. He has told them that he knows what they are going through because he too has experienced these feelings, and the family has seen their effect on him.

Entry into the family system should not be attempted in the very early phases of treatment, but only after a solid working rapport has been established and the therapist feels that support will come from some family members. If this technique is attempted prematurely, the family will reject the therapist, and possibly even tell him that he needs help. In one family, for instance, the single therapist found himself reacting to the mother much as had the nineteen-year-old schizophrenic son. While this woman bedazzled her son with a series of contradictory statements, denials of what had been said moments before, guilt-provoking comments, and double binds, the father and older sister sat back impassively and said nothing. When the therapist attempted a review of this material, he got the same treatment the son and the rest of the family had received from the mother. He found himself to be another son, feeling much as the schizophrenic son had described himself. At a later point in treatment, when rapport and trust had become more firmly established, he attempted this technique once again. When he said that he was feeling like the son, he received firm backing from the father and older sister, while the son himself opened up with much material relating to his confusion. They then all worked on trying to identify the causes of the mother's actions and the family's past passivity to the mother's destructive behavior toward her son.

In another family—consisting of two married daughters who came to the sessions, the twenty-four-year-old schizophrenic son, and the middle-aged parents—I found myself totally unable to understand the father. He would report incidents at work or at home that sounded rambling, confused and boring. Everyone sat back, said nothing, but claimed to understand him. When I asked what they understood, they each gave a different answer but felt quite comfortable about the differences and made no attempt to reconcile them. I also noted that most communications went through the borderline schizophrenic mother who then edited the material for distribution. I found myself repeatedly requesting the father to clarify his remarks. I also suggested that he talk directly to me or the other members of the family. The father responded by covert hostility. I often found myself turning to the mother for clarification of the father's remarks. While I did not understand the father very clearly, his wife's interpretations of what he reported frequently bore only the fuzziest resemblance to what he had said. The father had given his daughters unusually generous gifts, had given one son-in-law a sinecure in his wholesale organization, and had promised his other son-in-law an easy, well-paying job when he finished post-graduate work. The mother had offered several relatives her home where they lived like retired successful executives. Only the schizophrenic son refused to work for his father, claiming he had tried it briefly, had been well paid but had had nothing to do. He slept until 2 P.M. every day. I could feel within myself the lure of dependency gratification, and felt I could use this feeling in the service of the therapy. I sensed a partial longing to be part of this family, live with them, play golf daily or go fishing, work for a few hours every few days and make $200 a week, sleep late, and have delicious meals waiting for me any time of day or night. When I drew the family's attention to these various family patterns—the father's ramblings, the communication through the mother, the fostering of dependency—I got nowhere. Everyone wanted things just as they were. Only the son was in pain, but his weird associations didn't make sense to the family. Then I tried to enter the system. I started by commenting that one of the daughters seemed seductive to me, and was indirectly telling me that I could have her anytime I wanted her. (There had been an earlier seduction of the brother by this sister who had paraded about the house in a bra and panties.) I said that I was tempted, but afraid that everyone in the family would get upset; also, that I wasn't sure what the sister really wanted because I had the feeling that if I made any advances, she would respond with shock and anger. I said that I was tempted to join the family, to be taken care of. Could they make room for me? I started negotiating for a position in the father's business, discussed details, talked about living-in arrangements. While there was an obvious pseudo-quality to my request to become another son, the family tended to take my desires somewhat seriously, and this approach caused a great uproar. Somehow I was too much of a load for the family system to handle. Everyone wanted to talk at once. The mother lost control of the communication channel and started to express resentment against her life pattern of always being the family member upon whose shoulders the problems were dropped. She told her husband to involve himself with the rest of the family and leave her alone. The father, now more coherent, then said that he was afraid of me and of his schizophrenic son and had therefore always avoided him. The son ceased his delusional expressions and told of his being sexually aroused by his mother, a condition that had started years before when he had asked her for sexual information.

After that phase, which lasted at least 12 sessions, the family abandoned its static pattern and much meaningful interaction began to take place. This phase revealed considerable sexual confusion on the part of every family member, brought out hidden dyads and alliances, and the parents' own fear of dependency. I was able to identify the sources of the problems, who was confused, in what way, and how each person handled his confusion. Ultimately, the son was able to return to work, and the family's permanent guests were asked to make other arrangements. All this took place over many months, with progress and regression, anxiety and great tension. But a significant breakthrough had occurred, facilitated by my temptation to get into the system and to use this feeling in the service of the treatment. The next phase consisted of a clearer expression of problems that each member now felt as his own, and a willingness to work on his problems. They became much more honest with me and with each other. I suspect that at the next therapeutic plateau, I may again attempt to penetrate the system, depending upon how I would spontaneously react at that time.

To react temporarily as a family member can frequently uncover, in a single session, a specific dynamic that otherwise would remain obscured.

For example, during one session the mother, sons and daughter of a certain family were bitterly attacking the stepfather who had married into a family of teen-age children. When I asked why they were angry, I received very specific but limited replies. The father mismanaged this, failed to do that. Later in the session, I found myself provoked by the father, couldn't understand it and didn't try to. I joined the family in the attack. I felt that I had suddenly become accepted as one of the family. Then I stopped, turned to the mother and said I didn't understand why all of us were attacking the stepfather. This time she said that the father was just like her mother, stubborn, self-righteous, controlling. The children said that he was moving into the family, and wanted to take over, just like their maternal grandmother who was always interfering and tempting them with bribes to undermine the mother's position.

This example illustrates how feeling as one with the family yields information that the outsider does not readily receive. I have employed these brief entries into their system with a number of families, trying to sense the appropriate moment when they will tolerate it long enough to achieve this technique's limited goal. The element of irrational family expression must be clear. Such controlled freedom and creative use of self is often mandatory in treating very sick families, hopelessly mired in their closed and static systems.

I have suggested here that one therapeutic technique that could be employed in family therapy is to enter into the family system, either briefly to uncover a specific dynamic, or for a longer period to effect a major change in the system. Once the therapist obtains entry, the system no longer remains tenable and changes can take place. Entry may be necessary at different phases of an interactional impasse. And while it is possible for co-therapists to successfully enter a system, my experience has been that it is easier for a single therapist to do so.

V

ISSUES, PROBLEMS, AND CONCEPTS

IN FAMILY TREATMENT

This section deals with the more conceptual aspects of our experience in regard to family functioning, family pathology and family system. The first chapter reviews the implications of the home setting for family treatment, including the reorganization of the self-image that is required of the therapist by the change of the treatment locus, an assessment of the advantages and disadvantages of the home setting for family treatment, and finally, an estimate of the future for family treatment at home, both for the purpose of a theoretical exploration of family dynamics as well as a practical modality of treatment.

There are two chapters on resistance, an area midway between the level of direct, immediate experience and the level of abstract theorizing. The final group of conceptual chapters—dealing with the importance of the "well" sibling in the "sick" family, the role of significant peripheral persons, the transfer of illness, and the concept of change—represents an effort to generate concepts about the dynamics of the schizophrenogenic family.

Implications of the home setting

for family treatment

Alfred S. Friedman

Chapter
17

The single most unique feature of this project is that our family treatment has been conducted in the home on a regular and continuous long-term basis. We know of no other project that has adopted this feature as its main procedure, or has had as much of this particular kind of therapeutic experience as we have had. We shall therefore first report our rationale for selecting the home as the locus or setting for conducting family treatment; and then relate some of our observations and conclusions about the advantages and disadvantages involved in using the home as the setting for family treatment.

The home visit in psychiatry and social work has not always been regarded with favor and has been out of style for many years. Even in the field of general medical practice, it has become a frequent complaint in recent years that it is difficult to get a doctor to come to the home. Now, with the new emphasis on conceptualizing emotional illness in terms of family and social roles, and with the advent of a new family therapy, the place of the home visit needs to be reassessed.

Ackerman[3] had already reported that there was an advantage to making the diagnostic evaluation of the family in its own setting in the home, in that it allowed a more accurate behavioral picture of the family interaction. To us, the next question followed naturally: once we have gone out to the home for this purpose, why not return there regularly and conduct the family therapy on the spot, rather than admitting the patient to the hospital? In any event, we might learn something if we pursued our inquisitiveness in this direction.

In our original effort to develop a rationale for this approach, we had set down ten specific speculations or predictions of possible advantages to accrue from working in the home. They were as follows:

1. Treating the whole family in their own home adds a new dimension of reality and meaning to the psychotherapeutic experience. Meeting in the home setting renders the very concept of a family therapy, as distinct from therapy of the individual, more immediately meaningful.

2. Observation of a family in the natural setting of its own home,

rather than in the clinic, provides a diagnostic advantage. The family cannot as readily hide its real ways of living and relating to each other, or present a false façade of adjustment, when seen in the home, as they often do in the office. This observation also provides a short cut to understanding the patient and his or her problem or illness. It gives immediate tangible meaning to the patient's behavior and symptoms, and the therapist can differentiate more quickly between what is reality and what is distortion or misrepresentation in the patient's thinking, than he can by interviewing him in the clinic or office.

3. There is often an advantage in maintaining the responsibility for the patient within the family, and not permitting the family to deny or exorcise this obvious "sick" or "bad" part of itself by sending the patient to an institution. It is very tempting for the family to push the major responsibility for this difficult problem onto the doctor or the public authorities, and then perhaps to suffer guilt for their actions later. When a family hospitalizes an actively psychotic member they are often relieved of the incentive to cope with the problem, and to make efforts to change the pathological family system. Keeping the psychotic member in the home, and conducting the treatment of the family in the home, provides us with an additional leverage for working on the family system.

4. It is rational to attempt to insure the improvement the patient may make in the hospital by assisting the family to provide a more supportive and less pathogenic environment for him on discharge.

5. A specific advantage of conducting treatment in the evening in the home is that it allows for the active involvement of the father in the treatment. Too often fathers of patients have abdicated their authority and fatherhood role or have capitulated to the mother's authority. The disturbed patient is to some extent a helpless victim of a strained relationship that exists between the parents, and of the withdrawal of the father.

6. The transfer value of psychotherapy conducted in the realistic milieu of the immediate family and home will be greater than that of psychotherapy practiced in the socially isolated context of the office. Problems of transfer of what has been learned by the patient in psychotherapy are reduced to a minimum by this approach. In conventional psychotherapy the patient has to transfer what he has learned in his therapy, secondarily, over to his relationships with the members of his family.

7. Anxieties related to entering a treatment relationship which are sufficient to keep the patient or family from coming to the clinic can be overcome by the treatment team going to the home.

8. Many patients are unwilling to go to a mental hospital and are taken there by their families by means of subterfuge, threat or force. This does great damage to the family relationships and results in further estrangement of the patient from the family.

9. There may be less anxiety for the patient and for the family in their own familiar surroundings in the home than there is in the new and strange environment of the clinic and the forbidding atmosphere of the consulting room.

10. If a man's home is his castle, and the therapist is admitted there with his permission, this arrangement may reduce some of the usual inferiority-superiority implications inherent in the patient-doctor relationship. It may also reduce some of the hostility toward the professional authority figure when he is visited in his own office. The hostility related to status has been shown to contribute a serious barrier or resistance to psychotherapy, particularly in unsophisticated families of lower socioeconomic level.

Brown[27], in his association with the Community Extension Service of the Massachusetts Mental Health Center, surveyed attitudes of psychiatrists in Boston regarding home visiting. He found a wide variety of reactions, from enthusiastic approval to extreme criticism. Some who approved of the idea of home visiting never did it themselves, either because of the type of practice they conducted or because they found it impractical: ". . . I think home visiting is wonderful; I have absolutely no negative feelings about it—but because of the typical office practice I have, I have not done any home visiting and do not plan to." "Perhaps the reason I don't do home visiting is that it is difficult to maintain objectivity, perhaps the wish for distance between myself and the family is involved. After all, my first job is psychotherapy with the patient. . . ."

The nature or structure of a psychiatrist's practice seemed more important in determining his use of home visits than did his attitude toward the method. Psychoanalytically-oriented psychiatrists did not do frequent home visiting, even when they were positive in their attitude. But a number of general psychiatrists and neuropsychiatrists reported frequent home visits.

Some respondents were quite negative in their attitude: a) "It's a great time-waster and interferes with appointments. The doctor feels, in general, he must have a sense of control, and why take a chance by going into the home. If the symptoms are severe the hospital is called for and there is no need for the doctor to make a home visit. . . ." b) "If you go alone you see everybody—which is difficult; or just the family, and then the patient is a 'naughty child'. . . ." c) "If the patient is too ill to visit the doctor, then he is ill enough to be hospitalized." d) "One of the reasons I dislike home visits is that there is too much secondary gain. This has to be avoided. The risk of ready availability of home visits can lead to acting out on the patient's part in order to get the doctor to come."

There were also some very positive attitudes to home visiting: "Psychiatrists are the very people who preach that 'You should be sensitive and close to people's needs'—and yet they hide themselves in one phase of practice—sitting on one part of their anatomy, listening to only one member of the family's troubles. They are guilty of the very thing that they are always criticizing others for. . . ."

One prominent psychiatrist said, "There has to be a conservation of time and energy of a doctor's practice in these busy times, and one cannot expect a doctor to do extensive visiting. However, there is no doubt they should do a lot more, if for no other reason than to get to know the community better, as well as their patients' situations. Conversely, this sort of activity gives the community a chance to get to know the psychiatrist better, something that's badly needed. . . ."

Brown concluded that psychiatrists in general are fully aware of the importance of family to the patient, but still remain *patient-oriented* and for the most part do not see their role as being one of the family psychiatrist. He speculated that the current social movement in psychiatry, which is breaking down the rigid barriers between home and hospital, might lead to a renaissance of interest in home visiting as an important psychiatric modality.

Mickle[80] surveyed 266 psychiatrists in private practice, members of the northern California Psychiatric Society, regarding home visits. He found that 91% had at some time made a home visit, and nearly half had made two or more visits during the past year. He speculated that psychiatrists have a reputation for not making home visits because many of the visits were made reluctantly. The psychiatrist would have preferred to see the patient in his office, but the patient was too disturbed to come or to be brought to the office. Also the referring source preferred the psychiatrist to make the visit. The most common reason given for visits made during treatment was the sudden worsening of the patient's condition. Although most psychiatrists interviewed made home visits reluctantly, it appeared that in some cases their willingness to make the visit prevented hospitalization of the patient.

Querido's[90] Amsterdam plan, initiated in 1927, was the first reported program of home evaluation and care of psychiatric patients. He pointed to "the importance of studying the conflict *in situ* for the understanding of the genesis and the mechanisms of psychopathological dynamics." His group developed a program for long-term care of psychotic patients in their own and in foster homes. They found that 70% of the referrals for hospitalization could be taken care of in their program.

The Worthing Experiment[107] in England is another example of a program in which evaluation and treatment of mentally ill patients was made available in the home. The authors of this program reported that they were able to avoid hospitalization in 75% of "short stay" patients, and in 33% of chronic patients.

In the United States in recent years there have been several new demonstration projects which have experimented with conducting evaluation and emergency or short-term treatment in the home. Pasamanick's[87] group in Columbus, Ohio, has evaluated the effects of drug regimen and public health nursing care of schizophrenics in the home. They found that: 1) the patients on drugs were more successful in remaining at home and not requiring hospitalization than placebo cases; 2) the home care patients, whether on drug or placebo, were in the home a greater percentage of time than the patients assigned to a hospital control group; and 3) that the family, social and economic problems encountered by the patients remaining in the community indicated the need for a more comprehensive treatment program than just drug and nursing care.

Jules Henry[50] spent about 500 hours making observations in homes of families that had a psychotic child. He raises some challenging questions: "The parents, blinded by their own disorientation, confusion, and misery, sometimes half mad themselves, make dreadful mistakes; but only an observer who sees these with his own eyes can really know exactly how the tragedy was prepared. How can a parent who is psychologically blind perceive what he did to his child? How can he recall for a psychiatrist his innumerable acts, especially since most people are unaware of what they are doing?"

Henry discusses a mother in one of the families he visited as follows: "Mrs. P. is what clinicians call a sub-clinical case—a person recognized as having a potential for pathogenic behavior but superficially well adjusted. It is really in relation to her children that a visitor for a week can come to understand how this woman, apparently so "well-adjusted," can produce a psychotic child. This fact is central to understanding why, in general, apparently "lovely" parents may have a disturbed child. An infant organism cannot prosper on a culturally valued façade; it makes no difference to a mind dying from lack of social stimulation that its mother is popular."

Egan et al.,[35] Rafferty et al.,[91] Levine,[70] and Morgan,[83] are among other groups who have very recently reported working in the home with families who have disturbed and psychotic children. Egan supervised psychiatric nurses who made frequent visits to the home, usually when a mother felt overwhelmed or in a crisis situation with her small children. The nurse often talked with the mother and child and had occasional interviews with mother and father. They reported that they found that their method could be "an alternative to twenty-four hour care, a help with the emotionally battered child, and an assistance in reaching unreachables. . . . With certain situations it can be used by the less than maximally trained person under supervision. Costwise, it is more expensive than out-patient care, but usually considerably less expensive than in-patient care. Home treatment should be an integral part of any comprehensive mental health center." They reported that higher socioeconomic class families had more difficulty in accepting therapy in their domicile, and were more concerned about what the neighbors would think than lower socio-economic class families. The defenses of the lower class families are not so high or so sophisticated. When a professional person shows so much interest as to come to their home to work with them, they may respond positively and it may actually raise their feeling of status. As limitations and problems of the home setting for treatment, they mention that they were unable to institute effective treatment in families which had a paranoid parent, and in families which had an acting-out adolescent who absented himself from treatment or caused many interruptions. It seems to us that success with such problems may depend on the level of training and experience of the treatment personnel, since we were able to institute effective treatment in at least some of the families in which we encountered similar problems.

Levine[70] reported in 1964 the results of a "Treatment in the Home" experiment, conducted by the Henry Street Settlement of New York City. Seven foreign-born families of low socio-economic class, with pervasive socio-pathological problems, and with children who had been suspended from school, were treated by a social worker who made regular visits to the home. "It was expected that bringing the service to these people in their own setting would reduce suspicion and convey an informal, friendly interest, divested of the authority of other agencies with which they were familiar—such as the courts, Department of Welfare, school and police. The social worker brought with him arts and crafts material and simple games which all members of the family could play. The essential elements of the treatment technique were demonstration, activity, intervention and discussion." Family conflicts were acted out in play. Verbal interpretations and abstract conceptualizing were avoided. Improvement in the behavior of the children was reported in six out of seven of the families treated.

Morgan[83] described "extended home visits" in which a social worker spent two or three days in the home with each of six schizophrenic families. As a participant observer in the ongoing life of the family in its own home, this investigator performed both social and psychological roles in the family. He permitted himself to be incorporated by the family, to become part of the family psychopathological system. A deeper level relationship developed, but he needed the help and consultation of the staff to regain his objectivity. He had to submit to a personal uncovering process by the psychiatric team, dubbed a "post-visit debriefing procedure," in which his countertransferences were worked through, and his insight into the family was extended and clarified.

Schwartz et al.,[98] found that home visits have a definite teaching value in a training program for psychiatric residents. They believe that there is no substitute for the visual impression of the home setting, and that in the office interview the home and family interaction are not susceptible to "verbal conveyance with the same degree of meaning with which they are initially perceived." They speculated that the patient seen in his own home would tend to be less anxious, ill at ease and defensive than when seen in the doctor's office. In some cases the lesser defensiveness of the patient in the home enabled him to reveal his pathology more readily. This observation is consistent with our own experience that families seen interacting in their natural home setting appeared crazier than they did while sitting around the room during a session in our clinic.

Perry,[89] who reported on the implications of home treatment as practiced by the Psychiatric Home Treatment Service of the Boston State Hospital, appears to have approximately the same reservation as Egan[35] as regards working with the middle-class family in their home:

". . . public health psychiatry via home treatment will, initially at least, deal with a stratum of the population which has a high incidence of presumably avoidable hospitalization; which will not be able to afford private treatment; and which, unlike otherwise similar populations on a lower socioeconomic level, will share enough of the values and verbal modes of interaction which characterize present-day psychiatry so as to make it relatively easy for psychiatric staff to relate to them."

Toward the end of this statement Perry appears to make a further limitation on the indications for home treatment, by requiring a relatively high degree of verbal interaction and a value system similar to that of the therapist. To the extent that these latter conditions are necessary for success of treatment, they would apply, in our opinion, at least as much in the office setting. Perhaps this is also what Perry meant, and perhaps he would agree with us that these are not contraindications to using the home setting for family treatment.

At least one expert in the field of family therapy, John E. Bell,[11] has differed with our opinion that there are advantages to working in the home. He has stated, "I insist on holding conferences in an office rather than in the home. In the latter the therapist is a guest, subject to the conventions of that status. His freedom for determining the conditions of the conferences is restricted. In an office he can take direction of the situation. The setting there supports the authority of his actions. It cleanly separates the authority of the therapy from the authority in the home, where the therapist should not aspire to be an authority. As director of the therapy sessions, he can predetermine his role, communicate it to the family, relate to the family accordingly, and thereby facilitate the therapy in ways he chooses." At a later stage, after more experience in the home, Bell revised his opinion and informed us in a personal communication: "With regard to your use of the home as a setting for family therapy, I have revised my point of view to lower-class families where it seems to have been shown that the home is a more desirable setting than an office. This still does not seem to be the case with the middle-class family."

In considering this difference of opinion, we wonder whether it is sufficiently explained by the fact that Bell did not commit himself to working in the home to the degree which we did, or whether he worked as consistently in the home as required to become adapted to the method. We found that some of our therapists honestly expressed experiencing initial anxiety related to feeling like a visitor sitting in a strange living room, rather than being a host in their own office; some even likened it to feeling "like a sitting duck out on a patrol on the front lines of the enemy." But this only occurred during the first phase of our work, and was a feature of a new, unknown experience. Our therapists no longer feel this anxiety in going to the home of a new family. It may also be that the successful maintenance of the degree of authority and control necessary for therapy, depends more upon the personality, technique and expertise of the therapist than it does on the setting in which the therapy is conducted. Family doctors have gone into homes to conduct treatment for generations, and have managed to maintain adequate authority in that setting.

Some family therapists may interpret the fact that they go to the family rather than having the family come to them, as a reduction of their professional prestige. While the therapist does not have to feel this way about it, it is true that the usual custom is such that except in an emergency, the patient seeks out the therapist rather than vice versa. If the therapist interprets his going to the family as a narcissistic devaluation, both he and the family are likely to fall into a trap, and this may continue as an unresolved conflict between them, due to its countertransference component.

Thus, we did find that it was possible for our therapists to maintain their "structured role" adequately in the home setting, and that the "boundaries of the identified groups" remained at least as strong in the natural setting of their own home as in the artificial setting of the therapist's office, thus satisfying some of the conditions for family treatment which Bell requires.

Some Observations about Home Treatment

When a psychiatric emergency arises, and a family calls up the clinic about a sick or troublesome member who needs immediate attention, it is well to reserve judgment about who actually is the sickest member or the biggest problem in the family. A child who is presented as the problem may turn out *not* to be the sickest member of the family. Often there is a husband and wife, each declaring the other is mentally abnormal; and each justifying his own behavior in a convincing fashion. Sometimes this involves interlocking paranoid systems. In these situations, family group interviews in the home are the quickest, most effective way of assessing the situation; and friends, neighbors and local community agencies who have had contact with this family may also be interviewed.

When we start to treat the whole family rather than the individual in handling an emergency situation, it may be more natural to go to the home, rather than to wait for the disturbed individual to be brought, often unwillingly or by force, to the office of the psychiatrist or physician. The individual who is severely phobic or withdrawn, or is a suicidal or homicidal risk, may be too frightened or too resistant to facing his real problems to go to the office or hospital for treatment. There are many cases, including suicidal risks, who will not go for psychotherapy for themselves although they may want help desperately—partly because they feel that the problem, and the blame, is just as much that of the rest of the family as it is their own; but they will participate with good motivation if family treatment is offered, or if a therapist comes to the home.

There are practical and physical reasons which require going to the home in certain emergency cases—to avoid the use of police force, for instance, or the use of subterfuge and threat by the family who is trying to get the patient to the hospital. Some of the emergency situations involve concern over possible homicide, fear of danger to the patient, other family members, or to the community. But, as mentioned before, the therapists' regular visits to the home and their apparent unconcern about the possibility of violence was usually sufficient to reassure the parents that hospitalization was not necessary.

Our experience has also shown that family therapy in the home results in relatively less attrition of cases, fewer terminations by default or stalemate, and fewer absences from sessions. This may be partly because the families become a more or less captive audience when you go to their home, and it is more difficult for them to find adequate reasons not to attend the sessions. It is unlikely that some of the schizophrenic and paranoid families we have treated would have remained in office-based therapy for the length of time that they have continued to participate in therapy in the home. In addition, office sessions are often canceled due to the physical illness of a family member; home-based therapy need not be interrupted since the session can be moved from the living room to the bedroom of the sick member. In the case of one family several sessions were even held in a hospital room to which the family member had been confined for treatment of a skin condition.

Working with these families in their own homes has demonstrated to us how socially isolated most or all members of the schizophrenic family are; their distrust of all outsiders makes it extremely difficult for them to form a treatment relationship. The therapists, coming to the home regularly, slowly become a part of the family unit, and a relationship develops which may well become the prototype for future social relationships between the members of the family and members of the community.

One of our original purposes in conducting family treatment sessions in the home in the evening was that it would actively involve the father in the treatment. Although the schizophrenogenic role of the mother has been recognized for many years in the etiology of schizophrenia, it was not until recently that the role of the father has been examined more closely. In the vast majority of our cases the father is passive, submissive, unreachable or ghost-like and ineffectual. He contributes to the genesis and maintenance of the schizophrenic condition in the family by his abdication to his more powerful, domineering, smothering-mothering wife and to her relationships with the schizophrenic off-spring. We have referred to some of these fathers as "imitation" or "cardboard" fathers. In occasional cases the father plays the smothering-mothering role while the mother is aloof, unavailable or overtly rejecting.

When we have gone to the home for our work with the families, we have more quickly learned about the dynamic significance of some influential relative or family friend in maintaining the current family system or homeostasis, both in its pathological and adjustive aspects. A grandparent, an aunt or uncle may be living under the same roof or down the block and maintaining close contact with the family, usually through the mother. The sooner this key relative or friend is included as a member of the family treatment unit, the better.

Family ghosts, skeletons in the closet, and family secrets have usually been exposed more quickly when the therapeutic work started in the home. In one recent case, the maternal grandmother had been dead for two years, but her room in the family home had been locked and left untouched, with all her clothes and effects intact. No family member dared go into the room. The presence of the treatment team in the home was required to unlock the morbid fear and guilt which resided there, and to bring fresh atmosphere into the family relationships.

The therapist, as a participant-observer, has the opportunity to experience directly the emotional climate of the home, and to see through the facade to the underlying unverbalized family problems. When a family comes to the professional office they often dress in their "Sunday best," and treat the therapist with certain stereotyped references. Inasmuch as the families are more relaxed and natural in their homes, they drop some of the façade of adjustment which they present to the outside community and in the doctor's office. They often appear crazier when seen in their own homes. You see the life-space of the family, and their non-human environment in all its detail, filled as it is with their possessions, their reading material, etc., symbolizing their interests, identifications, and sublimations. As you observe the family members and their animal pets move about in this life-space, you are presented with rich material for quick understanding of the dynamic forces and problems of this family. You are in a better position to make irrefutable interpretations based on direct observation of family behavior just occurring. A child moving towards, away from, or in between the parents, can inform you non-verbally of his feelings and problems. The father of the house communicates some important feelings by whether or not he offers you his armchair in the living room to sit in, and by the manner in which he does it—feelings that he cannot talk about directly. The mother's interest in the home as expressed in its decor, its neatness or sloppiness, and her behavior as hostess informs you of how she feels about her feminine role and about her competence as a homemaker and mother. One mother had spoken of how important it was to her feelings about herself and her home that she was now getting the modern kitchen which she had wished for a long time. If the team had not continued to work in the home they might not have seen how she subsequently developed great resistance to having this kitchen completed, and might not have been able to use this evidence to bring into the open her ambivalence about her feminine role.

The family assigns the seating arrangements and picks what room the sessions are to be held in. We have held sessions in every room in the house—the kitchen, the dining-room, the living room, the bedroom, the bathroom, the basement or on the patio outside the home. There is more freedom in the home to move about and family members express their feelings in a less stereotyped manner than within the constricted confines of the average office. When a family member becomes anxious he can go to the refrigerator to get food, he can walk into another room, he can go and get a personal possession to show to the therapist—such as an album or pictures of friends or relatives—or he can invite a friend or member of the community to the session by merely picking up the telephone. All of these things and many more have occurred during the course of treating families in their homes.

Certain unique therapeutic incidents which occur during home family treatment are obviously unlikely to occur in other treatment setting, and are, therefore, unavailable for the therapists' understanding and use. For example, in the Island family (Chapter 4), the schizophrenic daughter repeatedly slashed herself with a razor blade around her ankles and legs. This occurred on several occasions while the family therapy sessions were in progress. It was very enlightening to the therapist to see the lack of concern on the part of the parents and the brother about this type of behavior. He intervened directly by taking the razor blades away from the schizophrenic girl, ordered the parents to get rid of razor blades in the home, and impressed the girl sufficiently with his concern about this kind of behavior that it did not recur after the early phases of therapy. If the therapist had not directly observed the event in the home, but had merely been listening to an account of the episode in his office, he might have been unwilling to guess at the accuracy of the account, and might have hospitalized the patient. The event as it occurred in the home allowed the therapist to focus his attention on the peculiar communication within the family and to teach the family members to attempt new and more effective ways of handling crisis situations.

The mother in this family often complained that the girl would never put on a dress or be properly attired. This was indeed true, but it was later shown that the mother had resisted several requests by the girl over a period of a year to buy her a dress. The girl actually did not have a single dress that could possibly fit her, since she had become very obese during her years at home. The mother had to be challenged by the therapist to produce the girl's dresses before she would accept the fact that this was true. This kind of reality testing could not have been employed if treatment were conducted outside the home.

In a case where the parents had assured the therapists that they had followed their suggestion to change the boy's exclusive ice cream diet, the psychotic son talked about a plot among liars, and stated that he could reveal the deception of his parents because the therapists came to the home, and he knew that they would be willing to take a look in the refrigerator and see the tremendous quantities of ice cream the parents were still keeping there.

In the Ichabod family (Chapter 7), much of the family dissension centered around the children's invasion of each other's bedrooms. On the first home visit, the children's bedroom arrangement was inspected by the treatment team, and it was found that they shared a bathroom which had no outlet to the outer hall but only to their bedrooms. The daughter showed the team her bedroom, as well as three peepholes her brother had made in the bathroom door. Only after the team had seen the arrangement of the home were they able to get the parents to let the girl use their bathroom, and to put a lock on her side of the other bathroom, thus providing some privacy for the children.

In still another family, during a critical phase of the treatment in which the father and son were in conflict, the father demanded that the two male therapists stop visiting the home. When they continued nevertheless, he revealed in a subsequent session that he felt the same sense of intrusion about their visits as he had experienced earlier in his life when his father, who had deserted him and his mother, had unexpectedly returned home. He also expressed fear of his son's closeness to the mother. Working through these feelings led to a decrease in suspiciousness in the family.

The presence of animal pets in the home is often advantageous in forming a relationship with a withdrawn, psychotic family member, or diagnostically in understanding the family relationships. Pets display behavioral reactions that are extensions of the behavioral reactions of the family members. Pets are very sensitive to emotionally charged affective states within the family unit. In several psychotic families with whom we have worked the pet animal was treated as if it were human, and the schizophrenic member of the family was treated as if he were a pet or an appendage. In one family, for example, the father insisted that all family members fill out the Leary Interpersonal Check List on the dog. He had acquired this dog after the death of a favorite five-year-old daughter, had unconsciously transferred this libidinal relationship to the dog, and had a closer relationship with the animal than with his schizophrenic son. After the family had been treated for about a year and the Leary Interpersonal Check List was being completed again, he stated that it was ridiculous for the dog to be included in the test—thus revealing a more realistic appraisal of the pet's role and a friendlier relationship to his schizophrenic son.

The relevant point here is that the home treatment setting facilitates observation of behavior in relation to family pets which in turn can add to the understanding of the family libidinal relationships and to other family dynamics.

In another instance, the father was being pressed by the therapist to assert himself more as the male and family's authority figure. He became quite anxious at this point, and walked over to the cage where the family kept its large tropical bird. He let the bird loose so that it flew around the room, creating such havoc that it broke up the therapy session for fifteen minutes. Here was an example of resistance to therapy so obvious and dramatic, that hopefully it could be interpreted to even the most naive patient.

Discussion and Conclusion

It may be that for some highly intellectual and verbal middle-class families, the doctor's office is sufficiently comfortable; but for non-verbal families and for many children who cannot express their feelings verbally or sit in a restricted space for an hour, the doctor's office is a more anxious and uncomfortable place than their home. Many families have told us that our coming to their homes rather than their having to go to an office, held special meaning for them; they felt we were more human and could be trusted more.

Our original concern that the therapists coming into the home would be considered intruders—particularly by the parent most responsible for isolating the designated patient from intimate contact with others—was not justified by our experience. It is true that our teams were "thrown out" by such parents on one or two occasions; but, in general, the families did not continue to react for long as if their privacy was being invaded and as if they were being spied upon by strangers. Most families incorporated the therapists into the family system all too quickly.

The family in their own home may tend to react to the therapist more on a peer level and to perceive him more realistically in his role as a technical expert, as a real person with feelings of his own who is not necessarily perfect and all-powerful. The therapist's attitude and behavior is no doubt most crucial in determining the quality of the therapist-family transference and role interaction; but the setting, the rules, and the structure of the therapy also play a role.

The family may appear to regard the therapist in home visits with less deference than when they visit him in the office. It is debatable whether this is a real difference or simply the absence of an artificial veneer worn when visiting the office. An inexperienced family-therapist may react to leaving the security of his office with a loss of self-assurance, or experience a reduction in his professional prestige in going to the family in the home rather than having them come to him. He is in an unfamiliar setting. He may feel weak in being away from his associates, his hospital, his nameplate, his diploma, his telephone, etc. He may also feel some reservation in making authoritative observations or confrontations to the "host" while he is a "guest." He may then impede to an extent the family members' tendency to develop a transference image of him as a competent authority figure. In spite of these possible complications, there is evidence that whole families have developed dependency transferences to therapists even when the therapy has been conducted in the home. In some families the parents are all too willing to assume the role of the dependent child towards the therapist, symbolically or in overt behavior, and to ignore their own children's dependent needs while seeking to obtain dependency gratification from the therapist. In this sense, a family group may enter into a transference relationship with the therapist as if he were a giving and understanding grandparent who is benignly intervening in the family problem. Some families, thus, may tend to become over-dependent and, whether they are seen in the home or in the office, expect the therapist to take over their problems.

In summary, there are advantages as well as complications and disadvantages involved in using the home setting for family treatment. There has not been sufficient experience as yet, nor have the necessary carefully controlled studies been conducted, to enable us to arrive at a definitive assessment of all these factors. Nevertheless, we must conclude from our observations thus far, that the advantages prevail over the disadvantages. If it were not for the greater personal inconvenience to the therapists in making the trips to the home, we would unreservedly recommend the home setting as the setting of choice for the treatment of most families.

Some specific advantages that we found in the home setting for family treatment, revised from our original rationale and predictions mentioned earlier in this chapter, were these:

1. It is possible to successfully treat many cases which traditionally were hospitalized and to maintain more of the responsibility for the family problem and the designated patient within the family. To achieve this appears primarily to be a matter of shifting one's philosophy and orientation of treatment from the traditional neutral-passive approach to a more active and flexible approach, and a willingness to provide emergency or crisis care which may require a longer initial contact than the traditional formalized one-hour session. There are however still some cases where the treatment of choice is hospitalization.

2. The handling of family emergency and crisis situations seems clearer and is often more effective.

3. The number of treatment dropouts is smaller than in individual psychotherapy.

4. There is a greater likelihood to involve the father actively in the treatment.

5. It reduces some of the usual inferiority-superiority implications that are inherent in a patient-doctor relationship.

6. Our therapy teams were able to maintain their professional as well as their structured therapeutic role adequately in the more informal, fluid, and active setting of the home.

7. The home setting is as appropriate and effective, although not always as essential, for families of higher socio-economic status with a good educational and intellectual background, as it is for families of lower socio-economic status.

8. The family's motivation for treatment was not reduced in any significant way. No treatment time or effort was wasted on families whose motivation had not been adequately tested. From the traditional point of view one might assume that a family would have to come to the therapist's office for treatment and pay substantial fees in order to prove their motivation for treatment. These traditional notions regarding motivation for therapy, however, do not seem to apply to all types of families, and probably need to be reevaluated in the light of more recent experience.

9. It has afforded us a closer view of the relationship of a schizophrenic and his family to the community.

10. Regarding cost to the community, it is less expensive than hospitalization of the patient but more costly than individual out-patient psychotherapy.

New issues will undoubtedly appear as the story of family living and family pathology unfolds through the medium of family home treatment. Whether or not these issues turn out to be advantages or complications in the process of therapy, they will present a unique opportunity to learn about family problems and about schizophrenia. Finally, we recommend that every family therapist make a few home visits to sample the uniqueness of this particular professional experience. For diagnostic purposes, at least one session in every case of family treatment should be scheduled in the home.

Resistances in family therapy of schizophrenia

in the home

John C. Sonne

Chapter
18

In considering the question of resistances relative to a family therapy approach to the schizophrenogenic family, one addresses oneself to processes occurring in the interpsychic communication system of the family. The resistances seen here are in the area of interaction and may be thought of as alloplastic resistances in contrast to autoplastic resistances, occurring intrapsychically.

Another way of conceptualizing the resistances would be to say that they are observed in the matrix of the schizophrenogenic interpsychic communication system, rather than thought of as occurring in an intrapsychic complex. The resistances are seen in the socially shared psychopathology of the "undifferentiated ego mass"[19] of the family. They operate to maintain family homeostasis[56] and impede or preclude psychic growth.

Many of these resistances, as seen in the interaction, appear to have a rather striking similarity to the political maneuverings of various candidates and parties in a political arena, and we have found it convenient and natural to use such terms as maneuver, strategy, split, alliance, and ploy, to name a few. Certain resistances seen in the interpsychic communication system may also be seen to have a similarity to certain intrapsychic resistances. For example, interpsychic doubting is similar to intrapsychic doubting. Perhaps we are seeing in the matrix of interpsychic communication the models of, and for, intrapsychic operations.

Some of the alloplastic resistances we have encountered in working with schizophrenogenic families have been described in detail elsewhere —for example, the absent-member maneuver (Chapter 19), and the significant peripheral person resistance (Chapter 21). Many other resistances have been mentioned in the descriptions of therapy in the first half of this book. This chapter will attempt to list and describe briefly, without extensive commentary, the majority of the specific resistances we have seen operating, and report in detail one specific resistance, the termination ploy. Resistances are not listed in the order of appearance or importance.

1. The resistance usually encountered first is the family's focusing on one member as "The patient." This, of course, immediately challenges the basic premise of socially shared psychopathology and calls into question the family therapist's role as explorer of family interaction.

2. Another resistance is to strip the therapists of their professional credentials by saying such things as, "You're really very nice people, it's nice to have you visit us. We enjoy your company." This tendency on the part of our schizophrenogenic families was most marked, and their common lack of respect for our knowledge often exceeded that seen in individual therapy with psychotic patients who would be delusional about their physician. Often, the families received the therapists' opinions and observations as if they were utterances from small uninformed children.

3. Attempting to split the co-therapy unity is a resistance somewhat akin to credential-stripping resistance in that it represents an attempt to take away power and sexuality from the co-therapists, leaving them isolated and estranged.

4. A member of the family may function as a competitive "non-therapeutic" therapist, playing a role as the good, knowledgeable sophisticate. In this he may actually be hostile to the family and to the therapists, succeed in arousing the family's ire and contempt, and divert these feelings from himself to the therapists.

5. A manifestly healthy member may absent himself from the therapy sessions and rationalize his absence as of little significance. This resistance we have called the absent-member maneuver.

6. A significant peripheral person in the social orbit of the family may support family psychopathology and overtly or subtly oppose the therapists' efforts toward change.

7. Family members may switch the subject in such a rapid, elusive way that often only after it has been switched for some time do the therapists realize the switch has occurred. For example, a mother may be arguing with her son and he will successfully turn the attack to his sister, then sit back.

8. Questioning as a resistance has been perfected to an art, and is used to turn away a question, to punish, or to obtain a retraction by signaling doubt. Multiple choice questions with no acceptable choice are often used, serving as seeming efforts of control or brain washing.

9. Reporting.

10. Description and self-righteous judging are resistances which consume time and block meaningful interaction. They are of the same type as "the patient" resistance in that they are "individual" rather than "shared" in their frame of reference.

11. The marital relationships may be withheld from the therapy and implicitly or explicitly declared out of bounds by the family.

12. Dyadic alliances between two family members, overt or covert, may function as resistances. For example, a member under "attack" in the therapy may find comfort in the alliance and avoid insight.

13. A member may interrupt or "cross monitor" a potentially meaningful interaction between two other members.

14. A special example combining both the alliance and the interruption occurs when one member starts a battle, is joined in alliance by a third, retires

from the fray, then attacks his ally. This latter combination might be called "destroy your ally."

15. The entire family may behave in a conspicuously passive fashion, waiting for the therapists to initiate and define issues, then will either attack him or fail to respond.

16. The family may "gang up" on the therapists and for that mission achieve a rare agreement and unity.

17. The family may focus on physical symptoms.

18. The family may use pets to occupy time, to leave the room, to express their feelings toward the therapists. For example, in one family, whenever the father became too excited, his dog would bark and he would take her out behind the house for a few minutes.

19. Family myths or legends may be perpetuated in the family system.

20. Secrets—for example, knowledge of actual incest—may be known to part or all of the family and not revealed to the therapists.

21. A major resistance underlying all the foregoing appears to be an attempt to keep meaningfulness from the interaction. We might speculate that there is a deep fear of psychic growth because psychic growth involves an awareness of impending biological death.

22. Termination, or the threat of termination, may be used as a resistance.

We have had several families request at different points that therapy be discontinued. Often the request seemed to be reasonable. At other times, although we felt there was an unsolved problem present, we tended to feel that the decision to continue or discontinue rested in the hands of the family, and felt inclined to abide by their request. We have in time, however, come to regard this request primarily as a strong and desperate resistance, which we have labeled the "termination ploy." If we stop to consider that we are working with a psychotic illness, it is not too surprising that we would see family defenses of psychotic intensity coming into play in treatment. In individual treatment, if a person were operating on a delusional premise that would endanger his life or preclude treatment, he might be hospitalized against his will. In our setup, we are visiting the family in the home and resistances will be expected to take a different form, but probably still one of psychotic intensity, thus posing a problem of technique. Whereas the psychotic in the hospital will want to leave and cannot, the family in their home might be expected to tell the therapy team not to come any longer. Although it sounds simple when stated as above, the requests to stop were not easily or readily seen as resistances in actual practice. And when they were seen as resistances, the way to handle them loomed as a major problem of technique. The following will illustrate this kind of resistance and its possible meaning in family dynamics and in the transference.

A family composed of father, mother, and two sons, age twenty-five and seventeen, was referred for treatment when the seventeen-year-old boy was hospitalized after twice sending the fire department to a non-existent fire at the home of his brother's girl friend. The girl friend and the older brother would have sexual conversations on the phone, the father and the older brother would get into arguments about this, and the younger brother wanted some peace in the family. The younger brother had had a long history of psychiatric treatment. It had been recommended that he be put in an institution away from home years ago. At the outset of treatment he was withdrawn, rolled his eyes involuntarily toward the ceiling, was having serious difficulty with his school work, and was terrified that he would die of blood poisoning if he had a minor cold. He was effeminate in manner and speech. He complained that his father beat him and that the family was not good to him. The twenty-five-year-old was an overtly cheerful, somewhat effeminate, anxious young man who professed a knowledge of psychiatry and played an initial role of co-host and of one who is outside the problem. The father was bombastic; the mother was quiet and posed as ignorant.

Much took place over the first year of therapy, with a shift occurring for the better in the relationship of the seventeen-year-old to the father. The father calmed down. The seventeen-year-old finished high school and obtained a job. This was a major development, but I do not want to deal with it at this time. There were many stormy sessions, often with tirades by the father against his "lunatic" sons. The house, which was an unpresentable shambles when treatment started, began to be redecorated, and financial problems began to be handled more effectively. The older son gradually presented some of his problems, in that he had had about fifty jobs since quitting high school to go to work to help the family, who at that time was supporting father's invalid mother. His jobs would often be lost because of sickness, mostly abscesses on his scrotum. He reported it had reached the point where his doctor had told him that if he had another serious abscess he would have to be castrated.

After one and one-half years of therapy, the nominal patient—the younger brother—was much improved, and the older brother was steadily employed and no longer suffering repeated illness. By mutual agreement, after several requests by the family, we terminated therapy for a trial period. We had reservations about the level of health arrived at, but did not feel that we could effectively push the issue at that time. The family said that they wanted to try living on their own.

About six months later the social worker received a phone call from a businessman who said that the older son had locked himself in the bathroom at work, was crying and wouldn't come out unless his employer called the social worker. It developed that he had become involved with a girl and was afraid that his father would break up the romance. We suggested that we arrange a family meeting. There was some opposition by the father, but we did meet. At the meeting the father expressed reluctance to have any more sessions and suggested that the older son handle his problems in individual treatment. He didn't think this was a problem that concerned the entire family. During the session the father gradually became more distraught. He told his son that he could bring his problem to him and asked the son to express himself. But as soon as the son did this, telling how he had gone to his girl's house and been told by the family that she would break his heart and that he shouldn't see her, and how he had sat on the door step for hours and cried, the father interrupted. He told the boy he shouldn't be so dependent on girls, and recited a long list of the older son's faults, saying that he was a flop, no good, and he could get out. He beleaguered his older son for not bringing his problems to him earlier, before things were out of control. When the son, lips trembling and eyes brimming with tears, told his father he was afraid of him, his father scoffed and said, "No, you're not." Later, gathering courage, the older son recalled an earlier episode to illustrate how he felt his father interfered: One time, during a family session, the son's girl had called and the father had grabbed the phone, ordered the girl not to call anymore, and hung up. The son at the time had compliantly said to the therapists that he felt his father had behaved properly. This time, recalling the episode, he said in anger, more bravely, that his father had had no right to do that. The father became more enraged, and angry remarks flared back and forth. The son then recounted how one night his girl said she couldn't date him because she had to go to a religious service. He spied on her to make sure, and found out that she had lied. When father heard of the spying, he exploded. Standing in the middle of the room, facing his wife slightly to the left, and his son to his right, his eyes on fire, he shouted to the son: "We don't want any more of your problems here!" His eyes darted quickly from his son to his wife and he repeated his statement. The rhythm of his speech and body were to stay with the son until the word "here," when he swung to face his wife.

He then turned to the therapists and said that the sessions had to stop. There was no discussing it reflectively. The father agreed, amidst the noise and shouting, that he was frightened of his feelings but didn't know why, and we were just to stop coming. He didn't care why. It was enough. Remarks about the value of continuing fell on deaf ears. Interpretations produced no shift in his ultimatum. Threats and counterthreats developed. We refused to stop. The father stormed out in the backyard with his dog. The mother and the two boys were cowed. The younger boy, who had been the original patient, had been silent for the most part, but said at this point that it was hopeless to try to get to his father, so why bother.

The next week, the older son was in the hospital with a mild concussion. He had been in an auto accident. We insisted on meeting in the hospital. The mother was the only member who overtly seemed at all interested. This session, again, was extremely stormy. The older son was in terror, lying sweating on the bed. The younger son said that doctors had a racket and rejected therapy. Mother shushed him and said the therapists would know when to stop. Father wildly challenged the psychiatrist, saying such things as: if he were driving a big trailer-truck and the psychiatrist were driving one, he'd push him off the road. We were not to come. He denied that anyone was sick in the family. After about an hour of this fury, the psychiatrist said that we would make a compromise and would stop by in a month to see how things were going. With this, he became tearful, grasped the psychiatrist's hand, and said to make it two weeks.

The next session at home was dramatic. The wallpapering of the house had been completed. The family proudly and cordially showed us all about. The father had joined a club for the first time in thirty years. The family had been on a couple of outings together. The older son had found a new girl. When we reviewed the past hectic month reflectively, the father said that what had made him mad was that when he had said to stop, the psychiatrist had insisted on continuing, and when he said stop again, the psychiatrist insisted and insisted. He said later that if he himself had really wanted to stop, deep in his heart, he would have said absolutely No. This we felt was highly significant. He had said to stop, with as much feeling as anyone in any of our families has said anything. We did not feel that his later remark was saving face. We felt he really was saying, "Don't believe me when I tell you to stop coming." The manner in which he handled this order to stop was reminiscent of countless times we had seen him decimate one or the other of his sons and threaten to throw them out of the house. His attack on us, however, was stronger than any we had seen toward his sons. He had said earlier in meetings, talking about his threats to his sons which had been quite unrestrained and had terrified the sons, "I never did throw you out, did I?"

When asked if our insistence that we continue reminded him of anything, the father immediately recalled that when he was a boy of nine, his alcoholic father had left home, leaving him with the responsibility of caring for his mother. The father's father would return episodically and intrude in the relationship between father and father's mother. There would be violent fights and father would beat mother and son. The transference to the psychiatrist became clear to everyone. The transference to the older son as an intruding father in spying was clear also and everyone was able to see in retrospect why the father had panicked when he had heard that the son had spied on his girl friend. The girl friend symbolized father's mother, as well as father's wife, whom father feared losing. The older son's fear of father breaking up his romance was also related to the general fear of the males in the family that their women might be taken away. The father openly discussed his jealousy of the therapist in relation to his wife.

This session represented a major breakthrough into the area of sexuality. The following session the father discussed operations, and wondered if the psychiatrist might not understand him better if he gave him a physical examination. He revealed he goes to a male doctor, the other members go to a female doctor. The older son spoke of a wish to become a corpsman. He and father were much more comfortably aggressive with each other. Father was accepting of his son's girl. The men proudly showed us a highly elaborate electric train set in the basement. They also talked of plans to buy a new home in a better neighborhood.

Shortly thereafter—when the older son made a move to reshift our meeting night so he could go to night school, after we had gone to considerable trouble to shift it so he could go to corpsman school, and that deal had fallen through—we resisted another change. Father this time strongly but rationally supported the therapists, held the line with his son who then arranged his classes for another evening.

Much more sexual material came up. They had seen "Butterfield 8," and "The World of Susie Wong"; they played us a record of risqué songs. Father and sons began work in an area of bringing mother more into the therapy as a patient, entering deeper into a new phase of treatment, with the men dealing with mother's giving ability and the question of favoritism.

The termination ploy served as a means of protecting the father's castration and homosexual anxiety. It was impossible to deal with this problem by any other method than doing the opposite of what he demanded. Since his violent insistence on termination was on a delusional basis, to have gone along with it would have left the family psychotic. Social mores; the idea that a man's home is his castle; respect for a man's freedom; distaste for violence; and fear for our own personal, physical and mental safety, and of possible and probable professional or social criticism—these were all factors opposing our decision to insist. Moreover, beyond purely practical matters involved in the decision, we had to gamble with the family's welfare on winning therapeutically, by continuing to forcefully press treatment in the face of this homosexual panic. We saw the crisis as requiring a decision about therapeutic technique, based on a dynamic understanding of the family psychopathology. We felt that we understood the dynamics and couldn't interpret them if we weren't there, so we stayed. If the family had successfully terminated, the family pathology would have remained—with all the males semi-castrated, the older son in a latent incestuous dyad with his mother, the father seeing his mother in his wife, and father and sons in latent homosexual dyads.

It is possible to see an interrelationship between the absent-member maneuver and the termination ploy. It would seem that rather than analyze the dynamics of the absence, the family would have preferred to terminate treatment.

In this case we can see a potential absent member in the older son, who initially functioned in the healthy, psychiatrically knowledgeable co-therapist, co-host role. These characteristics have become clues to us, heralding and designating the potential absent member. Throughout treatment the older son made several bids to leave for one reason or another: to go to school, to work at night, to get thrown out by his father, or to get sick. This behavior was seen and handled as a resistance. It was followed by the appearance of the termination ploy which, when explored, revealed dynamics centering around departing and returning competitive males.

In considering family resistances in general, it is pertinent to relate them to resistances seen in the treatment of one individual. In this regard, any of the above resistances may be likened to acting out of an individual patient in analysis to avoid a conflict area. The family is the patient, and with part of the problem fixed in physical relationships unavailable for scrutiny, treatment is stalemated, just as in individual acting out.

Conversely, in individual treatment, the therapist can be viewed as dealing with family resistances at a distance. In individual treatment, if a patient shows resistance, he is in effect maintaining and reinforcing his pathologic family ties, and symbolically or literally is running back to or is beckoned by his family. What we see in family treatment are the resistances in their fullest form, and at a more immediate and more ramified level. Individual resistances, when the intrapsychic processes are considered in their relationship to the family, can be seen as family resistances. And the resistances in the family during treatment, although at times seemingly motivated by one person, are a function of the relationships of all the family members with each other. Without the cooperation —implicit or explicit—of the rest of the family, resistances of an individual member are quickly weakened.

The absent-member maneuver as

a family resistance

John C. Sonne, Ross V. Speck and Jerome E. Jungreis

Chapter

19

The concept of socially shared psychopathology[67,44] can be applied in the treatment of families by working with the relationships with the family members physically present so that the intrapsychic images, memories and fantasies may be expressed in the presence of a potentially creative constellation of significant relatives.[3,81,22,33] We have been especially alert to any evidence of socially shared psychopathology in the schizophrenic family and addressed ourselves to defining and conceptualizing this pathology when we saw it. We hoped in this to gather clues pointing towards a more effective therapy of schizophrenia.

During the course of our treatment experience with a "schizophrenic family" we observed that in eight of the first ten families treated, a member, usually a manifestly healthy member, would absent himself from the treatment sessions, either intermittently or permanently. We made the additional observation that in two other families there was an absent family member who was absent from the outset of treatment, but who was revealed to have had close contact with the treatment experience, to have talked with the attending family members a great deal about the treatment sessions, and to have given opinions to them which were often made the basis for crucial family decisions. We became interested in these absences and have come to call the phenomenon of the absence of a family member from the family therapy sessions an absent-member maneuver. In considering possible meanings of the absent-member maneuver, we have asked a) what function the separation performed, b) whether the absent member was sick or healthy, c) what light examination of the absent-member maneuver might cast on our understanding of the shared family psychopathology so that we might conceptualize further, and d) whether family treatment could unfold to deeper levels of understanding and change after such a separation, if it were permanent.

When we first observed these absences, we regarded them as especially significant viewed in the context of socially shared psychopathology. Our suspicion that we were dealing with an important phenomenon was strengthened when we observed further that the families did not miss the absent member when he was not present at the therapy sessions, and moreover were bland in reaction to our expressed interest in the meaning of the absence. Additional evidence that we were noting a subtle cover-up was that in contrast to the blandness about the member's actual absence from the therapy sessions, the family revealed in their inflection, attitude and comments a continued intimate interest in the general behavior and opinions of the absent member. Likewise, the absent member exhibited continued interest in and curiosity about the family therapy sessions. Also, the timing of the disappearance or appearance of the absent member in relationship to the topic being dealt with in the therapy sessions, as well as the gradually expressed thoughts and feelings of the absent member and the family about each other and the therapists, lent further evidence in support of the importance of the absent-member maneuver. This evidence led us to infer that the absenting was a maneuver of perhaps crucial significance in the reinforcement of the schizophrenic family's resistance to maturation, and that it served as a family way of handling the anxiety generated in family therapy when fixed and stereotyped relationship patterns are threatened with exposure.

Examining this maneuver has continued to support our view that it is a defense against family anxiety; using the maneuver as a conceptual tool, we examined the deeper and more vulnerable socially shared defenses the maneuver served to protect in the family. What seemed to stand out when we became alerted to the absent-member maneuver was that it functioned to protect a psychopathological dyadic alliance. In this we have seen the absent member as a part of the socially shared family psychopathology and not "healthy".

We would define a psychopathological dyadic alliance as a complex relationship between two people which is non-maturational and delusional in nature, and which is composed especially of a shared distortion of the role of a third or other person in the family group. For example, in a psychopathological dyadic alliance we may see father and daughter jointly deny the mother's role as mother and wife. There are other distortions in the alliance obviously, in the images they have of each other, but we feel the distortion of the role of the third person or others to be the primary distortion. Further examination reveals that the absent-member maneuver not only protects one psychopathologic dyadic alliance, but indirectly several, and has led us to the proposition that the schizophrenic family is composed of multiple dyads representing pre-Oedipal psychic defenses. For example, in a psychopathological dyadic alliance father and daughter may have a special latent incestuous relationship, mother and son may have a special latent incestuous relationship, father and son, and mother and daughter may have latent homosexual relationships, and mother and father, although physically intimate, are latently divorced.[23]

We have been impressed by the enormity of these pathologic dyadic defenses which underlie the absent-member maneuver, and have derived from a consideration of the proposition of the dyadic composition of the schizophrenic family a further hypothesis, namely, that beneath these dyadic defenses there is a deficiency in the family members of what we have defined as a family image.

We would define the family image as the intrapsychic representation of a shared family multiple relationship growth experience over a prolonged period of time. This family image is represented intrapsychically along with intrapsychic object representation. We consider the time dimension of the psyche important in this image and would stress that part of the intrapsychic framework of an individual is composed of the experiences one "has gone through." Of primary importance in the family experience image is the representation of "the having gone through" or the resolution of the Oedipal experience with successful handling of rivalries and disappointments, and a creative use of the family traditions. The family image would be present in the parents, having been incorporated by them in their childhood during their experience with their parents, the grandparents.

We have seen the schizophrenic families repeatedly functioning in family therapy sessions in pathologic dyadic alliances and have come to think of the schizophrenic family, with its fixed dyads and with its clinically identified schizophrenic patient, as having a family image deficit. A member absenting himself from the therapy sessions, which are oriented around family growth, furthers the maintenance of a family image deficiency in the minds of all members. We see the family image concept as important not only in family therapy of schizophrenia, but as an important component of emotional maturity in general. Hence it would have application beyond schizophrenic families.

As for the importance of the absent-member maneuver in reference to therapeutic progress, we have come to question whether therapy can unfold to deeper levels of family understanding if this powerful resistance is successfully implemented. Although the members of a schizophrenic family are often physically adjacent, they are frequently unaware of or unwilling to admit the many fantasies they project onto each other and the affect associated with these fantasies. Many disguised fantasy patterns keep the physical relationships from libidinization and development. The family members are physically adjacent, poorly integrated emotionally, and bound together by unconscious fantasies. The relationship patterns are extremely rigid and non-shifting and one of the goals in therapy is to realign, both qualitatively and quantitatively, the intra-family relationships to allow flexibility and shifts. If one member absents himself from the treatment session, an unconscious affect-laden fantasy pattern of the family may be maintained, or go unnoticed; or be more difficult or impossible to recognize, delineate, or analyze.

Viewing the family as the biological unit being treated, one member absenting himself could be likened to a patient in individual therapy acting out a conflict to protect it from analysis. The whole family is "the patient." If a family member leaves permanently with or without the manifest consent of the others, then, in terms of treatment conceived in a framework of socially shared psychopathology, the absenting member takes part of the family with him, and there is no longer a real family in treatment. When a family member absents himself, the family therapy is threatened because one or more relationships are automatically frozen or immutable until the relationship can again be scrutinized with the absent member present.

Our experience with the absent-member maneuver has stimulated certain thoughts about absenting in general. The story of "The Prodigal Son," expressions such as "Absence makes the heart grow fonder," "Give him the absent treatment," the biblical story of Joseph, and the possible significance of absences in the psychopathology of everyday life may be reexamined in terms of some of the concepts formulated in this paper. The following case histories illustrate the so-called absent-member maneuver.

Family A

The twenty-four year old, younger daughter in this family of five was absent from the 14th session on. At this session the therapists were told by the father, age sixty-five, that she would not be able to make any more appointments. The father relayed to the therapists as her reasons the distance to her parents' home, the late hour of the evening meetings, and her husband's need to rise in the early morning to give an important academic lecture series. Although her absenting herself was treated as a significant event by the therapists, the family showed only moderate reaction to her leaving. Therapy continued for several months in her absence, with themes of open conflict between the thirty-two-year-old older daughter and the mother, age sixty-three and between the thirty-year-old overtly schizophrenic son and the father. The mother and daughter fought over the elder daughter's independent way of life. The father-son conflict presented itself as a hovering, anxious recitation to the therapists by the father of his son's clinical picture during the week, with the son expressing himself poorly and in vain. The father also showed mood fluctuations synchronous with those of his son. Minimal material unfolded dealing with the absent younger daughter. Therapy was progressing, but dragging.

At the 30th session, despite her earlier message that she would be unable to attend, the younger daughter returned. She attended four sessions, some of them very turbulent, and then left again, this time in anger. Her reason for returning, expressed to Therapist A, was that she felt so bad seeing how sick her brother still seemed to be. She soon showed herself to be hurt because her brother did not appreciate her efforts to help him. She was angry at him for being so inconsiderate of the parents. She looked and acted guilty at having been absent from the sessions, and presented, in addition, an attitude of, "Now, I'm here, let's not waste my time."

A few weeks after her return, during a session when both sisters were absent because of a snowstorm, the father was confronted by Therapist A with his clinical attitude toward his son. This had been done many times, but this time he became violently furious.

The following meeting, with the entire family present, the younger daughter attacked Therapist A verbally most violently and uncontrollably; using obscenity; leaping from her chair in rage to point her finger within an inch of his face demanding that he work harder; saying that he had no right to treat her father with disrespect and that he was frustrated in his therapeutic efforts and was attacking her father as an excuse. She also attacked the therapists for saying that they viewed each member of the family as sick. She was, in the main, protective of the father's being confronted by anyone in the group. The father was also extremely angry at Therapist A, but had more control in his attack, and, to the therapists, seemed in no way in need of protection from his daughter. He was expressing himself more vigorously and effectively than at any time heretofore.

Following this highly spirited meeting, the younger daughter phoned her mother that she was so angry that she would no longer attend. The father at this time phoned Therapist B, saying that he had not been so angry in twenty years, not since the time when he had been so enraged at the older daughter that he had to leave the room for fear he might kill her. He went on to say that he was so angry at the therapist who had confronted him that he intended to have his two sons-in-law at the next session to "beat him up."

The younger daughter was absent at the ensuing session. This time, however, she was extensively discussed by the rest of the family. They were unanimous in expressing the view that she occupied the role of the "good" child, the parents' favorite. Father said openly and directly to the older daughter, and to the group, that the younger daughter had always been more sympathetic than the older, and had understood him better. She could be counted on in time of need and sickness and did not think of herself first, as did the older daughter. Mother agreed, telling the therapists of a time when the younger daughter, even though married and with a family of her own, had been sensitive to the fact that her mother needed a new sweeper and had bought her one because the mother was so busy in the store. However, mother's support sounded hollow to the therapists, who felt it represented sweetly veiled hostility.

The older daughter's view of the above relationships, expressed to the group at large, was that she herself, and not her younger sister, understood the father better than anyone, despite what the father said. She also felt that the younger sister should not do things for the parents which the parents should do for themselves. She said that her sister had told her that she felt mother and father needed sympathy for their suffering with the brother's illness, whereas she felt understanding was more important, and that the parents should not be protected. She felt that her younger sister was the most fragile member of the family and cited an episode when the latter had exploded through her façade of calmness when she and her husband returned to live at the parents' home for a while. The younger daughter had railed at her sister for having left her to handle all the parents' problems, then returning and taking over. The older daughter likened this outburst to her sister's behavior in the preceding week's session. She said that she felt the parents did not understand their younger daughter; she added that her sister confides to her her resentment against them for imposing on her and exploiting her, but that she never expresses it directly to them.

In retrospect, the therapists recalled that the younger daughter in the second meeting had abruptly and insistently asked whether therapy was just to help her brother or the entire family, and had expressed her own view that the entire family needed help. Yet she was the only member who did not admit in some way to having a personality problem, and she was the one who absented herself.

The power of the alliance between father and the younger daughter continued behind the scenes, with their being reported by all the remaining members, including the father, as more openly sympathizing with each other. The father stated to the therapists that he was only physically present in the sessions following the younger daughter's angry departure, that he was only there out of consideration for the other members' desire to continue, and that he was determined not to participate. However, in actual fact, he could not restrain himself from episodically expressing himself with animation. During this period he was diagnosed by X-ray as having developed a duodenal ulcer and was put on a diet by his family physician.

At session 38 the younger daughter suddenly reappeared, with her husband impatiently waiting outside, to say that—acting as family spokesman—she wished to express the family's desire to terminate treatment. The brother had continued to improve during this interim, having progressed from his hallucinating, suicidal, eloping, hospitalized state at the outset of treatment. He was expressing himself eloquently and logically much of the time and had remained out of the hospital for eight months, longer than any period over the past five years. All the other family members were complaining that treatment was making them sick.

Although the youngest daughter posed as the healthiest member of the family, and her initial leaving was viewed in the main by the family as understandable and reasonable, subsequent events pointed to her as the cornerstone of the parents' pathology, and by extension the family's pathology. The older daughter had openly rebelled against the mother, and despite the mother's opposition, we felt that she was the most respected by the mother. The father also, although critical of her lack of attention, at other times expressed indirectly his admiration of his older daughter by referring to some qualities in her rebellion with great pride. The son had developed an overt ambivalent psychosis and was struggling ineffectively toward maturity. The younger daughter—married and living farthest from the parents' home—and the most cooperative child according to the parents, proved to be the most resistive to therapy; she was the most brittle and the person least able to tolerate anxiety.

We wish to reemphasize that the younger daughter's initial leaving was viewed by the family as reasonable, and little reaction was expressed to it. It was dealt with by the therapists as a significant event with some evoking of supporting material, but not till she returned and left again, did it become manifest what her role in the family was and what her leaving meant.

It would seem that her leaving served multiple functions. She was jealous of her brother returning to the home situation. She was hurt at not being able to run things. She could not tolerate the stimulation of her own hostility to her parents in therapy. In the main, however, she left to maintain a silent alliance of a behind-the-scenes intimacy and understanding with her father, which could have been exposed and dealt with if all had been present in family therapy. She could not tolerate seeing her father threatened in a way which would actually eventually strengthen him, for it would disturb her own intimate relationship with him and force her to deal with her hostility to her mother, and her own seductive handling of and by her father. She would also have to deal with her hostility to father for not being more manly. In leaving, she maintained a position of apparent superiority over the older daughter, being more powerful by being absent than her sister was by being present.

Her first leaving was at the time of her brother's discharge from the hospital to the home instead of going to a state hospital. She was not present while her sister struggled with the father in an effort to break the psychopathologic dyadic relationships. When, even in her absence, the brother was making some progress in confronting the father especially, she returned to protect the father. When therapy continued she left in a further effort to isolate the father, and herself as well, from actively relating to the rest of the family. When therapy still continued after her second departure, she returned and stopped the sessions. The therapists felt at the time of termination that the family was less than entirely happy with the younger daughter acting as spokesman, and that this resistance was on the verge of being broken.

Family B

This family treatment was a little more complex in that living together was a nuclear family composed of a fifty-four-year-old father, a forty-six-year-old mother, a twenty-six-year-old son, a nineteen-year-old son, a ten-year-old daughter, and the extended family: the mother's older brother and his twenty-four-year-old son.

The father was a passive, ineffectual individual who was completely domineered by his wife. The mother and the other family members told about the wealth of the mother's brother and how he owned a famous night club and was friendly with the stars of the entertainment world. The mother constantly alluded to how successful her older brother was and how unsuccessful her husband and all the other males in her life were.

The twenty-six-year-old son had not spoken to his younger brother (who was the schizophrenic patient) for about a year, ever since the latter had thrown a knife toward him during a quarrel at the dinner table. In the fourth family therapy session the older brother absented himself permanently from the sessions by remaining in the kitchen of the home, ostensibly doing work or watching television. The mother gave her assent to his absence and repeatedly pointed out how obedient this older son was to her. By her attitude and remarks she revealed that she wanted to maintain control over him and did not want their relationship to change. This was related to her strong desire to keep all the men in the family dependent upon her and the multiple Oedipal situations unresolved. Thus his absence from the sessions functioned to maintain a pathological dyadic relationship with the mother and inhibited further efforts on the therapists' part to produce change in the family.

During the 10th family session the therapists discovered that the family had failed to even mention that the mother's older brother, a widower, lived in the home. His absence from the family therapy sessions was accepted by all members as reasonable because he was such an important person. The therapists were blocked in their attempts to persuade the family to have this uncle join the sessions. In this family, therefore, we see an absent-member maneuver which began even before treatment started. The mother's brother represented "the power behind the throne" in the family. His importance strongly reinforced the omnipotent role of his sister; the fact that he lived in her home and was to some extent dependent upon her, further exaggerated and emphasized her role as head of the family. At least one aspect of the "family romance" from her own childhood was still maintained in her adult life. In addition, she had control of and attention from four other males who were competing for her. This constant competition of the five adult males for the one adult female created constant family strife and aggression. The 19-year-old son, who was the schizophrenic patient, appeared to be constantly trying to assert a strong male role in the family and thus reverse his mother's role to a more feminine one. This could not succeed, however, because of the strength of the mother and the need of the other male members to give way to her wishes. The apparently healthy motivation of the schizo-phrenic patient to reverse his mother's role in the family was interpreted by the family members as a portrayal of his illness. If the uncle had been present in the sessions, the therapists would have had an opportunity to confront the family directly with how his apparent success in life was being used by his sister to undermine her husband and the other males in the household.

The nineteen-year-old brother had flunked out of college on three occa-sions, had been unable to keep a job, and had shown disturbed behavior for several years. He showed a strong ambivalent relationship to his mother with underlying identification with her, and yet most of their relationship was overtly manifested by mutual strong verbal attacks and insults. He repeatedly attempted to get his father to assert the masculine role in the family, but the father could not do this. In default the son would then be extremely aggressive and order his mother to prepare all sorts of extra meals for him, would have his mother wait on him hand and foot, and would throw food off the table because she had not served him properly.

The ten-year-old sister came to a few sessions for brief moments, but the mother always encouraged her to leave so that she played a very small open role in the family therapy. The mother seemed to want to limit her young daughter's interaction with the male members in the household, and this further set up her role as the key person through which all interpersonal communications in the family were channeled. Thus another secret alliance (dyadic relationship) was isolated from fur-ther scrutiny or possible change.

The twenty-four-year-old cousin was present from the second to the 13th session. His role was that of an admired but at the same time resented sibling who basked in the glory of his absent father's importance. The nineteen-year-old brother and the therapists requested that he attend the sessions, although the mother was somewhat less than enthusiastic about this. He stayed for about 12 sessions and then excused himself saying that he was opening a business and also he did not feel that he needed therapy for himself. Although he had not worked for some three years, he then opened a food business. It failed in less than six months, but the thera-pists were blocked in their attempts to have him stay in the sessions by the unanimous approval of his leaving, shown particularly by the mother, but also by the father and the nineteen-year-old son. He absented himself from the family sessions following a direct attack by the mother in which she stated that he was really not her child, although she had raised him, and in which she berated him and accused him of being lazy. The nine-teen-year-old son approved of his absence from the sessions at this time as the cousin had been very critical of his behavior for several sessions.

The family sessions revolved for the most part around the mother, the father, and the younger son, and the therapy lasted for a total of 35 sessions. Throughout all the sessions each member of this triad related to each other with verbal tirades and threats; and when there was a lull in this, they attacked the therapists. The parents saw therapy as a chance to see their son attacked by the therapists with their role that of passive observers. When the therapists did not do this, they became very angry and berated them for not doing their job. The mother constantly belittled the son and accused him of eating in a non-human way and of not working. The son fought back and stated that she couldn't cook and couldn't do anything but meddle in other people's affairs. The family therapy came to a termination following a session in which the father was more direct than he had ever been in his life with the mother and in which he pointed out strongly that she was "too devoted" to the children and that she had been irritating him for twenty-five years. The schizophrenic son used this opportunity to join with the father in opposing the mother, and pointed out that she needed treatment. For the first time the mother became quite anxious, upset, felt that she had lost control of the family, and admitted that she had needed help for years. Following this session she called one of the therapists on the phone to state that she wanted no more therapy for the family, and despite the therapist's repeated suggestions that this should be discussed further, she acted as a family spokesman to terminate. She would not allow other members of the family to talk to the therapist on the phone and refused to allow the therapists to enter her home.

This case illustrates the absent-member maneuver occurring in four members of the same family and functioning to protect pathologic dyadic relationships in the family. The multiple absent-member maneuver reinforced the family pathology by maintaining the fixed, paired, static relationships between the mother and father, mother and each son, mother and uncle, mother and daughter, and mother and cousin. This family could not tolerate the anxiety generated by the disruption of these dyadic relationships. The absent-member maneuver thus functioned as a successful resistance to change in the family relationship patterns.

Discussion and Summary

We have had a number of other examples of this problem in family treatment. One of them, the Island family, has been discussed in detail in Chapter 4. The case report shows that the absence of the brother of the designated female schizophrenic patient from a series of sessions follows the same pattern and principle which we have described in our first two case illustrations.

In these cases we attempted to illustrate the absent-member maneuver as a family resistance to treatment which serves to maintain fixed and stereotyped dyadic relationship patterns within the family. The absenting member cannot be conceived of as healthy, but as involved with and continuing intrapsychically a pathologic family image.

Further examination and exploration of the absent-member maneuvers observed during treatment suggest that the fixed and stereotyped relationship patterns maintained in the schizophrenic families were unresolved Oedipal patterns. The schizophrenic families had great difficulty tolerating over a prolonged period of time the anxiety and instability of a three-person relationship, composed of two members of one sex and one of the opposite sex, in which one heterosexual relationship is genitally fulfilled and the other heterosexual relationship is resolved symbolically. This three-person relationship, instead of being resolved, fragments into fantasy heterosexual and homosexual relationships which are extremely conflictual, poorly repressed and maintained with use of denial and projection. We feel that three-way (triadic) relationships are much less well developed in the schizophrenic family than in more normal families. The passive father in the schizophrenic family may have been cut out of the significant relationships with his children,[23] thus impairing the child's reality testing from an early age, and also setting up the early model of the intense binding of the schizophrenic patient to the mother. The three-person tension occurring in the transition from dyad to triad[103] which is necessary for growth and development, is dissipated repeatedly and the Oedipal conflicts remain unresolved. Intrapersonal patterns among the family members are primarily dyadic and symbolic and static, rather than triadic and maturational.

This failure to conceptualize the possibility of a three-person family relationship growth experience is shown in a family member's inability to believe that a three-person heterosexual experience can be had without incest, homosexuality, or murder.[113] Hence he has difficulty developing an internalized image of a three-person heterosexual growth experience over a prolonged period of time, or a family image. The intense one-to-one relationships occur with great frequency in these families and interfere markedly with the multitude of shared relationships seen in more normal families. This family image may be an important need for maturation without which the family member is crippled.

In our concept, anxiety is generated when these intense binding, paired relationships are threatened. This has been repeatedly pointed out in the cases presented in this chapter where jealousy, fear of loss of protection, threat to control, loss of relationship, dissolution of secret alliances, etc., were the basic fears which caused a family member to be absent from the family therapy sessions.

In summary, the absent-member maneuver is a resistance encountered in family therapy which allows the maintenance of psychopathologic dyads and serves as a way of avoiding the anxiety which is inherent during the construction of a three-person heterosexual growth experience over a prolonged period of time, which may be called intrapsychically a family image. Although we have been alerted to, and have focused on, the absent member and have seen him as sick beneath his healthy role portrayal, we wish to stress also that this maneuver is a total family maneuver with which the rest of the family more or less cooperate. There are many more dynamics in this process which need further elaboration; we have speculated on only a few of them. The therapeutic handling of this resistance, especially, needs additional work.

The "well" sibling in the "sick" family:

a contradiction

Alfred S. Friedman

Chapter
20

Can a family which has a schizophrenic adolescent member have other offspring who are emotionally well-adjusted? Or is the occurrence of schizophrenia in a family member to be considered as evidence of maladjustment and psychopathology of a family system—with the implication that all family members, including the apparently "well" siblings, are an integral part of the psychopathology in the system? Our experience in conducting conjoint family treatment with these families leads us to believe that the latter condition holds in many, if not all, such schizophrenic family units.

The foregoing does not state that we believe we have proven that all siblings of schizophrenics are also schizophrenic, or even latently schizophrenic. We do not believe that this is so. Nor have we conducted the necessary controlled studies comparing our patient families with average or normal families in our society, to establish that the children in the alleged normal families have less severe problems or less pathology than the children in our patient families. We believe that this is probably so, and we are currently beginning controlled studies to test this hypothesis. What we are saying here is that we have repeatedly been surprised and impressed to find after several months of intensive work with a family, that the siblings of the adolescent schizophrenic member have themselves very severe problems and symptoms.

The "well" siblings are inevitably a part of the emotionally meaningful organization of family relationships, even when they believe themselves to have separated emotionally and to have broken the familial ties. We have found that certain siblings would stay aloof from the family therapy from the beginning, pretending to have no vested interest in what might be discussed. Actually, they did not want their anxieties and motives uncovered. When the family therapy then began to have an effect, they would openly criticize it and actively attempt to break it up. When we insist on including these siblings in the therapy group from the outset, there is more opportunity to control this acting out by observing the family cliques and splits in operation, and by bringing them into the open and analyzing them. The failure to include all members of the operational family organization from the outset in the composition of the treatment unit will probably later result in serious resistances and obstacles to progress in therapy.

We had previously accepted for therapy some nuclear family units consisting only of the parental pair and their schizophrenic offspring. We do no longer accept such partial therapy units, but require as a beginning minimum the participation of all unmarried siblings living under the parental roof. From our experience with conducting family therapy in the home, we further learned the importance of including, as an integral part of the therapy unit, not only all siblings, but grandparents, close relatives, and others who shared the twenty-four hour living experience.

Ackerman,[3] Jackson,[57] and Wynne[118] have each independently reported having similar experiences and have arrived at similar conclusions. Jackson describes the family therapy unit, as it is considered by his group, to be as follows: "The members of the family include parents, children, other significant relatives such as grandparents and aunts or uncles, and other significant non-relative people, with the selection dependent on relationships and not necessarily on blood ties." Once the membership of the therapy group has been formed, a specific group structure develops which has its influence on the process of therapy. As in other forms of group therapy, it is essential for the effectiveness of the therapy to maintain a consistent, stable group composition over a period of time. Frequent absences and changes in group composition interfere with the adequate exploration of family tensions, splits, and relationships.

When a family member is frequently absent from the therapy, this signals to us a probable resistance on the part of some or all of the family members to the family therapy. In the preceding chapter we have conceptualized this particular form of resistance as the "absent-member maneuver." [105] (See Chapter 19.) It occurs when the libidinized symbiotic partnerships are threatened with exposure, and when the envious and competitive feelings of the other family members toward the symbiotic pair are also threatened with exposure. Wynne[118] postulated that "both alignments and splits are functional in the homeostatic maintenance of families as social systems," and observed that the very intense splits in schizophrenic families somehow seem to bind the family together. He regarded the absence of a family member from a therapy session as "acting out a split within the group." In our discussion here, we shall focus attention on the covert purpose of the absence of one member, a sibling, from the family therapy: the acting out of a secret alliance with, and resistance for, another family member who is physically present in the therapy session.

The absent sibling is most typically in "secret" alliance with one of the parents. The absence symbolically represents that parent's original need and wish to maintain this exclusive symbiotic relationship (which is a continuation of a childhood pregenital fixation on one of his parents), and to continue the emotional divorce in the marriage, because of the fear of attempting a marriage relationship on a more phallic and genital psycho-sexual level. (This alliance may be on a different level from the symbiotic bind between a parent and the schizophrenic child, and the sex of the child may be one of the differentiating factors here.)

The family acts dumb toward the special important nature of this parent-child alliance described above, and toward the implications of this child's absence from the family therapy. This pretended secret helps to avoid the intense anxiety that would be stirred up in the whole family, if a concerted effort were made to break up the alliance, or to talk openly about their feelings regarding the special close relationship to the one sibling. Should the therapists also become party to avoiding the anxiety by ignoring the absence of the sibling from the session, the working through and altering of the pathological family relationships would probably be less likely to occur.

Clinical Examples

We shall illustrate the importance of including the well sibling in the family therapy by presenting three clinical examples. The first deals with the Island family, where the apparently healthier sibling had already made some progress in gaining his freedom and in detaching himself from the nuclear family problem. He said that he wanted to write off his responsibility to the family, and was therefore ambivalent about participating regularly in the family therapy. One could accept, or even sympathize, with this attitude. It is part of the American pioneer tradition that a young man of twenty-one, who is single, should move away from his family, and establish an independent place for himself in another location. However, when this boy was persuaded to attend the therapy sessions, he gradually learned that a flight is not required in order to gain independence. These healthier siblings are sometimes capable of making a unique contribution in the treatment sessions, to the family's efforts to solve its problems. But just as often they are revealed to have serious problems of their own, and to need the family therapy for themselves. As the therapeutic process develops, the focus of family disturbance and pathology is seen to shift back and forth from one family member to another. The sibling who in the beginning is seen as aloof, uninvolved, and functioning in the community at a level superior to the primary patient, may at a later stage of treatment appear to be the primary focus of the pathological family process.

An example of the shift of the focus of the family problem is the same young man referred to above. He had described himself originally as fairly independent of his parents and as having a number of good friends and an active social life outside the home. A year later, when he was drafted into the Army, these defenses crumbled and he could not tolerate to be away from home. He was stationed at a camp close to his home, and he came home on every possible occasion. He complained of recurrent headaches, couldn't concentrate, and developed other somatic symptoms. He felt that basic training was such a terrible ordeal that he feared he might not survive it. He withdrew, kept to himself in camp, and did not socialize with other soldiers. After his tour of duty was over, he went through a seclusive phase, staying at home practically all the time with the other members of the family. He related this reaction, in therapy, to feelings he had had earlier in life, of being isolated socially and of not belonging. (Social phobia was in fact a symptom which pervaded this whole family, even to the family pet animals. The dog and the cat were at times fearful of going outside the house. The original referring symptom of the primary patient of the family, the twenty-four-year-old daughter, was that she had been at home for several years, fearful of all social contact.)

The second example concerns a family that has also been previously mentioned, (see Chapter 19). We have found that it is often advisable, or even necessary, to include in the family therapy unit siblings who have married and moved out of the parents' home, but still maintain regular and close contact with the parents. In one such close-knit family a married sister of the male schizophrenic patient was the most dominant, aggressive member of the family, and continued to play an important role in family decisions. She was in a close alliance with her father, and supported him in his destructive battle with his schizophrenic son. We could not conceive of a very effective family therapy without her, and she agreed to come regularly for the sessions, bringing her baby with her from her home in a town fifty miles distant from the parents' home. When a crisis occurred at a later stage of the therapy, she stayed away from the sessions for several weeks, saying that her husband was too busy to drive her to the sessions.

Our final example, taken from the "V" family referred to in the following transcript, deals with the absence of a daughter from the therapy session. Incidentally, this family did not inform us until the second session that a maternal aunt had been living with them for seven years. We had no way of knowing this, since we had started out with this family in the clinic instead of in the home. The father did not tell us until the second session that he had very strong feelings about this aunt's presence in the home, and felt that she was in an alliance with his wife against him. He now revealed for the first time his suspicions of seven years' duration about the secret vault which his wife owned jointly with her sister, and his conviction that it contained some of his bonds and money. We took the position at this point that the aunt was important enough a figure in the family relationships to be included in the therapy unit, but the wife resisted the suggestion strenuously.

If we had started the work in the home, instead of in the clinic, this inclusion of all household members would probably have occurred more spontaneously and naturally; and there would have been less opportunity for the parents to use the absent-member maneuver as a resistance, and to maintain the stalemate in their marriage relationship. At first look, the split in the family appeared to be the result of a secret alliance of the females in the family—mother, sister, and daughter—and to be primarily their problem. The father however did not follow through when offered an opportunity to inspect the secret vault immediately after that same therapy session. It became clear that the split in the marriage served his purpose as well as the mother's. He preferred, probably for unconscious reasons, to retain his jealousy, anger and suspicion of the mother's collusion with the aunt, and to project onto this alliance, rather than face his own heterosexual problem in his marriage.

The transcript demonstrates how the mother and daughter cooperated to keep the daughter out of the family therapy. The mother admits her anxiety that the daughter will become "sick" like her schizophrenic son, if she participates in the family discussion, implying that the daughter might be contaminated by closer contact with the father and son. The mother either does not perceive or does not spontaneously admit her aggressive purpose, or her libidinal need, to keep the daughter in a bond with her, and for both to remain aloof and hostile towards the father. The transcript illustrates how it is difficult on first contact to differentiate the behavior of the daughter from the mother, and to determine whether they decided independently, or jointly, that the daughter stay away from the family therapy.

We do not at this stage of the case understand fully why the mother is so threatened by the possibility of the daughter's presence in the therapy. We might approach this problem with the following theoretical speculation: family therapy provides a setting for multiple group interactions which in turn reveal basic drives and needs. The therapist may capitalize on these interactions to activate the self-revelations of members by relating their current interactions to their past crucial experiences. If a family member who is a key relationship figure to other family members is absent, there will be less opportunity for exposing certain pathological dyadic relationships and for reactivating in the therapy the related crucial self-revelations of the past. In the case of the "V" family, the therapeutic participation and interaction of all three parties to the mother-father-daughter triad would be the minimum required for understanding the significance of this particular alignment in the family—that is of the apparent alliance of mother and daughter against father. Some of the possible historical predisposing factors to this alignment, considering only the mother's past, would be the following:

1. The mother's bond with the daughter is a continuation or a reactivation of an ambivalent bond she originally had with her own mother which she was never able to resolve.

2. She had an excessively intense and close immature attachment to her mother, and is prone to separation anxiety and excessive fear of loss of the mother object; or the specific pre-Oedipal fear that she would lose her mother to her father.

3. The mother was overprotective, possessive, and instilled in the daughter associated fears of dirt and sexuality.

4. The fear of her own aggressive wish to get rid of her mother, which would also leave her abandoned.

5. The fear of her Oedipal wishes toward her father, and her tendency to avoid them by maintaining a hostile distance from him (and from her husband now), and the fear of retaliation from the mother.

All of these, and possibly others, could be reactivated in the therapy by uncovering the suppressed anxieties and jealousies inherent in the current relationships between mother, father, daughter, and son. Some of them would obviously have less chance of being uncovered and analyzed without benefit of the daughter's interaction.

Transcript from Tape-Recorded Multiple-Impact Session with the "V" Family

The following transcript is taken from the joint family-team planning session of a "multiple-impact" evaluation session. The multiple-impact procedure was developed by the Galveston project of the University of Texas Medical Branch, Department of Psychiatry.[76] We have found the method to be as effective with families of schizophrenics in uncovering the family problems and in accelerating the family's initial involvement in therapy, as they have found it to be with families of adolescents with behavior problems. In this procedure, four staff members spend three to four hours with the family in a sequence of individual interviews, pairing and overlapping interviews. Following this, the family meets alone for a "coffee break" conference to exchange reactions on what has been stimulated, while the treatment team meets to plan strategy. The procedure finally culminates in the joint family-team session in which key problems are reviewed and a treatment plan is formulated.

Only three members of the "V" family participated in this session, the mother, the father and the twenty-four-year-old schizophrenic son. The twenty-two-year-old daughter was absent, and the staff did not as yet know about the maternal aunt who lived with the family. The four staff members quoted below are Dr. Friedman, Dr. Speck, Mr. Jungreis, and Mrs. Lincoln.

Mrs. L.: "As I listen to all of the talk about Janet, and try to work out a problem that exists between Janet and her father, I realize that Janet should be here. You know, I don't think this family therapy is going to work without Janet being here."

Joey: "I don't think so either. She's going to break this up, in her own way . . ."

Father: "I don't think so either. (Gradually working up to assert himself) You can blame my wife for that . . . yes, I'll put all the blame on my wife for that . . . positively."

Mother: (Starts crying.) "I get the blame constantly. I don't care what happens. I get no sympathy. . . . All right, I'll blame myself. (Voice rising, trying to divert attention from father, as he starts to report what she had said at home, the night before, about this issue). Look at me, I'm crying now."

Father: "Last night, I said to my daughter, 'You should go to the family therapy session,' and she (mother) was the one who said 'I don't want her to go,' right to me. I picked the least line of resistance, I guess, like you've been telling me. Maybe I'm wrong, maybe I should fight her."

Mother: (Denying) "Janet decided not to come completely on her own. You could never get her to come here."

Dr. F.: "This is something that has been bothering me during all this discussion here tonight, the fact that Janet did not show up for the meeting. She told me on the phone last night that she definitely would be here a 8 o'clock tonight. It is now 9 o'clock and she is not here. I reminded her on the phone that you (to mother) had said that you did not want her to be part of the therapy, but that we were definitely recommending to her and to you that she come for this one evaluation session at least, so that we could discuss the question together. The last thing that she said to me was that in spite of your feeling about it, she would promise absolutely to be here tonight, but she is not here. The fact that it bothers me is not too important, except that it points to something you all do with each other and to each other."

Mother: "I am surprised. She didn't tell me she was coming here tonight."

Dr. F.: "There was a whole discussion that went on between us on the phone during the last two days between you and Joey and me about it. In spite of this discussion Janet told me last night that you had never informed her that we were asking her to come only for this one session, to evaluate the question."

Mother: "Oh, I see, but it was because Janet didn't tell me that she would be here tonight. She was home sick with an eye infection, and she shouldn't have been out of bed. Then she went out in the evening to the dentist."

Joey: "Janet lies a lot. She was taught this, and I could see exactly how you (to father) did it. This went on all the time like I told you, he'd sit down with Janet, and it would be completely capricious and completely gratuitous, and he'd say, 'Last night I looked at the speedometer of the car before you went out and I checked it again this morning, and you went 60 miles. I demand to know where you went.' He would reduce her to tears with this inquisitorial stuff, and he taught her to lie. Secondly, whenever Janet doesn't want to keep a date or something, she (mother) picks up the phone and makes all the excuses for Janet. Like Janet is very extroverted, and after she went to New York for the first time with a guy and made him spend $26.00

or something like that on her, and then she didn't want to go out with him anymore. Janet will say to her mother, 'tell him I'm sleeping, tell him I don't want to talk to him,' and she (mother) will answer half of Janet's phone calls, leaving Janet irresponsible."

Mother: "Didn't you ever hear me say 'Janet, take your own phone calls.'"

Joey: "You lie by taking it."

Mother: "Well, if she refuses, somebody has to answer the phone. What's that got to do with lying?"

Dr. F.: "She told me she would absolutely be here tonight and she's not here."

Mother: "I can't get over it."

Joey: "What do you mean you can't get over it. She's doing that all the time. It's a pattern for her."

Dr. S.: "This is very interesting because Joey pointed out that in a number of ways when he flipped one way, Janet flipped the other way. For instance, he said that when he was getting good marks in school Janet was getting very poor marks, truanting and so on."

Mother: (Interrupting) "Truanting? Oh!" (In a tone of disbelief and exasperation.)

Joey: "Well, maybe she didn't cut, but she got D's and E's, didn't she?"

Mother: "She never cut classes or did anything like that."

Joey: "I beg your pardon."

Dr. S.: "The point is, when Joey started getting bad marks, Janet's marks started coming up."

Joey: "Yes they did. She never got an A or B in her life until after I had left med school and then she became a medical technician."

Mother: "No, you are wrong. She never got A's or B's all through school but got very poor marks. It was only after she took up the X-ray courses that she got A's. She never cared much for school. She used to sit there and be in a dream."

Dr. F.: "(To mother.) I get the impression now that you are quite proud of Janet when you say these things about her. I noticed earlier when I stated that Janet had directly misled me in telling me that she would definitely be here tonight, that you immediately began to beam and smile as if you were proud of her this way, this was your Janet and the way you wanted her to be. She apparently does some things that are quite questionable and which indicate that she has some problems, but you want to ignore it."

Mother: (Sighs dramatically in self-pity and exasperation at being confronted.) "She is honest."

Father: (To mother.) "The truth of the matter is that you did not want Janet here."

Mother: "I admitted it, but if she wanted to come she could have been here. . . ."

Joey: (Interrupting her.) "With all this pressure from you . . . never."

Mother: (Continuing.) "When she said she didn't want to, I said that's all right with me."

Joey: "Oh, no." (Then mimicking her.) 'It's not what I want. I'm not doing it. It's all right if you don't want to be here Janet, but I'll tell you what to say over the phone, Janet.' (Then to team.) "It's that kind of thing, the way they (parents) put the pressure on us (on Janet and himself). It's just like their trying to get me to go to med school."

Dr. F.: "You see, Mrs. V., it has been obvious that there is a very poor relationship between Janet and her father. Their best chance to reach a better understanding would be here. Now, if you don't want Janet to be here, it might appear that you don't think it is possible for them to reach a better understanding, or perhaps you prefer the situation the way it is."

Discussion and Conclusion

The unusual degree of active confrontation of the family members, and particularly of the mother, by the team during this part of the session, was part of a planned strategy of the evaluation—to determine whether family therapy would be effective if the daughter did not participate. Such aggressive confrontation is not often used by our teams in the early family therapy sessions.

One can see, even in this brief ten-minute excerpt, how complex and rapid are the shifts in alignment and the splittings that occur during a session. The son, for example, sometimes joins in the team's challenge to his mother's manipulations; but just as often diverts this effort to attack his father. Underneath these manifest splits in the family, the indissoluble bonds between the son and the mother on one side, and between the son and the father on the other, are only hinted at and not yet adequately exposed. The mother's bond with her daughter and their joint alliance against the father is, of the various alignments, the one most clearly in evidence. We should not be surprised however to discover at a later stage in therapy that some of the apparent intense hostility between daughter and father only serves to defend against the anxiety aroused by the possibility of intimacy between them, and to hide from themselves and others an underlying libidinal attraction. This hostility is further charged by their past mutual hurts and disappointments in each other, and by the intensity of the frustration of their desire for each other.

Father's jealous involvement in his daughter's relationships with boyfriends is suggested in the discussion about his interrogating her and checking the mileage on her car's speedometer after she has been out on a late date. Her sexual maturation and independence threatens him with the loss of his little girl, and angers and depresses him. The hostile, disturbed communication between them is misleading in that it does not adequately reveal the underlying mutually provocative and stimulating aspect of their relationship. Obviously none of them understand what it is that they are caught up in. But the schizophrenic son, who has made a project of analyzing himself and his family, appears to understand more than the others.

Several of the mother's statements regarding the daughter, quoted in the transcript, suggests that the mother perceives and uses the daughter as a narcissistic extension of certain of her own wishes and personality traits. We observe how obviously pleased and proud she is when her daughter behaves in an aggressive and phallic-competitive manner toward males. If the mother did not have the opportunity to gratify these wishes of hers vicariously, by identification with the daughter's behavior, she might be more vulnerable to her own underlying feelings of inadequacy and castration. She has to this extent externalized her problem, and constructed within the daughter a defense against her own anxiety.

The daughter very likely served her own purpose in feeding her mother's hostility towards the father, in order to perpetuate the emotional and sexual divorce in the marriage. If she wanted to insure that mother and father did not get closer together, she could perhaps do no better than to stay away from the therapy and to sabotage it. If she were to come into the therapy and become involved in a transference with the therapist, or work through some of her dependent bond with her mother, then mother might have to turn more to her husband for emotional relationship and satisfaction. The daughter's bond with the mother combines both the hostile and positive attitudes toward the mother, and covers a deeper split in their relationship.

Only after such pathological dyadic relationships are analyzed, broken up and reformed, can a more satisfactory triadic relationship between both of the parents and the child develop. It becomes increasingly clear how important the daughter's participation is for the successful therapy of her schizophrenic brother, and for the successful therapy of this family.

The role of significant peripheral persons in alloplastic resistances of schizophrenogenic families

John C. Sonne

Chapter 21

In working with families with a schizophrenic offspring, we have noted that frequently a family member, presumably a healthy member, would absent himself from the treatment sessions, his absence being rationalized by himself as well as the rest of the family as of little consequence. (This phenomenon has already been described in Chapter 19.) Such a maneuver serves primarily to preserve a psychopathological dyad between the absent member and a present member, allaying the anxiety mobilized when this dyad is threatened in therapy. We postulated that a "family image" deficit was present in the family.

In the present chapter I would like to describe some instances in which an absent person, *not* a member of the immediate family, is involved with the sick family in such a manner as to interfere with maturation, although the surface appearance of the relationship would suggest that it serves a helpful and salutory function. I have chosen to call this person a *significant peripheral person*. The following experiences with three schizophrenogenic families are illustrative of this alloplastic resistance.

Case I

In this family of three, the primary patient was a sixteen-year-old schizophrenic boy who was housebound. He had not attended school for four years and had let his hair grow down to his shoulders. He lived with his mother and father in a one bedroom apartment, he occupying the bedroom and mother and father sleeping on the floor of the living room. His hobbies were the center of the family activity. He had a pet bird which flew loose about the apartment. He stayed up till the early morning hours taking colored films of the late black-and-white television shows. He ate a gallon of ice cream a day. Most of the family spare money went into his coin collection. His parents had refused to have him hospitalized despite a strong and repeated recommendation by the school psychiatrist.

He had been seen for a brief period at a child guidance center prior to this recommendation, but had soon refused therapy. His mother had developed a relationship with the social worker which she continued, despite her son's stopping treatment. She had been encouraged to "get something for herself" and had gotten a job and taken up painting. However, she remained fantastically tolerant of her son's peculiar behavior.

The significant peripheral person interacted with the family by means of a regular Wednesday-night visit between the patient and himself to go over coins. The friend, about the same age as the patient, had been a regular visitor for years and was the most frequent, and practically the only, visitor to the home. All the family members liked him and seemed not at all embarrassed in his presence by the weirdness of their home situation, nor did he appear nonplussed, aware of anything unusual, or—least of all—critical. When the two therapists asked him how he felt about the patient's behavior, he replied, "A true friend never questions his friend's behavior." This significant peripheral person did not appear bizarre, and was reported by the family to be a good student and school athlete.

Case II

A family consisting of mother, father, the twenty-seven-year-old primary patient—a chronic schizophrenic son—and a twenty-year-old, prim, non-dating, bristlingly hostile daughter were referred for family therapy by their lawyer. It became exceedingly clear in the first three sessions that there were explosive forces in the family. The father was refusing to recognize or consider any of his son's communications to him and was constantly depreciating his son's feelings, talent and aspirations.

Mother was protecting the son, an aspiring engineer, in his isolation in his bedroom at home, where he spent hours perpetually planning for a big government contract which never materialized. She seldom had company for fear it would upset her son. The father's smouldering resentment of his son quickly came out and he told how, at one time, he had become furious when his son burst into the parents' bedroom in the middle of the night. He had threatened to kill him. The father had an unusual closeness to his daughter, fostered her church work, but held tight control of her activities and her finances. One of our research team likened the father to a smiling Nazi storm trooper. We all considered this one of our most difficult families.

At the last moment of our third session, after we had closed and said we would see the family next week, the father said, "Three of us, my daughter has a church meeting." We had already clearly expressed our concept of the importance of working with the entire family. The daughter became enraged and out of control when her contemplated absence was investigated. The father relented and said they would all come. During the week between this and the planned fourth appointment, the power of an alliance with the lawyer, the significant peripheral person, became manifest. A sequence of phone calls began with a call from the father to our secretary cancelling the fourth meeting which, we had made clear, meant termination. Both therapists made phone calls to the mother and the father. The mother brought out a time years ago when she had left her husband and later returned. She said everything that the therapists had said in the three sessions was true, but that therapy was upsetting her husband. She said she had a good home with him and did not want to cross him. If he wanted to terminate treatment, she would not protest, even though she agreed with the therapists that her daughter's absence was not essential. She also agreed that her husband and daughter were a mutual protection team. She had benefited from the sessions in separating some from her son, and was having her first large house party in years. She was worried about her husband in that he had been so disturbed from the therapy that he was making errors at work. (The son, in answering the phone regarding arrangements for the initial appointment, had declined a certain time suggested because "my father has a very important job" which caused a time conflict).

The father was irate, berated us for bothering his wife and for being too blunt in the therapy sessions. He let it slip that he had consulted his lawyer about his disagreement with us. We then called the lawyer, the male therapist calling first. Illuminating his relationship to the family, the lawyer expressed his belief that the son was the main problem. "They had trouble with their son, but did not get the help for him they had hoped for (in private individual therapy) and it was more than they could afford." He mentioned that he had suggested family therapy to them a year ago, but felt that the family had been shabbily abused by us; he was incensed by what he had heard from the father at church the other day. He said a family such as this, particularly the father, whom he had known for twenty years, and who has always done to perfection every job ever asked of him, needed to be treated with extreme gentleness. They had been through a lot with their son. Also the sister's proposed absence was no rationalization, for she was an important church woman who was cited by the Bishop the preceding year. The lawyer knew the family well from church. He acknowledged the father was stern, even foreboding, but added, "Aren't these the qualities that make him effective in his work?" Furthermore, "Is there much you can do to change a man of his age?"

It became clear that the lawyer had used the father, was somewhat afraid of him, wished him unchanged and protected, and doubted that he could change. He had waited nineteen years of their twenty year relationship to suggest therapy and this was mainly to help the father with his suffering at the hands of his son. The female therapist subsequently called the lawyer who then mellowed somewhat and agreed to call the father and encouraged him to continue family therapy, but this was ineffective. The father had already fortified himself in the relationship with the lawyer who defended the family psychopathology.

Case III

This brief segment from the Rituell family, described in detail in Chapter 5, also illustrates the significant peripheral person. The reader may recall that the family composed of mother, father and a twenty-five-year-old schizophrenic son was primarily preoccupied with time-consuming, grotesque religious rituals performed throughout the day and night by the son. This had been going on since the son's medical discharge from the Army two years previous, following a homosexual panic centering around his sergeant. The son would take four hours before breakfast to say prayers, and insisted that the family and he take literally such precepts as bowing before religious pictures and symbols in the house every time they looked at them or passed them. He felt it was sinful to look at a woman, or for his father to look at his mother, and would repeat and force them to repeat prayers of atonement. He was haunted by homosexual impulses while walking the street and a fear of sodomy.

He began to attend a religious group meeting shortly following his army discharge and there met a physician who confessed to him that he too had had trouble with homosexuality and had solved his problems by turning to religion. The physician, who is described as Dr. O. in the case history of the Rituell family, recommended to the patient that he lead an orthodox Jewish life and he would then have no problems. He perpetually held his head down in the same manner the patient did and also practiced many religious rituals to a fanatic degree. He said to the therapists that if he ever did anything in the practice of medicine that risked a person's life he would give up medicine. He encouraged the patient to call him any time and so would be called at 1 A.M. to answer such questions as "How shall I wipe myself. There is some shit in my anus. I can't get it in and and I can't get it out." The patient would ask him if his suit was all right, whether his food was sufficiently kosher or whether he had prayed properly. The family was somewhat annoyed at the son's closeness to this peripheral person but treated his pronouncements with respect. The therapy team spoke with Dr. O. on several occasions and he attended several therapy sessions. He appeared unquestionably to be a figure of much more importance to the family than the therapists. He sidestepped the therapists' attempts to get him to question his role in relationship to the family and often in mock humility pooh-poohed himself as a person of little importance. He was known to other members of the team to be a decidedly peculiar individual. Also of interest is the fact that the patient had previously formed a similar social liaison with a psychiatrist whom he had met in the woods while both were netting butterflies. This psychiatrist committed suicide in the ensuing year. The eventual movement that took place after over a year of therapy was that the patient left home, left town, and joined a sub-culture of borderline religious fanatics who saw life in terms of harmony with the significant peripheral person's Weltanschauung.

Discussion

In Sophocles' "Oedipus Tyrannus"[77] the people wish to get at the root of Oedipus' malady. Creon quotes Phoebus, the king: "A fell pollution, fed on Theban soil, Ye shall drive out, not feed it past all cure." In the families used for illustration, there is an involvement with a significant peripheral person who seems to be playing a role in feeding the sickness past all cure. We have found such a person or persons in the orbit of a majority of the schizophrenogenic families we have worked with, and in others we have had the haunting feeling that there is someone about who is helping sustain the pathologic family system. Jackson[56] has written of family homeostatic mechanisms operating within the family to maintain equilibrium. He did not in this paper speak of significant peripheral persons, and defined the family as if it were a more or less closed emotional system. I would postulate that the system would have to be unstable unless an intermediary peripheral relationship existed which drained off and/or supplied energy to the family system. The peripheral person relationships appear to be unambivalent and with attributes of omnipotence attached to the significant peripheral person. To ally oneself as a family with such an omnipotent figure gives sanction to the family's peculiarities, and "love" is obtained by them through the medium of their unique peculiar symbol system rather than through a symbol system more in harmony with biology. Hence, the symptoms are maintained as being of value, and motivation for a search for their determinants is dissipated. Not infrequently such a peripheral person is a professional person who has "kept the patient (primary patient) out of the hospital," but who has also played a role in masking anxiety which in turn masked not only the patient's pathology, but the family system pathology as well. These people often don't want to "let go." They want to "keep the door open," or they have made an ambivalent referral to family therapy, or they become so upset hearing about the first few family sessions, or being a part of one, that they support the family's resistance, or become emotionally disturbed themselves at the threat of losing the relationships with the family. It is as if the peripheral person were the only good mother. He has established a symbiotic-like relationship with the family, based on an exchange or mutual validation of peculiar symbol systems—a symbiosis which the peripheral person is unable or unwilling to break, make turbulent or creative. In the face of such pseudo-gratification, which "feeds the sickness beyond all cure," the therapist is impotent. Interestingly enough, in *Case I* the therapists felt that, although they had failed with the family because of its quick alliance with another peripheral person, they may have effected a cure of the peripheral person who ceased his bizarre relationship to the family and married.

As yet there are no extensive studies dealing with the peripheral person, and many questions remain unanswered. Why, for instance, does he want to play the role he does with the family? Does he feel useful and important by contrast with this family in conspicuous distress? Does he, like Dr. O., fortify his own defenses by helping the family deny their illness? Does he have his unconscious dream of omnipotence fulfilled by being essential to the family? Is he society's representative for repression, like the lawyer in *Case II*? Further study of these people might give us greater understanding of the schizophrenogenic family and possibly a clue to more effective treatment.

Although this chapter is in the nature of a preliminary delineation of the peripheral person resistance and is not an exhaustive study, a few additional thoughts about this resistance are worth mentioning. It might be argued that these peripheral persons are indeed friends. A friend is defined in the American College Dictionary[8] as: 1) one attached to another by feeling of personal regard; 2) a well-wisher or patron, or supporter; 3) one who is on good terms with another, one not hostile. Synonyms are: companion, comrade, chum and crony. The word "friend" comes from the Old English and is the past participle of a verb "freogan," meaning love. It is related to the Old English word "freo" which is cognate with the German word "frei," originally meaning "dear," or "favored." "Friend" is also related to the word for the fifth day of the week, Friday, which comes again from Freo, the name of an Old English goddess identified with Venus. The boy visitor in *Case I* said, "A true friend never questions the behavior of his friend." This may sound good. Perhaps we all might think off hand that we should like to have such a friend, or that we are such a friend. Yet, on reflection, we would probably realize that in our relations with friends there is an area of creativity, or therapy, which is always taking place, or might take place at any given time. We are apt in a conversation to say, "Well, maybe, but the way I see it is so and so," contrasting our view with our friend's view. Or we may question, "What are your motives and what are your goals?" We also expect the expression of appropriate and genuine feeling, either explicitly defined, or clearly demonstrated in inflection. If we don't understand, we are likely to ask for clarification, and out of this interaction each person emerges with feelings modified either infinitesimally or greatly. If this were not so, there would be no mutual psychic enrichment through relationships. Other things would happen, but nothing creative would happen. An exchange of information might occur, or a sharing of an activity, but these things alone are not creative. A good friendship contains what might be called creative turbulence, a quality lacking in the significant peripheral person relationships.

Further, I would like to postulate that peripheral person relationships, in addition to lacking the quality of creative turbulence usually seen in friendships (a quality not included in the dictionary definition), contain a factor that is specifically non-creative, or non-therapeutic. I believe a lot could be learned about "non-therapy" from a study of this resistance. Psychotherapy or creative turbulence does not occur in certain relationship contexts, but does occur in others. What do these negative relationship contexts do? Whitaker and Malone[116] list certain "don'ts" of psychotherapy—to do them would be comparable to doing "non-therapy," i.e., something that would aid maintenance of the sick state. The dictum, "primum non nocare," implies possible harmful action. The peripheral person in *Case III*, Dr. O., abided by this dictum, yet did harm for fear of doing harm.

Let us regard the family system as open and interacting with the peripheral environment. No biological structure can remain unaltered over time, and no psychic representation can go unaltered over time, nor any interpersonal system. For a psychic image or an interpersonal system to be fixed over time even though it is alive and in a state of dynamic equilibrium with it's cultural milieu, we could speculate that the cultural milieu, or a representative of it, may extract a "psychic growth factor" from the aliveness of the family system and replace the building blocks of the system with unchanged replicas, which reinforce the static, timeless, unnatural, unbiologic structure of the sick family. I would postulate that the significant peripheral person is involved in the dynamic replacement of essential pathologic family constituents, which are reconstructed unchanged because something that might be called the "psychic growth factor" is in some way extracted by the peripheral person. What the peripheral person may also provide to the family is some psychic nutrient comparable to sugar in the metabolic energy processes.

The psychic growth factor, since it is in the psychic sphere, might be likened to inspiration, hope or enthusiasm. Quite literally, it would seem in some cases that the relationship to the schizophrenogenic family not only may have provided the peripheral person with being viewed as omnipotent, but may actually have enhanced his power over other people, or have been necessary for the maintenance of his power. For example, the lawyer says, "He did everything I ever asked of him." The doctor reassured himself that his own solution to homosexual fears was a powerful one. The visiting boyfriend was perhaps cured, whereas the family stayed sick. In some ways, these peripheral persons benefited and gained from their association with the sick families. It would seem that the peripheral persons offer the families "great expectations" but actually exploit them. This relationship may be thought of as increasing the entropy of the family system. Entropy is a thermodynamic concept applied by this author to the interpsychic communication system of schizophrenic families and to family therapy, in a paper presented recently at the Sixth International Congress of Psychotherapy, London, August 1964, entitled "Speculations on Psychic Energy, Thermodynamics and Family Intrapsychic Communication."

The transfer of illness phenomenon in

schizophrenic families

Ross V. Speck

Chapter

22

Our experience in the conjoint therapy of the schizophrenic family led us to the observation that various types of transfer phenomena are regular and practically daily events among the members of the schizophrenic family. By transfer we mean a conveying or exchange from one person to another. A change in one family member effects changes in the others. An attempt will be made in this chapter to illustrate clinically as many types of transfer phenomena as possible and, at the same time, to classify them. Although our group has been carefully studying the transfer of illness phenomenon in the schizophrenic family for a number of years, it should be explicitly stated that what is unknown far exceeds the known.

Don Jackson[54] and others have written about a homeostatic balance of forces within a given family unit. Clinically there is much evidence to substantiate give-and-take, push-pull, or compensatory factors which operate continuously and mostly out of awareness within any family unit living and interacting within the same life-space environment. This clinical evidence will be presented throughout the chapter. In addition, there is evidence to suggest that changes in family structure are likewise compensated for. Structural systems within a family may consist of the marriage system,[23] the parent-child system, the sibling system, the structural excess or deficit ystem (other relatives or friends living or interacting in the home), and the human-pet system.

The sources of the ideas presented here are manifold. The most important source has probably been "schizophrenic" families with whom we have communicated and interacted in their own home over the past several years. In addition, the author has treated several "non-schizophrenic" families in a clinic setting, and has had experience in private practice in an office setting with both schizophrenic and non-schizophrenic families. Although a conceptual model has progressively developed in these various treatments, each case has been approached as an individual experiment in therapy,[48] with new techniques and hypotheses to be tested. At the same time, the therapists were there to learn about and study any interesting phenomena related to the family or its interaction. A fourth source of information about relationships in families was the therapist's own family and the families of friends where some of the intimate secrets of family life were exposed. A fifth source of thought-provoking material was anecdotal accounts about families from clinical colleagues and from other research workers, who were interested in families as units of study. Frequent conversations with Ray L. Birdwhistell and Albert E. Scheflen in the course of their film analyses of the process of psychotherapy were particularly helpful to me. Lastly, our weekly research conferences with the other members of the family therapy research project undoubtedly have had much influence on my own thinking.

Some Concepts of Illness

When a therapist undertakes to treat a family as a unit,[29] he is already making a departure from conventional medical treatment. Although the general practitioner has treated "families" for years, he works completely in the medical tradition of treating each individual person as the unit to be treated. He may use knowledge about other family members in applying his "cure" to the individual patient. However, the G.P. has his own medical concept of what constitutes illness and he sticks quite closely to the individual medical classification. The family therapist, however, works very little within the medical framework. He treats a sociological unit, the family, sees emotional illness in terms of the total family, and has no prepared classificatory system into which he can classify a malfunctioning family. The whole concept of illness when seen at the family level and at the cultural level takes on a markedly different perspective from that seen at the individual level in traditional medical concepts.[24, 25, 30]

Definitions of illness from a sociological point of view vary greatly across cultures as well as within cultures. For example, certain primitive societies[15] regard as "normal" what is to other societies an obvious disease. Skin diseases and injuries are so common among the Kuba of Sumatra that they do not find these conditions at all abnormal. Similarly, hookworm disease in North Africa was regarded as a normal condition and public health measures to correct it were strongly opposed. In addition, social class[96] defines whether an individual considers certain symptoms as illness or not. Actually, the higher the social class, the more illness is perceived in the typical medical frame of reference. For instance, Samuel Bloom[15] has a table indicating the percentage of respondents in each social class recognizing specified symptoms as needing medical attention. In Class I, 100% of those interviewed indicated that blood in the urine was a symptom needing medical attention. In Class II, 93% of the respondents concurred, while only 69% of Class III respondents concurred. Class III respondents generally showed a marked indifference to most symptoms. Different incidences of varying types of mental disorders have been reported in different cultures. If a culture accepts a certain set of physical, emotional or psychological attributes as "normal" for the culture, then regardless of how the medical profession may label these attributes, the individual member possessing them will not be thought of as "sick" and he will not be assigned any of the privileges, demeanor, obligations or deferences in terms of the sick role.

The Transfer Phenomenon in Schizophrenic Families

Attempts to document some of the types of transfer phenomena which have been observed in our clinical work with schizophrenic families, reveal that there is no good way as yet to classify clinical situations where symptoms or roles are exchanged between two or more people. One method of classification might take into account the involved structural part of the family unit; another might involve etiology of the phenomenon; still another might be related to role theory. A clinical description of several types of transfer phenomena follows, as does an effort to account for the transfer phenomenon from six different theoretical points of view.

Our experience with schizophrenic families reveals serious psychopathology[105] to be present in all members of the family who are living and interacting in the same dwelling. Just why this has been so much overlooked in the past is an interesting question. The most likely answer, however, is that the clinician has devoted his energies to a description of the schizophrenic patient and, perhaps, has let the family off the hook by blaming the patient for the family's individual idiosyncrasies. On the surface, many of these families show few unusual features, however, very little contact with them is necessary before even a relatively unsophisticated observer can detect patterns of family functioning which are apt to set this particular family aside from other families in the immediate community. As I was writing these lines I received two telephone calls. The first was from the director of the children's unit in a psychiatric hospital. He had called the week before to have the father of a schizophrenic child who is under hospital treatment hospitalized for a paranoid psychosis. This morning, the mother of this child was showing disorder of affect, disturbances of thought processes, and autism. She needed hospitalization. It is as if a contagion has occurred in the family.

The second call was different. A young physician telephoned to see if we could admit his twenty-five-year-old wife because of a post-partum depression. The husband sounded totally unconcerned. Despite delusions, hallucinations, thought disorder, and rages plus previous mental hospital admissions, he said his wife was just mildly upset and needed only a three-month stay at our hospital under sedation. The husband in this case presented the problem with the same affect in which one might order a second cup of coffee. Experience tells us that his problems would probably be as extensive as those of his wife. Marital pairs frequently assume the superadequate—inadequate balance (Bowen).[20] There is little doubt that if the wife were to improve, the functioning of the husband would move from the superadequate to the inadequate direction. Another way of saying this would be that his sickness had been revealed (instead of concealed), or that a transfer of illness had occurred from the wife to the husband.

The transfer of illness phenomenon frequently occurs in the parent-child system in schizophrenic families. This probably is related to the phenomenon of symbiosis, which is most frequent between the mother and the schizophrenic family member. But we have seen symbiosis between the father and the symptomatic patient, as well as between another sibling and the symptomatic patient. Schizophrenic families are conspicuous by their intense dyad formations and any change occurring in one member of the dyad is frequently reflected in the other.[105] A clinical example of this phenomenon occurred in the Island family (Chapter 4). At the beginning of therapy the mother was neat, attractive, and weighed 125 lbs. After a year of therapy, the daughter was progressively showing more rebellion at her mother's over-protection; she had lost weight, and looked neat and attractive. The mother now weighed 175 lbs., was sloppy, unattractive, and depressed. In this same family, the mother tended to get depressed practically every time her daughter showed therapeutic movement or was happy, or if she made any relatively mature decision. It was as if the mother could not tolerate the anxiety generated by the threatened dissolution of a non-maturational dyad. Her depression functioned to maintain the immature symbiotic relationship with her daughter, and she thus is seen to have a greater need to have a symbiotic relationship with the sick daughter than to have a mature and "individuated" relationship with a less sick daughter.

The mother never showed any overt affection to the father. Yet she was amused whenever her husband chased the schizophrenic daughter about the house, tickling her and playfully panting after her. She was thus her husband's ally in maintaining an incestuous dyadic relationship between the father and daughter. Whenever the daughter began to show signs of maturation, or of being able to function independently, the mother would become depressed or physically ill. Whenever the daughter was withdrawn or regressed or dependent, the mother would become cheerful and able to function in her usual role as leader in the family. The shifts and transfers of sickness observed in this family were of such high order and degree of frequency as to make verbal presentation difficult. The following brief chart illustrates shifts and transfers as observed at yearly intervals, but it must be remembered that such shifts can occur at any moment, daily, weekly, or almost continually.

TIME	FATHER	MOTHER	DAUGHTER	SON
Start of therapy	Worried over heart condition	Worried over weakness caused by pelvic surgery 8 years ago	Schizophrenic, weight 195	"Well" student
One year later	Less preoccupied with heart, defensive denial	Depressed, sloppy, poorer functioning	Much improved, less withdrawn, weight 125	Slightly depressed and anxious
Two years later	Depressed	Depressed	Further improvement	More depressed
Three years later (near termination of therapy)	Less depressed, more cooperative with family therapy	Less depressed, more angry with therapists	Further improvement	Less depressed, still over-protective of sister.

In another family, when the schizophrenic patient became acutely disturbed, the three other overtly non-disturbed members of the family were temporarily put on tranquilizers, with the expected result that the temporary disturbance in the family disappeared. Experiences such as this one strongly reinforced our belief that the family of the schizophrenic patient played as important a role in the genesis and maintenance of the psychopathology as any intraindividual factor, be it biological or psychological.[64]

We have repeatedly observed in hospitalized patients that one of the crucial phases in treatment is around the time of discharge from the hospital. Both schizophrenic patient and the family members feel increased tension. It is extremely common for a patient to have shown marked amelioration of psychotic symptoms in the hospital, but to have to be readmitted within a few days or weeks after return to his family. Nearly as common is the phenomenon of the primary patient's maintaining his improvement, but another family member living in the home having to be admitted to the hospital, often with a similar illness. I know of three cases, within a year, where a family member took his life within the first month after a schizophrenic patient had been discharged from the hospital as much improved. Conversations with other psychotherapists of schizophrenia confirm our clinical impression that transfer of illness—both physical and psychological— is by no means rare within the family of the schizophrenic. Bowen[18, 19] writes of a phenomenon where the psyche of one family member interacts with the soma of another.[34] In one such family which we have treated, the father has hypertension. The mother has diabetes, the one son has acute schizophrenic episodes, and the other son gets attacks of arthritis. When the son becomes psychotic, the whole family takes care of him, feeds him, and they wear themselves out. This son then shows marked improvement, and the other members of the family get flare-ups of their physical illness, and pay little attention to him. In the course of the psychotherapy of this family, this process has had several cycles. The mother once stated, "This family is like a Yo-Yo. We throw Joe out and then we bring him back in."

Abrahams and Varon[1] report that two out of six fathers died of coronary attacks during therapy from which they were physically excluded. The author had one case where a non-fatal coronary occlusion occurred in the father between the fourth and fifth family therapy session and another case where a non-fatal coronary occlusion occurred early in the family therapy in the father. I know of a case where a fatal coronary attack occurred in an uncle after his first family therapy session. The mother and schizophrenic son of one family, for instance, joked about the father's "nervous" heart. The mother flatly stated that the father had pampered himself all his life over a non-existent cardiac ailment. However, she worried continuously if her son missed taking his vitamin pills even for one day. The son was a husky, athletic, twenty-one-year-old in excellent physical health. After the father had a mild coronary attack, the therapist found that the father had been getting some irregular and inadequate treatments for a very severe hypertension of many years duration and that he had rheumatic heart disease. The mother also was found to have a severe hypertension. However, she persisted in her role as family diagnostician and was contemptuous of medical advice. She continued to insist during this phase of treatment that the family was enjoying the best of health, both emotional and physical, that they had experienced in a long time.

In another family, when the schizophrenic son was regressed and actively psychotic, the mother was ill with asthma, hypertension and pseudo-paralysis of the right hand. The father functioned well. When the son started to show improvement, the mother's symptoms disappeared and the father became depressed and went to bed and had to be looked after. The mother then indulged him. This cycle repeated itself. There were also cycles of sickness in this family between the schizophrenic son and his brother.

There is evidence to suggest that the patterns of illness cycles in schizophrenic families are not limited to the human members of the family. We have repeatedly observed that the pet animals[106] of the schizophrenic family show fluctuations in both behavior and health coincidental with the fluctuations in the behavior and health of the human family members. The observable animal behavior seems to have a direct relationship to the behavioral trends within the family. There are families where phobic humans have phobic pets. In one family, the mother, father and schizophrenic daughter all had a fear of leaving their house. The dog and cat also refused to leave the house and appeared to show fearful behavior when they were encouraged to leave. In our work with psychotic families, pets are regularly in the sessions which we hold in the family's home. The pets often seem to reflect the feelings of the family members. For instance, if the family is angry with the therapist, the pet is apt to be angry also; or if the family is friendly, the pet's behavior tends to be friendly also. It is not uncommon for pets to become ill in the family when significant human members of the family become ill. In psychotic families when aggression and behavioral disturbance become of high order, it is not unusual to see a cherished pet become ill, get injured or killed. This is usually followed by a period of mourning within the family and a marked lessening of the aggression and behavioral disturbance.

One might ask whether the above examples from cases truly constitute transfer of illness. At least theoretically, the schizophrenic family can be seen as non-maturational and as a closed system. The quality and/or quantity of relationships between the members of the schizophrenic family and the outside world are altered. Wynne[117] has spoken of the rubber fence, and Bateson[9] of the closed corporation in describing the schizophrenic family. It is common for schizophrenic family members to admit that they feel great guilt or reluctance in dealing closely with individuals outside the family unit. The schizophrenic patient is frequently blamed for the failure of socialization of other members. Schizophrenic families tend to isolate themselves from the rest of the community. It seems quite possible to me that schizophrenic families remain fixed, rigid, unadaptable, closed, with symbiotic dyads as a function of their inability to interact on a meaningful basis with the larger culture. An extension of this statement might be that more "normal" families are more open systems and that psychopathology or maybe even physical illness might be exchanged, diluted, or transferred in an ongoing interactional process with the larger culture.

An interesting research project has been carried out by Ruth Peachey[88] in which she asks the question, "Is it possible that apparently unrelated episodes of illness in families will, over a period of time, form repetitive patterns characteristic for a given family?" The data was taken from the records of her general medical practice. In 14 out of 21 families studied, a definite patterning of illness was discovered, and Peachey gives some clinical examples of transfer of illness or transfer of symptoms. Since her initial study, Peachey has further evidence of patterns of illness in "normal" families.

Significance of the Transfer of Illness Phenomena

It should be apparent that the transfer of illness phenomena in schizophrenic families is still virgin territory as far as our understanding of the basic mechanisms is concerned—though we have no doubt that we are dealing with regular, observable, and important patterns in these families, and can demonstrate these patterns to behavioral scientists and psychiatrists. The following is an attempt to speculate about the theoretical significance of the transfer of illness phenomenon by approaching it from the point of view of contagion, of complementarity, of primitive social organization, of role theory, of energy transfer, and as related to Franz Alexander's concepts in psychosomatic illness.

Contagion

This is probably the oldest theory embracing the transfer concept and has its origins in the work of Lasegue and Falret.[67] D. H. Tuke's "Dictionary of Psychological Medicine"[111] states that the term "communicated insanity" is the best equivalent for the French term "folie à deux." "Double insanity," "simultaneous insanity," and "imposed insanity" are given as synonyms. Four types of "communicated insanity" are distinguishable: 1) "Cases in which an insane patient distinctly infects another person with the same mental disorder." 2) "Cases in which a person becomes insane from companionship, not in consequence of the direct transference of morbid ideas, but as a result of shock or the strain of nursing such a patient." 3) "Cases in which two or more persons become insane simultaneously from the same cause." 4) "Cases in which one lunatic infects another lunatic with his special delusion." Types 1 and 4 embrace the idea of communication of mental disease from one person to another. A. Gralnick[44] reviewed the literature and 103 cases of "folie à deux" in two papers on the subject. He traced the history of the concept and found that in 1838, Ideler spoke of "the infectiousness of insanity," in 1846, Hoffbauer wrote about "psychic infection," and Wollenberg, in 1852, spoke of "familial mental infection."

Gralnick[44] also listed the following synonyms for folie à deux:

Seguin—contagious insanity.
Parsons—reciprocal insanity.
Ireland—collective insanity (a family of eight with similar
      psychoses).
Tuke—associated insanity or psychoses of association.
Carrier—insanity by contagion.
Rhein—conjugal insanity.
Gordon—influenced psychosis.

Tuke's definition of folie à deux: "A mental disorder occurring in two or more predisposed individuals who have been intimately associated, which is characterized by delusional ideas of a persecutory nature that may be transferred from one to the other." Three main factors are felt to be important to the contagion—close-association, dominance and submission, and relationship.

The transfer of illness theme in schizophrenic families is an extension of many of the elements which made up the folie-à-deux syndrome. The idea that only delusional ideas of a persecutory nature are transferred from one individual to another is broadened to include the psyche of one individual interacting with the psyche or soma of another individual, so that multiple shifts of psychological, "emotional," or physiological states between individuals can occur.

The idea of contagion as an etiological factor in the transfer of illness phenomenon in the schizophrenic family does not seem too plausible. In the schizophrenic family, folie à deux is the exception rather than the rule. Also, in psychiatric hospitals it is rare for one patient to be able to infect other patients, attendants, nurses or psychiatrists with a similar set of symptoms even when a close identification occurs. Contagion does occur at a higher social level, though. In Freud's time in Vienna, major hysterical attacks were quite common among the upper middle-class; today they seem less common. However, such phenomena still can be observed with regularity in Southern lower-class Negroes, and in some isolated sub-cultural groups.

It is possible that Lasegue and Falret, when they were writing their famous paper,[67] had already come to grips with important concepts in the understanding of the schizophrenic patient and his family, but that they were prevented from enlarging upon them by focusing upon the relatively infrequent folie-à-deux phenomena. Their concept that only delusional ideas of a persecutory nature could be transferred from one individual to another in particular limited the further development of the understanding of the transfer phenomenon in the schizophrenic family.

Complementarity

Social systems such as the family or other larger entities are in a state of balance—a steady state, where a change in input alters the output. If a husband, for instance, is a stern disciplinarian, his wife becomes more permissive; if she becomes more of a disciplinarian, he may become more permissive. Marriages appear to be made in the unconscious, so that a conscious character trait in one, e.g., the husband, is matched by an unconscious one in the spouse, and vice versa. Marriage partners have a strong tendency to select each other with the same types of pathology or fixation although on the surface they may seem to be at opposite poles. Bowen's superadequate-inadequate concept is an example of this. When the husband feels adequate and free from anxiety, the wife is helpless and dependent; if she becomes adequate and free from anxiety, he becomes dependent.

It seems possible that complementarity can involve several individuals synchronously in a family. In addition, there must be an effect upon those who live with the partners involved in the complementary reaction. In other words, any interaction within a system such as the family will produce an effect upon the total transaction.

Primitive Social Organization

When illnes becomes manifest in a family, an increasing preoccupation with confining the pathology and treating the sick member can be observed. This is in contrast to the time when a family is functioning in a healthy manner, a time when there is growth, maturation, and mobility. The schizophrenic family operates like a small, primitive culture[119] where the basic needs of life are most important. The sick role, with its accepted dependency and immaturity, brings early life, aggression, and primitive sexuality to the fore. Murder and incest become, at times, even conscious themes in the family life. The sublimated mask has been stripped off. One difference, though, between a primitive culture—such as the Iatmul described by Bateson—and a schizophrenic family in our own culture is that primitive cultures have well-defined taboos to handle incest and murder, sex and aggression, while members of a more advanced culture only know they should not live out their fantasies, and are being pulled towards the primitive via the regression in the illness. A psychotic family might be compared to a family in a primitive culture. It is very difficult to treat a psychotic family. The family itself is caught up in a violent destructive struggle and any intruder, such as a therapist, who attempts to change the prevailing social order, becomes a target for similar destructive impulses. The family therapist can only hope to dilute the intensity of the destructive process by having his own team, which will hopefully function in a manner similar to what Slavson has called the dilution of the transference.

Role Theory

Schizophrenic illness is seen as a sick-role assignment by the family, as a restitutive effort to wall off the "creeping insanity," or as primitivization occurring within the family unit. This fits in well with clinically observable phenomena in schizophrenic families. Some families seem to need a scapegoat and are highly selective as to who is best qualified to play this role. This could be thought of as a projection mechanism within the family. It is not uncommon to see schizophrenic families in which the family as a unit appear to function much more capably when one member is psychotic. In one such case when the chronic schizophrenic patient showed marked improvement and returned to his home, his father shot himself two weeks later, and his brother, who had been in college, left to stay at home. We have repeatedly seen families where the father functioned well in his work until the schizophrenic member showed signs of recovery; at that point, the father became depressed, anxious or so disturbed as to threaten his breadwinning function in the family.

Energy Transfer

Schizophrenic families tend to wall themselves off from interpersonal contact with the larger social system; because of their markedly decreased interaction with the outside world and the increased interaction within the family units themselves, they could be considered a relatively closed system. The normal family, however, is seen as an open system, complete with inputs, outputs, and energy transfers. The schizophrenic family knows no such transfers—here energies and forces accumulate and build up which in a normal family are discharged and exchanged via ongoing maturational experiences with multitudes of other interacting human beings. There is some evidence also that the incidence of illness—both physical and emotional—in members of schizophrenic families is higher than in "normal" families.

Relation to Franz Alexander's Concepts

Franz Alexander[5] assumes that family tensions occur which specifically affect the blood pressure system, the respiratory system, the gastro-intestinal system, and others. If the family is the unit and sickness is in the unit, one individual may express a symptom physiologically through the tissues, and another may express it psychologically, or in behavioral terms as in schizophrenia. There may be an inherited or congenital point of weakness, called the X-factor by Alexander, which in one family member may be in the physical, in another in the emotional or psychological sphere.

Both somatic and psychological illness may be related to the transfer phenomenon. Peachey[88] cites a case of a father coming to the physician because he fears that he has rheumatic fever. He was reassured that he did not have rheumatic fever. The next month his eight-year-old daughter was brought to the same physician, and she was diagnosed as having acute rheumatic fever. This father and his daughter had shown repeated patterns of alternating visits to the physician. The choice of illness and the manifestation sometimes have an additional secondary use within the family. In one family, when the younger schizophrenic son gets face pains, the three other members rub their own faces in the same area. The discomfort is transferred to the other family members. In the same family, the diabetic mother occasionally gets an insulin reaction and becomes stuporous, talks in a confused psychotic fashion and has to be looked after in bed—all behavioral reactions that closely mimick those of her schizophrenic son when he is in an acute episode. It is difficult to say whether the son in his psychosis is mimicking the mother in her insulin reaction, or whether the mother in her insulin reaction is mimicking the son in one of his psychotic reactions.

A recent paper by Veiga[112] cites several interesting examples of what we call the transfer phenomenon. In one of her cases—a family of six—"four of the members became ill almost simultaneously with various conditions which ranged from complications of obesity through severe skin disorders and the very real threat of psychotic breakdown in one of the parents" following admission of a child to the hospital. Veiga sees the illness of the child as an externalization of the family's unconscious conflict, much in the way an unconscious conflict is represented by the symptoms in an individual.

Since the above theoretical notions do not account for all the manifestations of the transfer phenomena, further observation and study is needed for a better understanding and treatment of it.

The concept of change in conjoint family therapy

Ivan Boszormenyi-Nagy

Because of its relevance for pathology, the assessment of change is of fundamental significance for the psychotherapist. Pathology, whether it is conceived in physical or psychological terms, traditionally connotes a deviant (altered or changed) state of an organism. As to psychiatric conditions, that which has been altered can be best defined either in intrapsychic or in interpersonal terms. It is apparent that of all recent developments in psychiatry, family therapy has been most emphatic concerning the multipersonal texture of psychological health and illness. This chapter is specifically concerned with questions of individual and interactional changes, accompanying conjoint psychotherapy of families comprising at least one clinically schizophrenic member.

I shall first discuss general criteria of change; then an hypothesis for the main dynamic dimension of change; and finally, the implications of insight for change, along with some general concluding considerations.

Criteria of Change in Family Therapy

The literature on evaluation of change effected by psychotherapy is far too voluminous and multifaceted for a review here. From the point of view of family therapy, it is especially premature to focus on detailed questions of evaluative methodology before the main conceptual issues of the criteria of familial change are clarified. Furthermore, family therapy experience teaches the therapist new dimensions of evaluation regarding even individual psychotherapy. However, even from the vantage point of individual psychotherapy, one cannot escape the conclusion that it is impossible to define change in the total dynamic functioning of a person without reference to his most intimately interpersonal, familial exchanges.

A truly systematic discussion of change in families undergoing psychotherapy ideally ought to be based on operationally definable process concepts of psychological health and maturity of both individuals and families. At the other extreme of the scale, a clinical-empirical evaluation of change may simply rest on the presence or absence of descriptive psychiatric (symptomatic) evidences of traditionally defined pathology. Since space does not permit even a tentative utilization of such a highly useful conceptual analysis as Hill and Hansen's[51] identification of interactional, structural-functional, situational, institutional, and developmental frameworks that are applicable to family studies, the observations in this chapter will be based on the author's six years of experience with conjoint (institutional, home, and office) family treatment and on team discussions held at the Philadelphia Psychiatric Center and the Eastern Pennsylvania Psychiatric Institute.

The family therapist has to develop a long-range process view of therapy in order not to get lost in the sequence of kaleidoscopically changing "microscopical" events. For the moment, an event may strike him as an impairment, while seen in its overall temporal context the same event may represent an important element of progress. A large category of phenomena classified under "regression in the service of the ego" (Kris[65]) belongs here. Temporary disorganization of a formerly always composed member, for instance, may indicate the beginning of a rearrangement of his contribution to the total family pathology. Loewald[73] characterizes the course of psychoanalysis as consisting of "periods of induced ego-disorganization and reorganization." In the same significant paper, he suggests a guideline for the analyst in his evaluation of the direction of movement and the placement of his interpretations. The guideline issues from a construction, even if rudimentary, by the therapist of a reference image of the patient's core personality. In other words, according to Loewald, the analyst extrapolates into the future that intrinsic construction of long-range change which he has inferred from the minutiae of his observations of the patient's here-and-now behavior as well as of his conscious and unconscious account of his past.

Many an apparent change in families turns out to be a simple manifestation of a never-ending relational seesaw movement. Several of our treatment families have come to use the term "Yo-Yo" for this pseudo-progress quite spontaneously. It is only through understanding the long-term gratification economy of all participants of the symbiotically close familial relationship that the therapist can learn whether, for instance, a young girl's leaving home means increased autonomy or rather a travesty of individuation through the subsequent intensification of her symbiotic involvement. In other words, any apparent change may actually contribute to reinforcement of the underlying developmental stagnation.

Developmental (directional) concepts underlie any dynamic consideration of psychic health. Change is the essence of life processes and the direction of change points from conception to death. On the other hand, certain changes, e.g., physical growth, are appropriate for the young only. Slowness of the aging process irks the adolescent, whereas it is most welcome to the elderly. Turning now to relational development, personal overinvolvement and underinvolvement appear to be phasically alternating requirements and goals throughout the individual's lifetime, although the general direction of change points to more involvement on a more individuated (mature) basis; early infantile uninvolvement as a start yields to more and more complex and deep involvements throughout adulthood.

Although it is difficult to apply developmental process concepts in evaluating anybody's emotional maturity, at least it can be categorically stated that the individual's life adaptations ought to be aimed at the preservation of his own self. The same criterion of health cannot be applied, however, to the nuclear family. If the nuclear family remains ideally adjusted to self-perpetuation after the offspring have grown to biological maturity, one can assume that certain dynamic facets of the family's life support stagnation. Perhaps the parents cannot let the grown-up children go, despite their best conscious intentions; or the children may have grown up to be frightful of true individuation and of genuine extra-familial involvement. Naturally, the period in which the offspring attains separation age (launching stage) is stressful for any family. We have found, especially, that many families comprising schizophrenic members are close social systems which tend to discourage such intruders as boyfriends, girlfriends, potential marriage mates, etc. Of the many possible criteria of family health or maturity, we can emphasize the one which, by a flexible preparedness for giving up the family's togetherness itself, allows individuation and separation through formation of new relationships on the growing offspring's part. We can epitomize our developmental outlook with the statement that "family maturity" is not determined by the extent of individual accomplishments or of manifest discord, but by the state of the equilibrium between forces supporting individuation and those building roadblocks to personality growth and relational diversification in various members.

Considerations of developmental arrest lead us to the more general and rather central concept of *fixation*, fundamental to post-Freudian psychiatry. It is customary to consider a rigidity or lack of flexibility as the central factor in all psychopathology. Searles,[99] in a paper centering on the significance of change in psychotherapy, describes change itself as a major source of life anxiety. Some therapists claim that *any* change in response to psychotherapy is beneficial. With qualifications, this holds true of family therapy. In this connection it is interesting to note that whereas the student of psychopathology tends to look upon illness as fixation, stagnation, or arrest of change, members of the family often view psychosis as a change for worse from the patient's "good" pre-psychotic, static condition. Family members often wish to change the primary patient back to what he used to be prior to the onset of psychosis and, according to good clinical evidence, unconsciously they wish him to remain there.

Directional considerations of familial change can highlight the intricate connections between intrapsychic and interpersonal dimensions of change. In this regard, it has to be recognized that, thanks to the contributions of Freud, Abraham, Melanie Klein, Fairbairn and others, intrapsychic changes can be formulated in the interactional terms of a quasi-interpersonal conceptional dynamic. To use a common example, any act of actual, interpersonal "giving" alters the giver's emotional balance not only with regard to the receiver, but with regard to his own super-ego as well. Another example highlights the manner in which a seemingly new relationship essentially represents the elaboration of an internalized old one. For instance, the apparently interpersonal, here-and-now relationship of a young woman with her baby may be—dynamically speaking—the heir of her relationship with her own mother (Benedek[14]). To the extent that she is excessively fixated to an old relational tie in a new relational context, the mother's attitude will become the source of major family pathology (Boszormenyi-Nagy[17]).

The evaluation of observed interactional changes is, of course, of primary importance for the family therapist. The interlocking of developmental changes ("epigenetic" changes, Erikson[36]) of individuals no more reveal the overall family process than adding the properties of hydrogen and oxygen reveals the properties of water. Since the family is a multilevel organization, its changes have to be conceptualized on each of its significant levels. The emergence of any simple event, e.g., a heated discussion, can signify change in a) an individual member's habitual behavior, b) the nature of dyadic or other sub-group interactional patterns (coalitions, displacements, etc.), and c) the overall style of the entire family. Changes observed on each of these three levels will have to be integratively evaluated in terms of long-term process considerations. Naturally, the life of an individual is just as much a process as is the life of the brother-sister infatuation or of an entire nuclear family.

While not losing sight of possible evidences of changes in individual members, the family therapist has to maintain an eager interest in noting changes that occur in the dyadic or triadic patterns of the family system of relationships. For instance, newly emerging trends of father-daughter or mother-son involvement may characterize a certain phase of family therapy. One can be drawn into detailed examination of the Oedipal features of these involvements and yet the true significance of such relational changes cannot be evaluated without an understanding of the qualitative changes of each participant's subjective need gratification systems. A father who, returning home late in a drunken state, accused his daughter of promiscuous behavior, turned out to be struggling with a projected resentment toward his long deceased mother rather than with heterosexual jealousy in a father-daughter context. The impact of such changes to other dyadic or triadic configurations is even more important to note. Perhaps the most significant dynamic consequence is that a newly emerging need-gratification system between two members will inevitably effect the balance of relational gratifications as far as the other members are concerned. In the above example, there seemed to be no evidence of jealousy on the mother's part, who rather appeared to be a co-beneficiary with her daughter in a wished for, emerging expression of her husband's needs for family. Ultimately, the question of change has to be decided in the context of the total relational system, involving all members.

Many typical examples of dyadic or triadic changes can be cited from clinical experience with families containing a psychotic member. Quite frequently the initial phase of conjoint therapy with such families is characterized by an ostensible parental alliance feuding with an unmanageable "sick" child. The parental alliance is all the more obvious since the parents share the responsibility for the psychiatric hospitalization of the psychotic member. This arrangement, however, tends to yield to one in which the psychotic child gains immense significance as a mediator in the middle of a meaningless, often emotionally "burnt out" parental marriage. This picture may easily change again into one in which the most significant pseudo-alliance in the family appears to be a hostile, ambivalent, primary identification type relating between a forceful, phallic mother and her psychotic daughter. In the case of families with a young psychotic male, a corresponding configuration often is a homosexually tinged, ambivalent attraction between a mothering type father and his son. This inverted Oedipal phase then is apt to yield to a heterosexual arrangement within the family's inter-member involvements. The latter may in turn coincide with extra-familial heterosexual experimentations on the offspring's part, whereupon a defensive closeness between the parents may reoccur as a transitory defensive maneuver and the whole cycle may start again, causing the observer to wonder whether he has seen anything but phases of cyclic oscillation in an essentially unchanging conspiracy of static relationships.

Change is the direct opposite of conformance with fixated family ideologies or "family myths" (Wynne et al.[117]). One has to develop a sensitive ear to parental statements like: "What a pity that Loretta (twenty-one-year-old daughter) has such a poor figure; otherwise she would have been engaged or married a long time ago." With the help of the therapists' warm interest in her femininity, this schizophrenic girl learned that she was not as incapable of attracting men as suggested by her mother, and she started to date afterwards.

Certain family myths can distort the personality development of the offspring by stamping a configuration of negative identity upon them. The most insidious of these identity indoctrinations take place unconsciously, instigated by the parents' superego or ego lacunae (A. Johnson[59]). By this is meant that the parents' consciously disapproved though not deeply repudiated anti-social impulses may find their outlet through their unintentional encouragement of anti-social behavior in the offspring. These unconscious encouragements usually have typical double binding characteristics, especially when they come in the form of cautions against the child's potentially dangerous anti-social impulses. An interesting form of power schemes used by mothers can be built on the family myth of the dangerousness of the members' impulses. The mother can then be seen engaged in complicated schemes of protecting each member from the potentially dangerous effect of his impulses upon another member. Such complex, shared mechanisms of impulse discharge and control clearly cut across individual ego boundaries and their change can only be defined in terms of the overall family system. When the family therapist becomes convinced that almost any change in the rigid family myth would be beneficial, he may find it difficult or impossible to revert to his earlier positions where he expected change in terms of character or impulse-defense configurations of individuals.

A Hypothesis of the Basic Dynamic of Familial Change

It is proposed here that psychological sequelae of object loss are of the most profound significance for the two main criteria of maturity: personal identity and capacity for interpersonal relationships. The incomplete mourning process which in its most general sense diffusely penetrates man's entire individuation, prevents the formation of distinct ego boundaries and leaves one preoccupied with the inner representation of the partially delineated, past relational objects. The incompleteness of the self-object delineation is conducive of an unconscious tendency for projecting the lost person's internal image upon persons of one's here-and-now actual environment. In its extreme, this tendency manifests itself in transference neuroses and delusions; in its milder form it pervades all our closer (familial) ties. This basically object conservative or restorative effort can be very costly as far as the prospects of healthy interpersonal relations are concerned. Various members, especially the growing child, will unconsciously conform to and pose demands for reciprocally shared restorative efforts aimed at retaining deserting though desired early parental images. In certain families the inability for object relinquishment may increase progressively from generation to generation, due partly to physical absence, but even more likely to the inadequate parental model of ego-delineation.

Family pathology then can be conceptualized as a specialized multi-person organization of shared fantasies and complementary need gratification patterns, maintained for the purpose of handling past object-loss experience. The very symbiotic or undifferentiated quality of transactions in certain families amounts to a multipurpose bind, capable of preventing awareness of losses to any individual member. Another aim of the "symbiotic" family organization is the prevention of threatened separations. Separations can occur on interpersonal-interactional and on structural levels. The maturation of a sixteen-year-old daughter, for instance, can cause anxiety in the parents both on account of threatened actual parent-child separation and on account of a reinforcement or return in the parents through identification with their daughter of their own fear of individuation. These fears may compel the parents to revitalize their involvement with the daughter through guilt, scapegoating, infantilization, parentification, or some other means. In one family of this type, the parents developed a concomitant "myth" according to which their only real problem was a marital disagreement over how to discipline their seventeen-year-old daughter. Their discord with each other became so violent that it took close listening and observation on the family therapists' part to detect how the parents' shared role-playing helped them to deny and act out at the same time their anxiety concerning the daughter's maturation.

The above, hypothetical core dynamic of families is assumed to be the determinant of both family need-complementarity (Boszormenyi-Nagy[17]) and family myth (Wynne et al.[117]). Family pathology amounts to a sensitively regulated system of interdependent displacements regarding the members' affect responses and object choices. The stronger the system as a whole, the less it permits meaningful and mature relating among the members. Deceptive pseudo-involvements, required by the family myth, serve to obscure the incomplete state of individuation of the participants of the system. Vicarious gratifications, projections, and revenge fantasies transferred from early lost love objects prevent the members from definitively working through those steps of maturation which are concerned with the painful process of relinquishing archaic internal objects. The unconscious conspiracy for preventing each other's maturation can therefore be hypothesized as the causative dynamic, underlying the members' symbiotic partnership.

As far as change is concerned, these family systems present well disguised but powerful obstacles. An implicit aim of family pathology is to immobilize real growth in another member because growth leads to the eventual loss of the other member: the source of real or imaginary satisfactions. Inasmuch as imaginary familial satisfactions are partly of a transference nature, they are analogous to certain phases of clinging-type therapeutic transference. Whereas the intrapsychic part of the interrupted object relinquishment process is essentially identical in both situations, in family neurosis the individual member is faced with an accomplice in shared postponement of maturation instead of an agent of the secondary process in the person of the therapist. This is an additional, interactional reason why the consequences of the psychotic member's separation from his family so often produce in him overtly familial object-restitutive efforts as symptoms (delusions or hallucinations).

If the various manifestations of family pathology (projections, incomplete individual boundaries, vicarious gratifications, projective and distorted identifications) are useful only as a means for maintaining the delay of mourning work, the family may itself come to symbolize for its members the denied lost object, perhaps the mother (Josselyn[60]). Furthermore, it is conceivable that the individual members' primary process needs become largely submerged in the family system and consequently the members become more or less free of typical neurotic (intrapsychic) symptoms. If, on the other hand, one member "changes" with respect to his reliance on the system, one or several of his complementary partners will suffer from "individual symptomatology." The family homeostatic forces will then resume their work as the "betrayed" partners start exerting pressure on the escaping member so that he should resume his compliant family role. Thus, explicit scapegoating often originates from one member's attempts at escape. If scapegoating alone does not compel the escapee to return, he can often be driven into overt psychotic despair with consecutive physical expulsion (hospitalization). The unconscious purpose of the whole game is restoration of the family system, i.e., the imaginary possession of a primal family on the part of most or all members.

Having learned about the underlying mechanisms that prevent genuine interpersonal growth in the family of the schizophrenic does not relieve the frustrations of the therapist who is concerned with change. The therapist will be eager to "attach" any one of the pseudo-involvements manifested between family members, yet he will soon discover that the causal roots of these "sub-system" manifestations involve the total family system. Without affecting the shared motivation of *all* family members for denying and deferring external and internal object losses, the therapist's efforts are largely wasted on mere symptomatic manifestations.

Naturally, the outlook for ultimate change will be determined by the balance between deeper motivational forces of growth or stagnation in the family; and the therapist's role is divided between being a point of crystallization of these forces and an active technician of change. He will, by necessity, have to enter the family system while at the same time protecting himself against being absorbed into it.

The family therapist has to remember that, in any type of psychotherapy, the development of a deep (regressive) relational experience and subsequent exploration are the *sine qua non* of lasting therapeutic effect or change. Criteria of depth are the same in family as in individual psychotherapy. Great intensity of affect may be generated and emotionally charged past attitudes may get forcibly projected (transferred) on other members or on the therapists. Gradually, the barrier against the expression of angry, frustrated or rejecting feelings toward one another will be overcome. Experimentation with trial separations unleashes long repressed frustrations and fosters a more genuine intermember relating. The process of piercing a pseudo-involvement on one member's part stimulates, if motivation permits, a replication on another member's part.

With each experience of newly achieved freedom for rejection of transference distorted pseudo-involvements the wheel of arrested mourning processes turns and the family equilibrium advances one step from symbiosis toward potential individuation.

One treatment family came to a meeting with the explicit agreement among father, mother, and married daughter that the psychotic son was to be helped through hospitalization rather than through family therapy. They were unanimous in their opinion that all of their other problems were routine and their only real trouble resided in the intolerable behavior on the boy's part. The therapists' adamant refusal to consider any therapeutic planning other than full conjoint family sessions, gradually led to a violent outbreak of marital disagreement and a decision on the father's part for continuing family explorations instead of hospitalizing his son. In the ensuing, highly emotional exchange, the mother described how she used to scratch her son's back for long intervals while refusing him the right to occupy himself with any hobby of his own. The daughter subsequently admitted to her own marital unhappiness and ascribed her "bad" nature to similar traits in her and in her mother's personality. The session ended in a generalized relief of tension, probably as a result of more genuine, emotionally free relating. That the family system could yield this quickly was probably possible only on a transference-cure basis. The strong stand taken by the therapists established them as targets for transferred parental object needs.

The stage of regression or primary process-type relating brings the family therapist deeply into the family system. A sensitive and suspicious, socially highly accomplished father appeared to be heavily relying on support from one of the therapists for his surprisingly angry rejection of his martyr-like wife. In the subsequent session he displayed a highly ambivalent and guilt-laden behavior toward the therapist. The next day he called to announce that the family wanted to halt therapy for several weeks. As he later associated, the therapist became the heir of a desired yet hated, deserting parental figure who would have to be rejected either symbolically or in reality in order to allow individuation to take place. Often the family terminates at this point or provokes the therapist into terminating treatment. However, as far as long-range change is concerned, even though such termination is premature and the subsequent reunion of the family has a paranoid flavor, it might foreshadow a more mature, more individuated pattern of acting at least on the part of one or possibly all family members.

Premature termination may not be in itself a desirable treatment goal but its prognostic significance merits conceptual exploration. A family's arrested life process may pick up from the point of termination and its homeostatic steady state might get adjusted on a new functional level. More specifically, since we have hypothesized that the main cause of stagnation was a fear of object-relinquishment, an ability to relinquish the therapist as a quasi-familial object may, though it does not have to, signify a newly-won capacity for growth through an emancipation effort in the context of transference.

A family's prognostic evaluation can be made from the balance between the changes they have made and their resistance to change while undergoing conjoint therapy. The first ominous prognostic sign usually is a proof of genuine unwillingness by one or several family members to become deeply involved in an intensely emotional therapeutic group process.

A twenty-one-year-old psychotic girl who used to write bizarre suicide notes to her family, soon became non-psychotic in her overt behavior shortly after family therapy had been started. Yet even while she was overtly asking for discontinuation of the family therapy sessions, she kept sending disturbed letters to the therapists, most likely in order to document her deeper needs for help. Quite in contrast to the daughter, the mother consistently refused to become involved in the therapy process. In the beginning she showed her resistance by not having anything to say or by considering the repetitious discussion of the few "crazy" symptoms of her daughter as the only valid subject area. She consistently refused to talk about her own past memories and fell more and more into the habit of discouraging even the other members of the family from doing so. In the end she began missing sessions and she only occasionally darted through the room where the meetings were held. Finally, she told the therapists not to come any more because her daughter was well now. The therapy had to be discontinued. Several months after termination the mother called to tell the therapists that her daughter had been admitted to the local state hospital and that she hoped she would be cured there by means of physical treatment.

The following example illustrates the thesis that a mere capacity for regressive, deep involvement is not in itself sufficient for an ultimate good prognosis. The mother in this family of a nineteen-year-old schizophrenic boy started out rather cool and aloof in the conjoint treatment sessions and remained so for several months. She would have nothing to say except for well-guarded conventional statements until, approximately at the end of the second year of treatment, she became childishly flirtatious and talkative. Thus, in this sense there has been a definable behavioral change in the mother, yet she was unwilling to connect this behavior with associations from her past. She specifically refused to agree to having her father attend a single session. In one of the last sessions with this family, in which the members seemed to be emotionally freer than ever before, she asked to be excused or else she would have to "do" on the sofa. A few weeks later the family terminated therapy in an abrupt manner, at a point where evidences of change in the family seemed insignificant.

Change in the Family System vs. Change in Individual Members

Without intending to question the validity of individual-based concepts of psychotherapeutic change (Luborsky,[74] Siegal and Rosen,[102] Wallerstein[114]) for the family therapy situation, we would like to stress the importance of developing a conceptual system for evaluating change on the level of family interaction as a system. Regardless of whether one agrees with the collectively deferred mourning process as the fundamental dynamic mechanism of the pathology of the family system, some kind of a dynamic regulatory principle has to be assumed to operate on a collective group level of the family. It has to be postulated that the emotional gratification economy of each member is, to a high degree, regulated by the nature of the family's group transactional process. It is logical to assume that the system's change cannot be expressed in terms of a mere additive summation of each family member's shift from id to ego mechanism, decreased anxiety, or other criteria of individual structural rearrangement.

The following is an example of a family system of gratification: a family was referred for conjoint therapy because of the psychotic behavior of a sixteen-year-old, extremely muscular son. This boy had quite openly threatened various family members with murder. Curiously, the mother was not nearly as much concerned about her son's threats as were the father and the recently married ("escaped," in her own words) nineteen-year-old sister. As it turned out, the boy's threatening, unreasonable behavior represented a vicariously displayed manifestation of the mother's own, warded-off, murderously hostile attitude toward her husband and her daughter. The latter two gave evidence of their deeply isolated feelings of anger toward the mother through occasional, surprisingly direct and intense outbursts of angry denunciations. Yet, it was also obvious that the son's "craziness" filled the role of a welcome "lightning rod" for all members' explosive tensions and thus his behavior, although consciously censured, was reinforced by the "pleasure economy" of the homeostatic family system.

The question as to the family-therapy counterpart of the Freudian expectation that where there is id, ego shall be, remains unanswered so far. We have claimed that family therapy cannot become productive without a transitory phase of regressive, "free" interaction. This question appeared related to the requirement for a regressive therapeutic transference relationship in psychoanalysis. Naturally, in both cases successful therapy ought to result in a better integration of all functions, leading to more satisfaction in life. Man's satisfaction depends, to a great extent, on his capacity for channeling innate drives into socially and biologically workable patterns of action. The process principle of change demands that the organization of every member's patterns of action be flexible enough to keep pace with the changing requirements of the individual needs for "self-actualization" (Maslow[79]) and society's expectation for the emergence of new nuclear families from old ones. The very existence of such a purposeful normal adaptation suggests that a surpra-individual family principle has to regulate what ostensibly appear to be the satisfaction goals of individuals. Any lasting change in any member or in the family as a whole has then to fit into the dynamic constellation of the timetable of the family's growth process.

It would be an exaggeration to assert that in family therapy the only significant criterion of change is that which occurs on a group level of the entire family. Changes in the configurations of libidinal or aggressive needs as well as in the degree of the autonomy of ego functions of each and every member have to be watched for significant *indicators* of re-arrangements on a multiperson level. One father, for instance, achieved the status of an independent entrepreneur during the treatment period, for the first time in his life. Another father who had been essentially idle for many years decided to undertake a work-training course. In several families parents became able to sleep together again after many years of relational defeat and mutual avoidance. In quite a few cases, the psychotic offspring—under the impact of family therapy—resumed school work, dating, or employment. All of these changes in individuals or in inter-acting dyads and triads involved complementary changes on all other members' part. The main guideline in evaluating the degree of healthy contribution of any family change issues from the members' joint capacity for replacing gratification systems of stagnant possessiveness with those of fresh, new involvements and with pride in everyone's gain toward individuation.

The family therapist finally has to be cautioned against overlooking, for reasons of his own needs, *lack* of significant change. Although verbalization of previously non-verbalized behavior is ultimately conducive to many new insights, some family therapies are maintained for reasons other than motivation for change. Certain families may continue conjoint family treatment only because they obtain dependent support from and a convenient target for parental type transference in the therapist. Dynamically then, rather than changing the family system, the therapist becomes merged with that aspect of the system that stands for a generalized parent object. Through his own altered emotional position in the family, he may be inclined to distort his perception of the family's interaction. In other words, what may represent a change from the therapist's point of view, may not really be a change for the family's pleasure economy.

In summary, I wonder whether any pathological family system can have a good prognosis as to significant change unless there is evidence that the members can meet the following minimal criteria in a relatively short time: 1) a sufficient emotional spontaneity for the creation of an atmosphere in which they are impelled to make statements which they feel uneasy about after the session; 2) an ability to explore their past emotionally significant relational ties in relation to the interactional structure of the current family and the family therapy situation; 3) a willingness to include any of their relatives or friends, or whomever else the therapists suggest, in their meetings; and 4) evidence of changes in the family's patterns of interaction, e.g., changes in long-established sleeping arrangements, tolerance of the offspring's social experimentation, etc.

VI

THE EMERGING PICTURE

The continuing search for a conceptual model of

family psychopathology

Howard E. Mitchell

Chapter

24

As stated at the beginning of this book, it was our intention to lead the reader from an initial frame of reference concerning family functioning relevant to family therapy in the home through a statement of our methods to the heart of the volume—a series of illustrative family case histories reported in the distinctive style of each treatment team. We then presented some objective-evaluative data and specific topics of clinical and theoretical interest which caught the fancy—and to some extent the fantasies —of our group. What follows now is an elaboration upon the rough parameters of the conceptualization of family functioning outlined in Chapter 1. We approach this difficult task by asking ourselves, "In what ways did our initial concept of family dynamics change as a function of the experience of treating the schizophrenic and his family as a unit in the home?"

Adequate response to the above question required a review of the rather crude parameters of our beginning model in order to appreciate in what respect our ideas had been modified or changed. In what ways were we prepared to alter or elaborate upon our original thinking? In the process of many of these discussions the team struggled with the additional problem of having to distinguish between an explanation of our ideas about family functioning and the goals of family treatment. Implied in the latter is the matter of how change in family functioning is altered and redirected. The social scientists and clinicians still grope among vague concepts with which they attempt to establish criteria for differentiating the functioning of non-pathological families from that of pathological families. We recognized and derived some tenuous support from the fact that ignorance in this regard is not unique to our group but plagues the whole field of family research. It has been more fashionable to study family pathology than "healthy family functioning." In fact, a more accurate appraisal of family research is that the study of successfully functioning family units has hardly been undertaken at all.[84]

The entire area of understanding the day-to-day functioning of the family is one about which social scientists have some theory but with which they have had little experience. The practitioners, however, have had considerable experience but have little theory. Looking back over the past generation, there are a few studies of the family functioning by social and psychological scientists. Psychologists certainly have been little concerned; sociologists, as typified by the late James Bossard,[16] have focused their efforts upon studying particular rituals or delineating aspects of normal family living. Cultural anthropologists have concentrated on gross seasonal descriptions of societies and families within those societies, with little regard for the week-to-week, day-to-day, not to mention minute-to-minute occurrences. Thus, anthropology as well had little to offer in the way of description or theory regarding detailed processes of change in family living.

Fortunately, we are presently witnessing a change in this pattern and social scientists and clinicians are getting together and combining their skills. Unfortunately, it still remains fashionable to devote most of these efforts to studying family pathology and few to non-pathological families. Therefore, our views of family functioning are necessarily biased by our experience with these markedly pathological family units. We regret that a comparable experience with non-pathological families is not available to us or others in the field. No clinical investigators have as yet reported extended contacts with an entire family unit in the home in which crucial issues of family functioning were discussed and observations made concerning patterns of interactions, resolutions of conflicts, the nature of communication networks and the overall pattern of family functioning. Reports are not available on observations of non-pathological family units over time on the various levels of functioning necessary to account for the complexity of the phenomena observed. An awareness of the totality of the operation of the family social unit encompasses an appreciation of:

1. Each family member as a biological organism.

2. Each member's intrapsychic dynamics (with their representations in a variety of interpersonal relationships ranging from delimited to extended ones).

3. The functioning of the family as an organic unit.

4. Broader social reference systems "outside" the family to which individual members and the family as a whole relate.

The integration of skills by social scientists and practitioners is beginning to produce fruitful theoretical results as witnessed among others in Gregory Bateson's[9] leadership in the Palo Alto group, and the recent contributions of Rhona Rapoport[92] of the Harvard University school of Public Health Family Research Project. Hence, we are hopeful of avoiding in our conceptions of family therapy research something which Rosenthal[95] has criticized in two recent collections of clinical papers dealing with the treatment of schizophrenia—namely, the fact that the conceptual frame of reference was formulated in metaphysical language and divorced from bodies of relevant scientific facts about human behavior.

It would appear no longer necessary to justify the need of making explicit the conceptual base for treating families as a unit. Nevertheless, we might do well to quote from Rhona Rapoport on this issue. "Any treatment approach which consistently takes into account the impact of significant relationships, such as those in the family, depends, implicitly or explicitly, on a framework for analysis of such relationships. To the extent that a framework is explicit and systematic, its clinical and theoretical use may be increased."[92]

As mentioned in Chapter 1, we early recognized the importance of ordering our thinking around a beginning model and working toward the elaboration of our initial frame of reference as dictated by our experience and the thinking of others in the field. Therefore, we set about the latter task aware of the limitations of experience and knowledge in this field as well as those based upon our own myopia.

All team members gained from the experience a new perception of the functioning of the family as a whole rather than an awareness and reaction to its individual members. We had begun with varying degrees of conviction as to whether the schizophrenia manifested in a given family member was or was not a symptom of the family system's problems, but, increasingly, the research team agreed with Bowen[18] who had earlier implemented this point. He saw the schizophrenic family as an "undifferentiated ego mass" in which each individual member had insufficient ego boundaries and was not adequately differentiated from the others. Therefore, what we offer as an emerging model begins with a discussion of aspects of normal versus pathological functioning of the family as a unit in our society, highlighting those features of family functioning that enable us to demonstrate the salient aspects of our experience.

Total Family Functioning

We also begin at the organizational level of family functioning because we have *post hoc* adopted Chapple's[31] notions as a broad working hypothesis, notions developed in the mid-thirties and demonstrated later by Chapple, Arensberg,[32] and Richardson.[93] According to Chapple, organizational change takes place in a three-fold sequence: changes in the organizational environment—in this case total family functioning—are followed by interaction changes, which in turn are followed by changes in action and in attitudes or sentiments of individuals. It is the intent of family therapy to bring about changes at the organizational level.

Family therapy as we have practiced it represents an intervention upon the family as a group in the sacredness of the home atmosphere by representatives of the community—the therapy team. This intervention is a crucial experience for the family because they have withdrawn from all agencies and their representatives in the community, maintaining only the most limited and superficial contact.

In the crude parameters of our beginning conceptual model we drew heavily upon sociological theory in viewing the family as a social system embedded in a larger social system. We also leaned toward what Bell and Vogel[13] have termed a structural-functional descriptive analysis of this system, and nothing in our experience caused us to alter the soundness of these original propositions.

The conceptual model developed to demonstrate features germane to our experience consists of two levels. The initial level deals with the functioning of the family as a unit via a schematic representation. Then we consider the interactional components of the family and attempt to relate our observations of dyadic and triadic transactions to the clinical observations of others at this level and to some theoretical constructs from systematic psychology. Emphasis is placed on a discussion of the initial level which has been largely neglected by family therapists. Most family therapists have based the characterizations of the family largely upon notions about the interlocking peculiarities of the personalities of husband and wife, or the problem has been conceptualized in terms of an interpersonal process such as communication or perception. The core difficulty in the marital relationship—which has been described principally in terms of the patterns of marital conflict—is extreme marital schism with associated mutual distrust and derogation, and the masking of disagreement and conflict to achieve what Wynne[117] has called "pseudo-mutuality." These characterizations of marital conflict patterns are presented in detail at the second level of our conceptual analysis. We shall also consider the character of the husband-wife relationship, an important factor, but feel it is better understood as a crucial dyad in the larger framework of total family functioning.

Bearing in mind the previously mentioned limitations of experience and knowledge about "normal" family functioning, a comparable reference is made between such families and "abnormal" units in the initial schema, Figure 24-1. In this figure we present our conceptualization of the functioning of the family in health and sickness at the global level, that is, the functioning of the family as a unit in its articulation with other social systems in society.

Looking first at the top of Figure 24-1, representing the "Normal Family System," we note that the system has its internal and external boundaries. Within the internal boundaries of the family are its members symbolically marked "Mo" for mother, "Fa" for the father, and "C_1" for one child and "C_2" for another. The vectors uniting the family members represent reciprocal transactions at a variety of levels, verbal and non-verbal communication, sentiments and feelings, as well as action toward one another. The vectors flow in all possible directions and any combination of dyadic or triadic relationships may develop dependent upon the maturation of a particular parental-child relationship, the development of identification patterns, environmental circumstances and external pressures upon the family system.

The spheres appended to the family social system are to represent other reference systems with which the normal family is in daily articulation. The size of the reference systems are intended to show the amount of time and energy devoted to each in the average successfully functioning American family. Hence, a great amount of time is spent at work by the father (Fa) and possibly by the mother (Mo) if she chooses to be gainfully employed outside the home. Less time is spent with kinship figures in the current nuclear family, and spheres drawn to show kinship figures are therefore relatively small.

It is significant that the sphere of work overlaps the external boundary of the family which is intended to demonstrate the amount of impact that these systems have upon each other in the majority of families in our culture.[31] The parents' vectors flow both toward and away from the sphere of work to the family social system. This indicates that parents take to their jobs feelings about their families and share them with fellow workers and employers. On the other hand, it is common to observe that satisfactions and dissatisfactions about the job and other personnel associated with one's work, are brought home and become an integral part of daily conversations at the dinner table, and in the living room—often they are carried into the intimate atmosphere of the bedroom as well.

The sphere representing "Recreation" appears at the bottom of the top figure. It is drawn fairly large, and depicted to rival the sphere of work in size. This was done in keeping with the increased time devoted to leisure time activities and recreation by the average American. To the left of the family system is another fairly large unit, "Social Institutions," with a blister-like appendage called "Community Agents." The social institutions primarily referred to here are schools, churches and synagogues, law-enforcing agencies, health and social welfare institutions. "Community Agents" as represented by the teacher, minister, rabbi or priests, law enforcement officer, physician or social worker may operate as representatives of these aforementioned institutions or operate independently, as in the case of the physician in private practice. Most of these community agents have established in our society a natural entrée into the family as the needs of the family and its members warranted their entrance. The nature of the circumstances determines the extent to which these agents of humanitarian services penetrate into the inner boundaries of the family as well as the duration of influence. For example, the minister who develops a close relationship with a family in his church and from whom counsel is requested or offered, often becomes deeply involved in the families' inner-most dynamics.

The unit representing "Friends" is pictured in close articulation with the family system and placed next to "Recreation." Of course, with given families it might be more appropriate to place "Friends" in closer proximity to "Work," "Kinship Groups," or "Social Institutions," to show

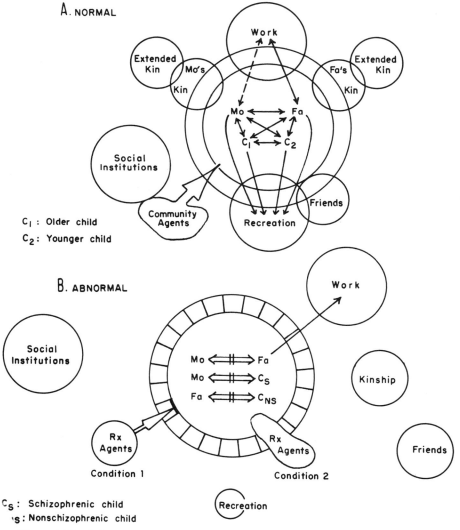

Figure 24-1 Schematic representation of "normal" vs. abnormal family functioning in society.

that their social acquaintances mainly derive from other reference systems outside the family. Moreover, for simplicity of presentation we have not attempted to show all the possible vectors which would demonstrate all the transactions between individual and sub-groups of family members and friends.

The "Abnormal Family System" is drawn at the bottom of Figure 24-1. By the Abnormal Family System we mean one typical of the family units treated in our project and whose case histories are presented in this book.

The external boundaries of the Abnormal Family System are drawn as thick, cross-hatched, well-fortified walls used to defend the family from environment, often perceived by all members as threatening and productive of anxiety. The boundary serves as the families' "iron curtain" to ward off a hostile, misunderstood and misunderstanding environment. It serves as a first line of defense about which we have attempted to characterize the families treated and to suggest that assessment of the degree of its pregnability-impregnability might serve as a prognostic indicator for family therapy in the home or clinic.

The project team often remarked about the extreme isolation of these families who had produced a schizophrenic member. There was little intermingling and contact with relatives, let alone friends, outside the family. This is demonstrated graphically in the self-report of family members in Chapter 8, "Quantitative Family Evaluation Measures."

"Schizophrenia", write Kohn and Clausen[62], "poses a problem at the core of social-psychological theory—the problem of the relationship of the individual to his society, of the personality to its social matrix." If we consider the family to be the primary unit of illness or maladjustment, the psychological problem for the schizophrenic family might be regarded as the divorcement of the family unit from society. Curiously enough, although isolated from the community, most of the families studied had some key individual external to the family system who exerted power and influence on the family. In one family it was an attorney, a friend of the father's; in another it was a boyfriend of the primary patient, and in another, a physician, etc. In fact, it appeared that there was little chance of bringing about significant change in some of the families treated unless these key individuals were also engaged in the therapeutic endeavor. Such a key peripheral person would accommodate himself to the family's psychopathological defense pattern, for his own needs, and the family could accordingly remain a relatively rigid, closed system.

Not only were these disturbed families regarded as isolated, but they were increasingly appreciated as closed rather than open social systems. Patterns of living were rigid and fixed instead of being flexible and modifiable. These families might be viewed as a conceptual counterpart of the encapsulated paranoid schizophrenic individual, who although delusional and withdrawn in some spheres of behavior, remains capable of a high level of functioning in other defined areas of performance. For example, in a number of the schizophrenic families, a pattern was observed in which, although the father was physically active and busily engaged in one area of activity outside the family—usually work—the family system was characterized as closed in terms of freedom. So little affect was fed into and out of it from the father's activities that it had little effect. The manner in which roles within the family were perceived and enacted was seldom altered by the male leader's experience outside the family. This is thought to be largely a function of the emotional distance and of the minimal affective interchange between him and his fellow workers.

Shown at the bottom of the "Abnormal Family System" are Conditions 1 and 2. These represent the crucial intervention of the therapeutic agents into the family system in order to perform family therapy. Therefore, these conditions are unique to the therapeutic enterprise and are not meant to depict pathological family functioning in a general way.

Condition 1 is meant to typify the situation in which the family mobilizes its defenses in order to keep the therapists on the periphery. These defenses are manifested in a variety of ways, ranging from the mother who seeks to reduce the therapeutic effort to a social occasion to outright hostile rebuffs at the front door of the home.

Condition 2 represents the typical antithesis of the first condition. In this situation the therapists are freely permitted to invade the sanctity of the inner boundaries of families' feelings and sentiments. The family tries to swallow up the therapists to satisfy certain needs, but not to change the operating defense system.

Both conditions are defensive in nature. Their unwitting purpose is to maintain the status quo of the dynamic pattern of family living. What is needed further in our model is an overriding concept which would account for the self-correcting feature of successfully functioning family units which enable them to overcome transitory imbalances resulting from internal or external pressures. This is provided—most vividly—in Haley's paper in which he distinctively elaborates upon Don Jackson's earlier notions about the homeostatic quality of the family system.[47]

Haley states that "When one begins to conceptualize the family as a group of people who respond to change in each other in an 'error-activated' way, it becomes possible to view the family as a homeostatic system. Such a system contains within itself self-corrective processes which permit it to continue to function in habitual ways. It is these points of self-correction which must be changed if a change in the family system is to occur."

"A homeostatic system is like the heating system of a house which is connected with a thermostat; the system governs itself . . . If the room is too hot, one cannot say it is the fault of an element in the system. It is not the fault of the heater because it is controlled by the thermostat, and yet the thermostat is not to blame because it is controlled by the heat produced by the heater. . . . The only way to make a change in any element of the system is to change the 'setting', the correction point which regulates the range of all the elements in the system."

Past attempts to discuss problems of families have concentrated upon a single element. We do not now consider the "fault" to be either that of the "bad" schizophrenic child or of the "schizophrenogenic" mother, or of the " inadequate" father. The total system must be influenced if any of the elements are to change.

We see the range of temperature as symbolizing the range of role behaviors permitted by forces internal and external to the family. The modern American family which is operating in a state of equilibrium, permits a broad range of role performance. As Rapoport and Rosov[92] have pointed out, competing cultural values and flexible social norms actually serve to increase the opportunity for personal preference and each member contributes to shaping the organization of family life. Specific role content, the "proper" performance of different family members, and the preferred relationship between them are subject to flexible settlement which can vary considerably from one family to another. The range, therefore, of behavior of family members—the things they do, the roles they enact—is set largely by them and others.

Trouble arises in very disturbed families when each individual member attempts to be the one who sets or establishes the limit. Haley[47] goes so far as to say that "All activity in a disturbed family centers in a struggle at this level. If father suggests going to a movie, the merits of the movie are not the issue as they might be in a more normal family; the issue is whether or not to do what father says." Eugene Brody[26] while working with the Yale group of family therapists, expressed the same point of view. Brody and his associates observed in the family of psychotic patients a pivotal person whom they designated as the *key member.* "The attitudes and behavior of the key member, by virtue of his position in the family power structure, exerted more influence on the family group and its component members than did those of any other individual in the family." It soon became apparent to Brody and his fellow workers that this key member was frequently able to impede the successful adaptation of a post-hospitalized patient to the family group.

Our observations are consistent with those of Haley and Brody on this point. It is not surprising, therefore, that extremely disturbed families under the leadership of so-called key members became extremely defensive over the encroachment of not one but two external agents (the co-therapists) who invaded the home and "tampered with the thermostat."

Key Interactional Sub-Systems

Family therapists have traditionally placed the greatest emphasis on dyadic interaction patterns as the etiological key of the family's pathology. Although we have made our bias clear in terms of the pathology being a total family affair, five key family sub-systems are delineated in our conceptual framework in order to understand better the components of the total family system. This is necessary in light of practical considerations related to the treatment effort. We have seen in the case histories that at certain times the therapists focused on particular dyadic or triadic relationships. The five sub-systems are:

1. The core marital relationship.
2. Past and current relationship of parents to their parents.
3. The parent-child relationship.
4. The sibling pair relationship.
5. The human-animal relationship.

In the "Normal Family System" in Figure 24-1 the vector between husband and wife is drawn to indicate a free flow of affect and communication on all levels in both directions, whereas in the "Abnormal Family System" the vector between the marriage partners is cross-hatched to indicate that communication lines are blocked and disrupted. Furthermore, the quality of this core relationship is static rather than dynamic.

Ackerman[3] writes, "The special problems of marital pairs and parental pairs can best be understood in terms of the mutuality and interdependence of the respective family role adaptations, the complementarity of sexual behavior, the reciprocity of emotional and social companionship, the sharing of authority, and the division of labor." He goes on to say that as the marital pair moves on to parenthood, the problems of the latter add another level of complexity to family relations. The degree to which there has developed a healthy satisfying marital relationship determines to a great extent the character of subsequent dyadic relationships between each parent and the child. The core sub-unit in the normal functioning family is the marital pair which has socially learned during the marital union to fit their two personality systems together in such manner that not only their individual needs are satisfied, but that—in a gestalt-like way—the emotional toning of the ensuing relationship enhances the quality of each individual's ego development.

On the other hand, in the "really disturbed family," as Haley[12] calls the family who has succeeded in "driving a child mad," we observe a core marital relationship which is pathological and deficient. In fact, review of this matter by the therapeutic team over the five-year-period of working together led to the consensus that in most cases the pathological dyadic relationship between the husband and wife in both the parents' families of origin, and in the current intrafamilial environment is in conflict. In both sets of families there has been resistance to change which may be based upon an unconscious fear of the destruction of the family *status quo*, as suggested by Jungreis and Speck in their account of the Island family in Chapter 4.

In the successfully functioning family, one has to evaluate the sibling dyads according to the age of each sibling and the difference in ages between them. These factors determine what we expect the quality of relationship to be, and the degree to which the relationship might fluctuate before being termed deviate. For example, in a young family comprised of a six-year-old sister and a two-year-old brother, we would expect even under the most favorable circumstances that there would be emotional tugging and pulling between the siblings as each tries to get his share of attention and love in order to feel secure and mature. There will be frequent occasions in which big sister will direct, command, and put her tattling little brother in his place. He will make full use of his greatest asset to get even with her and to limit the extent to which she plays her substitute mother role. In the normal family life moves on, and both parents, secure within their relationship to one another, are able to differentiate between reasonable differences between their children and the question of how the needs of both may best be met in their family living.

If we were to work with the same sister and brother twenty years later, status differences would be minimized, and they would relate as one young adult to the other, enjoying one another's new allegiances to their own spouse and family.

On the other hand, the character of the sibling relationship in the abnormal family appears to become fixed at an early period. Maturation and development do not mediate any change. As a result, one is able to predict early in the life of the family what the later character of sibling relationship will be, barring the advent of significant therapeutic intervention or the family's "flight into health" from their sick condition.

Perhaps related to the above is the observation that the sibling or siblings other than the schizophrenic member appeared to detach themselves increasingly from the primary patient. This maneuver was ostensibly utilized to disengage themselves from the family pathology in order to maintain their strength of ego. In keeping with the premise of family illness as basic to the building of this model of family functioning and disfunctioning, these maneuvers represent the unconscious need of both siblings to maintain a status difference between them.

Ross Speck has dealt meaningfully with some of the nuances of the human-pet interactional system which operates in these families (*see* Chapter 22). In the malfunctioning family unit the pets themselves are drawn into the family pathology, and the thin line separating the human system from that of the pet seems even thinner here. The separation between the human and animal world is perhaps becoming indiscriminately small in our society—witness the elaborately built kennels, shelters and animal hospitals referred to as animal hotels and motels. Indeed, the author recently observed in an Eastern metropolis that he was driving behind a "School Bus for Animals."

The Individual Actors

Finally, we turn our attention to the individual actors or units in the family drama. Since this volume has been stimulated by and is based upon an experience of therapy with the total family unit, we have emphasized the functioning of the entire family rather than its sub-systems in our conceptual treatment. Moreover, we have modified Chapple's[31] working hypothesis developed in a setting of industrial social psychology, to serve us as a guide in this respect. It is becoming increasingly apparent that changes in individual family members had better follow rather than precede changes in interactional family sub-systems and in the family system as a whole. Our modification of Chapple's hypothesis is that changes in organizational structure and functioning of the family are followed by interaction changes of dyads and triads which are in turn followed by actions and sentiments of individuals.

We will not discuss the individual psychology of family members as they are involved in the healthy versus unhealthy family functioning. We do, however, have some specific ideas about possible conditions of the individual which need to be delineated in order to complete our thinking model. A great part of our experience, and certainly of our evaluative techniques, involved a phenomenological description of perception. According to Heider,[49] a phenomenological description of perception means the nature of contact between the person and his environment. How each family member perceives important dispositional and psychological properties of himself and other family members has received attention. The schizophrenic and his family maintain their tenuous adjustment to the environment by first limiting and then distorting the environment they have to observe, as we have discussed in the isolation of family unit. In such families there is an inability to discriminate perceptually self and others. This is not the case in the "normal" family; individual differences are discerned and appreciated. Hence, family members are permitted a wider range of behavior and role performance. There is greater flexibility of role than in the extremely troubled family environment. In the latter type family, relations are perceived in primitive terms and roles enacted accordingly. It is as if these troubled family members are incapable of perceiving patterns of interrelationships at a higher level. They ascribe roles as a function of their disturbed perceptions, and a principal dimension deals with the degree of power and control others have over the self.

Control over the environment is an effect of perception. When the individual is able to observe freely a wide range of his environment, he has more control over it. Since the window through which disturbed family members view the world is narrowed, the sensation of adaptation to their surroundings is seriously limited. Therefore, it is not surprising to note that a key issue revolves around who "sets the thermostat and exerts control" in the family system so aptly described by Haley.[47] Still unanswered is *how* this is accomplished. We suggest that such an explanation await a fuller development of the recent marriage between clinical observation and the social sciences.

Epilogue of the authors

Chapter
25

Family treatment is a relatively new field of endeavor, and we are only at the beginning stages of our effort to conceptualize the psychopathology of family functioning. As can be seen from the foregoing, a number of individuals and groups across the country—ours included —are attempting to bridge the gap between thinking about pathology in individual terms and thinking about it in family terms. Much work remains to be done in the future; the intrapsychic and transactional spheres will have to be integrated, in order to refine the techniques of family therapy, and to establish specific indications for this method of treatment.

The discoveries that have been made in family treatment represent a major conceptual challenge to contemporary psychopathology and personality theory as a whole. One challenge is to perceive the family as something more than merely the addition of three, four, or five individual personalities, or the interaction between two or three family members. We must perceive the individual not just as having separate introjects derived from each parent, but as having introjected or internalized a whole global family pattern, consisting of a constellation cf affective reactions, as well as attitudes and myths regarding human relationships. The old formulations no longer suffice. Another challenge is to find the specific kind of intervention that is required for an arrested or malfunctioning family to achieve its potential as a creative, expanding laboratory for need satisfactions, maturation, and individuation of its members—the action mechanism or model, for instance, that has to be introduced into a family system whose members are fixated on indecision, discussion, speculation, and disagreement, and who rarely take decisive, constructive action.

While we are striving for this new and different perception of family problems and for corresponding new ways of treating the whole family, we are aware of the powerful tools which we already possess for helping families, including our own personalities and insights, our capacities to engage freely with a family in the expression of genuine feelings and to learn from the experience.

There are perhaps a dozen professional teams in this country who over the past ten years have begun to explore the methods of family therapy. In addition, hundreds of mental health centers, clinics and family service agencies are starting to experiment with this method, and trying to learn the appropriate techniques. Child guidance clinics are generally slow in leaving their traditional approach, but a few have begun to use the conjoint family approach as an initial diagnostic and evaluative procedure. This experimentation is all to the good; but there is an acute need for training, and for operating guidelines that will facilitate diagnostic, prognostic and therapeutic decisions based on multi-personal, interactional and family-system concepts. The approaches to family therapy are varied in regard to settings and techniques, as well as to philosophy and treatment goals. We are just beginning to understand some of the problems and complications of this method, as well as some of its potentialities. Much study and research is required to isolate specific issues for controlled observation and analysis. We also need more specific criteria to help us determine the cases in which family treatment is indicated as the treatment of choice. There are basic questions as regards methods for assessing the mental health of a family, for identifying and classifying types of family dysfunction and pathology. The traditional diagnostic typology and nomenclature of individual psychopathology is not applicable here, although we still use it for lack of a new and better language.

To sum up, these were some of the main conclusions and observations of our experience as reported in this book:

1. It is possible, with the home family treatment approach, to successfully treat schizophrenia and to avoid hospitalization in a majority of cases, particularly those which had traditionally been hospitalized. The advantages of the home setting appear to us to clearly outweigh the disadvantages. If it were not for the greater personal inconvenience to the therapists in making repeated visits to the home, we would recommend the home setting as the setting of choice for the treatment of most families.

2. During the course of family treatment, hospitalization of the designated psychotic offspring was necessary only on very rare occasions. When this occurred it was kept to a minimum period of hospitalization, and integrated into the overall, long-range planning of the family therapy.

3. A team of two co-therapists was usually able to foster an uncovering process that revealed the true family problems and patterns of interaction, and to achieve some therapeutic resolution of familial conflicts with apparently long-term positive effects in a number of very disturbed schizophrenic families. In other cases the results were less substantial and therapy may only have provided supportive help during a crisis, or resolved some current problems. Almost invariably, though, pressure was taken off the psychotic child or adolescent when the total family problem was elucidated. Excluded from this generalization were only those families who terminated after one or two sessions, and who had never really accepted the idea of family treatment.

4. While most of our therapists preferred the co-therapy team method when dealing with very disturbed families, we also found that it was possible to work effectively as a solo family therapist. The practical considerations of staff-time and cost may not always permit the use of co-therapy teams. Additional experience and research will be required to determine the type of family in which a single therapist may be as effective or more so than a co-therapy team.

5. Our aim has been to provide more than temporary support, and to achieve more than a symptomatic change, or transfer of illness from one family member to another. Our rationale for engaging in an intensive form of family treatment, and employing active techniques when working with these very pathological families has been that their dysfunctional family habits and interactional cycles are often rather difficult to modify because of their rigid, ingrained and conditioned character. We have sought not only to dissolve underlying conflicts but to clarify simultaneously to each family member the rigidity and the conflict-provoking character of his interactional habits.

6. The main operational procedure and dynamic of therapeutic work has been along multipersonal, interactional and familial lines, with an analysis of the pathological family system. We do not exclude, however, the analysis of the intrapsychic dynamics of the designated patient or of any family member in the presence of other family members.

7. The extent and degree of psychotic regressive symptomatology of the designated patient was not the main determinant in our prognostic considerations regarding family therapy, nor was the degree of improvement or accomplishment.

8. Active psychosis in a child seemed to protect the rest of the family from overt psychotic manifestations. Although many of the parents appeared to have a psychotic degree of denial and paranoid projection, they nevertheless maintained an adequate degree of social and vocational functioning as long as the child was actively regressed and symptomatic.

9. Our experience reaffirmed the often reported existence of an intense pathological symbiosis between the mother and the schizophrenic child. We were also impressed with the role the father played in maintaining and furthering the schizophrenic process. Whether he achieved this by passive, ineffectual abdication of his role as husband and father; by aiding and abetting the symbiosis; by engaging in splits and alliances; or even by taking over the pathological mothering role—he was always an essential participant in the pathological system. The father's role in the maintenance of the pathological system has not been sufficiently studied in the past.

10. Parents of a schizophrenic tend to dwell on the sickness and symptomatology of their problem child, and on their desire to help the child. It may be that the presence of the symptoms seals the symbiosis, and as long as the symptoms can be discussed the symbiosis is fortified. The initial phase of family treatment, however, often results in transferring the symptoms and the sick role from the schizophrenic child onto another family member.

11. Families with a schizophrenic member are relatively closed off from meaningful emotional interaction with the outside world, and often have a funereal, "dead," resigned, and empty quality about them in spite of the underlying chaotic, destructive tendencies. They behave as if all their emotional needs were to be gratified within the family unit and as if it were "taboo" to look outside for gratifications.

Such a family system tends to react initially to the intervention of therapeutic agents in one of two pathological ways: by mobilizing its defenses to keep the therapists on the periphery, or by permitting the therapists to invade the sanctity of the inner boundaries of its feelings and sentiments. The family will try to swallow up the therapists to satisfy certain needs and incorporate them into their pathological system, but without changing the operating defense system. At the same time the family, as a functionally helpless organism, attaches itself to the therapists. In this process, the therapists' understanding and support may be sufficient to relieve the immediate, acute stress in the family, so that the active psychotic phase of the schizophrenic member subsides. But the therapeutic endeavor must progress beyond these initial defensive family reactions in order to arrive at a more significant and basic change. A variety of techniques and methods are currently being explored by us and others to achieve this more basic, intensive working-through and restructuring of the pathological family system. Not the least of the therapeutic factors or agents is the self-awareness of the therapist and the depth of his insight into his inner experience. The professional qualifications, personality and family background that are required to become an effective family therapist also warrant additional study.

REFERENCES

1. Abrahams, J., & Varon, E.: Maternal Dependency and Schizophrenia, New York: International Universities Press, 1953.
2. Ackerman, N.: "The Emergence of Family Psychotherapy." Paper read at the Conference on Psychotherapy and the Family, Temple University, March, 1961.
3. Ackerman, N.: The Psychodynamics of Family Life: Diagnosis and Treatment of Family Relationships, New York: Basic Books, Inc., 1958.
4. Albert, R. S.: Stages of Breakdown in the Relationships and Dynamics Between the Mental Patient and His Family, *Arch. Gen. Psychiat.* 3:682-690, 1960.
5. Alexander, F.: Psychosomatic Medicine, New York: W. W. Norton Co., Inc., 1950.
6. Allport, F.: A Structuronomic Conception of Behavior, Individual and Collective, 1. Structural Theory and the Master Problem of Social Psychology, *J. abnorm. soc. Psychol., 64:*3-30, 1962.
7. Arieti, S.: Psychotherapy of Schizophrenia, *Arch. Gen. Psychiat., 6:*112-122, 1962.
8. Barnhart, C. L. (Ed.): American College Dictionary, New York: Random House, 1947.
9. Bateson, G., et al.: Toward a Theory of Schizophrenia, *Behav, Sci., 1:*251-264, 1956. *Palo alto - "Double Bind" + "family homeostasis"*
10. Becker, A.: "Handling of Psychiatric Emergencies in the Home." Paper read at the Tenth Annual Conference of Mental Health Representatives of State Medical Associations, Chicago, Ill.: February, 1964.
11. Bell, J. E.: A Theoretical Position for Family Group Therapy, *Family Process* 2:1-14, 1963.
12. Bell, J. E.: Family Group Therapy, Public Health Monograph #64, USPHS, 1961.
13. Bell, N. W., & Vogel, E. F. (Eds.): Modern Introduction to the Family, Glencoe, Ill: The Free Press, 1960.
14. Benedek, T.: "Sexual Functions in Women and Their Disturbance" in S. Arieti, American Handbook of Psychiatry, New York: Basic Books, Inc., 1959.
15. Bloom, S. W.: The Study of Human Behavior: An Introduction to the Sociology of Medicine, Preliminary Manuscript: 95-105, 1961.
16. Bossard, J. H. S.: Ritual in Family Living, Philadelphia: University of Pennsylvania Press, 1950.
17. Boszormenyi-Nagy, I.: The Concept of Schizophrenia From the Perspective of Family Treatment, *Family Process, 1:*103-113, 1962.
18. Bowen, M.: The Family as the Unit of Study and Treatment: I. Family Psychotherapy, Workshop, 1959, *Amer. J. Orthopsychiat., 31:*40-60, 1961.
19. Bowen, M.: "A Family Concept of Schizophrenia" in D. D. Jackson, (Ed.): Etiology of Schizophrenia, New York: Basic Books, Inc., 1960.

20. Bowen, M.: "Family Psychotherapy in Office Practice." Paper presented at the Conference on Psychotherapy of the Family, Temple University, March, 1961.

21. Bowen, M.: "Family Relationships in Schizophrenia" in A. Auerback, (Ed.): Schizophrenia, New York: The Ronald Press Co., 1959.

22. Bowen, M., et al.: "Study and Treatment of Five Hospitalized Family Groups, Each with a Psychotic Member." Paper presented at the 34th Annual Meeting of the Am. Orthopsychiat. Ass., Chicago, 1957.

23. Bowen, M., et al.: The Role of the Father in Families with a Schizophrenic Patient, Amer. J. Psychiat., 115:1017-1020, 1959.

24. Brodey, W. M.: Image, Object and Narcissistic Relationships, Am. J. Orthopsychiat., 31:69-73, 1961.

25. Brodey, W. M.: Some Family Operations and Schizophrenia: A Study of Five Hospitalized Families Each With a Schizophrenic Member, Arch. Gen. Psychiat., 1:379-402, 1959.

26. Brody, E.: Modification of Family Interaction Patterns by a Group Interview Technique, Int. J. Group Psychother., 6:38-47, 1956.

27. Brown, B. S.: Home Visiting by Psychiatrists, Arch. Gen. Psychiat., 7:98-107, 1962.

28. Browning, C. J.: Toward a Science of Delinquency Analysis, Sociol. Soc. Res., 46:61-74, 1961.

29. Carroll, E. J.: Treatment of the Family As A Unit, Penna. Med. J. 63:57-62, 1960.

30. Caudill, W.: The Psychiatric Hospital As a Small Society, Cambridge, Mass.: Harvard University Press, 1958.

31. Chapple, E.: "Applied Anthropology in Industry" in A. L. Kroeber, Anthropology Today, Chicago, Ill.: University of Chicago Press, 1953.

32. Chapple. E. D., & Arensberg, C. M.: Measuring Human Relations: An Introduction to The Study of Interaction of Individuals, Genet. Psychol. Monogr. 22:22, 1940.

33. Day, J., et al.: "The Psychiatric 'Patient' and His 'Well' Sibling," 116th Annual Meeting of APA, 1960.

34. Dysinger, R. H.: A Family Perspective on the Diagnosis of Individual Members, Am. J. Orthopsychiat., 31:61-68, 1961.

35. Egan, M. H., et al.: "Home Treatment of Severely Disturbed Children and Families." Paper read at the 42nd Annual Meeting of the Am. Orthopsychiat. Ass., New York: March 18-20, 1965.

36. Erikson, E. H.: Identity and the Life Cycle, Selected Papers, Psychol. Issues, 1: #1, 1959.

37. Freeman, H. E., & Simmons, O. G.: Mental Patients in the Community: Family Settings and Performance Levels, Amer. Sociol. Rev., 23:147-154, 1958.

38. Freud, S.: Fragment of "An Analysis of a Case of Hysteria (1905)" in S. Freud, Collected Papers III (p. 61), London: Hogarth Press, 1953.

39. Freud, S.: "Observations on Wild Psychoanalysis (1910)" in S. Freud, Collected Papers II, London: Hogarth Press, 1953.

40. Friedman, T. T., et al.: Home Treatment of Psychiatric Patients, Am. J. Psychiat. 116:807-809, 1960.

41. Gans, R. W.: Group Cotherapists and the Therapeutic Situation: A Critical Evaluation, Int. J. Group Psychother., 2:82-88, 1962.

42. Gendlin, E. T.: Need for a New Type of Concept: Current Trends and

Needs in Psychotherapy Research on Schizophrenia, *Rev. Existent. Psychol. Psychiat.*, 2 Winter 1962.

43. Gianopulos, A., & Mitchell, H. E.: Marital Disagreement in Working Wife Marriages as a Function of Husband's Attitude Toward Wife's Employment, *Marriage and Family Living 19*:373-378, 1957.

44. Gralnick, A.: Folie A Deux—The Psychosis of Association, *Psychiat. Quart.*, *16*:230-263, 1942; *16*:491-520, 1942.

45. Greenblatt, M.: The Prevention of Hospitalization, New York: Grune & Stratton, 1963.

46. Gruenberg, E. M.: "Socially Shared Psychopathology" in A. H. Leighton, et al., Explorations in Social Psychiatry, New York: Basic Books, Inc., 1947.

47. Haley, J.: Whither Family Therapy, *Family Process 1*: 69-100, 1962.

48. Handlon, J. H., & Parloff, M. B.: The Treatment of Patient and Family as a Group: Is It Group Psychotherapy? *Int. J. Group Psychother.*, *12*:132-141, 1962.

49. Heider, F.: The Psychology of Interpersonal Relations, New York: John Wiley & Sons, Inc., 1958.

50. Henry, J.: Culture Against Man, New York: Random House, 1963.

51. Hill, R., & Hansen, D. A.: The Identification of Conceptual Frameworks Utilized in Family Study, *Marriage and Family Living*, *22*:299-311, 1960.

52. Homans, G. C.: The Human Group, New York: Harcourt-Brace, 1950.

53. Jackel, M.: Clients with Character Disorders, *Soc. Casewk. 44*, June, 1963.

54. Jackson, D.D.: "Family Interaction, Family Homeostasis, and Some Implications for Conjoint Family Psychotherapy" in J. H. Masserman, Individual and Familial Dynamics, Science and Psychoanalysis II, New York: Grune & Stratton, 1959.

55. Jackson, D.D.: "The Monad, the Dyad, and Family Therapy" in A. Burton, (Ed.): Psychotherapy of the Psychoses, New York: Basic Books, Inc., 1961.

56. Jackson, D. D.: The Question of Family Homeostasis, *Psychiat. Quart.*, *Suppl. 31*:79-90, 1957.

57. Jackson, D. D., & Satir, V.: "A Review of Psychiatric Developments in Family Diagnosis and Family Therapy" in N. W. Ackerman, et al. (Ed.): Exploring the Base for Family Therapy, Family Service Association of America, 1961.

58. Jackson, D. D., & Weakland, J. H.: Conjoint Family Therapy, *Psychiatry Suppl.*, *24*:30-45, 1961.

59. Johnson, A. M., & Szurek, S. A.: Genesis of Antisocial Acting-out in Children and Adults, *Psychoanal. Quart. 21*:323-343, 1952.

60. Josselyn, I. M.: The Family as a Psychological Unit, *Soc. Casewk. 34*:336-343, 1953.

61. Kluckhohn, F., & Spiegel, J. P.: "Integration and Conflict in Family Behavior" in GAP Report #27: August, 1954.

62. Kohn, M. L., & Clausen, J. A.: Parental Authority Behavior and Schizophrenia, *Am. J. Orthopsychiat.*, *26*:297-313, 1956.

63. Koos, E. L.: Families in Trouble, New York: King's Crown Press, 1946.

64. Koskoff, Y., & Weniger, F.: "The Adverse Effect Upon a Family Resulting From a Radical Change of Personality in One Member After Frontal

Lobotomy" in Life Stress and Bodily Disease, *Res. Publ. Ass. Nerv. Ment. Dis.*, 29:148-154, 1949.

65. Kris, E.: Psychoanalytic Explorations in Art, New York: International Universities Press, 1952.

66. LaBarre, W.: "The Biosocial Unity of the Family" in N. W. Ackerman, et al., (Ed.): Exploring the Base For Family Therapy, New York: Family Service Ass. of America, 1961.

67. Lasegue, C., & Falret, J.: La Folie A Deux (ou folie communiquée), *Ann. Med. Psychol.*, 18:321, 1877; and Michaud, Richard, (Eng. Trans.) *Amer. J. Psychiat., Suppl.*: October, 1964.

68. Leary, T.: Interpersonal Diagnosis of Personality, New York: The Ronald Press Co., 1957.

69. Lefebre, L. B.: On Being Historically Unaware and Existentialism and Psychotherapy, St. Louis, Mo.: United Campus Christian Fellowship Publications, July, 1963.

70. Levine, R. A.: Treatment in the Home, *Soc. Wk.* 9:19-28, 1964.

71. Lidz, T., et al.: The Intrafamilial Environment of Schizophrenic Patients: II Marital Schism and Marital Skew, *Amer. J. Psychiat.*, 114:241-248, 1957.

72. Lindner, R.: "The Jet-Propelled Couch" in R. Lindner, The Fifty-Minute Hour: A Collection of True Psychoanalytic Tales, New York: Holt, Rinehart & Winston, 1955.

73. Loewald. H. W.: On The Therapeutic Action of Psychoanalysis, *Int. J. Psychoanal.*, 41:16-33, 1960.

74. Luborsky, L.: "The Patient's Personality and Psychotherapeutic Change" in H. H. Strupp & L. Luborsky, Research in Psychotherapy, Proceedings of Conference APA, Division of Clinical Psychology, N.C.: May 17-20, 1961. Published by APA, 1962.

75. Maas, H.: Discussion of S. J. Beck, Families of Schizophrenic and Well Children: Method, Concepts and Some Results, *Amer. J. Orthopsychiat.*, 30:247-275, 1960.

76. MacGregor, R., et al.: Multiple Impact Therapy With Families, New York: McGraw-Hill Book Co., 1964.

77. Magill, F. N. (Ed.): Sophocles, Oedipus Tyrannus, New York: Salem Press, 1949.

78. Malone, T.: "Countertransference" in Whitaker, C. (Ed.): Psychotherapy of Chronic Schizophrenic Patients, Boston: Little Brown, 1958.

79. Maslow, A. M.: Motivation and Personality, New York: Harper Bros., 1954.

80. Mickle, J. C.: Psychiatric Home Visits, *Arch. Gen. Psychiat.*, 9:379-383, 1963.

81. Midelfort, C. F.: Family in Psychotherapy, New York: Blakiston Div., McGraw-Hill Book Co., 1957.

82. Mitchell, H., et al.: Areas of Marital Conflict in Successfully and Unsuccessfully Functioning Families, *J. Hlth. Hum. Behav.*, 111:88-93, 1962.

83. Morgan, R. W.: The Extended Home Visit in Psychiatric Research and Treatment, *Psychiatry*, 26:168-175, 1963.

84. Mudd, E., et al.: "A Study of the Relation of Marital Conflict to Mental Health." An investigation conducted by the Marriage Council of Philadelphia 1947-1954, Research Grant #MH57—The Promotion of Marital

Adjustment in Men and Women as an Aid to Good Mental Health.

85. Naegele, K. D.: Attachment and Aiienation: Complementary Aspects of the Work of Durkheim and Simme, *Amer. J. of Sociol., 63*:580-89, 1958.

86. Parsons, R., & Bales, R. F.: Family, Socialization and Interaction Process, Glencoe, Ill.: The Free Press, 1955.

87. Pasamanick, B., et al.: Home vs. Hospital Care for Schizophrenics, *JAMA, 187*:177-181, January 18, 1964.

88. Peachey, R.: Are There Family Patterns of Illness? Unpublished Master's Thesis, Temple University School of Medicine.

89. Perry, S. E.: Home Treatment and the Social System of Psychiatry, *Psychiatry, 26*:54-64, 1963.

90. Querido, A.: Early Diagnosis and Treatment Services, *World Ment. Hlth., 8*:180-189, 1956.

91. Rafferty, F. T., et al.: "The Disturbed Child at Home." Paper read at the 42nd Annual Meeting of the Am. Orthopsychiat. Ass., New York: March 18-20, 1965.

92. Rapoport, R., & Rosow, I.: An Approach to Family Relationships and Role Performance, *Human Relations, 18*:209-221, 1957.

93. Richardson, Jr., F. L. W.: Community Resettlement in a Depressed Coal Region, Applied Anthropology *I*:#1 & #3, 1941; 7:#4, 1949.

94. Rosen, J. N.: Direct Analysis, New York: Grune & Stratton, 1953.

95. Rosenthal, D.: Book Review of A. Burton, (Ed.): Psychotherapy of the Psychoses, New York: Basic Books, Inc., 1961; *Psychiatry, 24*:377-380.

96. Sanua, V. D.: Sociocultural Factors in Families of Schizophrenics: A Review of the Literature, *Psychiatry, 24*:246-265, 1961.

97. Schaffer, L., et al.: On the Nature and Sources of the Psychiatrist's Experience with the Family of the Schizophrenic, *Psychiatry, 25*:32-46, 1962.

98. Schwartz, D. A., et al.: Use of Home Visits for Psychiatric Evaluation, *Arch. Gen. Psychiat., 3*:57-65, 1960.

99. Searles, H. F.: Anxiety Concerning Change as Seen in the Psychotherapy of Schizophrenic Patients—with Particular Reference to the Sense of Personal Identity, *Int. J. Psychoanal., 42*:74-85, 1961.

100. Searles, H. F.: The Effort to Drive the Other Person Crazy: An Element in the Aetiology and Psychotherapy of Schizophrenia, *Brit. J. Med. Psychol., 32*:1-18, 1959.

101. Searles, H. F.: Oedipal Love in the Countertransference, *Int. J. Psychoanal., 40*:180-190, 1959.

102. Siegal, R. S., & Rosen, I. C.: "Character Style and Anxiety Tolerance: A Study in Intrapsychic Change" in H. H. Strupp & L. Luborsky, Research in Psychotherapy, Proceedings of Conference APA, Division of Clinical Psychology, N.C.: May 17-20, 1961, Published by APA, 1962.

103. Simmel, G.: In K. H. Wolff, The Sociology of Georg Simmel, Glencoe, Ill: The Free Press, 1950.

104. Snyder, W. U.: "Some Investigations of Relationship in Psychotherapy" in E. A. Rubinstein & M. B. Parloff, Research in Psychotherapy, Washington, D.C.: National Publishing Co., 1959.

105. Sonne, J., et al.: The Absent-Member Maneuver as a Resistance in Family Therapy of Schizophrenia, *Family Process, I*:44-62, 1962.

106. Speck, R. V.: Mental Health Problems Involving the Family, the Pet and the Veterinarian, *J. Amer. Vet. Med. Ass.*, *145*:150-154, 1964.

107. Springarn, N. D.: The Worthing Experiment, *Ment. Hosp.*, *10*:24-29, November, 1959.

108. Szasz, T. S.: On the Experiences of the Analyst in the Psychoanalytic Situation: A Contribution to the Theory of Psychoanalytic Treatment, *J. Amer. Psychoanal. Ass.*, *4*:197-223, 1956.

109. Tietze, T.: A Study of Mothers of Schizophrenic Patients, *Psychiatry*, *12*:55-65, 1949.

110. Titchener, J. L., et al.: Family Transaction and Derivation of Individuality, *Family Process*, *2*:95-120, 1963.

111. Tuke, D. H.: Dictionary of Psychological Medicine, Volume I, Philadelphia: P. Blakiston & Co., 1892.

112. Veiga, M.: "The Missing Child: Reactions of Parents and Siblings to the Hospitalization of Children Due to Mental Disorders." Paper read at the 40th Annual Meeting of the Am. Orthopsychiat. Ass., Washington, D.C.: March, 1963.

113. Wahl, C. W.: The Psychodynamics of Consummated Maternal Incest, *Arch. Gen. Psychiat.*, *3*:188-193, 1960.

114. Wallerstein, R. S.: The Problem of the Assessment of Change in Psychotherapy, *Int. J. Psychoanal.*, *44*:31-41, 1963.

115. Weakland, J. H.: "The Double-Bind Hypothesis of Schizophrenia and Three-Party Interaction" in D. D. Jackson, (Ed.) The Etiology of Schizophrenia, New York: Basic Books, Inc., 1960.

116. Whitaker, C. A., & Malone, T. P.: The Roots of Psychotherapy, New York: The Blakiston Co., 1953.

117. Wynne, L. C., et al.: Pseudo-Mutuality in the Family Relations of Schizophrenics, *Psychiatry*, *21*:205-220, 1958.

118. Wynne, L. C.: "The Study of Intrafamilial Alignments and Splits in Exploratory Family Therapy" in N. W. Ackerman, (Ed.): Exploring the Base for Family Therapy, New York: Family Service Association of America, 1961.

119. Yap, P. M.: Mental Diseases Peculiar to Certain Cultures: A Survey of Comparative Psychiatry, *J. Ment. Sci.*, *97*:313-27, 1951.

120. Zelditch, M., Jr.: "Role Differentiation in the Nuclear Family: A Comparative Study" in N. W. Bell & E. F. Vogel, (Eds.): Modern Introduction to the Family, Glencoe, Ill.: The Free Press, 1960.

APPENDIX

FAMILY THERAPY OBSERVATION RATING SCALE

Philadelphia Psychiatric Center

Name of family: _____ Date: _____

Family members present: _____ Therapists: _____

    Fa   Mo C_1 C_2 Rater: _____

I. EMOTIONAL CLIMATE
   Estimate the emotional climate of the family treatment session by circling the
   appropriate letter:

                  a. Friendly and relaxed
                  b. Evasive and guarded
                  c. Hostile
                  d. Other _____
                  e. Unable to rate

II. COMMUNICATION
   A. Indicate the three principal lines and direction of verbal communication
      among the participants (family members and co-therapists) observed during
      the session, using the following symbols:

      Mo = Mother, Fa = Father, C_1 = Child (older), C_2 = Child (younger),
      Th-A = Therapist A, Th-B = Therapist B

      For example:

      Fa $\longleftrightarrow$ Th-A Operating in both directions between Father and Therapist A
      Fa $\longrightarrow$ Mo   Mainly from Father to Mother

      Mo
      $\updownarrow$ $\searrow$ Th-A A triadic communication between Mother, Father, and Therapist A
      Fa

                         Verbal Patterns

      1. _____   2. _____   3. _____

   B. List the principal line and direction of nonverbal communication (all levels
      of behavior exclusive of actual verbal communication) among the participants
      (family members and co-therapists) observed during the session, using the
      symbols as illustrated in the above examples:

                        Nonverbal Pattern

   C. Indicate the person or persons about whom the communication appears to re-
      volve during this session. Communication network is defined here to include
      both verbal and nonverbal behavioral observations.

      For example:
      Mo   Mother central figure
      Mo-C_1 Mother and older child central figures

III. CLIQUES AND ALLIANCES

Indicate who seems to be allied with whom and against whom in this session.
For example:

$\overline{C_1, C_2}$ vs. Fa   Siblings against Father
Mo, Fa vs. Th-A, Th-B   Parents against Therapists

1. _____   2. _____   3. _____

IV. EMOTIONAL INVOLVEMENT

Rate the degree of emotional involvement of each family member and each therapist in this session. How emotionally involved does he appear to be? Does he
tend to show an underreaction, a failure of affective involvement, or an over-
reaction to situations?

Use the following five-point rating scale for each member and place the rating
in the appropriate space;

Involvement			Overinvolvement	
1. None	2. Inadequate	3. Adequate	4. Distinct	5. Marked, exaggerated

Fa _____   Mo _____ C_1 _____ C_2 _____   Th-A _____   Th-B _____

Critical Incident (Positive)

Describe in some detail the incident in this session that was most indicative of
positive therapeutic movement:

Describe what you think precipitated or facilitated this positive movement, and check
below the confidence you feel in this judgment:

Critical Incident (Negative)

Describe in some detail the incident in this session that seemed to block or interfere with positive therapeutic movement (Main resistance):

Describe what you think precipitated this blocking or interference, and check below
the confidence you feel in this judgment;

Rate the degree of confidence you feel in your selection of the above incidents:

	Quite confident		Moderately confident		Not confident
	1.	2.	3.	4.	5.

Positive
Incident

Negative
Incident

Sociometric Scale:

Rank order the family members according to your spontaneous feeling of liking them;
listing the one most likeable first, etc.

1. _____   2. _____   3. _____   4. _____   5. _____

FAMILY PARTICIPATION INDEX

Name _____ Date _____

Specify the activities in which you participate together with other members of your family. An activity in which you have participated at least once in the past six months would be checked as "occasionally." If however you participated more frequently than this, check it for "fairly often."

List the following symbols in the appropriate spaces below to indicate what you do with whom:

A parent when rating uses the following symbols:
- P = Marriage Partner
- S = Son*
- D = Daughter*

A child when rating uses the following symbols:
- M = Mother
- F = Father
- Si= Sister*
- B = Brother*

*If more than one, rank according to age by using number after the symbol; for example: D_1 for oldest Daughter, B_2 for second oldest Brother, etc.

Activity	Family members who partipate with you	
	fairly often	occasionally
1. Motion pictures		
2. Dances		
3. Competitive sports		
4. Spectator sports		
5. Outdoor activities, hikes, picnics, etc.		
6. Social gatherings with friends, parties		
7. Reading		
8. Artistic and creative		
9. Political and civic		
10. Hobbies		
11. Membership in clubs and organizations		
12. Business or professional activities		
13. Meals		
14. Talking together		
15. Religious activity		
16. Snacks		
17. Household maintenance and repair		
18. Listening to radio, watching TV		
19. Gardening		
20. Family circle meetings and parties		

DISAGREEMENT CHECK LIST

Name _____   Date _____

Specify all disagreements between you and other members of your family over any of
the matters listed below. Use the appropriate symbols and record them in one of the
three columns to indicate amount or intensity of disagreement that occurs on the
particular topic.

List the following symbols in the appropriate spaces below to indicate what you do
with whom:

A parent when rating uses the   A child when rating uses the
     following symbols: following symbols:
     P = Marriage Partner   M = Mother
     S = Son*   F = Father
     D = Daughter*   Si= Sister*
                                            B = Brother*

*If more than one, rank according to age by using number after the symbol;
for example: D_1 for oldest daughter, B_2 for second oldest brother, etc.

Area of disagreement	Amount of disagreement		
	a little	some	considerable
1. Household management	_____	_____	_____
2. Sharing of household tasks	_____	_____	_____
3. Financial matters	_____	_____	_____
4. Father's work (husband)	_____	_____	_____
5. Mother's employment (wife)	_____	_____	_____
6. Disciplining children	_____	_____	_____
7. School adjustment and education	_____	_____	_____
8. Matters of recreation	_____	_____	_____
9. Personal habits (smoking, cleanliness, drinking, eating, sleeping, etc.) Specify	_____	_____	_____
10. Health	_____	_____	_____
11. Religious matters	_____	_____	_____
12. Jealousy	_____	_____	_____
13. Dating	_____	_____	_____
14. Getting psychological help for family members	_____	_____	_____
15. About friends	_____	_____	_____
16. About mother	_____	_____	_____
17. About father	_____	_____	_____
18. About grandmother(s)	_____	_____	_____
19. About grandfather(s)	_____	_____	_____
20. About sister(s)	_____	_____	_____
21. About brother(s)	_____	_____	_____
22. About other relatives	_____	_____	_____

INDEX

INDEX

A

Abraham, K., 307
Abrahams, J., 298
Absent member, 84-85, 88, 95-96, 101, 249, 255, 256, 261, 263-64, 265-74, 276-84, 285
Ackerman, Nathan, 11, 27, 192, 207, 232, 233, 240, 276, 329
Addams, Charles, 208
Albert, Robert S., 11
Alcoholism, 179
Alexander, Franz, 300, 303
Allport, Floyd, 10
Amsterdam plan, 243
Anthropology, cultural, 321
Anxiety, 190, 241, 242, 250
    absent member and, 264
    change and, 307
    peripheral person and, 289
Arensberg, C. M., 322
Arieti, S., 207

B

Bales, R. F., 227
Bateson, Gregory, 299, 302, 321
Bell, John E., 4, 9, 190, 232, 233, 246, 323
Benedek, T., 308
Birdwhistell, Ray L., 18, 294
Blocking, see Resistance
Bloom, Samuel, 294
Bossard, James, 321
Boston State Hospital, 246
Boszormenyi-Nagy, Ivan, 308, 311
Bowen, Murray, 12, 17, 18, 216, 296, 298, 302, 322
Brody Eugene, 328
Brown, B. S., 242, 243
Browning, C. J., 11

C

California Psychiatric Society, 243
Change, 188, 191, 307-10, 311
Chapple, E. D., 322, 331
Child, 15-18, 216-17, 226, 230
    control, 17, 244

departure, 24, 306
isolation, 16
marital relations of parents and, 177, 229
married, 24
rearing of, 15-18
role, 92, 93, 188
Child guidance clinics, 3-4, 334
Clausen, J. A., 326
Communication
    between therapists, 218-20
    crossfire of, 208-9
    family spokesman, 201
    lack of, 176-77, 187, 192, 194, 215
    non-verbal, 168, 169, 172-73, 195, 211, 250-51
    patterns, 165-66, 171, 190
    private, 197, 203-4
    unconscious, 188
Community Extension Service, 242
Community Health Project, 11
Complementarity, 301-2
Countertransference, 26, 206, 210, 245, 247

D

Daughter, 24, 226, 230
Death of sibling, 82, 95
Delinquency, 11
Desertion, 310, 313
Developmental process, 188, 191, 306-10, 311
Dominance, 149-55, 178, 215-16
Doubting, 255
Draw-A-Person test, 22, 29
Dreams, 223, 224, 225
Drugs, 244

E

Eastern Pennslyvania Psychiatric Institute, 306
Egan, M. H. 244, 246
Environment, home as therapeutic, 21, 28, 169, 182-84, 207-8, 240-54
Equilibrium, 13